# The Literary Channel

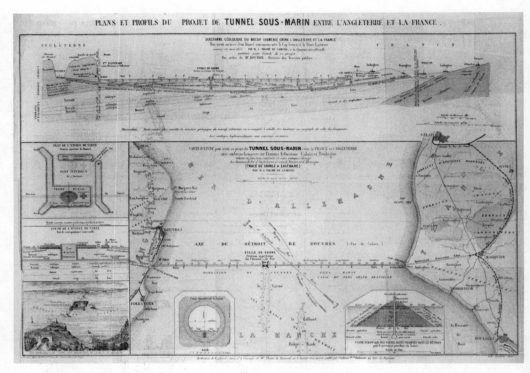

Plans of the project for an underwater tunnel between England and France by Thome de Gamond (ca. 1855). Courtesy of the Harvard Map Collection.

EDITED BY

MARGARET COHEN

AND CAROLYN DEVER

# The Literary Channel

The Inter-National Invention of the Novel

PRINCETON UNIVERSITY PRESS

PRINCETON AND OXFORD

Library of Congress Cataloging-in-Publication Data

The literary channel : the inter-national invention of the novel / edited by
Margaret Cohen and Carolyn Dever.
p.    cm. — (Translation/transnation)
Includes bibliographical references and index.
ISBN 0-691-05001-5 (alk. paper)—ISBN 0-691-05002-3 (pbk.: alk. paper)
1. Fiction—History and criticism. I. Cohen, Margaret, date. II. Dever, Carolyn. III. Series.
PN3451 .L58 2002
809.3—dc21        2001021484

British Library Cataloging-in-Publication Data is available.

This book has been composed in Minion with Gill Sans display.

Printed on acid-free paper. ∞

www.pup.princeton.edu

Printed in the United States of America

10  9  8  7  6  5  4  3  2  1
10  9  8  7  6  5  4  3  2  1
[pbk]

# CONTENTS

v

## ACKNOWLEDGMENTS

*The Literary Channel* began as a graduate seminar called "The Literary Chunnel," which we team-taught at New York University during the spring semester of 1996. Our thanks to the students in that seminar and to the Departments of Comparative Literature and English at NYU for sponsoring the course. The Department of Comparative Literature generously funded a conference that enabled us to bring the book's contributors to New York for a weekend of collective work in December 1999; our special thanks to Chair Richard Sieburth and to Susan Protheroe and Suzanne Daniels for organizing the conference. Warm thanks go to NYU's International Center for Advanced Studies, where Margaret Cohen worked on the collection while a Fellow in 1999–2000 and to Vanderbilt University, which granted a research leave to Carolyn Dever enabling her to prepare the collection during 1999–2000. We are grateful to David Cobb, head of the Harvard Map Collection, for his assistance with the cover image and frontispiece. The New York University Humanities Council generously helped defray production costs.

From its inception this volume has represented an unusually collective effort among its contributors. We thank April Alliston, Emily Apter, Joan DeJean, Lynn Festa, Françoise Lionnet, Deidre Shauna Lynch, Sharon Marcus, Richard Maxwell, and Mary Helen McMurran for their invaluable contributions, not only their essays but also their help with the introduction. We have learned much from dialogue with Karl Britto, Tita Chico, Shalyn Claggett, Julia Douthwaite, D. A. Miller, Franco Moretti, John Plotz, Tim Reiss, Marvin J. Taylor, Katie Trumpener, and Judith Walkowitz. We are grateful to Mary Murrell and Fred Appel for their constant support of the project and to our anonymous readers at the Princeton University Press.

Our families have provided encouragement, patience, and wisdom: Dan, Sam, and Max Klotz and Kathryn Schwarz.

**The Literary Channel**

MARGARET COHEN

AND CAROLYN DEVER

# Introduction

In the last decades of the seventeenth century there emerged a hybrid prose
genre that rapidly attracted the enthusiasm of readers across Europe and
then throughout the world. This genre was the modern novel oriented
around the twin focuses of "[t]he Romance . . . an heroic fable, which treats
of fabulous persons and things," and "[t]he Novel . . . a picture of real life
and manners, and of the time in which it is written," as Clara Reeve put it
in 1785.[1] When the novel first took shape, critics assigned it a marginal if
not suspect place in the generic hierarchy, treating it as " 'illegitimate' and
outside the range of recognized" forms.[2] By the time Reeve was writing,
however, the novel's authority was established, and by the mid-nineteenth
century it had become the dominant literary genre of modern culture.

But the novel's global appeal did not accompany its global production. Well into the 1820s and even the 1830s the great majority of novels,
and certainly the majority of internationally acclaimed novels, were written
in what Franco Moretti has called a novelistic "core" of France and Britain.[3]
This geographical concentration was at once quantitative and poetic, for
it produced the literary codes that are familiar hallmarks of the genre:
first-person narrations of complex interiority, the omniscient narrator, free
indirect discourse, dramatic dialogue, causally motivated plots of suspense,
and detailed, socially precise descriptions that helped to constitute fictional
historical and geographical categories.

Materialist histories of the novel have long explained the novel's
formal innovations as responses to the transformations accompanying the
advent of capitalist modernity. In more recent years critics have highlighted
above all the novel's implication in the project of empire and the consolida-

tion of the nation-state. They have also raised the question what the novel owes to changing conditions of literary production in either Britain or France.[4] There has, however, been little attention to the formative role played by a factor that intersects each of these inquiries yet retains its own discrete existence: the processes of literary and cultural exchange that occurred across the English Channel.

The modern novel did not develop along two separate, nationally distinct trajectories; it developed through intersections and interactions among texts, readers, writers, and publishing and critical institutions that linked together Britain and France. These intersections constitute a distinctive arena of cultural power that we call a *zone* because the notion of zone, particularly in its military and mathematical usage, suggests a structure produced through the intersection of other structures that are coherent formations in their own right.[5] A zone is a liminal formation at the confluence of independent formations; it both belongs to these formations and constitutes a distinct whole of its own. As the military notion of the zone makes especially clear, such liminal spaces are characterized by discrete practices that are implicated in but not necessarily identical with the practices of the formations coming into contact; those who visited the border dividing East from West Germany during the cold war may remember guards on opposing sides who knew each other by name and exchanged jokes across yards of barbed wire, broken glass, and land mines.

When the notion of the zone has been invoked in avant-garde writings on cultural modernity, it has identified sites of power and struggle with an ambivalent relation to hegemony. As Freud suggests in an analysis of the dream-work zone between consciousness and the unconscious, liminal spaces foster experimentation and harbor potential anarchy;[6] they have a particular affinity with emerging, ephemeral, and hybrid practices, though these practices themselves can become hegemonic, as the history of the novel's cross-Channel development will make clear. For the zone's liminality in no way means that it eschews the production of power. The cross-Channel literary zone is, specifically, a version of what Bourdieu has called the cultural field, though it exists at the international level, and is hence defined both by and in tension with the nationally based literary institutions of interest to Bourdieu. Like any cultural field, the Channel zone is characterized by the agglomeration of a range of formal and informal institutions that produce and distribute symbolic and economic capital. This volume argues that to understand the material factors producing the modern novel, we must recover the terms of its passage through the

Channel zone, the specific history of its cross-Channel construction and consumption.

Patterns of literary transmission and exchange between Britain and France shifted dramatically over the decades and centuries of the modern novel's development, and the chapters in this volume intervene at especially sensitive moments in this process. The historical as well as methodological range of the chapters should suggest the depth and breadth of the modern novel's cross-Channel genealogy. This is a story of cultural exchange and of cultures constituted through exchange, of novels imported and exported, published, reviewed, sold, circulated, and read together, of works translated from one national language to the other and then retranslated as their national origins are mislaid. Such processes both vindicate and challenge the imagined contours of the nation-state. If England and France have at times defined themselves by means of contrast with the other, through a complex process of displacement in which the representation of national difference played an important, even constitutive role, this "othering" helped shape the Channel zone itself. Yet exchanges within that space were not identical with the practices of power that defined English and French state hegemony. They were shaped by the political, economic, and social processes that bound the two nations in an inextricable competition for global economic and political supremacy throughout the history of the novel's development. But they also defined themselves against these processes, just as they partook of the concept of a national literature yet did not assume novels as coextensive with nations. Cross-Channel cultural exchanges were not, moreover, limited to the modern novel, though this genre played a key role in defining and perpetuating the literary and cultural authority of the dynamic zone at the intersection of two national traditions.

## The Inter-National Invention of the Novel

We elaborate our notion of the Channel zone with the help of both comparatist and nationally based critical paradigms that set the terms for describing the novel's relation to geography across the twentieth century. In the comparatist paradigm, the novel is a constitutively international genre. This paradigm reaches at least back to Georg Lukács, who linked the novel to a generalized historical and philosophical modernity that was not, however, rooted in a specific social formation. For Lukács in *The Theory of the Novel* (1920), the novel's codes were determined by its attempt to express what he famously described as the transcendental homelessness of subjectivity in a disenchanted world. Following his Marxist turn, Lukács did not fundamentally shift from an international view of the novel's aims. He did, however, transform the novel's engagement with existential exile into an engagement with the contradictions defining the development of capitalist modernity, as *The Historical Novel* and *Studies in European Realism* illustrate.

In the shift from Hegel to Marx, Lukács encountered a question that was to trouble materialist efforts to conceptualize the novel in global terms throughout the twentieth century: how was one to reconcile the novel's international presence with the fact that capitalist modernity developed unevenly, that it was rarely in sync in differing nations; and that the novel developed unevenly in different national contexts as well? The beginning of *The Historical Novel* suggests the importance to this question of the Channel zone, for despite his general lack of interest in the tradition of the British novel, Lukács speculates on the novel's eighteenth-century variation across Britain and France in particular, with some discussion, too, of late-eighteenth-century Germany. Rather than exploring this immensely rich subject, however, Lukács isolated a moment in the history of the novel when both poetic and social unevenness were minimal across nations, and he identified this moment as the teleology of the genre as a whole. For him, that historical moment encompassed the French Revolution and the Napoleonic Wars, "which for the first time made history a *mass* experience and moreover on a European scale."[7] The novelistic subgenre accordingly privileged in this paradigm was historical realism in the vein of Walter Scott. In this argument, however, Lukács rigged the game, admitting only a very narrow field of objects—the novels of historical realism—and a narrow literary focus, as he bracketed, for example, the entire eighteenth century. When Auerbach produced a remarkably similar account of the culmination of the novel in "modern tragic realism," he followed suit, treating the eighteenth-century novel as problematic and aligning the triumph of historical realism to "the first great movements of modern times in which large masses of men consciously took part—the French Revolution with all the consequent convulsions which spread from it over Europe."[8]

The power of an alignment between historical realism and the European wars produced by the French Revolution can be seen in its authority across the twentieth century. It shaped, for example, such important works as Jameson's *Political Unconscious* (1981) and Moretti's *Way of the World* (1987), which focus on a set of literary objects and historical events similar to those of interest to Lukács. But while such analyses do not fundamentally shift the phenomena to be explained, they do differ from the Lukácsian narrative in confronting head on the novel's formal divergence across national boundaries. They stress the concept of its uneven development, proposing that variations in the practice of capitalist modernity from nation to nation explain differences in national practices of the novel as a form. With this response, they offer a powerful tool for disarticulating the rise of the novel from realism and from the early nineteenth century and for reconstituting the existence of a unified zone of cultural power across national variations in history and poetics.

We also owe our conceptualization of the novel as a form constitutively engaged with boundary crossing to the comparative lineage instigated by Mikhail Bakhtin, whose first major work on the novel, *Problems in Dostoevsky's Poetics*, appeared in 1929. For Bakhtin, as for Lukács, the novel was an international genre, but Bakhtin was attentive to the insurgency, beyond classes, of language itself. In this, Bakhtin offers a template of novelistic heterogeneity that is crucial to our argument for the importance of attending to a trans-Channel literary field. For Bakhtin, the novel's rebellious energy led to its constitutive engagement with categorical logic. As Michael Holquist explains in the translator's introduction to *The Dialogic Imagination*, " '[N]ovel' is the name Bakhtin gives to whatever force is at work within a given literary system to reveal the limits, the artificial constraints of that system. Literary systems are comprised of canons, and 'novelization' is fundamentally anticanonical. It will not permit generic monologue. Always it will insist on the dialogue between what a given system will admit as literature and those texts that are otherwise excluded from such a definition of literature. What is more conventionally thought of as the novel is simply the most complex and distilled expression of this impulse."[9] In this narrative, the novel's class insurgency and its poetics are extensions of its resistance to hegemony and hierarchy. The novel is a form whose very stability paradoxically depends on a project of instability, which Bakhtin variously characterizes as both epistemological and ontological. What is suggestive about this argument in the context of a theory of a cross-Channel zone of novelistic production is the sense in which the novel establishes itself counter to systematic, organizing, canonizing logic. In his insistence on a dialogic novelistic imagination Bakhtin shifts the frame of reference through which cultural materialists have located the novel as an emblem of radical modernity in a fashion conducive to interrogating other foundational categories, including those of nation and national literary tradition.

Equally suggestive for our purposes is the fact that such instability is inseparable from linguistic instability represented in and by novelistic language, which is subversive because it is polyglot, ironic, and self-referential. "To a greater or lesser extent," Bakhtin writes, "every novel is a dialogized system made up of the images of 'languages,' styles and consciousnesses that are concrete and inseparable from language. Language in the novel not only represents but itself serves as an object of representation. Novelistic discourse is always criticizing itself" (49). This self-critical, even parodic tendency lends the novel a strategic "polyglossia," or subversive heterodoxy, and, Bakhtin continues, "[o]nly polyglossia fully frees consciousness from the tyranny of its own language and its own myth of language. Parodic-travestying forms flourish under these conditions, and only in this milieu are they capable of being elevated to completely new ideological heights" (61). As Bakhtin's application of a rhetoric of oppression and liberation to language suggests, the novel's polyglossia is political as well as epistemological; it is inseparable from the genre's democratizing ambition and effects.

Born of and as a hybrid form, cobbled together from the scraps and fragments of various storytelling modes, the novel, in Bakhtin's vision, is the repository for "an interanimation of languages." Through this attention to languages as fundamentally permeable, Bakhtin challenges the conceptual bases that would enclose novels within national traditions and also points to one starting point for a history such as ours: the importance of translation and the fact that national languages are "interanimated," originating piecemeal in terms and forms imported and exported across boundaries of national and cultural difference.[10] Once the clear boundaries of national language are challenged, other accompanying distinctions are problematized as well: "nation," for example, and literary canon. From a Bakhtinian perspective, it is simultaneously perverse and yet understandable that the novel would signify the coherence of national identity; it is a genre that dwells at borders whose policing is crucial to the nationalist project.

The space of the border is also at stake in our debt to the vital twentieth-century lineage that situates the novel within the framework of the nation. This lineage focuses on conceptual borders, certainly: it has been concerned with the destabilization of historical, ideological, and aesthetic categories as a key project of the genre.[11] But also important here is the geopolitical border, and particularly the border dividing England from

France: the cross-Channel comparative context has haunted nationally based histories of the novel as powerfully as it defined the developmental trajectory of the novel itself. In nationally based studies of the novel the novel's transnational contours have generally receded in favor of attention to distinct national traditions, aligned with the material histories, most notably for our purposes, of *either* Britain *or* France. But we would like to call attention to how the question of the Channel zone complicates these studies even though it is never raised directly, tending to emerge at the margins of discussion, in introductions that establish the paradigm to be studied, in footnotes or impressionistic comments designating material for future thought. When the novel's transnational constitution is directly confronted, it most often serves the function of contrast to explain what makes a British novel British, or a French novel French.

To give an example from the foundations of this tradition, Ian Watt grounds his influential analysis of the "rise" of formal realism in eighteenth-century Britain by situating his work within a context both transnational and transhistorical. "[I]f we assume, as is commonly done, that [the novel is a new literary form], and that it was begun by Defoe, Richardson and Fielding, how," asks Watt, "does it differ from the prose fiction of the past, from that of Greece, for example, or that of the Middle Ages, or of seventeenth-century France?"[12] The novel emerged, for Watt, from a globally diverse prose-fiction tradition, but the formal realism that constitutes its truly "novel" contribution was first noted as such by the French. Watt continues to evince his awareness of the cross-Channel genesis of the novel when he suggests that a specifically formal quality of English narrative realism was in fact a trans-Channel phenomenon: "[T]he novel's realism does not reside in the kind of life it presents, but in the way it presents it. . . . This, of course, is very close to the position of the French realists themselves, who asserted that if their novels tended to differ from the more flattering pictures of humanity presented by many established ethical, social, and literary codes, it was merely because they were the product of a more dispassionate and scientific scrutiny of life than had ever been attempted before" (11). The comparative context enables Watt to suggest the many yields of *réalisme* on both sides of the Channel: the novel is a description of the human condition in high states and in low, a description presented through formal conventions of time and place shaped by empiricism and by a new narrative emphasis on "dispassionate and scientific scrutiny."

But because the histories of class relations in Britain and France developed quite differently during the long eighteenth century, when defining novelistic codes were forged, Watt reiterates a distinct line between British and French traditions throughout his work. Watt makes the startling assertion that "[i]n France, the classical critical outlook, with its emphasis on elegance and concision, was not fully challenged until the coming of Romanticism. . . . French fiction from *La Princesse de Clèves* to *Les Liaisons dangeureuses* stands outside the main tradition of the novel. For all its psychological penetration and literary skill, we feel it is too stylish to be authentic" (30). French fiction's "inauthenticity" is a matter of a "stylishness"—classical, elegant, concise form applied to aristocratic plots— which seems anachronistic when compared with the (relatively) lower-class narratives of Fielding, Defoe, and Sterne. For Watt, like other literary historians working in the context of cultural materialism, such a contrast is not value-neutral: a repressive French high-cultural literary tradition is opposed to a more popular and, by implication, more democratic tradition in Britain. It was British fiction of the eighteenth century that reaped the benefits of a popular revolution in aesthetic taste, enabling formal realism to establish a footing that it failed to achieve in France until the nineteenth century, when France saw "the first great efflorescence of the genre . . . with Balzac and Stendhal" (300). The "main tradition of the novel" was thereby appropriated in the name of an appealing insurgency and celebrated the "rise" of the middle classes.

Watt's segregation of French texts from the main line of novelistic tradition was noted by Georges May, a historian of the French novel who remains similarly haunted by the novel's transnational genesis, at once acutely aware of it yet lacking the framework to theorize it as such. May's thesis in *Le Dilemme du roman au siècle XVIIIe* is that eighteenth-century French novelists were stymied by the contradictory demands of powerful literary critics that the novel at once idealize human nature, and thereby improve its readers, yet also represent people as they really are. May continuously looks across the Channel to find works that can treat realistic subjects without descending into libertinage: his works are rife with statements like that praising the "superiority . . . of Defoe or of Fielding over Prévost or Madame Riccoboni" for their ability to include a veritable human comedy in their depictions.[13] For May, English success turns on the ability to absorb the French attention to the depiction of interiority, forged in what he calls the golden age of the French novel in the 1720s and 1730s, and to fuse it with a social realism of detail.

Why can English writers do this? May's answer to this question is the same as Watt's: the close links between the eighteenth-century English novel and the newly empowered middle classes. May turns out to share the assumption that links the emergence of the modern novel with the "rise" of the middle classes; his problem is that this rise cannot be celebrated similarly in eighteenth-century *ancien régime* culture, when the bourgeoisie started to amass economic power but could find no way to bring it to political expression and where the beginnings of industrialization lagged far behind those of England (French industrialization gained momentum later, in the 1820s).[14] It is thus no accident that French literary history long treated the eighteenth-century French novel as somehow problematic.[15] And this is why materialist analyses of the French novel generally begin with the nineteenth century and the emergence of Balzacian realism against the backdrop of the post-Revolutionary triumph of the bourgeoisie.[16] Friedrich Engels diagnosed the uneven development of modernity motivating this divergence in nationally based historiographies of the novel when he wrote that "[t]he Industrial Revolution has been as important for England as the political revolution for France."[17]

The pressure to align the novel and capitalist modernity is tremendously powerful. But even when given the optimum field by the focus on a single national tradition, it is disturbed and complicated by the influential context of cross-Channel exchange. In order to understand all that such a homology suppresses, it is crucial to have a sense of what might have been, to understand that in fact a range of novelistic forms were crudely condensed into a single teleological model figured as the rise toward realism. This is an insight of feminist critics working on both English and French contexts, several of whom are contributors to this volume. In the process of searching for organizing cultural paradigms beyond the novel-nation homology, feminist literary historians observed the implication of patriarchy and fatherland and found in narratives and subgenres pioneered and consumed by women readers (notably the Gothic, historical romance, and sentimental fiction) imagined communities and literary codes that worked across the enclosing boundaries of the nation.[18] Feminist scholarship has joined such archival excavation with the epistemological interrogation that preoccupies both Bakhtin and McKeon. As a result, the feminist critique of power constituted in superpatriarchal categories such as "nation" has reaped the benefit of a materialist concern with the productive power of the market and also a poststructuralist suspicion of categories constituted in binary opposition to each other.

When *The Literary Channel* decenters the category of nationality from its unquestioned authority in dominant accounts of the rise of the novel, it pursues an imperative resulting from such scholarship: *to rewrite the category of nationality so foundational in traditional literary histories, it* is imperative to reorient the major landmarks and figures that have conventionally defined the canon of the novel along with the contexts that give them shape, with these contexts understood as broadly discursive literary and cultural fields. Feminist literary historians' challenge that the nation and the canon must be interrogated simultaneously has become, if anything, more urgent as it has evolved in tandem with postcolonial studies that have extensively historicized as well as theorized the constructedness of the "imagined geography of the nation," to use Benedict Anderson's celebrated phrase. In postcolonial analysis, the nation is clearly disarticulated from the state; it has become "one of the major structures of ideological ambivalence within the cultural representations of 'modernity.' " [19]

Such an ideological approach to the category of nation has, in turn, enabled nationally based studies of the novel to broach the nation as a problem to be investigated rather than as a self-evident framework organizing the analysis. William Warner's question at the opening to *Licensing Entertainment* emblematizes such a shift: "How," he asks, "do eighteenth-century novels that happen to have been written in England come to be understood, by the late nineteenth century, as the first instances of that complex and valued cultural object known as 'the English novel'?"[20] At the same time, postcolonial studies also paved the way for comparatists to rethink the novel's internationalism in offering a global account of modern capitalism, which developed its international practice well beyond early-nineteenth-century political upheaval and the emergence of the working classes onto the stage of history. Moretti's *Atlas of the European Novel* takes up this challenge, invoking Wallerstein's notion of the modern world system to ask not only how novels were shaped by the global rise of capitalism but how novels themselves form a cultural system across national borders.

## Transnational Culture before—and with—the Nation

In the introduction to *Nation and Narration* Bhabha cogently formulates one of the most powerful lines of inquiry opened by the postcolonial interest in questions of space and in the category "nation." Bhabha writes, "It is this *inter*national dimension both within the margins of the nation-space and in the boundaries *in-between* nations and peoples that the authors of this book have sought to represent in their essays. The representative emblem of this book might be a chiasmatic 'figure' of cultural difference whereby the anti-nationalist, ambivalent nation-space becomes the cross-roads to a new transnational culture."[21] But when Bhabha speaks of "a *new* transnational culture," he suggests how much remains to be discovered about the notion of the transnational when applied to cultural formations and, notably, how much remains to be written about its history. For transnational culture did not begin in the postmodern era, though there is a marked presentist trend in the way this concept has been energized in recent literary studies.

In its application to the postmodern condition the notion of the transnational foregrounds the simultaneously increasing totalization and fragmentation that characterize the processes of late capitalism, a phenomenon Lukács diagnosed in 1922.[22] Thus, in interdisciplinary studies the transnational interpretive frame is applied to multinational corporations with the ability to circumvent the state and thwart labor organizing on the local level. It also is used to describe political and economic nongovernmental organizations, whose relation to multinational corporations ranges from the critical to the complicit. At the same time, the notion of the transnational has been applied to the fragmented, immigrant labor forces whose transnational identity, or what Yasemin Soysal calls "postnational" identity, is encouraged by a multinational development of capital.[23] That immigrant workers are the marginal and displaced of late capitalism meshes with the specific political valence of the notion of the transnational when it is applied to contemporary cultural formations. Such formations are generally associated with minority, multicultural, and nomadic forms of cultural production, cultural forms that celebrate what Katharyne Mitchell, observing how the notion of the transnational designates at once the hegemonic economic formations of global capitalism and the cultures of marginality, ephemerality, and flux that resist them, has called "hybridity and pluralism."[24]

But while postmodern notions of the transnational will resonate with certain aspects of the cross-cultural exchanges depicted in these chapters, the volume also accounts for a history that differs from the present in several important ways. We are concerned, notably, with a transnational culture that was in no way postnational but rather predated the modern nation-state and took shape in tandem with its emergence. Analyzing the case of England, Linda Colley argues that modern British identity was forged in the process of a bitter and protracted struggle between Britain and France for hegemony fought out both in Europe and in the colonies. In her introduction, Colley offers a few dates to indicate the intensity of this struggle as well as its time frame. Britain and France,

prime powers on sea and on land respectively . . . were at war
between 1689 and 1697 . . . between 1702 and 1713, 1743 and
1748, 1756 and 1763, 1778 and 1783, 1793 and 1802, and,
finally, between 1803 and the Battle of Waterloo in 1815. And
. . . even in the interludes of token peace, the two powers repeatedly plotted against and spied on each other. Their settlers and
armed forces jostled for space and dominance in North America,
the West Indies, Africa, Asia, and Europe. French clerics, intellectuals and tourists scrutinized Britain's political system, moral
fibre and cultural achievements, and their British counterparts
did the same with regard to France.[25]

One of the principal cultural effects of this struggle, according to Colley,
was to enable the use of France as Other to construct what was distinctively
British about a unified modern Britain, and French historians have recently
started to explore the relevance of Colley's thesis to the case of France.[26]

From Colley's account, it would seem that dominant English and,
by implication, French culture throughout the rise of the novel tends to
reinforce the political hostilities reigning between these sister nations, but
in fact this conclusion is complicated by the narratives of Anglo-French
cultural exchange presented in this collection. For the very years Colley
designates as constructing modern British identity are precisely contemporaneous with the cross-Channel invention of the novel, which can be very
roughly dated (sticking, for the moment, with the already canonized classics) from Mme de Lafayette's 1678 *La Princesse de Clèves* to Sir Walter
Scott's 1814 *Waverley*. And as the chapters in this volume demonstrate
time and again, political hostilities diminished neither the intensity nor
the cultural centrality of Anglo-French intellectual and literary exchange.
To give only a few examples that also highlight the range of cultural links
at issue in the Channel zone, the strategies for representing interiority devised by French fiction in the late seventeenth century and the first decades
of the eighteenth century resulted in a series of English works that have
long been viewed as the culmination of formal realism published during
the 1740s, precisely as political tensions between France and Britain came
to a head during the period of the Jacobite rebellion. According to Robert
Dawson, "In 1760, in the midst of the Seven Years' War, there was . . . an
attempt to publish an English newspaper in Paris," and Pierre Le Tour-
neur's "magnificent translation of Shakespeare" appeared in 1776–82, contemporaneous with French-English rivalry over the issue of the American
War of Independence.[27] The Napoleonic Wars did not prevent writers and

readers on either side of the Channel from enjoying or reworking each other's fiction; indeed, as we will subsequently explain, the historical novel, perhaps the form most closely associated with imagining the origins of the modern nation, was facilitated by the generic fertilization catalyzed by trans-Channel exchange during this time.[28] And even as Victorian disciplinary society was bolstered through invective against French immorality, G. H. Lewes went off to his bookseller after finishing *Jane Eyre* only to find "the new volumes of unfinished novels by Alexandre Dumas, enough to have tasked the energies of the British Museum to catalogue," along with "volumes by Théophile Gautier, Michel Masson, Madame Reybaud, Jules Sandeau, Badon, Feuillet, Roger de Beauvoir, d'Arlincourt, de Gondrecourt," to say nothing of new books by Sand, Balzac, and Hugo. The transnational culture of the Channel zone differs from postmodern transnationalism not only in predating the nation-state and helping to shape its emergence but also by its position squarely at the center of national cultural formations, overdetermined and ambivalent as this position might be.

Colley writes of the extended conflicts between Britain and France that "the result was less a series of separate and conventional wars, than one peculiarly pervasive and long-drawn out conflict which rarely had time to become a cold war in the 20th-century sense."[29] That the novel could be forged in the cross-Channel crucible during such a prolonged series of "hot" wars is truly remarkable; can we imagined a major new literary or cultural genre resulting during the cold war in interchanges between American and Soviet intelligentsia and audiences even as the two nations' leaders promised each other Mutually Assured Destruction? In foregrounding the ways in which culture may offer alternatives to political and economic formations as well as support them, the literary Channel reveals the importance of a concept that we have already mentioned as crucial to dismantling the longstanding authority of "rise of the novel" narratives and that will figure prominently here: the notion of uneven development. Just as Britain and France could share novelistic forms even while they differed in their political and economic formations, the Channel zone could perpetuate a vibrant transnational culture in a climate of intense political hostility. This is what Louis Althusser distinguished as the semiautonomy of culture relative to economic relations. More recently, Pierre Bourdieu has elaborated Althusser's insight into the need to study literature as a space of social production in its own right, imbricated in the other spaces of power defining societies but also functioning according to its own logic and rules.

In this volume we focus on institutions that are above all poetic. They include, notably, what Jameson in *The Political Unconscious* describes as the "social contract" of genre, as well as historically specific ways of practicing translation.[30] At the same time, such poetic institutions were framed by salons and literary gathering places that offered homes to émigré intellectuals; a nascent media industry that transformed Richardson's *Pamela* into an international commodity within one year of its appearance; an Enlightenment republic of letters and science that was itself shaped in the Channel zone and helped to disseminate its effect; and Victorian critics whose reviews policed the boundaries of moral acceptability even as the surveillance effort itself reproduced the very moral transgressions it intended to combat.

## The Literary Channel

The chapters in this volume contribute to an archaeology of transnational culture in keeping with the twin objectives that Moretti proposed as basic to the study of literature's spatial implications: the imperative to consider ways in which space is imagined within literature and the imperative to consider the social importance of space in shaping literary forms.[31] Our collection rethinks the modern novel's contribution to the process by which "nation" in the abstract, and the nation-states of France and Britain in particular, emerged as "imagined communities" even as it offers case studies in the imagined construction of alternative transnational communities and the existence of a sociological zone of cross-Channel literary and cultural exchange. Because of the complexity of the processes we describe, we offer a brief overview of the major points of their development and mention some major figures, concerns, and texts that gave them shape.[32] This overview also allows us to provide further details about our previous claims concerning the historical specificity of the transnational cultural formations considered here.

In the late seventeenth and early eighteenth centuries the traffic in novelistic prose flowed far more actively from France to England than in the reverse direction. Following a more general pattern for the circulation of culture, the circulation of French texts in Britain was also encouraged by the return from France of the exiled Stuart court, the Restoration, and later the exodus of Huguenots in the wake of the revocation of the Edict of Nantes in 1685.[33] Especially prominent within the larger framework of exportation, and thus to the developing novelistic form in both countries, were the heroic romances of such authors as Scudéry, La Calprenède, and d'Urfé; as well as *Les Aventures de Télémaque*, Fénélon's epic of *Bildung*; the new "nouvelle," Scarron's *Roman comique*; historical fictions and fairy tales; and memoirs of aristocratic life written not only by Lafayette and Madame de Villedieu but also, as DeJean observes, by French women in exile, notably Anne de La Roche-Guilhen and Marie-Catherine LeJumel de Barneville, comtesse d'Aulnoy.

Early British novelists were not only informed by the influx of texts from France; they were also its facilitators. Aphra Behn, for example, translated heroic romances and also produced her own version with a racially complex twist in *Oroonoko or the Royal Slave* (1688). Eliza Haywood, like Behn, adapted *chroniques scandaleuses*, and Delarivière Manley emphasized her relationship with French letters in no uncertain terms: the preface to her *Secret History of Queen Zarah and the Zarazians* (1705) presents a theory of the novel appropriated quite directly from French sources; she published *The Lady's Paquet Broke Open* (1707 and 1708) appended to translations of the memoirs of the comtesse d'Aulnoy; and she produced what is generally considered her autobiography, *The Adventures of Rivella* (1714), under cover of the claim that it was translated from the French.[34]

During this period there were, to be sure, individual works that traveled from England to France. In the 1720s, for example, both *Gulliver's Travels* and *Robinson Crusoe* were prominent in French bibliographies and reviews, following upon the popularity of Barclay's *Argenis*, a romance written in Latin, and Bacon's *New Atlantis*. What is not clear, however, is whether these texts were received as "novels" or as travel narratives and philosophical tales, for in this period Continental writers looked to England primarily for writing in science and philosophy.[35] Meanwhile, the flow of French fiction, including the major novels of Prévost, Lesage, Tencin, Marivaux, Crébillon, Mouhy, Argens, Hamilton, Gomez, and Lussan, flooded the British marketplace throughout the 1720s and 1730s.[36]

The prominence of French texts in the British context enabled Bishop William Warburton to describe the novelistic lineage resulting in *Clarissa* within the terms of cross-Channel exchange: "[T]his great People (to whom, it must be owned, all Science has been infinitely indebted) hit upon the true Secret, by which alone a deviation from strict fact . . . could be really entertaining to an improved mind, or useful to promote that Improvement. And this was by a faithful and chaste copy of real *Life and Manners*: In which some of their late Writers have greatly excelled."[37] Richardson, however, was none too pleased with Warburton's comments and suppressed them "as soon as he could."[38] For Richardson, beginning with *Pamela*, was seeking a distinctively English novelistic form that would be close to life yet not licentious. In this effort he was writing against the popularity of texts such as Crébillon's *Les Egarements du coeur et de l'esprit*, itself a displacement of the *chroniques scandaleuses* produced by Behn, Manley, and Haywood.[39]

In *Pamela* and later in *Clarissa*, Richardson, as critics have argued, was concerned to represent a uniquely English form of moral virtue. By substituting domestic virtue for portrayals of worldliness and displacing worldly vice onto the French, Richardson continued the English interest in locating heroic subjects close to home. So it is perhaps ironic that Richardson's domestication of French worldly observation and complex interiority in turn paved the way for a new sentimental form in France, pioneered by Graffigny, Riccoboni, and Rousseau and featuring a newly authentic and distinctly unworldly narrator. As the case of Richardson should suggest, beginning in the 1740s, and in the context of the transnational nature of the republic of letters—salons in France, the global marketplace of coffeehouse culture in London—there clearly emerged a reciprocal economy of literary interchange across the Channel.[40] Prévost, for example, translated Richardson, who in turn was of great importance for catalyzing sentimental fiction in France, even as William Godwin, Charlotte Smith, Sophia Lee, and Clara Reeve all worked to translate or imitate Prévost.[41] Sarah Fielding, Henry Fielding, and Tobias Smollett were also prominent among the numerous English novelists favored in France during the 1740s and 1750s; as Sterne mentions in his letters, he may have been notorious across the Channel, but he was not yet translated.

And translation was indeed the medium through which much of this interchange was conducted. As Mary Helen McMurran argues in her chapter here, "National or Transnational? The Eighteenth-Century Novel," the modern novel began to emerge as writers simultaneously translated and rewrote a range of fictional prose genres; in this context rendering in another language was associated with *translatio studii*, "the transfer of culture through imitation, translation, or adaptation." The act of *translatio*, literally "bearing across," also involved *translatio imperii*, the transfer of power across space and time from one empire to another. McMurran demonstrates, however, that trans-Channel translations during the eighteenth century work—in both directions—to erode the presumption of nationalist hegemonies. Joan DeJean, in "Transnationalism and the Origins of the (French?) Novel," examines the role of French Huguenot translations to suggest that early modern translation not only disseminates culture from an imperial center but also works in an ambivalent fashion, simultaneously extending but also undermining that center's authority. In her account, the French Protestant diaspora that followed the revocation of the Edict of Nantes both exported and translated French generic practices—memoir novels and the fairy tale, notably—even as writers in exile promoted the importance of French as an international lingua franca.

DeJean's chapter on the role of the absolutist state in provoking transnational Huguenot culture underscores that cultural transnationalism of the early modern period predated the modern nation's emergence as an imagined community, a process not fully solidified, most scholars of nationalism agree, until the late eighteenth century.[42] Such antiabsolutism was an agenda shared by the modern cultural nationalisms also forming at the time. As the chapters concentrating on the first hundred years of the novel's emergence repeatedly emphasize, the literary Channel of the eighteenth century was hence in a triangulated relation to the passage from an absolutist to a modern nation-state. It offered an alternative to absolutism, however, that could not simply be identified with the modern notion of the nation replacing absolutism in the arena of political theory and practice.

In the trans-Channel literary context such a triangulated relation finds expression in the construction of a sentimental code of universal humanity that transcends the worldly interests of nation. The chapters of Lynn Festa, April Alliston, and Margaret Cohen foreground the transnational appeal of sentimental fiction, which was arguably the dominant literary subgenre traveling across national borders between 1740 and 1848. These chapters view transnational culture through the lens of a literary genre that has been implicated in hegemonic practices—helping to form modern class identity also bound up in normative notions of national identity—and that at the same time existed as a form of hegemonic literary culture in an Enlightenment republic of letters. Cohen's "Sentimental Communities" focuses on sentimentality as an aesthetic and political intervention that works to consolidate both national and transnational ties. Sentimental fiction, Cohen argues, addressed contradictions in emerging liberalism both across national borders and within the political formations dominating on either side of the Channel. In "Transnational Sympathies, Imaginary Communities" Alliston situates the function of sentimentality and the imagined communities it constitutes in relation to Anderson's arguments concerning that imagined community of sentiment above all others: the nation. In the process, Alliston reveals sensibility's unsettling tendencies, its creation of communities that work against national borders and patriline transmission. The "idealized personal bond of sympathy," Alliston argues, is identified with the disruptive liminality of the Celtic fringe and works to represent "utopian imaginary communities that transgress the limits defining nations—as well as national languages, class distinctions, kinship relations, and legitimate sexuality." Festa's "Sentimental Bonds and Revolutionary Characters: Richardson's *Pamela* in England and France" further complicates an understanding of sentimentality's triangulated relation to the nation by bringing in another form of international cultural production central to the Channel: the consumer culture that appropriated Richardson's *Pamela* in a range of reworkings and imitations across media and genres whose popularity was not yet opposed to high-culture Enlightenment taste.

In their shared focus on the sentimental novel Festa, Cohen, and Alliston argue for a major effect of cross-Channel literary exchange. By viewing the development of the novel in the context of a transnational literary zone, they reveal an alternative community consolidated most explicitly in the sentimental form: the nationally marked exchange of literary subgenres between the late seventeenth century and the 1760s produced an ideal of the human, as the subject of the novel was less nation than normative humanness without markers of exclusive national identity. Viewed in the transnational context, sentimentality is the subgenre most closely correlated with this ideal and helps to constitute a range of codes for representing the interior, emotional qualities that demarcate a distinctive shared humanity.

The trans-Channel invention of normative humanness also realigns how we appreciate a range of eighteenth-century genres with strong national associations. From this perspective, such national identification does not precisely reinforce monolithic notions of national identity; rather, it confirms the existence of a nongeneric universal humanity by showing how it can vary according to local contexts. Examples of nationally grounded genres that come to serve as counterpoint to such universal humanity include the novel of worldliness, which was produced above all in France and which eighteenth-century English critics condemned for its licentious depiction of manners. Similarly, contemporary French critics debated British writers' consistent attention to life in low society and the particulars of material existence, even while French translators such as Prévost purged British novels of their excessive interest in material detail. And even sentimental fiction, while fundamentally a transnational genre, not only acquires specific English and French articulations, as Cohen argues, but is a privileged site for formulating what Alliston calls the pan-European vernacular of "national character."[43]

A history of the novel narrated from the perspective of the Channel thus underscores the longstanding claim of feminist literary historians that "rise of the novel" narratives privileging realism displace the powerful presence of sentimentality in the literary field.[44] A renewed focus on the sentimental as the modern novel's core, its generic infrastructure, enables a reconsideration of the novel's engagement with the project of education; again, this was an effort pursued by writers in both Britain and France in the later eighteenth century. While the flow of British cultural transmission into France was dominated more by the scientific and epistemological insights of Scottish Enlightenment empiricism than by novels, Marmontel's moral tales, in contrast, were equally beloved on both sides of the Channel and gave rise to a didactic project for the novel made famous in each nation, as in Europe more generally, by Rousseau's *Emile* (1762) and Genlis's *Adèle et Théodore ou lettres sur l'éducation* (1782).

In this collection, the transnational didactic project appears in the form of its monstrous progeny, which Deidre Shauna Lynch gives pride of place in "The (Dis)locations of Romantic Nationalism: Shelley, Staël, and the Home-Schooling of Monsters." Lynch interrogates the Janus-faced ability of romantic fictions to invigorate cultural nationalisms and yet, in their more general dismantling of borders, mobilize a critique of national hegemonies. The novels of Staël and Shelley, Lynch contends, "jointly disarticulate 'mother' from 'nature' and 'mother' from 'country'" and suggest "that the lessons of Romanticism do not have to be those obtained through home-schooling." Women writers erode the comforting ideal of mother country and mother tongue, exposing the uncanniness— indeed, the monstrosity—at the heart of a newly Gothic domestic vision. Lynch also stresses the importance of the Celtic fringe, so important in the work of Edgeworth, too, in offering an unhomed homeland for such "dis-articulation."

The cross-Channel comparative context has long provided novelists on each side with a repository for all the characteristics of alterity. Even in the earliest French novels England figures as the "Other" nation-state whose existence plays a crucial role in defining a uniquely novelistic mode of history located at the intersection of private and public life. Thus, Lafayette's *La Princesse de Clèves* takes the distanced events of heroic romance and brings them to a court much closer to her audience's present, the court of Henri II, but also defines the private specificity of these events through an unrealized plot featuring a heroine beckoning from across the narrow sea. In this narrative the perverse history of Clèves and Nemours is a refusal of a distinctively public history in the form of Nemours' abandoned flirtation with Elizabeth; and it is also a counterpoint to the unlucky fate of Mary, Queen of Scots, who, the novel suggests, found the wrong way to mix politics and love.

Maxwell argues in the chapter "Phantom States: *Cleveland, The Recess*, and the Origins of Historical Fiction" that cross-Channel exchange is key in this process, for it serves to construct an *unheimlich* space that dismantles historical narratives binding family and nation together in a new alignment of personal and public history. In a reading of Prévost's *Cleveland* (1731–39) and Sophia Lee's *The Recess* (1785) Maxwell shows that the "phantom states" inhabited by royal pretenders serve as a metaphor "embodying, even justifying, dense literary mixtures of history and fiction." Historical novels offer a mode of imagining and also narrating history; the implication of the private sphere on the stage of history emerges through literary acts of Channel-crossing from Prévost to Lee, from Lafayette to Edgeworth, Cottin, Scott, Hugo, Dickens, and Balzac. When Balzac suggests that the novelist's ambition is to narrate the history of manners, forgotten by so many historians, he is in fact the inheritor of a long genealogy of transnational exchange.

Throughout the eighteenth century the cross-Channel zone of literary culture produced a vision of the universally emotive human subject abstracted from national difference and historical specificity. But with the rise of the nation as imagined community such universality itself bolstered a new, nationally articulated version of history. In turn, it became the basis of claims by novelists on each side of the Channel to offer novels that coordinated nation with narration. During the Napoleonic Wars, for example, patterns of cross-Channel exchange were notably uneven. In France, the value ascribed to English novels was emblematized by their prominence in works creating a newly French literary canon, such as La Harpe's *Lycée, ou cours de littérature ancienne et moderne*, even as, according to Marilyn Butler, "[f]or about a decade from 1802, . . . the importation or translation of books from France, which had before been a flood, was reduced to a trickle."[45] Yet at the same time, the nineteenth-century historical novel, so closely bound to the emergence of cultural nationalisms, was itself a product of Channel crossings, not only, as Maxwell has suggested, in the way such crossings created imagined phantom states but as a vital site of generic cross-fertilization.

It is striking testimony to the semiautonomy of the literary Channel that this process occurred across the Napoleonic Wars; from this perspective, Scott's *Waverley* (1814) was as much the conclusion of twenty years of cross-Channel exchange as a new beginning. It brought together a number of subgenres, read on either side of the Channel, concerned to make sense of the violence of the Revolution: the Gothic, dominated by Radcliffe and Roche, the novel of manners (Opie and Edgeworth were most important in France, Austen to a notably lesser extent), a picaresque and immoral French comic novel, and an explosion of French sentimental fiction in the post-Revolutionary period, some of it with an explicitly historical focus, such as Cottin's *Mathilde* and Genlis's *La Duchesse de la Vallière* and *Mademoiselle de Clermont*. The historical novel also was shaped, as Katie Trumpener has discussed, from the interrogation of nationhood offered by Irish- and Scottish-identified writers around the turn of the nineteenth century, who simultaneously belong to an English literary tradition and resist Englishness through the assertion of political and cultural independence.[46] Writers such as Morgan and Edgeworth, moreover, occasionally triangulated their alternative nationalist literary projects through generic allusion to French practices and through positive cultural representations associating the French with tolerant cosmopolitanism. Not only had the French historically been supportive of internal rebellion as a strategy to destabilize the British nation but such Francophilia allowed insurgent writers to mark their difference from the political and cultural xenophobia then prominent in Britain.

Once we become attentive to the Channel's implication in the colonial problematic, the England-France-colonies triangulation provokes reconsideration of the security of national borders even in those canonical authors most often credited with their defense. In "Gender, Empire, and Epistolarity" Françoise Lionnet reveals how such triangulation makes its way into Jane Austen's *Mansfield Park*, rereading the novel through its contemporary rewriting in Marie-Thérèse Humbert's *La Montagne des Signaux* (1994). Situating *Mansfield Park* in the context of its publication coincident with the signing of the Treaty of Paris and the accelerating abolitionist movement in Britain, Lionnet proposes that Austen foregrounds the unstable authority of writing, troubling novelistic distinctions between oral and written as well as official and vernacular languages. As the example of Humbert's text makes clear, this reformulates the power relations of colony and metropole within terms both gendered and melancholic. Lionnet suggests that Humbert, "writing from the antipodes, . . . refracts back to Austen the dynamics of transnational, postcolonial, and transcolonial cultural formations." Finally, Humbert and Austen, in dialogue with each other and through their use of the epistolary mode, make explicit the gendered nature of this extranational range of cultural formations.

If Scott's *Waverley* confirms the novel's new power to provide narratives of English national identity, it serves an analogous function across the Channel when it breaks upon the French literary scene about 1820. Initially viewed as popular entertainment, Scott's novels become increasingly valued, along with the international works they inspire, especially those of Cooper and Manzoni. This moment is worth underscoring for it marks the beginning of the transformation of the novel into an internationally based literary form and the power of this dissemination in turn to shape and dissolve the trans-Channel zone.[47] Previously, isolated works from beyond the Channel zone had played a formative role in the history of the novel. These works include premodern prose that was widely read and appreciated in the early modern period, ranging from Heliodorus's *Ethiopian Romance* to Cervantes's *Don Quixote*.[48] In the later eighteenth century the novels of Goethe celebrated in a cosmopolitan Enlightenment republic of letters figured prominently. But historical fiction inaugurated a moment of generalized international diffusion that dissolved the hegemony of the cross-Channel formation altogether.

Within France, the historical novel brought a solution to a problem that had troubled French writers of the 1820s: how to take account of the social divisions fissuring French society given the literary subgenres at writers' disposal.[49] To represent the diverse classes and groups comprising the post-Revolutionary nation was a difficult challenge for the idealizing codes of sentimentality, though Sand's novels indicate that it was possible. Scott, however, provided an effective way to incorporate social specificity into sentimentality via the use of social detail that had long been the province of the British tradition, where writers were markedly more hospitable to empiricism. Scott's novels combined a core of sentimentality with a strongly descriptive style and a historical, often heroic plot, and his poetic innovations inspired diverse experimentation by a range of French writers. Balzac and Stendhal, for example, adapted Scott's methods by dismantling the ethical content of sentimentality, turning its struggles into an amoral game to succeed, in keeping with the older French novelistic paradigm of worldliness.

The cross-Channel field gained a new impetus from a decisive development in the 1830s that would influence all literary production to follow: the invention of mass-market literature. A product of cheaper techniques of printing, the first genres of mass literature were the novel and the newspaper, forms that Anderson argues underpin the constitution of the nation as imagined community. But much as the new mass novel may have fortified an individual sense of national belonging, these works in fact were much more cosmopolitan than is sometimes emphasized, and indeed the first communities of mass entertainment owed a great deal to the transnational communities forged in the context of cross-Channel exchange. No subgenre of mass fiction illustrates this more clearly than the sensationalized mystery novel, pioneered by Sue and Dumas in France and by Dickens and Reynolds in England, which was a cross-Channel publishing event before it swiftly achieved international fame.[50]

In their popular serial form these texts were produced through the integration of a range of nonfictional and fictional subgenres for depicting the new metropoles of Paris and London as urban, and national, capitals. At the same time, when they displaced the moral and physical heroism of a Scott or a Cooper novel from liminal territories to be conquered in the name of the nation to the urban jungle of the newly industrialized modern city, urban serial novels also devised a new international common denominator in the form of the great metropolis. The international appeal of these works was reinforced by their use of sentimental codes that historically had had the power to catalyze communities across national borders. Perhaps as a result, they exponentially expanded the non-nationally based communities of consumption that Festa has described, already catalyzed by Richardson's *Pamela* a century earlier. These were rapidly resituated and rewritten to suit local context by authors around the globe into, for example, *Die Geheimnisse von Berlin*, by Paul Thiel (1845); *The Quaker City; or The Monks of Monk Hall*, by George Lippard (1844–45); *The Mysteries and Miseries of New York*, by Ned Buntline (1848); *Madrid y sus misterios*, by Ramon de Naverette (1845–46); *Los misterios de Barcelona*, by J. N. Milà de la Roca (1844); and, as late as the 1860s, *I misteri di Napoli*, by Francesco Mastriani (begun in 1864), and *Peterburskie Truschoby*, by V. V. Krestovski (1864).

No gesture more confirms the urban serial novel's cosmopolitan potential than mid-Victorian efforts to domesticate its internationalism, which Carolyn Dever describes in " 'An Occult and Immoral Tyranny': The Novel, The Police, and the Agent Provocateur." Victorian British pulp detective fictions seek to secure national boundaries through a familiar gesture of displacement across the Channel, registering a newly absolute equation of the French with vice, erotic transgression, and moral dissolution. Dever shows that such a mix of fascinated revulsion destabilizes codes of English domestic virtue as much as it secures them. Detective fiction, the most popular literary genre of the later nineteenth and twentieth centuries, first took shape, Dever argues, as an expression of ambivalence concerning the Victorian forging of mechanisms of soft power; that ambivalence was expressed by displacement onto a mythic vision of France, where absolutism and the Terror met in domestic catastrophe.

In the mid-nineteenth century the cross-Channel literary zone persisted as a sociological institution even as national literary fields became strengthened in conjunction with an increasing devotion to the nation as an imagined community. In the context of developing copyright laws, for example, the covers of the first four serialized numbers of Dickens's *Bleak House* (1852–53) read: "NOTICE is hereby given that the author of 'Bleak House' reserves to himself the right of publishing a Translation in France." This suggests the remaining power of the cross-Channel context as well as the revision of juridical categories of authorship that reinforced distinctions grounded in national identity. That Dickens changed his notice in the fifth number to read "The Author of this Work notifies that it is his intention to reserve the right of translating it" should only underscore the sense in which the Channel remains the first line of national defense.[51]

Another important strategy for bolstering the national defense was the identification of literary history with national culture, a project that emerged in conjunction with the institutionalization of nationally based literary studies in both Britain and France. As Warner says of literary history in the British context, "During the nineteenth century, the novel was gradually nationalized. Influential critics such as Hazlitt and Scott came to understand novels as a type of writing particularly suited to representing the character, mores, landscape and spirit of particular nations."[52] In France this process began with the Revolutionary-Napoleonic invention of modern cultural nationalism. Such nationalism found one of its principal supports in the creation of a centralized, comprehensive system of education in which a newly devised French literary canon played a prominent role.

The close links between a nationally based literary history and the cultural education of the citizen were epitomized in one of the first works to set this new canon's terms, Jean-François La Harpe's *Cours de littérature française ancienne et moderne* (1791–1804). Yet, as we have already mentioned, such was the prominence of the trans-Channel zone that La Harpe features the powerful eighteenth-century British contribution to the genesis of the modern novel and, indeed, demonstrates marked ambivalence over whether this work, along with the genre itself, should be nationally or universally identified. "For me, the premier novel in the world is *Tom-Jones*," he declares. Several paragraphs later, he has amended this statement to "*Tom-Jones* is the best written novel of England."[53] It should also be stressed that for La Harpe the cultural value of the novel is middling: he considers it a polite but in no way major literary genre, and his view is characteristic of critics on both sides of the Channel at the turn of the nineteenth century. The novel did not rise toward the pinnacle of the generic hierarchy until the 1830s and 1840s in France and the 1840s in England, a rise that was contemporaneous with the genre's taking on the ambitious project of representing a panorama of contemporary society. The trans-Channel perspective highlights how closely the novel's rising cultural value was aligned with the genre's insertion into a nationalist frame.

Once the novel became anchored squarely within national culture, the still powerful transnational connection was no longer likely to be expressed through an open rhetoric of homage and contestation, but rather obliquely, through "the overwhelming accumulation of negation, ellipsis, periphrasis, and metonymic allusions," as Sharon Marcus writes of the rhetoric of disavowal surrounding Victorian discussions of sapphism. In "Comparative Sapphism" Marcus suggests that Victorian critics mapped literary sapphism onto their cross-Channel literary Other as a means of moral displacement. "The sexual difference," Marcus writes, "between the French and British novel is also homosexual." Marcus locates the erotic politics of Victorian literary culture with its aesthetic politics, linking the British resistance to sapphism with a resistance to realism that critics expressed through their allegiance to idealism.

The death of Queen Victoria in 1901 offered symbolic closure to the nineteenth century and to the moral and aesthetic values of the Victorian period. But in some sense the century can be said to have ended a year earlier, in a highly symbolic act of Channel-crossing: following his release from Reading Gaol, where he had been imprisoned following his conviction on charges stemming from sodomy, Oscar Wilde left England to take up residence in Paris, converting to the Catholic Church at the moment of his death on 30 November 1900.

Wilde's retreat to France made literal a circuit of cultural exchange in which he had participated throughout his life as a poet, essayist, playwright, and novelist: the English aesthetes quite conspicuously embraced ideals of opulence and libertinism coded as French as a means of critiquing and rejecting the perceived rigidity of British social identity. Indeed, the aesthete's pleasures represent a veritable archive of Channel transgression. In Wilde's novel, Dorian Gray surveys the contents of Lord Henry Wotton's Mayfair library: "On a tiny satinwood table stood a statuette by Clodion, and beside it lay a copy of *Les Cent Nouvelles*, bound for Margaret of Valois by Clovis Eve, and powdered with the gilt daisies that Queen had selected for her device. . . . [T]he lad was looking rather sulky, as with listless fingers he turned over the pages of an elaborately-illustrated edition of *Manon Lescaut* that he had found in one of the bookcases. The formal monotonous ticking of the Louis Quatorze clock annoyed him."[54]

From the perspective of French decadence, the invocation of cross-Channel alterity worked similarly, in the service not of national self-definition but rather of subversion. This subversion might have been called the Lord Dudley principle, in honor of one of its first powerful French formulations, in Balzac's *La Fille aux yeux d'or* (1834), a novel whose representations of sexuality were, Marcus shows, crucial to the definition of literary realism as French in the Victorian context. The biological "author," as Balzac puts it, of Henri de Marsay and Margarita-Euphémia Porrabéril, the two characters in competition for the affections of the girl with the golden eyes, is a shadowy Lord Dudley invoked only through hearsay, whose ability to transgress boundaries is such that, when inquiring after the identity of the handsome Marsay upon first meeting him as a grown man, Lord Dudley is reputed to have remarked only, "Oh! he's my son. How unfortunate!"[55] In such usage the gesture of cross-Channel "othering" so prominent in the history of the novel takes on an altogether new significance; it becomes the means to subvert the categories constitutive of national identity and order, and bound up in this attack is the category of the novel itself.[56]

Displacement via England will hence be a paradigmatic gesture in a French decadent lineage crucial to defining avant-garde notions of transgression. This lineage finds its culmination in the Anglophilia of Des Esseintes, the hero of J.-K. Huysmans's *A Rebours*, and in Stéphane Mallarmé's protosurrealist efforts at an English grammar book (Mallarmé was himself an English teacher) in which he invents a hallucinatory, hilarious third language in the slippages between French and English. With this gesture Mallarmé turns cross-Channel othering to the alterity of what Kristeva and Barthes would later call textuality, which he aims against nationalism, consumption, pedagogy, and the clichés of touristic ethnography.[57]

Even after cross-Channel exchange had ceased to play a defining role in producing the modern novel, themes and issues from its history continued to resonate. In an afterword included to suggest the afterlife of the literary Channel into our own present, Emily Apter considers the contours of novelistic transnationalism in the new Europe, which takes the form of an intra-European novel engaged with shrinking national markers, a kind of "money market" or "middle management" literature subduing regionalist or minority narrative forms. In its millennial iteration, the supranational no longer transcends the oppressive dimensions to national organization but rather becomes the dehumanizing power of capital to annihilate specificity in the homogenous and sterile culture of global capitalism, while blatantly distasteful, indeed oppressive, nationalism becomes the last resistance of the universal human subject initially produced in the novel's international exchange.

Apter identifies this reversal transforming the literary Channel's complex interplay of novelistic genres into the anodyne generic of "Eurofiction" with the transformation of the literary Channel into the Chunnel zone. The year 1994 marked the inaugural run of a circuit of international exchange transforming the Channel into the Chunnel zone, in the form of the Eurostar linking London and Paris. The route's extension from Paris to Brussels, capital of the European Union, is an apt figure for the imperative to triangulate if we are to understand cultural crossings in the postmodern era. Transnational literary studies is also a development of the late nineties, and it is our hope that *The Literary Channel* not only recuperates previously marginalized literary and cultural formations but also suggests all that critics have to gain from such an archaeology. Claims about global and transnational culture now proliferate, as social processes of globalization are taken to a new level. These claims are often made with a historical amnesia that, while to some extent enabling, eventually ends up eroding the specificity of the very formations they are intended to describe. One effective way to approach the contemporary conjuncture is by exploring the practices of the past. Far from a detour, this inquiry illuminates not only the present's specificity but also those aspects of history that are currently very much alive.

The archaeology of inter- and transnational cultural formations poses a particular challenge to literary scholars, even comparatists, given the power of national identification as the logic organizing literary history since the nineteenth century. But the difficulty of this enterprise in no way diminishes its urgency, though it does heighten the need for collaboration, along with the need to accept, paradoxical as it might seem, that the only way to approach the global is through the fragmentary and the incomplete. In this volume we isolate key moments—points of inflection that are indicative but in no way exhaustive—across a broad historical arc. We will have met our aims if the range of our interventions suggests the alternative canons, social structures, and urgent methodological questions to be excavated from the Channel zone.

## Notes

1. Clara Reeve, *The Progress of Romance* (1785; reprint, New York: Facsimile Text Society, 1930), 111.

2. Ioan Williams, ed., *Novel and Romance, 1700–1800* (London: Routledge & Kegan Paul; New York: Barnes & Noble, 1970), 6. In England, critical recognition that the novel is a distinct new genre starts to emerge, according to Williams, around 1740 and is catalyzed by the publication of Richardson's *Pamela*. During the first decades of the eighteenth century "writers who did comment on fiction tended, like Shaftsbury in his *Characteristics* (1711), to attack it because it was ridiculous or indecent" (6). In France, critical attention to the novel occurred much earlier, for as Joan DeJean has shown, the genre figured centrally in late-seventeenth-century aesthetic debates between Boileau and Huet over the trans- and extranational components of French culture. Tellingly, Boileau excised the novel in formulating his "politicoliterary vision of conquest and assimilation," while Huet, who envisioned "a political system that . . . find[s] in a multinational heritage a source of strength," promoted the novel as a constitutively transnational genre (Joan DeJean, *Tender Geographies: Women and the Origins of the Novel in France* [New York: Columbia University Press, 1991], 176).

3. Moretti's work on the imaginary and social geographies that constructed the novel as a European form is tremendously important for us and in fact opens the door to a methodology at the intersection of sociology, cartography, and rhetorical criticism, whose details have yet to be entirely worked out. In the course of a suggestive sampling correlating geography and novelistic production of the eighteenth and nineteenth centuries Moretti found that "for the entire period of the novel's take-off (1720–1850) . . . most European countries import from abroad a large portion of their novels . . . whereas France and Britain form a group to themselves, that imports very little from the rest of the European continent: a fact which has a very simple explanation—these two countries *produce* a lot of novels . . . so they don't need to buy them abroad" (Franco Moretti, *Atlas of the European Novel, 1800–1900* [New York: Verso, 1998], 151). Moretti subsequently elaborates that "while trying to quantify 'the rise of the European novel', for instance, we quickly realized that there was not *one*, but (at least) three such take-offs: the first around 1720–1750 (in the core: France, Britain, and a little later Germany); the second around 1820–1850 (for a half a dozen countries or so); and a third one, later still, for all the others . . . [w]ith France and Britain always in the core" (173–74). Moretti borrows the notion of the core from Immanuel Wallerstein's description of the international geography of global capitalism. The richness of Britain's internal divisions for literary production emphasizes the need to make sure that the opposition of core and periphery suggests neither term as a monolithic formation, a caution that has been applied to Wallerstein's theory more generally. For "Britain" in fact includes England's internal colonies, which play a role in the genesis of such key novelistic forms as the historical novel (see Katie Trum-

pener, *Bardic Nationalism: The Romantic Novel and the British Empire* [Princeton: Princeton University Press, 1997]).

4. There is also a critical lineage reaching from Mikhail Bakhtin through Tomas Hägg, and most recently Margaret Anne Doody, that has written eloquently about the modern novel's prehistory in antiquity. Doody, notably, discusses the processes of rewriting and reading by which classical forms were transmitted to the early modern era. Generic analyses of the premodern novel have yet to be integrated fully with accounts written from the perspective of modernity that stress what is innovative about the eighteenth-century version of the genre. It has often been suggested, for example, that the modern novel not only records but helps to create a distinctively new notion of psychological subjectivity and a distinctively new sense of spatiotemporal coherence and causal motivation. At the same time, critics working on the classical novel have pointed to continuity between antique and modern creations of psychology and depth. Recent awareness of the way in which literary genres have been shaped by the politics of empire may offer a powerful materialist tool for linking novelistic genres that predate capitalism with the modern novel, whose emergence has always been linked to the inception of capitalism in its full-fledged modern form. On the need to situate claims about the novel's distinctive modernity in relation to the antique practice of the novel and its vitality across the literary history of Europe, see Doody, *The True Story of the Novel* (New Brunswick, N.J.: Rutgers University Press, 1996). See also Mikhail Bakhtin, *The Dialogic Imagination: Four Essays*, ed. Michael Holquist, trans. Caryl Emerson and Michael Holquist (Austin: University of Texas Press, 1981); and Tomas Hägg, *The Novel in Antiquity* (Berkeley and Los Angeles: University of California Press, 1983).

5. We are indebted to Emily Apter for highlighting the zone's ability to illuminate the study of literature in transnational contexts. See, notably, Apter's *In the Translation Zone: Language Wars and Literary Politics*, forthcoming from Princeton University Press. See also her "On Translation in a Global Market" and "Balkan Babel: Translation Zones, Military Zones," *Public Culture* 13, no. 1 (2001): 10–12 and 65–80, respectively. A critical bibliography on the notion of zone includes the work of Gilles Deleuze, Félix Guattari, and Paul Virilio, as well as Hakim Bey's *T.A.Z.: The Temporary Autonomous Zone, Ontological Anarchy, Poetic Terrorism* (Brooklyn, N.Y.: Autonomedia, 1991) and Mary Louise Pratt's *Imperial Eyes: Travel Writing and Transculturation* (London: Routledge, 1992). See, too, Apollinaire's "Zone," in Guillaume Apollinaire, *Alcools: poems*, trans. Donald Revell (Hanover, N.H.: Wesleyan University Press, University Presses of New England, 1995), as well as Thomas Pynchon's notion of "The Zone" elaborated in *Gravity's Rainbow* (New York: Viking, 1973).

6. Sigmund Freud, *The Interpretation of Dreams*, in *The Standard Edition of the Complete Psychological Works of Sigmund Freud*, trans. and ed. James Strachey (London: Hogarth Press and Institute of Psycho-Analysis, 1953), vol. 5.

7. Georg Lukács, *The Historical Novel* (1937), trans. Hannah Mitchell and Stanley Mitchell (London: Merlin, 1982), 23.

8. Erich Auerbach, *Mimesis: The Representation of Reality in Western Literature*, trans. Willard R. Trask (Princeton: Princeton University Press, 1953), 458.

9. Michael Holquist, in Bakhtin, *Dialogic Imagination*, xxxi.

10. Timothy Brennan offers an alternative reading of Bakhtin's significance for studies linking the novel and nation in "The National Longing for Form," in *Nation and Narration*, ed. Homi K. Bhabha (New York: Routledge, 1990).

11. Thus Michael McKeon writes: "What is required is a theory not just of the rise of the novel but of how categories, whether 'literary' or 'social,' exist in history: how they first coalesce by being understood in terms of—as transformations of—other forms that have thus far been taken to define the field of possibility" (*The Origins of the English Novel, 1600–1740* [Baltimore: Johns Hopkins University Press, 1987], 4).

12. Ian Watt, *The Rise of the Novel: Studies in Defoe, Richardson, and Fielding* (Berkeley and Los Angeles: University of California Press, 1957), 9.

13. George May, *Le Dilemme du roman au dix-huitième siècle* (Paris: Presses Universitaires de France; New Haven: Yale University Press, 1963), 183. Unless otherwise indicated, all translations from French originals cited in this introduction are by Cohen.

14. Thomas DiPiero's observation apropos of Watt can be extended to May. Both fail "to consider historical developments in French history that, although they lacked the *éclat* of revolution, still had profound effects on social, economic, and cultural life . . . it is an oversimplification to adhere to a rigid formula dictating the conditions necessary for the production of prose fiction" (*Dangerous Truths, Criminal Passions* [Stanford: Stanford University Press, 1992], 11). DiPiero's introduction offers a good account of some of the impasses encountered by French critics overly swayed by Watt's model. At the same time, DiPiero himself perpetuates the generic orthodoxy of Watt, since he gives us an eighteenth century without sentimental fiction.

15. Peter Brooks's *Novel of Worldliness* (Princeton: Princeton University Press, 1969) offers another good example of the discomfort provoked by the eighteenth-century French novel's difference from Watt's paradigm. Brooks opens this work by astutely criticizing the weight of *The Rise of the Novel* on accounts of the French novel: "[M]ost study of the novel has in fact consciously or unconsciously shared an outlook formed by the great tradition of nineteenth-century bourgeois realism and its modern transmutations; attention to the eighteenth century has been directed and filtered through this optic in a search for origins. While such an approach has given a fine and subtle account of the major eighteenth-century English novelists in Ian Watt's *The Rise of the Novel*, it can only falsify and distort the French fiction which interests me in this study" (3). At moments, however, Brooks himself looks longingly across the Channel to British fiction of the eighteenth century, belittling the beginnings of bourgeois culture in France. For Brooks, as for so many other critics informed by Watt's narrative, that paradigmatic cross-Channel genre, sentimental fiction, plays a minor role.

16. Important critics in this lineage include Barbéris, Moretti, Prendergast, Terdiman, and even Barthes in his own way. Macherey's focus is also indicative of the problem we are describing: his studies move from Robinson Crusoe to French novelists of the nineteenth century, first Balzac, then the popular fiction of Verne.

17. Friedrich Engels, *The Condition of the Working Class in England*, trans. and ed. W. O. Henderson and W. H. Chaloner (Oxford: Basil Blackwell, 1958).

18. For the diverse methodologies that have led feminist critics to rethink literary exchange beyond national borders, see, for example, the writings of April Alliston, Nina Auerbach, Joan DeJean, Catherine Gallagher, Nancy Miller, Felicity Nussbaum, and Patricia Spacks.

19. Bhabha, *Nation and Narration*, 4.

20. William Beatty Warner, *Licensing Entertainment: The Elevation of Novel Reading in Britain, 1684–1750* (Berkeley and Los Angeles: University of California Press, 1998), 19. Stating that that eighteenth-century British "debate about the novel" "assumes that the novels of different nations belong to the same cultural field" and that in fact "eighteenth-century British cultural critics often gave France precedence over England in the invention of several different species of romances and novels," Warner suggests that novels became nationalized "coextensive with the nationalization of culture and the rise of the discipline of English literary studies" (20, 19).

21. Bhabha, *Nation and Narration*, 4.

22. See Georg Lukács, "Reification and the Consciousness of the Proletariat," in *History and Class Consciousness: Studies in Marxist Dialectics*, trans Rodney Livingstone (Cambridge: MIT Press, 1971), 83–222.

23. Soysal characterizes the current conjuncture as a moment when "contemporary membership formations have superseded the dichotomy that opposes the national citizen and the alien, by including populations that were previously defined as outside the national polity. Rights that used to belong solely to nationals are now extended to foreign populations, thereby undermining the very basis of national citizenship" (Yasemin Nuhoglu Soysal, "Towards a Postnational Model of Membership," in *The Citizenship Debates*, ed. Gebon Shefir [Minneapolis: University of Minnesota Press, 1999], 191).

24. Katharyne Mitchell, "Multiculturalism in Canada," in *Global/Local*, ed. Rob Wilson and Wimal Dissanayake (Durham, N.C.: Duke University Press, 1996), 219, 220. Other collections that offer useful examples of how the notion of the transnational is currently being used to rethink postmodern cultural formations include *Scattered Hegemonies*, ed. by Inderpal Grewal and Caren Kaplan (Minneapolis: University of Minnesota Press, 1994); *Between Women and Nation: Nationalisms, Transnational Feminisms, and the State*, ed. Norma Alarcón, Caren Kaplan, and Minoo Moallem (Durham, N.C.: Duke University Press, 1999), which includes articles by a number of contributors to *Scattered Hegemonies*; and *Streams of Cultural Capital: Transnational Cultural Studies*, ed. by David Palumbo-Liu and Hans Ulrich Gumbrecht (Stanford: Stanford University Press, 1997).

25. Linda Colley, *Britons: Forging the Nation, 1707–1837* (New Haven: Yale University Press, 1992), 1.

26. Edmond Dziembowski, notably, has raised the question of the importance of wars against Britain in the emergence of a modern notion of the nation in France (see Edmond Dziembowski, *Un Nouveau Patriotisme français, 1750–1770: La France face à la puissance anglaise à l'époque de la guerre de Sept Ans*, Studies on Voltaire and the Eighteenth Century, 365 (Oxford: Voltaire Foundation, 1998). An earlier volume in the series, vol. 292, entitled *The Channel in the Eighteenth Century: Bridge, Barrier, and Gateway*, ed. John Falvey and William Brooks (Oxford: Voltaire Foundation, 1991), offers a range of case studies documenting the intensity of Anglo-French cultural exchange during the eighteenth century. On the eighteenth-century French fascination with British culture, see also Josephine Grieder's *Anglomania in France, 1740–1789: Fact, Fiction, and Political Discourse* (Geneva: Droz, 1985).

27. Robert L. Dawson, "Books Printed in France: The English Connection," in Falvey and Brooks, *Channel in the Eighteenth Century*, 140, 139. The English newspaper was the bilingual *Papiers anglais*, which "were to provide selections from some of the best British gazettes of the day" (140 n. 1). Dawson observes that the English were far more likely to learn French than the other way around since French was the international lingua franca of the eighteenth century.

28. Such cross-Channel interchange was in part facilitated by the wars; émigré intellectuals in England played an important role in the history of the novel both following the Huguenot expulsion and in the wake of the French Revolution. But these wars were also inconveniences to the flourishing cross-Channel literary and cultural fields, as witnessed by the "surge of traveling from England to the Continent" when peace was declared following hostilities; the peace of 1763, for example, produced an explosion of Continental travel narratives written by British expatriates such as Smollett and Sterne.

29. Colley, *Britons*, 3.

30. Fredric Jameson, *The Political Unconscious* (Ithaca: Cornell University Press, 1981). We insist on genre as a basic way of categorizing literary works in accordance with the Jamesonian principle that genres not only represent society but are themselves social products; they are the material formations by which poetics interpellate readers by addressing social contradiction. We also use genre in accordance with Bourdieu's notion that genre is a historically located position situating writers within the contemporary literary field rather than an abstract system of classification. On how Jameson and Bourdieu's notions of genre may productively be integrated for the contemporary practice of literary history, see Margaret Cohen, *The Sentimental Education of the Novel* (Princeton: Princeton University Press, 1999).

31. See Moretti, *Atlas of the European Novel*.

32. The following account is indebted to all the chapters in this volume and also to the generous contributions of Julia Douthwaite, Deidre Shauna Lynch, Sharon Marcus, Richard Maxwell, and Mary Helen McMurran. Any inaccuracies are solely the editors'.

33. On the introduction of French romance into England, see Thomas Philip Haviland, *The Roman de longue haleine on English Soil* (Philadelphia: University of Pennsylvania, 1931); and Annabel M. Patterson, *Censorship and Interpretation: The Conditions of Writing and Reading in Early Modern Europe* (Madison: University of Wisconsin Press, 1984). For information about the literary traffic from France to Britain in the Restoration, see also Robert Adams Day, *Told in Letters: Epistolary Fiction before Richardson* (Ann Arbor: University of Michigan Press, 1966); and David F. Foxon, *Libertine Literature in England, 1660–1745* (London: Shenval, 1964).

34. We thank Deidre Lynch for information about Delarivière Manley.

35. We owe this question, along with many details in this overview, to Mary Helen McMurran. For details on the flow of translations in each direction see her "Translation and the Novel, 1660–1800" (Ph.D. diss., New York University, 1998).

36. See May, *Le Dilemme du roman*, 76.

37. William Warburton, preface to vol. 3 of *Clarissa Harlowe* (1748), republished in Williams, *Novel and Romance*, 123.

38. Williams, *Novel and Romance*, 122.

39. On Richardson's relation to the *chroniques scandaleuses*, see Catherine Gallagher, *Nobody's Story: The Vanishing Acts of Women Writers in the Marketplace, 1670–1820* (Berkeley and Los Angeles: University of California Press, 1994).

40. On this subject, see Dena Goodman's *The Republic of Letters: A Cultural History of the French Enlightenment* (Ithaca: Cornell University Press, 1994).

41. Our thanks to Richard Maxwell for this information. For more on the translation of sentimental fiction in England, see Josephine Grieder, *Translations of French Sentimental Prose Fiction in Late Seventeenth-Century England: The History of a Literary Vogue* (Durham, N.C.: Duke University Press, 1975).

42. "The dates that are often singled out as signaling the advent of nationalism include 1775 (the First Partition of Poland), 1776 (the American Declaration of Independence), 1789 (the commencement and second phase of the French Revolution), and 1808 (Fichte's *Addresses to the German Nation*)," write John Hutchinson and Anthony D. Smith in their preface to the collection *Nationalism* (New York: Oxford University Press, 1994), 5.

43. See also Alliston's forthcoming *Character and Plausibility: Gender and the Genres of Historical Narrative, 1650–1850*.

44. John Richetti's tremendously useful *Popular Fiction before Richardson: Narrative Patterns, 1700–1739* (Oxford: Clarendon, 1969) constitutes an exception to this neglect, though Richetti does not entirely escape reading fiction through "the dark glasses of late realism," as Alliston points out in "Female Sexuality and the Referent of Enlightenment Realisms," in *Spectacles of Realism*, ed. Margaret Cohen and Christopher Prendergast (Minneapolis: University of Minnesota Press, 1995), 21.

45. Marilyn Butler, *Romantics, Rebels, and Reactionaries: English Literature and Its Background, 1760–1830* (New York: Oxford University Press, 1982), 115. Our thanks to Deidre Lynch for this citation.

46. On this subject, see Trumpener, *Bardic Nationalism*.

47. See Moretti's *Atlas of the European Novel* for suggestive numbers concerning the shift of novelistic production outwards from the Channel, notably the previously quoted section on 173–74.

48. On the novel's global premodern antecedents, see Bakhtin, *Dialogic Imagination*; Doody, *True Story of the Novel*; and Hägg, *Novel in Antiquity*.

49. On this subject, see Cohen, *Sentimental Education of the Novel*.

50. On this subject, see Richard Maxwell, *The Mysteries of Paris and London* (Charlottesville: University Press of Virginia, 1992). Our thanks here to Maxwell and Sharon Marcus.

51. In the developing context of international copyright legislation France paved the way with an 1852 law that extended the copyright protections afforded works of French authors to works by foreign authors as well. This prompted the widespread call for a binding international agreement, which fourteen signature nations, including France and Britain, achieved at the Berne Convention of 1886.

52. Warner, *Licensing Entertainment*, 20.

53. Jean-François La Harpe, *Cours de littérature ancienne et moderne*, 3 vols. (1791–1804; reprint, Paris: Firmin Didot, 1851), 3:192.

54. Oscar Wilde, *The Picture of Dorian Gray* (1891; reprint, ed. Peter Ackroyd, New York: Penguin, 1985), 51. On decadence, see Linda Dowling, *Hellenism and Homosexuality in Victorian Oxford* (Ithaca: Cornell University Press, 1994). On Wilde, see Richard Ellmann, *Oscar Wilde* (New York: Knopf, 1987).

55. Honoré de Balzac, *La Fille aux yeux d'or* (1834; reprint, Paris: Garnier, 1966), 393.

56. On the decadent use of England in nineteenth-century French literature, see Rhonda K. Garelick, *Rising Star: Dandyism, Gender, and Performance in the Fin de siècle* (Princeton: Princeton University Press, 1998).

57. We cannot resist the brief example of Mallarmé's list of supposedly good English proverbs to help French readers remember English exclamations: "1. You cry *hem!* When there is no echo. 2. *What!* Keep a dog and bark myself. 3. It is time enough to cry *oh!* When you are hurt. 4. *Back* with that leg" (Stéphane Mallarmé, *Thèmes anglais*, in *Oeuvres complètes*, ed. Henri Mondor and G. Jean-Aubry [Paris: Bibliothèque de la Pléiade, 1974], 1156).

# PART I

# The Novel without Borders

JOAN DeJEAN

## CHAPTER ONE

# Transnationalism and the Origins of the (French?) Novel

Nabokov: American novelist, born in St. Petersburg.

*Oxford Companion to Twentieth-Century Literature in English*

Who were the most important early French novelists? Indeed, what do we mean when we say that a seventeenth-century writer was French? Once we begin to examine the grounds on which we determine the nationality of early modern writers, the answers to questions such as these no longer seem predictable.

Rather than continuing to write and rewrite the history of what we think of monolithically as The French Novel, we might begin to imagine a transnational history of the novel in French—and the novel in English, and so forth—a history that would encourage us to focus on all the geographic eccentricities of the genre's production and to question the absolute Frenchness of novelists such as Jean-Jacques Rousseau, a citizen of Geneva who composed many of his major works in his native country and in England; the Frenchman Voltaire, who also wrote both in England and in Switzerland; and Isabella van Tuyll van Serooskerken, known to French scholars as Isabelle de Charrière, who composed her extensive oeuvre in French but was of Dutch origin and worked in Switzerland. The time may be right for a history of the French novel in which we interrogate the meanings previously assigned these terms in order to open up *novel* to the full range of its possibilities, and, above all, to make the contours of *French* far less precise. What did it really mean to be a French novelist? How many novelists were truly and completely French?

This type of literary history would not be equally valid for all periods or for all geographic blends. For example, the nineteenth century, during which the novel became increasingly nationally based, would be less fertile ground for such geographic mixing. During the first century and a half of its existence, however, the novel was seldom the product of a single national literary tradition. During its formative period the modern novel was most often the result of massive shifts of influence back and forth across the English Channel—from 1660 to 1750, the prose fiction created both in England and in France was massively "French"; from 1750 on, it became increasingly "English." Those who study the novel are aware of these facts; all too seldom, however, do we take them into account when we think of how the genre took shape.

When it comes to issues of national status, in particular the function of the nation-state as a convenient marker for the classification of writers, scholars of the early modern period would do well to consider the ways in which this marking function was negotiated by twentieth-century studies. Literary history may at last be taking a cue from art history, which has long officially recognized the power of wandering artists to transform national traditions by making these artists "citizens" of those countries whose artistic history was permanently altered by their foreign presence.

Think, for example, of the two roughly contemporaneous artists now known as Rogier Van der Weyden and Corneille de Lyon. The first, born Rogelet de le Pasture in Tournai, was rechristened to reflect the fact that he owes his fame to his place in Netherlandish art. The second, born in either The Hague or Antwerp, was renamed because his career was played out in Lyon and at the French court. More importantly, the places in which they worked quite literally determined their place in art history: Corneille de Lyon has been officially assimilated as a French painter; his canvases are always hung alongside those of native-born French artists, while Van der Weyden's are never placed with those of the French tradition.

It is, of course, true that in the late fifteenth and early sixteenth centuries national status did not yet have the significance it acquired during the period when both the modern novel and the modern nation-state were coming into being. It is also true that artists of the day, often dependent on ducal and princely courts for patronage, were far more likely obliged to live out their careers on foreign soil than were artists of subsequent generations. Nevertheless, their example is still relevant later in the early modern period, and for the novel in particular. For many reasons, some of which I consider here, no genre has had a history more closely bound up with nomadic conditions of production than the modern novel. To forget this and write the novel's history as though each national tradition were an entity unto itself, as though each had developed without the stimulus of foreign artists, is to blind ourselves to a particularly significant type of literary interconnection.

Today, the country of a writer's birth is no longer seen as the sole determinant of national affiliation. Home now takes account of the country in which the body of the author's work was produced and the language in which that work was written. On this basis, Nabokov, to name but one example, is now referred to as an American novelist. Students of the early modern period, precisely the period during which no literary development was more significant than the so-called rise of the modern novel, have to date failed to share this assumption that national origins may be decided in more than one way. Early modernists have so far simply taken it for granted that it is easy to know which writers are French: French writers are those who wrote in the French language, no matter where they practiced their art. This unquestioned assumption has helped create a literary history that in general fails to account for the true geographic complexity of early modern literature.

I propose to reconsider the national affiliation of a few of the modern French novel's early practitioners. Even a small sampling is sufficient to indicate that the French cultural scene during the second half of the seventeenth century contained a strain of transnationalism that literary history has never seen fit to record. It also suggests that some of the major early novelists long considered part of the French tradition may well have been not quite so French as we have always assumed.

---

At its origins in late-seventeenth-century France the novel was widely considered a transnational genre by those who were giving it shape. In 1670, in his *Lettre-traité de l'origine des romans*, Pierre Daniel Huet—the genre's first great theoretician and the close collaborator of the two writers who guaranteed the novel's transition into its modern form, Madeleine de Scudéry and the comtesse de Lafayette—portrayed the genre as truly international.[1] The novel was, Huet argued, a form with multiple origins all over the globe, a form then transmitted in complicated fashion from one "nation" (a term he repeats incessantly) to another. In addition, and more importantly, Huet characterized the novel as a transnational genre, one passed on most prominently by nomadic artists, artists with no fixed national allegiance, and a genre that was therefore limited by no national borders.

In its most striking moments Huet's thesis describes how, at key junctures, the novel took on characteristics of the new culture in which it was implanted, while retaining aspects of its past national affiliations.[2] To make his point, he endows the novel's history with a primal scene, set in medieval Provence, which begins when storytellers work together to develop tales they call "romances" *(romans)*. From there, the storytellers spread out "across the world" to provide entertainment at the greatest courts. Sometimes a great lord, "thrilled with pleasure" at a wandering artist's recital, would "strip himself of his garments in order to dress [the storyteller] in them" (71). Huet subsequently returns to this scene in order to broaden its implications. The custom of royal divestment, he explains, was practiced in many countries, for instance, by French lords and also by their Arab contemporaries, the kings of Fez. The novel, Huet suggests, is a genre built on the refusal to recognize impermeable frontiers: its practitioners travel freely and take on the nationality of the king who gives them his clothes, and this acceptance of otherness benefits the assimilating society (77).

Huet's treatise may have seemed prophetic when, in 1685, the revocation of the Edict of Nantes, which had guaranteed freedom of religious expression, made a nomadic existence integral to the French cultural scene: the revocation forced numerous French artists and writers into the pan-European Protestant diaspora, obliging them to practice their art outside of France. One group thus exiled played a major role in the development of the modern novel: the French women novelists who created their works in Protestant countries such as England.[3] Literary history has always called these novelists simply "French." With its meditation on the manner in which national traditions are transformed by nomadic artists, as well as on the "nationality" of the artist who wears the clothes of a foreign prince, Huet's treatise suggests, however, a different take on their classification.

When we consider the artistic and the literary history of the twentieth century, we are accustomed to immediately taking into account the formative role played by such capitals as Paris, Berlin, and, more recently, New York as centers of cultural exchange and blending, as responsible for the creation of truly international art. We are, unfortunately, far less likely to have this reflex when it comes to pre-Revolutionary cultural phenomena. And yet, during that formative period for the novel, the 1680s and 1690s, Paris and London were positioned with respect to each other in important ways, just as they are today: vying for cultural dominance, with the brain drain flowing across the Channel in London's direction.

One enormous difference distinguishes then from now, however. In the 1680s the position of linguistic power was the reverse of what it is today. French was just inaugurating its long reign as cultural lingua franca. This in turn made possible a phenomenon virtually nonexistent in the literary world since Latin's disappearance as the dominant literary language: French-born writers were suddenly able to function as writers in a foreign setting. In addition, they were able as never before to become part of a foreign cultural scene in their native language. (It is, of course, true that by helping make the use of French widespread in the countries in which they took refuge, the exiled Protestants also played a key role in transforming the language into the new lingua franca.)[4] An important origin of the modern novel's history thus coincided with a moment when London played the role of international capital, a capital made international in part by the sudden influx of refugees fleeing religious persecution across the Channel.

By no means all the Huguenot women novelists went into exile in London: both Catherine Bernard and Charlotte Caumont de La Force, for example, converted to Catholicism at the time of the Revocation. The numbers of Huguenot women who did flee to London were, however, sufficiently important to cause Anne-Marguerite Du Noyer to remark in her protojournalistic chronicle of the Protestant diaspora, *Lettres historiques et galantes* (1714), that "all of England is full of French women, who have abandoned their husbands for religious reasons."[5] When this chapter from the history of women is written, we will surely find that numerous writers were part of this crowd.

Consider the one French Huguenot woman writer whose story is reasonably well known, Anne de La Roche-Guilhen. Since her first publication dates from 1674, her career was already solidly established by the time of the revocation of the Edict of Nantes. From 1683 on, her works were published by Dutch rather than French editors, a first sign of her disaffection from the Catholic cultural power base. It is not clear exactly when she emigrated, but it seems to have been shortly after the revocation, for when the first Royal Bounty Fund was established in 1686 to provide financial aid to the refugees who had flooded into London, she was among the recipients.[6] From then on, La Roche-Guilhen was a prolific French novelist—on English soil. By the time of her death, in 1707, she had published nearly twenty novels written in French in London, including her best-known works, for example, *Le Grand Scanderberg* (1688), *Histoire des favorites* (1697), and her fictionalization of Sappho's life (1706).

La Roche-Guilhen was part of the first generation of writers to profit from her native language's rise to new prominence: the French editions of her novels were undoubtedly read, first in England and France and then far more widely, as the novel went on to conquer a European and ultimately a global readership. Her invasion of the English cultural scene did not, however, end with these editions. A significant number of her novels also appeared in English translation, proof that she reached a less cosmopolitan audience as well. These English editions point to a second trajectory of La Roche-Guilhen's influence over the novel's development outside of France, one that does not necessarily intersect with that of the importance of her works read in French.

At times, the story told by the translations simply repeats that of French editions. *The Great Scanderberg*, for instance, is a clear winner in both categories; it was the novel most often reedited in French, as well as that most frequently translated into English. La Roche-Guilhen's career in English translation is also full of surprises: one could hardly have predicted, for example, that *Zingis* (1691), a novel subsequently republished in French in collected works but never again as an independent volume, would have been, of all her novels, the one most quickly translated into English (in 1692), nor that it would have been translated twice in the same year. In addition, the history of La Roche-Guilhen's English translations shows just how durable her influence proved to be: some translations were reissued well into the eighteenth century, at least a decade, and in one case (*The History of Female Favorites* in 1772), a full half-century, after the novels had ceased to be edited in French. The example of La Roche-Guilhen suggests that the early French novel may have had a double life, a truly separate history on each side of the Channel, and furthermore that novelists we might consider minor, based on what seems to be the span of their influence in France, may have had a far greater impact on the novel's development outside of France than we might have imagined.

This possibility becomes far more likely when we consider a second example, the career of Marie-Catherine Le Jumel de Barneville, comtesse d'Aulnoy. D'Aulnoy was among the French women who emigrated for the reason Du Noyer cited, to "abandon" her husband, although she, unlike the women Du Noyer had in mind, elected exile in London not for religious reasons but, more likely, purely and simply to escape a notoriously bad marriage.[7] Modern scholars have questioned whether d'Aulnoy's sojourns on foreign soil, in England and in Spain in particular, actually took place. Her contemporaries, however, did not hesitate to confirm her claims and to make her stay in London part of the historical record. In a review of her *Mémoires de la cour d'Angleterre*, for example, the *Journal des Savants* referred to her presence there. And Du Noyer noted that "Madame d'Aulnoy formerly spent time at the English court. . . . Since she had made many friends in that country with whom she had continued to correspond, her house became the clearing house for all persons of quality who came from London to Paris."[8]

D'Aulnoy's contribution to the beginning of a literary Chunnel was far more crucial than Du Noyer's image of the keeper of a Franco-English salon would suggest. In the years between 1690, when she is thought to have been in England, and her death in 1705 d'Aulnoy composed virtually all of her oeuvre. The ten works that form the core of her production were all translated into English, often with remarkable speed. These translations continued to be reedited, and new ones appeared with truly unusual regularity throughout the eighteenth century. Only twice between 1701 and 1781 did more than three years go by when none of her works were reissued in translation.[9] In the early years of d'Aulnoy's life in English her 1691 *Relation du voyage d'Espagne* and her two memoir novels, *Mémoires de la cour d'Espagne* (1690) and *Mémoires de la cour d'Angleterre* (1695), were particularly prominent; collections of her fairy tales appeared with increasing frequency as the eighteenth century unfolded.

The full significance of such a publication history becomes evident when we compare it with the trajectories of the writers literary history always showcases as the preeminent figures of their generation. Thus, for instance, in the image now promoted of the fairy-tale genre, so wildly popular in late-seventeenth-century France, Charles Perrault was incontrovertibly the leading practitioner of the form, whereas the view from England suggests a distinctly different story. Both Perrault's and d'Aulnoy's fairy tales were initially published in French in the early 1690s. Perrault first appeared in English only in 1729, however, by which time d'Aulnoy's tales had been published and republished six times in England, beginning in 1691.[10]

The example of the novel gives us a similarly nuanced picture and perhaps an even more surprising window onto the manner in which French literary history has skewed our sense of the development of French prose fiction. In the unquestioned image of the final decades of the seventeenth century Lafayette reigns virtually alone, as the creator of the most authoritative model for the novel just as it was coming into its own on the European scene. Certainly, her publication record in France supports this view. In the late seventeenth century and throughout the eighteenth century Lafayette's major works were reissued in an unbroken succession of editions. During the same period d'Aulnoy was virtually forgotten: during the entire eighteenth century the *Mémoires de la cour d'Espagne* were republished only three times in French, and only early in the century (in 1716, 1733, and 1736); there was a not a single new edition of the *Mémoires de la cour d'Angleterre.*

The two authors' contemporary publication records in English offer, however, diametrically opposed images. Lafayette was, to be sure, quickly translated: English editions of her 1678 novel *La Princesse de Clèves* appeared in 1679 and 1688; her 1669–70 novel *Zayde* was translated in 1678 and 1690.[11] Lafayette's English influence, however, appears to have been relatively short-lived. During the entire eighteenth century *La Princesse de Clèves* was reissued only in 1720, 1769, and 1777; *Zayde* reappeared in English merely twice, in 1729 and 1737.

The paucity of Lafayette's record becomes blatant when that record is compared with d'Aulnoy's. While d'Aulnoy's two court-memoir novels and her story of travels to Spain were particularly prominent, a number of her novels were reedited in English from one end of the eighteenth century to the other, with a regularity, furthermore, that casts a pall over Lafayette's record. D'Aulnoy's *Mémoires de la cour d'Angleterre* was already in its third translation in 1708; *Mémoires de la cour d'Espagne* appeared in its third translation as early as 1701. And d'Aulnoy's *Relation du voyage d'Espagne* was the most spectacular success of all. Under various titles, including *Travels into Spain*, it first appeared in 1692; the 1697 edition was already advertised as the fourth, and new editions appeared in 1703, 1705, 1708, 1717, 1722, 1726, 1735, 1738, and 1740. It is believed that there were additional editions, but no copies appear to have survived. Nor did the *Relation*'s life in English end at that point: I merely stop listing new publications because from 1740 on not only did d'Aulnoy's life in English translation become less intense but—and this is the crucial point— by then the mold of the eighteenth-century English novel had been cast.[12]

In 1740 Samuel Richardson, the English novelist who, more than anyone else, brought the genre back to France, revitalized the French tradition by showing how its original, seventeenth-century models had been refashioned on English soil; in that year Richardson literally invaded the European literary scene with *Pamela*. In 1741 he offered the French still another look at "their" epistolarity revised and corrected with the publication of his letter manual, *Letters written to and for particular friends, on the most important occasions*. And already in 1742 *Pamela* was available in French translation. Now, I am not suggesting that Richardson's view of the first generation of the French novel was shaped only by those French novels that were translated most often into English and therefore most frequently read by the Anglophone public. I am suggesting, however, that we would do well to be far more attentive to that public's preferences in French fiction during the early decades of the eighteenth century. Those preferences were hardly random: it is as if the English public for French fiction somehow instinctively sensed where the novel was headed.

It is thus no accident that whereas the major part of d'Aulnoy's fiction, like the novels of her French precursors, Scudéry and Lafayette, was written in the third person, the novels singled out for a particularly intense life in English in the late seventeenth and early eighteenth centuries were precisely those narrated, as almost all eighteenth-century prose fiction would be, in the first person. Her *Relation du voyage d'Espagne* is part journey novel told in letters, part an account of a foreign sojourn told in letters, two forms with a prodigious future in the eighteenth century. Her two court-memoir novels, unlike those of Lafayette, have contemporary settings, a change of significant importance for a century during which the novel examining the historical past was virtually abandoned. All these novels seem to be accounts of true stories and were taken as such by their early readers. All of them could be characterized as "realistic" or "journalistic," to the extent to which these adjectives are applicable to early modern fiction. It is therefore easy to detect her influence on the types of novel Defoe made famous. It also seems evident that, along with Prévost and Marivaux, she prepared the way for the fictional model represented by Richardson. In these transnational products of the Huguenot diaspora, written in French in London during the transition from the seventeenth to the eighteenth century, we find, therefore, the first clear intimations of the forms that the novel would explore during the formative decades 1730–50, when the genre was seeking a new transnational incarnation.

D'Aulnoy's strange fate—quickly to become a virtual nonentity in her native country even as she attained impressive status in England— leads me to pose a very basic question: To what extent was d'Aulnoy truly a French novelist? Does she, along with the other women writers who developed their talents in London, belong instead, to an extent worthy of some form of official recognition, to the English tradition of prose fiction?

---

I take as the inaugural moment for the modern novel in France Théophile de Viau's 1619 *Première journée* because of its opening manifesto for literary "modernism": "Il faut écrire à la moderne" [We have to write in the modern style].[13] Théophile's narrator begins his story by announcing that he "was only banished yesterday"; the *Première journée* is, in other words, the first day of his life in exile. For the moment, he has only been exiled from the court, but he is preparing himself for exile from his homeland: "If I am forced to leave France, no matter where I want to go in Europe my name will have won acquaintances for me."[14]

Théophile was banished because of his poetry; however, when he wanted to raise the issue of exile, he composed, for the first and only time in his career, a novel in French. The idea that an important origin of the early modern novel was defined by the menace of a forced departure from French soil seems particularly appropriate, for we could view the first two centuries of the novel's history in France as defined by those moments at which novelists were forced into exile.

Thus, the line of demarcation between the first two generations of novelists is drawn by the departures after the revocation of the Edict of Nantes. Then, throughout the eighteenth century the contributions of writers in exile punctuated the French novel's history. Nowhere was this influence more spectacular than in the case of the abbé Prévost, one of the formative novelists of the first half of the century and one of the first translators to give Europe a French Richardson. Much of Prévost's writing was done outside of France: repeatedly, he either chose to exile himself from his native country or was forced to leave. To commemorate his nomadic existence, he even rebaptized himself "Prévost d'Exil" and "Prévost d'Exiles." Finally, the emigration provoked by the revolution of 1789 marked the end of the early modern novel's trajectory. The fiction produced by émigrés such as Germaine de Staël at the same time ended the eighteenth-century novel and provoked the genre's redefinition in the early nineteenth century, by which time the novel was becoming increasingly directed toward national rather than international communities.

Undoubtedly because its history was thus punctuated by exile, for the first two centuries of its existence the novel was the genre that, more than any other, encouraged the French to examine the basis of their cultural unification, to recognize, if only dimly, that this unification was founded less on the existence of a real community than on what Benedict Anderson terms "imagined communities," communities independent of the boundaries that delimited the French state. This could explain why all early polemics concerning the novel, beginning with Théophile's and Huet's manifestoes, were also attempts to generate debate regarding the foundations and the limits of French society.

In raising these issues I have no hope of eliminating the channel that separates English and French literary history. I would like to suggest, however, that our view of the first two centuries of the modern novel's history would be far richer if we became actively concerned with exploring the ways in which individual production and the novel in general were shaped by the diasporic conditions in which the genre was often produced. In the cases considered here, for example, how would our view of the Huguenot novelists be changed if we considered them somehow on the frontier between two developing traditions of prose fiction? In addition, beyond these individual examples lie two general questions. How many of the English novel's early contours were shaped by the French presence in London? Conversely, how did the French novelists writing outside France "contaminate" the purity of what we are accustomed to think of as the French novel?

## Notes

1. I will accept here as a given the argument that the novel first took on its truly modern form—that it became the novel of interiority, as opposed to such precursor forms as the romance and the picaresque—in France during the second half of the seventeenth century, when Scudéry radically altered the romance genre by introducing a new emphasis on sentimentality and Lafayette carried this emphasis over into a vastly more compact form. Certain theorists, in particular those working on the English tradition, have downplayed the French novel's foundational role. The most recent scholarship on the history of the English novel has, however, granted an important place to the French novel's influence on the development of a tradition across the Channel. See, e.g., Michael McKeon's *The Origins of the English Novel, 1600–1740* (Baltimore: Johns Hopkins University Press, 1987). See also Margaret Doody's *The True Story of the Novel* (New Brunswick, N.J.: Rutgers University Press, 1996), in particular her remarks on the widespread translation of French fiction into English in the 1650s (269).

2. Huet's *Lettre-traité de l'origine des romans* was published as an extended preface to Lafayette's novel *Zayde* (Paris: Claude Barbin, 1670), thereby linking the theory and the practice of transnational fiction at one of the French novel's principal origins. On Huet's vision of the novel's transmission, see esp. 10–11. On his privileging of nomadic writers, see 71. The dominant meaning of *nation* in Huet's day was "a people," but his understanding of the term clearly prefigures our own, post-Revolutionary usage. Huet's history of the novel records the contributions of different cultures and different parts of the globe to a degree truly astonishing for his day. His intellectual proximity to Scudéry and to Lafayette and collaboration with them on such

novels as *Artamène, ou le grand Cyrus* (1649–53) and *Zayde, histoire espagnole* are facts worth remembering for anyone seeking to record the (French) novel's transnational heritage.

3. Because of this volume's focus, I shall consider only novelists who worked in England. Anyone interested in the effects of the Protestant diaspora on early prose fiction would also do well to examine those women who worked in the Low Countries in the early eighteenth century (e.g., Anne-Marguerite Du Noyer), particularly in view of the fact that the Low Countries would soon produce one of the most remarkable "French" novelists of the eighteenth century, Belle de Zuylen/Isabelle de Charrière.

4. The very term *lingua franca* originated in just this period. The first example given by the *Oxford English Dictionary* is from Dryden in 1678. In his 1691 *Dictionnaire universel*, Antoine Furetière introduced a French equivalent, *langue universelle*. Both his definition—"that which is understood throughout the Mediterranean"—and the example from Dryden make it clear that the new expressions referred to mixed languages developed to facilitate commerce. The new terms are nevertheless evidence of the widespread belief at the moment of French's new validity that there could be a "universal language."

5. Anne-Marguerite Du Noyer, *Lettres historiques et galantes*, 7 vols. (Cologne: Pierre Marteau, 1711–14), 3:37–38. Du Noyer's *Lettres* are a mine of information on the contemporary cultural scene from the perspective of a Protestant exile. On Du Noyer's journalism, see Nina Gelbart, *Feminism and Opposition Journalism in Old Regime France* (Berkeley and Los Angeles: University of California Press, 1987).

6. Alexandre Calame, *Anne de La Roche-Guilhen, romancière huguenote, 1644–1707* (Geneva: Droz, 1972), 35–36. Calame's study is the best source of information on La Roche-Guilhen. Myriam Yardeni's *Le Refuge protestant* (Paris: Presses Universitaires de France, 1985) provides a good general introduction to the emigration brought on by the revocation.

7. The breakup of d'Aulnoy's marriage and the wild charges made against her at that time have been recounted far too often, since it will undoubtedly never be possible to learn just what the reality behind the lurid tales actually was and since there probably wasn't much reality at all: similar accusations were not at all infrequent at this period. On the use literary history has made of these accusations, in particular the charge that she conspired with her mother to have her husband convicted of treason, see my *Tender Geographies: Women and the Origins of the Novel in France* (New York: Columbia University Press, 1991), 158. Melvin Palmer rehearses the speculation that she fled Paris after being accused in the plot against her husband ("Madame d'Aulnoy in England," *Comparative Literature* 27 [1975]: 239).

8. *Journal des Savants*, 1695, 143; Du Noyer, *Lettres historiques et galantes*, 3:28. D'Aulnoy begins her 1695 *Mémoires de la cour d'Angleterre* (2 vols. [Paris: Claude Barbin, 1695]) with a direct request that the reader believe that the novel was based on a personal sojourn in England, a sojourn that was the basis for her knowledge of "very agreeable and singular adventures about the English court" (1:1). Shir-

ley Jones Day demonstrates that both the *Mémoires* and the 1690 *Histoire d'Hypolite, comte de Duglas* "contain references to aspects of English life not found in print elsewhere" (*The Search for Lyonnesse: Women's Fiction in France, 1670–1703* [Bern: Peter Lang, 1999], x–xi; see also Mary Elizabeth Storer, *La Mode de contes des fées, 1685–1700* [1928; reprint, Geneva: Slatkine, 1972], 23–27). On d'Aulnoy and the other women novelists of her generation, see Jones Day, *Search for Lyonnesse*.

9. No translations appeared in the periods 1728–35 and 1741–49. Only after 1781 did the frequency with which d'Aulnoy was translated finally drop off dramatically; nonetheless, early translations continued to be reissued throughout the nineteenth century. Palmer, "Madame d'Aulnoy in England," is the best source of information on d'Aulnoy's life in English.

10. The problem was not that Perrault was considered an insignificant figure by his English contemporaries. His 1699 work *Les Hommes illustres* appeared in English in 1704. Those same contemporaries, however, obviously associated the fairy tale with a woman writer, the practitioner who had spent time on English soil. In French, Perrault's first tale appeared in 1696; d'Aulnoy had initiated her involvement with the genre in 1690.

11. In the English editions *Zayde* was identified, as it was on the title page of the original edition, as "by Mr. Segray," that is Segrais, a reference to Jean Renault de Segrais, who was a friend and collaborator of numerous seventeenth-century women writers, from Anne-Louise d'Orléans, duchesse de Montpensier, to Lafayette. While the novel's authorship was an open secret in France, it is not clear whether this information crossed the Channel along with the text.

12. A comparison with the time necessary for the translation of some major nineteenth-century French novels may help give a sense of the rapidity of d'Aulnoy's translation history. *Le Père Goriot* was finally translated into English twenty-six years after its original publication; it took twenty-nine years for *Madame Bovary* to make it into English, and seventy years for *Le Rouge et le noir* (Franco Moretti, *Atlas of the European Novel, 1800–1900* [London: Verso, 1998], 156–57).

13. I cite Théophile from *Oeuvres complètes*, ed. Guido Saba (Paris: A. G. Nizet, 1978), 14. *Première journée* is often referred to as *Fragments d'une histoire comique*, a title first used by Georges de Scudéry for the edition he published after Théophile's death (Rouen: Jean de La Mare, 1632).

14. Théophile de Viau, *Première journée*, 19, 20. At the time of his initial exile, the one alluded to in *Première journée*, Théophile, a Protestant, probably went to southwestern France. However, for centuries it was thought that he went to London, and the question has never been resolved (see Antoine Adam, *Théophile de Viau et la libre pensée française en 1620* [Paris: Droz, 1935] 163).

MARY HELEN McMURRAN

## CHAPTER TWO

# National or Transnational?
# The Eighteenth-Century Novel

Several persuasive studies have shown that fictional narrative and nation-building became intimately related in the nineteenth century.[1] The novel-nation relationship in particular has been analyzed from two different perspectives. One perspective focuses on the nationalist agenda of novels; as an instrument for consolidating national identity and portraying the nation as a cohesive unit the novel helped construct the "imagined community" of the nation. Novel and nation are also linked in studies of the institutionalization of literature in the nineteenth century. As histories of the novel, criticism, and novel collections came to be organized on the basis of the national origin of the writers and their native language, an exclusively nationalist framework was set for the novel, as well as for its reception and study. These associations between nation and novel, national culture and its narratives, seem applicable to the eighteenth century and the novel's emergence, or "rise," until we look at translation.[2]

During the eighteenth century translations of novels in Britain and France not only were prevalent but offer a privileged site for posing questions about national boundaries and their presence in the novel. Translations have often been studied with a view to cultural contact, explaining how a source text moves into a target language and culture. Scholars frequently find evidence for the appropriation or nationalization of the foreign literary work, in which the outsider text is rewritten to conform to the target culture's ideologies and literary standards.[3] Yet this is not how translation functioned for the novel in the eighteenth century. Translations were not necessarily the result of a simple conversion of a recognized original into a target language. Many translators were novelists themselves—from Aphra Behn, Penelope Aubin, Eliza Haywood, Tobias Smollett, Oliver Goldsmith, Frances Brooke, and Elizabeth Griffith to Alain-René Le Sage, Denis Diderot, Marie-Jeanne Riccoboni, and abbé Prévost, among others—and they were often conscious of blending the two processes.[4] Because these writers did not always acknowledge their source texts or mixed translation with original writing, much translation of prose fiction in eighteenth-century Britain and France was marked by the permeability of the two languages and cultures. Just as translations of novels in the eighteenth century did not represent a move from one cohesive nation and national literature to another (to the extent that an established cultural and literary value system inflected the translation, its reception, and its influence), the contact between France and Britain cannot be properly described as the simple intersection of two distinct others but was a more fluid interaction based on a history of cultural intimacy.

I argue here that prose-fiction translation was not only a practice of converting French to English, or vice versa, but also a cultural and literary dynamic predicated on *translatio.* Literally "bearing across," *translatio* had a range of meanings in the Middle Ages, including extended metaphor, the transfer of souls from earth to heaven, and the transfer of relics from one place to another. More significantly for my purposes, it was used in the phrase *translatio imperii,* that is, the transfer of power from one empire to another, and then *translatio studii,* the transfer of culture through translation, imitation, and adaptation. Although instances of *translatio* do not abound in eighteenth-century writings, comments made in a variety of contexts indicate that the movement of literary works through translation and imitation was all too obviously the norm, if not cause for increasing discomfort.[5] We shall see that historians of the novel in the eighteenth century specifically acknowledged *translatio* as they detailed the long-term historical transmission or transference of fictions from one language and country to another, showing that the novel had traditionally crossed between languages and national boundaries, continuously challenging an easy fit between the novel and the nation. As both a writing practice and a larger conceptual apparatus in *translatio,* translation was central to the eighteenth century's view of the novel.

There is, however, no getting rid of the nation; the word is used in eighteenth-century writings about the novel, and the nation was becoming a meaningful category for producing and organizing novels by the turn of the nineteenth century. "Nation" was also a working political and cultural concept throughout the eighteenth century, as it had been even earlier. But it is largely agreed that for most of the eighteenth-century *nation* did not yet imply the modern notion of nation-state and its forms of nationalism. These phenomena are usually dated from the very end of the eighteenth century, with the French and American revolutions, into the nineteenth century, with the beginnings of industrialism.[6]

So, there is no reason to claim that the novel was *national* or *transnational* until we can understand how these terms operated in the eighteenth-century novel. To articulate the significance of *translatio* as a model of transnationality and the nation as a loose alternative, providing some form of boundedness, also reveals that these views were not yet firmly antithetical in the eighteenth century; every moment that seems to mark the novel's national definition is all too easily subject to reversal, just as every argument for the novel's pure transnationality is foiled by the strength of the nation over the novel. In order to demonstrate the openness of this question in the eighteenth century, I use three kinds of literary-historical evidence that best display the difficulty of separating the novel's transnational and national tendencies. First, a bibliographical survey of translations establishes the dual orientation of the eighteenth-century novel market as both national and international; second, essays on the history of prose fiction written in the eighteenth century reveal a collision of meanings and inferences for both *translatio* and "nation." Third, blatantly nationalist discourse around the exchange of the British and French novel in translation turns out to be less decisive as a sign of the nationalization of the novel than it appears.

In the larger perspective of the French-British contact zone, prose-fiction translation directly addresses the shared process of consolidating the novel across the Channel. This is merely one mode and one phase of a history of almost overdetermined political, linguistic, and cultural contact between France and Britain, but by focusing *between* the two countries, and by focusing on a genre they brought into being together and even understood as culturally self-reflecting, translation resituates the questions about the novel and the complex set of relations between the two countries within the zone. Unlike many studies of the novel's relationship with the nation, studies of prose-fiction translation can investigate the novel without assuming the nation as an a priori category and can take the British-French contact zone as their primary focus, working from both sides of the Channel at once.

## The Translation Market

How prevalent was translation in the novel market? In the case of Britain, my survey of novel publishing from 1660 to 1770 shows that translations of French romances and novels constituted as much as 36% of the published prose fiction in a given year and hovered around 15–30% up to the late eighteenth century.[7] Thus, the market was dominated by national-language novels, but it made no efforts to close itself off from foreign imports. The situation can be usefully compared with the current situation in English-speaking countries, where foreign books of all languages and genres make up only 2–4% of published books.[8] Measuring the popularity of novels in terms of the frequency of reprints yields an even more liberal and welcoming attitude toward foreign fictions. A study of bestsellers in Britain from 1700 to 1740 reveals that four of the eight best-selling novels were translations: Fénelon's *Télémaque*, Cervantes's *Don Quixote*, the medieval *Guy of Warwick*, and the *Arabian Nights*, which was translated from the French translation. Of the twenty most popular novelists in the period 1750–69, judging by editions printed, six were foreigners: Marie-Jeanne Riccoboni, Voltaire, Marmontel, Cervantes, Rousseau, and Marie Le Prince de Beaumont.[9]

The situation in France was similar. Before 1750 there were very few translations of British novels, but then their share increased to approximately 20% of the published prose fiction in a given year through the rest of the century, roughly the same as the percentage of French novels in English translation for the same period. Daniel Mornet's study of eighteenth-century private libraries shows that among readers, however, British novels were as popular as French novels, if not more so. He lists the nine novels most often encountered in these library catalogs, choosing those that had appeared on the market between 1740 and 1760. Except for Françoise Graffigny's *Lettres d'une Peruvienne*, Mornet found more copies of *Pamela*, *Tom Jones*, *Clarissa*, and the anonymous *History of Charlotte Summers* than of the other most popular French novels.[10] Thus, foreign novels were allowed to gain a respectable foothold in the publishing industry, and buyers' choices apparently were not nationalistic either because of natural attachment or as a consequence of an imposed agenda. On the contrary, consumers seem to have been attracted to the foreign fictions.

To test the hypothesis that novel publishing was not nationalistic, it is helpful to look at collections of novels, since a tendency to nationalize might be evident in the selection of works for reprinting as a group and thus developing a canon. In France, the most popular novel collections of the eighteenth century, such as the *Bibliothèque des romans*, *De l'usage des romans*, the *Bibliothèque de campagne*, and the *Bibliothèque universelle des romans*, the latter a collection of excerpts only, all included translations not only of British novels but of Spanish, Italian, and ancient Greek and Roman novels as well. A survey of novel collections published in Britain from 1660 to 1800 reveals a similar mixture of translations with novels in English. Of 133 collections of novels, romances, tales, and so on, the majority, 93 of them, included all or some translations, and 19 were not determinable, leaving only 21 as exclusively British.[11] Most of these were collections of anonymous pieces and were oblivious to nationality as a category for writers, narratives, or overall organization. Even a title such as *Moore's British Classics*, of 1800, included Montesquieu's *Persian Letters*.

Anna Barbauld's collection *British Novelists*, of 1810, however, represents a radical departure. It contains no translations and nothing more than sixty years old. In identifying the logic of collecting in terms of writers' national identity and language Barbauld clearly reversed the trend of mixing translations with native-language novels. The last lines of her introductory essay even indicate that she intended to initiate a national novel for Britain: "It was said by Fletcher of Saltoun, 'Let me make the ballads of a nation, and I care not who makes the laws.' Might it not be said with as much propriety, Let me make the novels of a country and let who will make the systems?"[12] Barbauld's analogy between ballads as law-giving and novels as systematizing assumes that the nation or country is an imposed limit to law and system and argues that fiction deeply informs a society. Yet the claim that novels form not just laws but systems, that is, whole sets of principles applicable in any arena—political, philosophical, social, cultural—is an essentially expansive move away from ballad and nation as older, more localized forms to country and novel as new, larger ones. She seems well aware of forging a national novel for modern Britain.

Barbauld was one of the first to recognize the novel's power to influence the nation's readers and to suggest that the novel could have a national agenda. But this potent rhetoric comes as a final flourish in her introductory essay to the collection, "On the Origin and Progress of Novel Writing." This introduction is a long, multicultural history of the novel, encompassing ancient, medieval, Renaissance, and early modern fictions from all over Europe. She also remarks on the difficulty of choosing novels for the collection and indicates that her choice to exclude translations may have been more arbitrary than calculated.[13] If Anna Barbauld's *British Novelists* represents the novel as a new national institution, her introduction represents the novel as a category that passes across boundaries of language and nation. Thus, the nation's entrance into the novel was of a piece with the novel's shared, international history.

## *Translation* and the Idea of the Novel

To understand Barbauld's perspective on fiction, we need a better grasp of eighteenth-century readers' experience of the novel and their sense of its definition as a category. As the eighteenth-century bestsellers and collections demonstrate, older fictions and foreign ones were grouped together with recent native-language novels. Works such as Heliodorus's *Theaganes and Chariclea*, Achilles Tatius's *Clitophon and Leukippe*, and Longus's *Daphnis and Chloe*, written in Greek and dating from late antiquity, were continuously a part of the contemporary novel market because they were retranslated and published in the eighteenth century. *Daphnis and Chloe* was published more often in the eighteenth century than in the sixteenth, when it first became popular in French and English translation.[14] Tatius's *Clitophon and Leukippe* was translated anew in 1720 as *The Amours of Clitophon and Leucippe illustrated in Six Novels*, specifically reorienting its title and organization to better match the model of eighteenth-century fictions.[15] In addition, French medieval fictions like the *Gesta romanorum* and Peninsular chivalric fictions like *Don Bellianis* were regularly consumed in translations, adaptations, and chapbook form throughout the eighteenth century.[16] The sixteenth- and seventeenth-century Spanish and French picaresque novels were also retranslated and republished in eighteenth-century England.[17] Not only had the novel traversed numerous national borders in its long history, there was no consistent distinction between the earlier romance and a modern novel; in fact, the two were elided for many, such as Walter Scott, who called the novel "modern romance."[18] A growing novel readership was presented with a wide mixture of foreign and native-language fictions, old and new narratives, as part of a single continuum.

Though translations were an important presence in the eighteenth-century novel market, translation was more than a category of books to consume; it had a particular symbolic resonance. From the Middle Ages through the eighteenth century prose fictions were sometimes translated from languages most likely to be understood, and from books most widely available, rather than directly from an original.[19] Thus, some translations were translations of translations, some were adaptations and imitations rather than translations, and some were translations with no originals. Occasionally the translations of some of the older narratives were the only versions available, the unique means by which a lost or unknown original manuscript survived.[20] These conditions regarding the circulation of fictional texts in translation are frequently represented in novels. In the eighth chapter of *Don Quixote*, for example, with the hero's sword in mid-air, Cervantes suddenly suspends the story because, the narrator informs us, the source text goes no further. The search for the continuation follows the narrator to the streets of Toledo, a famous medieval translation center, where he comes upon a boy selling parchment books and discovers an old Arabic manuscript version of the "famous Spaniard" Don Quixote's story. The narrator, we find, does not read Arabic and needs a translator to finish the novel, but as he tells us, a "Spanish-speaking Moor" was not difficult to find. Thus, the rest of the novel is the narrator's version of the bilingual translator's version of Quixote's story written by the Arabic historian Cide Hamete Benengeli.[21] Numerous French and British novels in the eighteenth century, from Montesquieu's *Lettres persanes* to Walpole's *Castle of Otranto*, continued to symbolize the pervasive fact of translation through the device of pseudotranslation.[22]

In the translations themselves the act of bringing a fictional text into a new language was also expressed in symbolic terms. In the elaborate paratexts of Renaissance and seventeenth-century prose-fiction translations, translation rarely meant simply rewriting a foreign text in one's own language. Often, the romance's eponymous hero's or heroine's translation is figured as travel from one country to another, framing the translation in *translatio* as migratory transference. The translator John Davies wrote in the preface to *Astrea* (1620): "Astrea finding so good entertainment in her owne Countrey . . . is now encouraged to crosse the seas, and to try what welcome she shall meete with here in England."[23] A poem to the English translator of Mateo Aleman's *The Rogue, or the Life of Guzman de Alfarache* (1623), also allegorized the successive European translations of the novel as the travels of the hero:

> When Guzman's Legend was allow'd in Spaine,
> And, though a Rogue, found Prince-like intertaine;
> He did o're Alpes and Pyrene Hils advance
> To tell his Tale in Italy and France
> With which their native cares being sweetly stung,
> He theevish stole their heart, and bound their tongue

To speake his praise. At last on Gallick shore
(Standing like Cesar) thence he did implore
Some Pegasus, or winged Argoes ayd,
To crosse the Brittaine Seas.[24]

This nostalgic image of Guzman as a troubadour-like oral performer traveling throughout Europe, a polyglot whose tale can be told and understood anywhere, depends on the belief that location is preeminently changeable, Guzman is convertible. These images reinforced *translatio* in its sense of moving across and simultaneously downplayed notions of change or potential loss that are often deeply ingrained in discussions of translation.

When Anna Barbauld introduced the *British Novelists* with her essay "On the Origins and Progress of Novel Writing" and foregrounded cultural and linguistic transference, or *translatio*, as the essential logic of the novel's story, she was following an established trend. Pierre Daniel Huet's *Lettre-traité de l'origine des romans* (1670), the first systematic and thorough treatment of the history of fiction, was used as a reference point in both France and England by scores of others writers tackling the subject.[25] Huet's treatise and other critics' essays are characterized by their breadth; their definitions of the romance and the novel often included verse and prose narrative, short tales, fables, and allegories, as well as long works; nonetheless, these historians of fiction understood romance and novel as a unified category even though its unity was not based on the definition of its form.[26] The fundamental premise in most of these histories of the romance and the novel was that fictions of all kinds were linked by their transmission throughout history, from one part of the world to another and from one language to another.

While literary scholars have noted the attempts of early novel critics to articulate a definition of the novel as a form or genre, we have ignored that the idea of the novel was also defined by the notion of transfer. The diversity of prose fictions in the eighteenth century defies a clear sense of a genre with defining formal features. Perhaps we should allow this challenge and refuse for the moment to define the novel as a form or genre. In light of the eighteenth century's experience of the novel, it is possible to conceive of the novel as transfer without focusing primarily on what was transferred and secondarily on the potential for transposition, as if what was transferred were a bounded, cohesive object in itself, with a nationality, so to speak. Transfer, or *translatio*, may have been a constitutive element of the novel's definition because what fictions had in common was the ability to speak across, to change form and language without obvious rules, much less impediments, resistance, or loss.

Huet and several others followed the path of the earliest fictions from Egypt, Persia, and Syria to ancient Greece and Rome and later Europe. Huet's essay begins:

> Ce n'est ni en Provence ni en Espagne comme plusieurs le croient qu'il faut espérer de trouver les premiers commencements de cet agréable amusement. . . ; il faut les aller chercher dans des pays plus éloignés et dans l'antiquité la plus reculée.

> [It is neither in Provence nor in Spain, as many believe, that one should hope to find the first beginnings of this pleasant amusement. . . ; it is necessary to go to countries further away and back to the most ancient times.][27]

Huet was following the narrative model of universal histories of civilization, partly based on biblical history and on *translatio imperii* as defined by Otto von Freising's medieval interpretation of the book of Daniel.[28] Freising's and others' readings of biblical passages became the basis for a historiographical theory of *translatio*, but it took on a consciously propagandistic flavor when used by Charlemagne and other European rulers to renew the Roman Empire.[29] *Translatio imperii* drew a direct path from the Roman Empire as a universalizing center of political as well as cultural domination to medieval Europe. Literary authors employed the complementary concept of *translatio studii*, the more specific theory of the transfer of learning from one culture to another. For Chrétien de Troyes, in particular, learning passed from Athens to Rome and from Rome to France. In the prologues to his romances Chrétien relied on the authority of the past but also emphasized his own renewal of chivalry and its noble aspirations in a new vernacular language.[30]

The introduction to a 1640 translation of the ancient Greek novel *Cleitophon and Leukippe* is a shorthand account of the way many seventeenth- and eighteenth-century writers took up *translatio*: "The Persians first affected up this kind of amorous literature. . . . You will not find it hard to believe that of old they introduced the beginning of Milesian fables in Asia which they ruled. Certainly they gave to the Arabs the fashion of this same kind of writing and the genius for it. The Arabs then transmitted it to the Spanish. From the Spanish we Gauls in turn took it, and from them indeed it also went elsewhere."[31] Here, imperial conquest provided only one aspect of fiction's transmission. The Crusades, routes of commerce, the travels of jongleurs—any sort of travel resulting in cultural contact—allowed fiction to be communicated, translated, and imitated.

Thomas Warton, in his *History of English Poetry* (1774), spoke about the transport of early medieval romance in this way: "[T]he Spaniards [were] captivated with the novelty of the oriental books imported by these strangers. . . . The ideal tales of these Eastern invaders . . . were eagerly caught up and universally diffused. From Spain . . . they soon passed into France and Italy."[32] Warton implies that the transmission of fiction from one culture to another was based on fiction's ability to captivate those who came into contact with it. In his 1755 dialogue the abbé Jacquin, following the track back to the Middle East as Huet had, explains fiction's movement during cultural contacts in the same way as Warton, saying that fiction was unusually attractive to the target culture: "La Syrie et l'Arabie étaient des pays trop voisins de l'Egypte, pour ne pas contracter facilement ce goût contagieux de la fiction" [Syria and Arabia were countries too close to Egypt to avoid easily contracting this contagious taste for fiction].[33]

The emphasis in these eighteenth-century accounts was still placed, as it had been traditionally, on a colonizing impulse. The foreign culture was understood as the source of power and cultural production. The native tradition, by contrast, was practically invisible, only a place or target for influence. The inherent attraction of foreigners' fictional narratives, however, complicates the imperialistic basis of *translatio*. Romance and novel, unlike rulers and empires, were not simply imposed. According to many of these historians of the novel, fiction conquered and enslaved like empires, but it conquered through attraction. No borders were closed, because foreign fiction was, by definition, desirable. *Translatio*, then, retained its sense of transfer, literally moving from one place and language to another, but without the original hegemonic structure.

Just as Barbauld reformulated novel collections to give the nation a new power to define the novel, many other writers between 1750 and 1800 began to write about the novel's history from a wholly different perspective by asserting the primacy of the nation. Differing and occasionally competing theories did not abolish *translatio*, as writers continued to show that the romance and the novel had moved from one language and region to another, but by the late eighteenth century critics had become interested in the notion of the progress of fictional narrative as a form, not simply in its transmission.[34] More importantly for my purposes here, the question of fiction's origins was also reopened. Many doubted the connections between medieval romance and the earlier fictions and disputed whether the origins of medieval romance were northern or southern European. In her *Progress of Romance*, Clara Reeve spoke to these difficulties: "This curious story . . . furnishes an additional proof that romances are of universal growth, and not confined to any particular period or countries."[35] Many authors were impelled by the assumption of universality to return to the question of origins and rewrite them. In the preface to *Roderick Random*, Tobias Smollett places the origins of romance in the "dark ages of the world," when a man who became famous for his "wisdom and valor" was the subject of stories that were circulated as incitements to virtue.[36] Walter Scott's "Essay on Romance" includes the following story of the novel's origins: "The father of an isolated family, destined one day to rise into a tribe, and in farther progress of time to expand into a nation, may indeed, narrate to his descendants the circumstances which detached him from the society of his brethren, and drove him to form a solitary settlement in the wilderness, with no other deviation from truth, on the part of the narrator, than arises from the infidelity of memory, or the exaggerations of vanity."[37]

Smollett's and Scott's versions of the origins of the novel, unlike Huet's scholarly account, are self-consciously fictional. And unlike Huet's and others' view that fiction was based largely on amorous tales that became a transmogrifying attraction across cultures, Smollett and Scott define fiction as the history of a local group. For Smollett and Scott, communal affect does not move outward and across nations through desire but instead is relocated within the tribe, clan, or nation, attaching its members to one another.

Smollett's and Scott's accounts imply that compared with the narratives of *translatio*, fiction is local and the purpose and structure of fiction in the locality are universal: fiction begins with the members of each culture or tribe telling their own stories to one another in the early stages of its growth and development. In the introduction to *O'Donnell: A National Tale* (1814), Sydney Morgan illustrates a similar view: "Literary fiction . . . has always in its most genuine form exhibited a mirror of the times in which it is composed; reflecting morals, customs, manners, peculiarity of character, and prevalence of opinion. Thus, perhaps, after all, it forms the best history of nations, the rest being but the dry chronicles of facts and events."[38] In France, the Marquis de Sade posited a full reversal of the assumptions of *translatio* in his *Idées sur les romans*. He concedes that novels have been written in every language and by every nation but clearly states that the native tradition is determined by its own national mores and received opinion: "[I]l est des modes, des usages, des goûts qui ne se transmettent point" [There are customs, mores, and tastes that do not transmit at all].[39]

Although it is fairly easy to read Sade's and Morgan's comments and Smollett's and Scott's narratives as signs that the nation was a new paradigm for fiction, we must ask whose nation is invoked in these accounts. For Smollett and Sade the nation is a clan or tribe; for Sydney Morgan a national tale is the story of the peripheral nation of Ireland directed against the English.[40] Moreover, these writers imply much more about the nation than they actually bear out. Despite their important implications for the nation and nationalism, Smollett's and Scott's scenarios, which focus on ahistorical locality, were still a very long way from the British nation or the French nation as these entities would have been evoked in a political context. The British and the French were large anonymous groups who did not yet clearly express a sense of exclusive attachment to the nation over other networks of loyalties such as religion or locality. At the same time, the national origins of fiction are lodged in explicitly transnational frames. Like the majority of those who wrote histories of fiction, Reeve, Smollett, Scott, and Sade trace its origins in a variety of cultures and languages that influenced one another.

## Bluffing about the Nation in Translation

So far I have suggested that the translation market and histories of the novel had a significant impact on the idea of the novel in the eighteenth century, but I have not addressed French and British attitudes about the novels they were translating during the period. These contemporary translations highlighted the zone of French-British contact as individual translators entered into the process of importing a novel and reviewers commented on that process. In fact, translation prefaces, along with commentary on the exchange of the novel between Britain and France, were important sites for inscribing the nation into the novel even as the translators themselves often performed the permeability of the two nations' novels, because a growing discourse in and around the novel underscored national identity. In Britain this discourse was expressed as a resistance to the deleterious effects on readers of translating French fiction. In France, where English literature and culture were newer discoveries, translations were frequently funneled through a discourse on national character.

Before the mid-eighteenth century the French romance and novel in the English language were generally recognized as formative with respect to the tradition in English. Several British writers recognized that they had long been the recipients and not the source of romances and novels because they translated and imitated the French. The preface to a 1673 translation entitled *The Drudge: or the Jealous Extravagant, a Piece of Gallantry* speaks of "Translation; that word that sounds so gloriously in this pretty French-ify'd Generation." The translator of Huet's *Lettre-traité de l'origine des romans* hoped that the reign of French translations of fiction would give rise to a native tradition: "And (tho' we have been hitherto, for the most part, supply'd with translations from the French) it is to be hoped . . . that some English genius will dare to naturalize romance into our soil; which (I don't doubt) it will agree with, as well as that of a neighboring country; since we are acknowledg'd to be very ingenious, in improving foreign inventions."[41] The number of French romances translated into English nods to *translatio* and its traditional one-way trajectory. The desire to "naturalize romance," however, indicates that the imitation or emulation of another culture's literary models can lead to "improving foreign inventions"—a hint that emulation becomes rivalry. In the mid-eighteenth century this same indebtedness could still be found, but a new desire to fight off French influence was also present. A revisionist claim that French importations were an unnatural transplant was voiced in a review of Smollett's *Peregrine Pickle*, which referred to "that flood of novels, tales, romances, and other monsters of the imagination, which have been either wretchedly translated, or even more unhappily imitated, from the *French*, whose literary levity we have not been ashamed to adopt. . . . But this forced and unnatural transplantation could not long thrive."[42]

Another potent example of reproachful rhetoric is found in the prefatory letters to Richardson's *Pamela*: the authors of the letters disdain the harm caused by the importation of French novels to the English character.[43] This relatively quick succession of positions goes from receiving to improving, to producing, to refusing the original source—from constituting one's own literary tradition through contact and translation, to ultimately overcoming it and then concealing the influence.

By the time the *Pamela* controversy broke out, the French novel was perceived not only as having an adverse effect on the British novel but as being dangerous because it represented Frenchness in its entirety. In *The Rise of English Nationalism* Gerald Newman identifies a mass of visual images and writings by moralists, journalists, essayists, novelists, playwrights, and others to argue that "[t]o be truly English was to live up to a stereotype generated in anti-Frenchness."[44] Newman also shows that the novel was one form of this nationalist cultural criticism, satirizing English imitations of French culture, as with Fielding's "French-English Bellarmine" in *Joseph Andrews* and Smollett's Dutton in *Humphrey Clinker*, to lampoon those who were Frenchified in dress, manners, and speech. Thus, comments on the novel seem to reflect ideas available more broadly, as James G. Turner put it, in the "Anglo-French culture wars."[45] Indeed, a proliferation of journalism and travel writing on the customs, manners, and character of diverse countries appeared in the eighteenth century, marking a sea change from seventeenth-century accounts. Earlier English travelers to the Continent had tended to observe places, monuments, and other physical conditions; eighteenth-century Englishmen visiting France and French travelers in England added commentary on the people and lifestyle, generally in the mode of negative comparison, widely distributing and reinforcing ideas about national character.[46]

On the other side of the Channel, novels being translated from English to French were imported very differently because unlike the English, who believed themselves to be under some quasi-imperial influence of the French and their prose fiction, the French were discovering the British novel through a relatively new introduction to British culture more generally. The Huguenot refugees in Britain, Voltaire, and others helped prompt the translation of fiction, but only after many works in theology, philosophy, science, history, and so on, had been translated and diffused by French speakers. The translation of fictional narratives like *Gulliver's Travels* was favored largely because they were vehicles for philosophical ideas circulating in Britain. English had never attained the status in France that French had gained in Britain, so French translators had no sense of being indebted to the English as literary models to imitate. On the contrary, translators did not hesitate to describe their struggles with rendering English and expressed a resistance to the English novel based on its failure to conform to established aesthetic criteria. The translator of Swift's *Le Conte du tonneau* (Tale of a tub) wrote: "[J]'ai fait tous mes efforts pour la rendre bonne malgré la difficulté terrible, qu'il y a à faire passer heureusement d'une langue dans une autre, tout ce que l'ironie a de plus fin, tout ce que la raillerie a de plus vif . . ." [I did my best to render it well despite the terrible difficulty of making pass easily from one language into another all the finest irony, all the liveliest raillery . . .] He went on to suggest that the translator's task was so arduous because the English "sont outrez, et libres à l'excès, dans leur tour d'Esprit, comme dans leur conduite, et dans leurs manières" [are exaggerated, free to excess in their witty turns as in their conduct and their manners].[47] In the preface to his 1727 version of *Gulliver's Travels* the abbé Desfontaines complained of Swift's low thoughts, annoying repetitions, and other things that were repulsive to the "good taste that reigns in France."[48] Prévost's translations of Richardson and

Pierre-Antoine de La Place's translations of a number of influential works, including *Tom Jones* and *David Simple*, were less than faithful because, they claimed, the English lack of balance, order, and proportion would not conform to French taste.[49] In addition, Elie Catherine Fréron, in his *Année littéraire*, Sébastien de Castres, in his *Trois siècles de la littérature française*, and others reinforced the image of the English novel as rough-hewn by praising these translators' infidelity. Castres said that La Place had rendered several good English novels into French "en les corrigeant d'une certaine prolixité, de certains détails minutieux, qui n'auraient pas été de notre goût" [in correcting a certain prolixity, certain minute details that would not have been to our taste].[50]

At the same time, however, English novels were praised for their naturalism and liveliness. In 1761, when Simon Iraihl recounted the English novel's success in France, he repeated what many others, including Diderot, were saying : "[Q]uelle image vive et naturelle de la vie ordinaire des hommes!" [What a lively and natural image of ordinary life!].[51] English literary style may have lacked balance, but by this same token it was energetic and natural compared with the French literary style. Whether blaming or praising, writers agreed that Englishness represented what Frenchness was not, and national differences between the English and French languages and national characters formed a lens through which many translators and critics viewed the novel exchange.

Thus, on both sides of the Channel national character seems to have exerted pressure on the novel. Of course, this consciousness of national character came about through transnational reflection; it was only within the zone of contact that such discourses of cultural and linguistic difference made sense since they were born of experience-based reflection. Nonetheless, this process of articulating national frameworks for the novel seems to indicate that transnational contact was increasingly directed against the idea of the novel as a single field of infinitely translatable, metamorphosing fictions. Instead, translation appeared to be a more tense process of mediating between oppositional national characters, languages, and hence novels. Like Reeve's, Scott's, Smollett's, and Sade's view that the novel's origins had been national all along, and like Barbauld's desire to create a national collection of novels, the nation was becoming a significant part of the perception of the novel at the moment that it passed from one language to another. But the comments quoted above aimed at rhetorical effect rather than explanations of the full reality of the literary field of the period. A new belief in the nation as a powerful, organizing force for the novel may have been expressed, but I think we can call their bluff.

These writers were not necessarily insincere, but their discourse should not be taken at face value. The French critics of Englishness (Desfontaines, Swift's translator, is a prime case) often knew very little about England, much less Britain. Few had ever been there, most had barely begun to learn English, and English-French grammars and dictionaries were relatively scarce in France.[52] Their ideas of Englishness were based less on experience than on hasty invention. In Britain, the new resistance to Frenchness also appears rather false given the continuing importance of French fiction. There was no real slowdown in translating; French novels continued to be influential, and some writers even argued for the moral purity of French novels despite the invective of Richardson's friends and admirers.[53] More significantly, there is ample evidence that the British and the French simply could not tell whose novel was whose. A number of anecdotes and bibliographical evidence shows that novels and short fictions that were translated from French to English or from English to French were then translated back into the language of the original. Aphra Behn's translation of Brilhac's *Agnès de Castro* (1688) was retranslated into French from her English version and appeared in Madame Thiroux d'Arconville's 1761 *Romans traduits de l'anglais*; and Eliza Haywood's novel *The Fortunate Foundlings* was loosely translated into French as *Les Heureux Orphelins* in 1754 and then brought back into English as *The Happy Orphans*.[54] In his biography of Samuel Johnson, Boswell tells the story of Mr. Murphy, who was persuaded to translate "a very pretty oriental tale" from a French magazine rather than go down to London to prepare his *Gray's Inn Journal* and only later learned that the French had been taken from an English original that had appeared in Johnson's *Rambler*.[55] The most ironic example of this ignorance of national origins is Richardson's *Pamela*. For Richardson and his group the novel was quintessentially anti-French, but when *Pamela* was first published in French, with no author's or translator's name on it, at least a few people guessed that it had been written by a French person.[56]

Everywhere that *nation* appears to have entered the novel—in the construction of the novel market, in discourse on the origins of the novel, and in commentary on translations of novels—it was evocative and potentially persuasive, but it was also quite vague, often signifying smaller localities, like the Irish or Welsh nations, or medieval clans rather than the whole British nation or the whole French nation as they were later understood. And it is not clear that "nation" had a claim above other modes of categorization. That is, the resistance to French fiction in some British writings was based largely on the perceived immorality of the French novel, so that *Frenchness* was just as much a name for worldliness and urban cosmopolitanism as it was for national character. Other claims on one's loyalty and other modes of understanding community, such as religion, locality, or center versus periphery, especially the dominance of Paris and London as the "World"—all these alternatives prevented the exclusive domination of the nation. Thus, the appearance of the nation in writing about the novel in the eighteenth century is not a significant marker of the cohesive, unified nation-states of the nineteenth century and their nationalisms. However, a new presupposition about the novel, namely, that it reflected its culture, was embedded in these uses of *nation*. One's country, whatever that may have included, became the source and limit for the content of the novel. This new vision of the novel as a mirror or container for its cultural surroundings suggests that the novel may not have been defined by its form but sprang in some natural way from a group of people intimately related by kinship or territory and that the story really belongs to them.

Yet, translation, and its fuller significance in *translatio*, has not been a mere backdrop and context for the nation's appearance. As *translatio*, translation was more than a practice; it was a conceptual foundation for the novel. Despite their nationalist discourses, the French and British persistently revealed that the novel was not bounded by a nation's borders but was continually available for appropriation across languages. Like the nation, *translatio* suffered from a similar conceptual looseness in the eighteenth century. Having lost the structural agenda of *translatio imperii* and *translatio studii*, the novel's *translatio* was not meant to reinforce and renew a lineage of powers but survived as another essential aspect of the novel: its fluidity and transmissibility or translatability. Despite all the work the novel would do for the nation, the novel's power to move, crossing cultural borders and language barriers, only increased as the genre became legitimized and formally cohesive. From nation to nation the novel has reinvented itself across national borders as a world literature.

———————

This chapter presents an extremely narrow view of the fuller, more complicated picture of the novel in Britain and France in the eighteenth century, of the more complicated reality of the nation during this period, and of transnationalism in some larger framework for the period. It remains to be seen whether readings of eighteenth-century novels themselves will bear out my argument that the question, National or transnational? remained open. Although I have refused to start outside the novel and find the nation in it, not wishing to assume that the nation already existed and was then applied to the novel, it also remains to be seen how the uses of the nation in the novel relate to its uses in other areas, especially political discourse. Last, and most importantly, I have argued for a continuity between a transnational past in the novel and an increasingly nationalized mode of novel production and reception, but there has been little attention given to models for transnationalism in the eighteenth century more broadly. A link between transnationalism and cosmopolitanism suggests itself here, but much work will be required to carefully define differences between these two theoretical constructs, much less to define their usages and practices in a variety of arenas in eighteenth-century culture.

## Notes

1. See, e.g., Benedict Anderson, *Imagined Communities*, rev. ed. (London: Verso, 1991); Doris Sommer, *Foundational Fictions: The National Romances of Latin America* (Berkeley and Los Angeles: University of California Press, 1991); Eric Hobsbawm and Terence Ranger, eds., *The Invention of Tradition* (Cambridge: Cambridge University Press, 1983); and Homi Bhabha, ed., *Nation and Narration* (New York: Routledge, 1990).

2. The nation is the framework for most of the major studies on the eighteenth-century novel: Henri Coulet, *Le Roman jusqu'à la Révolution* (Paris: A. Colin, 1967); Lennard Davis, *Factual Fictions: The Origins of the English Novel* (New York: Columbia University Press, 1983); Frédéric Deloffre, *La Nouvelle en France à l'age classique* (Paris: Didier, 1968); J. Paul Hunter, *Before Novels: The Cultural Contexts of Eighteenth-Century English Fiction* (New York: Norton, 1990); Michael McKeon, *The Origins of the English Novel, 1600–1740* (Baltimore: Johns Hopkins University Press, 1987); and Ian Watt, *The Rise of the Novel: Studies in Defoe, Richardson, and Fielding* (Berkeley and Los Angeles: University of California Press, 1957). A few exceptions to this trend are April Alliston, *Virtue's Faults: Correspondences in Eighteenth-Century British and French Women's Fiction* (Stanford: Stanford University Press, 1996); Robert Adams Day, *Told in Letters: Epistolary Fiction before Richardson* (Ann Arbor: University of Michigan Press, 1966); and David Foxon, *Libertine Literature in England, 1660–1745* (London: Shenval, 1964).

3. My understanding of translation in the eighteenth century goes against the grain of scholarly work in translation studies that is based on the notion of a literary system. See, e.g., Gideon Toury, *In Search of a Theory of Translation* (Tel Aviv: Porter Institute for Poetics and Semiotics, n.d.); Kitty van Leuven-Zwart and Ton Naajkens, *Translation Studies: The State of the Art, Proceedings of the First James. S. Holmes Symposium on Translation Studies* (Amsterdam: Rodopi, 1991); and Itamar Even-Zohar, "Polysystem Theory," "The 'Literary System,' " and "The Position of Trans-

lated Literature within the Literary Polysystem," *Poetics Today* 11 (spring 1990): 10–51.

4. For example, Walter Wright sees Marie-Jeanne Riccoboni's influence on the translator Frances Brooke in his *Sensibility in English Prose Fiction*, Illinois Studies in Language and Literature, 22, nos. 3– 4 (Urbana: University of Illinois, 1937), 41. Diderot adapted a scene from Laurence Sterne's *Tristram Shandy* in his own novel *Jacques le fataliste* without crediting Sterne. Smollett translated Cervantes and Le Sage, whom he also consciously imitated in *Roderick Random*. Abbé Prévost translated and adapted a variety of English ephemera without acknowledging his sources (see, e.g., Pierre Berthiaume, "Les Contes de Prévost et leurs sources," *Canadian Review of Comparative Literature* 8 [winter 1981]: 61–78).

5. On originality and imitation in the literary tradition see, *inter alia*, Brean Hammond, *Professional Imaginative Writing in England, 1670–1740* (Oxford: Clarendon, 1997); and Joel Weinsheimer, *Imitation* (London: Routledge & Kegan Paul, 1984).

6. See, e.g., Ernest Gellner, *Nations and Nationalism* (Ithaca: Cornell University Press, 1983); and Hans Kohn, *Nationalism, Its Meaning and History* (Princeton: Van Nostrand, 1955).

7. Numbers for English translations are based on my own survey; I counted all prose fictions listed as published, rather than merely advertised, during the course of a single year for every third year between 1660 and 1770. I include both new and reprinted fictional works. Over the course of these 110 years there was a modest overall decline in the percentage of prose-fiction translations from French, though not a steady decline. My sources were Charles Mish, *English Prose Fiction, 1600–1700: A Chronological Checklist* (Charlottesville: Bibliographical Society of the University of Virginia, 1967); the online database *English Short Title Catalog* for the years 1700–1739; Jerry C. Beasley, *A Checklist of Prose Fiction Published in English, 1740–49* (Charlottesville: Bibliographical Society of the University of Virginia, 1972); and James Raven, *British Fiction, 1750–1770* (Newark: University of Delaware Press, 1987).

8. Lawrence Venuti, *Scandals of Translation: Towards an Ethic of Difference* (New York: Routledge, 1998), 88.

9. Charles Mish, "Early Eighteenth-Century Best Sellers in English Prose Fiction," *Papers of the Bibliographic Society of America* 75 (1981): 413–18; Raven, *British Fiction*, 14.

10. Daniel Mornet, "Les Enseignements des bibliothèques privées (1750–1780)," *Revue d'Histoire littéraire de la France* 17 (1910): 449–96.

11. *English Short Title Catalog.*

12. Anna Laetitia Barbauld, "On the Origin and Progress of Novel Writing," in *British Novelists*, 50 vols. (London, 1810), 1:59.

13. Ibid., 4.

14. Giles Barber, *Daphnis and Chloe: The Markets and Metamorphoses of an Unknown Bestseller* (London: British Library, 1989), 24.

15. The title page falsely claims that the work had not yet been translated. The previous translation was *The Loves of Clitophon and Leucippe. A most elegant History written in Greeke by Achilles Tatius and now Englished* (Oxford, 1638). The choice of *Amours* for the 1720 translation makes reference to the many amorous tales translated from French in the Restoration and the early eighteenth century.

16. Arthur Johnston, *Enchanted Ground: The Study of Medieval Romance in the Eighteenth Century* (London: Athone, 1964), 29–30.

17. This was the case with Quevedo and Cervantes in particular. Charles Jarvis recounts the history of *Don Quixote* translations in Miguel Cervantes de Saavedra, *The Life and Exploits of the Ingenious Gentleman Don Quixote de la Mancha*, trans. Charles Jarvis (London: Tonson, 1742), iii–iv.

18. Walter Scott defines the romance in opposition to the novel in the first paragraph of his "Essay on Romance," but in his conclusion he redefines the novel as "modern romance" (Walter Scott, "Essay on Romance," in *Essays on Chivalry, Romance, and the Drama* [Freeport, N.Y.: Books for Libraries, 1972], 129, 216).

19. For example, in 1708 an English version of *The Life of Guzman D'Alfarache* appeared that had been translated, not from the original Spanish, but from the French translation. Other Spanish and Italian works, such as *Amadis de Gaul* and the novellas of Bandello, as well as ancient works like the *Characters of Theophrastus* and the works of Aesop, were translated from French into English rather than from the original languages.

20. See Pierre Daniel Huet, *Lettre-traité de l'origine des romans* (1670; reprint, ed. Fabienne Gégou, Paris: Nizet, 1971), 59, 63–64; and John Dunlop, *The History of Fiction* (1814; reprint, London: Longman, Brown, Green, & Longmans, 1845), 14.

21. Miguel Cervantes de Saavedra, *Don Quixote*, trans. J. M. Cohen (New York: Penguin, 1950), 74–78.

22. This phenomenon was not new in the seventeenth century; it can be traced back at least to medieval romance and chronicles like Geoffrey of Monmouth's *History of the Kings of Britain*. The *Histoire des Sévarambes*, another example of pseudotranslation, included a Babel-like story of the multilingual original manuscript in desperate need of translation (see Denis Veiras, *Histoire des Sévarambes* [1677], preface).

23. John Davies, quoted in Margaret Doody, *The True Story of the Novel* (New Brunswick, N.J.: Rutgers University Press, 1996), 272. The translator of Louis Du Bail's *The Famous Chinois* (1669) similarly personified the hero: "The Famous Chinois comes, as obliged, to waite upon you in habit of English phrase." *Amadis of Greece*, 7th part (1694), has a dedication to the "Beauties of Great Britain" by Amadis himself, who, like the book, "In your soft Arms and silken Laps he hopes to find that Repose, he has so long in vain been seeking thro' so many hard and perillous Adventures."

24. I.F., "To the Exact Translator of the famous History of Infamous Guzman," lines 1–10, prefatory material to Mateo Aleman, *The Rogue, or the Life of Guzman de Alfarache* (London, 1623).

25. Many of Huet's ideas were in circulation before his treatise was written, but there was no systematic treatment of the history of the romance or the novel (see Daniel Selden, "Genre of Genre," in *The Search for the Ancient Novel*, ed. James Tatum [Baltimore: Johns Hopkins University Press, 1994], 43).

26. Although Huet begins his treatise by defining the novel as "fictions d'aventures amoureuses, écrites en prose avec art, pour le plaisir et l'instruction des lecteurs" [fictions of amorous adventures, written artfully in prose, for the delight and instruction of readers] (46–47), he says that the earliest fictions were hieroglyphs and allegories. Most other writers either do not attempt to define the romance as a genre by identifying formal criteria or reiterate Huet's rather loose ones. Unless otherwise noted, all translations are my own.

27. Huet, *Lettre-traité de l'origine des romans*, 51.

28. See Ernst Curtius, *European Literature and the Latin Middle Ages*, trans. Willard R. Trask (Princeton: Princeton University Press, 1953), 26–30.

29. See Karlheinz Stierle, "Translatio studii and Renaissance: From Vertical to Horizontal Translation," in *The Translatability of Cultures*, ed. Sanford Budick and Wolfgang Iser (Stanford: Stanford University Press, 1996).

30. See ibid., 56–57.

31. Introduction to *Cleitophon and Leukippe*, quoted in Doody, *True Story of the Novel*, 260.

32. Thomas Warton, *History of English Poetry from the Twelfth to the Close of the Sixteenth Century*, ed. W. Carew Hazlitt (Hildesheim: Georg Olms, 1968), 93.

33. Abbé Armand Pierre Jacquin, *Entretiens sur les romans, ouvrage moral et critique* (Paris: Duchesne, 1755), 32.

34. Problems of historical interpretation also arose in the narrative of transference, especially in a late-eighteenth-century controversy over the origins of European romance, i.e., over whether it was French, Gothic, Scaldic, or from the Arabs via Spain. For an account of the differing opinions, see Dunlop, *History of Fiction*, 50–51. For a more recent account, see Johnston, *Enchanted Ground*.

35. Clara Reeve, *The Progress of Romance* (1785; reprint, New York: Facsimile Text Society, 1930), ix–v, xv.

36. Tobias Smollett, *The Adventures of Roderick Random* (London: G. Bell, 1925), 3–4.

37. Scott, "Essay on Romance," 134–35. Cf. Homer Brown, *Institutions of the English Novel* (Philadelphia: University of Pennsylvania Press, 1996), 14–15.

38. Sydney Morgan, quoted in *Nineteenth-Century British Novelists on the Novel*, ed. George Barnett (New York: Appleton-Century-Crofts, 1971), 19.

39. Marquis de Sade, *Idées sur les romans*, ed. Jean Glastier (Paris: Editions Ducros, 1970), 37, 34–35 (quotation).

40. Katie Trumpener, *Bardic Nationalism: The Romantic Novel and the British Empire* (Princeton: Princeton University Press, 1997), 143–45.

41. Pierre Daniel Huet, *Treatise on the Origins of Novel*, trans. Stephen Lewis (1715), preface. See also John Moore, "View of the Commencement and Progress of

Romance," in *The Works of Tobias Smollett, M.D.*, 8 vols. (London, 1797), 1:51: "Most of the prose romances, which appeared in England from the days of Chaucer to those of James I were translations from Spanish or French."

42. The review of Smollett's *Peregrine Pickle* is quoted in *Novel and Romance, 1700–1800: A Documentary Record*, ed. Ioan Williams (New York: Barnes & Noble, 1970), 161–62.

43. See Samuel Richardson, *Pamela, or Virtue Rewarded*, ed. T. C. Duncan Eaves and Ben D. Kimpel (Boston: Houghton Mifflin, 1971), 5, 7. I do not go into any depth about *Pamela* here since it is the subject of Lynn Festa's chapter in this volume.

44. Gerald Newman, *The Rise of English Nationalism: A Cultural History, 1740–1830* (New York: St. Martin's, 1987), 124. Linda Colley makes the same point about anti-French feeling in her arguments about British nationalism in *Britons: Forging the Nation, 1707–1837* (New Haven: Yale University Press, 1992), 85–92.

45. James Grantham Turner, "Novel Panic: Picture and Performance in the Reception of Richardson's *Pamela*," *Representations* 48 (fall 1994): 70–96.

46. On seventeenth-century travelers see John Stoye, *English Travellers Abroad, 1604–1667* (New Haven: Yale University Press, 1989). For an overview of eighteenth-century English travelers, see Constantia Maxwell, *The English Traveller in France, 1698–1815* (London: George Routledge & Sons, 1932). Important early observations of England writing in French include Béat de Muralt, *Lettres sur les Anglais et les Français et sur les voyages*, 2nd ed. (Cologne, 1727); and abbé Jean-Bernard Le Blanc, *Lettres de Monsieur l'abbé Le Blanc*, 5th ed. (Lyon, 1768).

47. Jonathan Swift, *Le Conte du tonneau* (La Haye, 1721), preface.

48. Jonathan Swift, *Voyages de Gulliver*, trans. Pierre F. G. Desfontaines (Paris, 1727), preface.

49. See Aphra Behn, *Oronoko* [*sic*], trans. Pierre-Antoine de La Place (Paris, 1745), preface. See also his preface to *Tom Jones, ou L'Enfant trouvé* (London, 1750). Similar statements of method are found in several of Prévost's prefaces to translations, including that in Sir Charles Grandison's *Nouvelles Lettres anglaises* (Amsterdam, 1754).

50. Sébastien de Castres, *Les Trois siècles de la littérature française*, 5th ed. (La Haye, 1781), 74.

51. Simon Iraihl, *Querelles littéraires* (Paris, 1761), 350.

52. The online British Library Catalog and *English Short Title Catalog* list numerous, frequently reprinted grammars for English speakers learning French, but the Bibliothèque Nationale lists only a few for French speakers learning English, and some of these were published in England. On Desfontaines, see Thelma Morris, *L'Abbé Desfontaines et son rôle dans la littérature de son temps*, Studies on Voltaire and the Eighteenth Century 19 (Geneva: Voltaire Foundation, 1961).

53. *Lettre à Monsieur l'abbé Des Fontaines sur "Paméla"* (Amiens, 1742), 7–8; *Pamela Censured* (1741; reprint, ed. Charles Batten, Los Angeles: William Andrews Clark Library, 1976), 6–7.

54. See John P. Kent, "Crébillon fils, Mrs. Eliza Haywood, and *Les Heureux Orphelins*: A Problem of Authorship," *Romance Notes* 11 (1969): 326–32.

55. James Boswell, *Life of Johnson*, ed. R. W. Chapman, intro. Pat Rogers, (Oxford: Oxford University Press, 1980), 252.

56. See Charles Bastide, *Anglais et français du XVIIe siècle* (Paris: Alcan, 1912), 290; and Aubert de la Chesnaye-Desbois, *Lettres amusantes et critiques sur les romans en general anglais et français, tant anciens que modernes* (Paris: Gissey, Bordelet, David, 1743), 43.

LYNN FESTA

# Sentimental Bonds and Revolutionary Characters: Richardson's *Pamela* in England and France

In the early 1740s Richardson's *Pamela* was everywhere. "Pamela," Horace Walpole wrote, suggestively conjoining the novel's promiscuous ubiquity to its heroine's ostensible purity, "*Pamela* is like the snow; she covers all with her whiteness."[1] "Many English books I conclude are to be bought at Paris," Walpole continued. "I am sure Richardson's works are, for they have stupefied the whole French nation."[2] As is well known, *Pamela*'s triumphant progress through London and Paris led to a proliferation of critical letters, apologies, polemics, parodies, imitations, sequels, and theatrical adaptations, not to mention paintings and prints, fans, china, and even two waxworks, "containing above a hundred Figures in Miniature, richly dress'd, suitable to the Characters."[3] In France, the novel spawned a comedy, a *comédie larmoyante*, a burlesque opera, and a farce, leading to ample metacritical commentary on the *Pamela* vogue; one of its theatrical adaptations would spark a small riot at the Comédie Française during the French Revolution, leading the Committee of Public Safety to debate the merits of this sentimental fiction in the midst of the Terror.

    *Pamela* serves as the crux to a set of relationships central to a cross-Channel analysis of the rise of the novel—between canon formation and national identity, between the emergence of the sentimental genre and the elaboration of a literary marketplace, between sentimental celebration of human reciprocity and the Enlightenment discourse of human rights. It was the first of the eighteenth-century sentimental novels—of which Richardson's *Clarissa*, Rousseau's *Julie*, Sterne's *Tristram Shandy*, and

Goethe's *Werther* are the most prominent—to incite a pan-European consumer frenzy. These novels stimulated an appetite for international literary goods that both created and capitalized on a cross-Channel zone of consumer culture, in which the circulation of texts forged a triangulated relationship between English and French readers through their shared interest in cultural products like *Pamela*. Such goods gave a tangible form to the overlapping appetites and intersecting cultural investments of France and England, fostering transnational bonds through shared acts of cultural consumption.

*Pamela*'s popularity, no less than its centrality to "rise of the novel" narratives in England and France alike, suggests ample comparisons between the two, but it is not my intent to take a traditional comparatist approach here.[4] In examining the fate of an English novel in France, I wish to pose a set of questions about the role of the sentimental novel in general and *Pamela* in particular in forging collective identities among readers as consumers in a literary marketplace, as participants in the imagined community of nation, and as emotional partakers in the universal drama of the human heart promised by the sentimental novel. The various ways *Pamela* was read solicit different forms of human communities—commercial, national, linguistic, sentimental-humanist—in a variety of not entirely compatible ways. In following the itinerary traced out by *Pamela* as both text and marketing phenomenon I want to suggest some of the ways the circulation of literary texts and their cultural by-products created a cross-Channel zone of consumer culture that shaped the novel as a genre.

In both content and form, sentimentality would seem to be the ideal genre for a transnational book trade. The sentimental novel represents forms of interpersonal communion that transcend national origins to embrace all humanity; it produces a community of weeping, powerfully moved readers united across cultural and geographic barriers by shared tears. The reciprocal movement of sentimental commodities forges material bonds between nations in a consumer zone that brings disparate audiences together in shared raptures over a literary text. But on the periphery of visions of ecstatic sentimental communion hover the interested exchanges of economic commerce. The cross-Channel traffic in sentimentality is manifested not only in scenes of collective feeling but also in the tangible consumption of texts like *Pamela* and its myriad consumer by-products. The French and English absorbed these texts into their literary forms and their reading appetites, giving shape to a transnational audience whose desires governed the works brought to market. At the same time, the proliferation of *Pamela* rewritings, theatrical adaptations, and marketing by-products in France suggests the ways consumers not only digested or absorbed texts "as is"; they also took them apart and put them back together in new forms, appropriating the original work to their own tastes and ends. The international literary market is a zone in which forms drawn from different countries sympathetically mingle and fuse, but it is also a site of dissension and cross-Channel rivalry. Thus writers concerned with the French appetite for English sentimental fiction employed a mercantile rhetoric calling for a cultural balance of trade between the two countries. Anxious to maintain the integrity and autonomy of their own traditions, such critics endeavored to harness wayward consumer appetites to a national cultural agenda.

The transnational consumer zone produced and distributed symbolic capital in ways that governed the meaning and reception of the sentimental genre, even as the rapid-fire interchanges between nations formed and deformed the cultural institutions and reading publics that gave shape to the modern novel. Thus *Pamela* has recently been read as part of Nancy Armstrong and Leonard Tennenhouse's effort to resituate the novel, "the perfect creole," in terms of an English-speaking diaspora that embraced the reading public on both sides of the Atlantic.[5] English identities, they contend, took form by being sustained in the face of cultural challenges (e.g., life among the Indians in Rowlandson's captivity narrative; the Gothic domesticity of Mr. B's houses in Richardson), and such challenges created the medium—the written word, the self as a tissue of words rather than a violable and vulnerable body—by which that identity was to be maintained. *Pamela*'s reception in France suggests the fragility of such sustained fictions of identity. The role played by *Pamela* in forging a collective readership depended not only upon its ability to reflect or maintain individual and national identities but also upon its capacity to generate a transnational community of consumers within an emerging literary marketplace. While readers' desires were manipulated or even disciplined by the novel, the proliferation of texts and marketable commodities based on *Pamela* suggests that its consumers garnered from the text what they would: sentimental tropes of readerly identification rarely work seamlessly to produce a uniform effect on a receptive reading public. The international consumer culture that emerged around the sentimental novel, that is, did not necessarily create coherent communities that aligned with other social or ideological affiliations (nation, family, class).

That the communities forged by the sentimental novel did not a priori line up with other cultural institutions was in part a product of tensions located within the genre. At the same time as sentimental novels like *Pamela* resolutely assert their English origins, for example, the genre's celebration of the singular universality of the "human heart" purveys a notion of human identity that knows no national borders. At stake here is how sentimentality can foster both national sentiments *and* universalized ideals that transcend the boundaries of nation. Inasmuch as the genre's fostering of reciprocal feeling extends humanity to those who fall within the novel's purview, sentimentality becomes implicated not only in a notion of national prerogative but also in the construction of a community of individuals to whom human rights are to be extended. And the values attributed to these communities in turn haunt the institutions that define the nature of the novel.

That *Pamela*'s reception transcended the boundaries of nation does not mean that French readers ignored its English origins. Quite the contrary. From *Pamela*, as one critic put it, arose "the vapors of the swamps of Albion[, which] engendered this philosophical epidemic that kills genius, places spirits in a ferment, and produces this anti-national taste of which the ravages are only too evident. . . . We abandon the true sources of taste, to search for new ones, and made sterile by our own fault, we debase ourselves to become the imitators and servile copyists of all that bears a foreign character."[6] By fostering a differential identity in opposition to the English, the reception history of Richardson's novel produced at least one version of "Frenchness." As the true wellsprings of French taste were abandoned in favor of English novelty, the French are said to debase themselves by becoming the sterile copyists of another nation's cultural production. Indeed, the mode for English novels was such that, as the *Journal Étranger* wrote, "[o]ur romance-writers are reduced to travestying their reveries under a foreign mask in order to be read."[7]

The preeminence of literary works of foreign origin menaces the cultural autonomy of French literary institutions. Thus, Richardson's role in forming—or *de*forming—the eighteenth-century French novel has often been debated, and the way Richardson's stock rises and falls is a creditable reflection of the vicissitudes of Anglo-French relations. The "rise of the novel" narrative in France has been marked by a tug-of-war about Richardson's role stemming from a national (and nationalistic) investment in the canon.[8] On the one hand, *Pamela* is often depicted as inaugurating the Anglomania that transformed the French public taste in the novel. On the other hand, *Pamela* and Richardson are normally relegated to footnotes in French narratives of the rise of the novel; the *Pamela* vogue is viewed as a pale precursor of the frenzy inspired by Rousseau's 1761 *Julie, ou la Nouvelle Héloïse*, usually considered to be the first French sentimental novel.

No matter how popular *Pamela* was, Richardson is not permitted to usurp Rousseau's position as originary author and genius within the Enlightenment canon.[9]

*Pamela* held sway over the ways individuals conceived of themselves as participating in an imagined community of consumers; the novel's reception demonstrates the way the emerging print market was formed by the reciprocal shaping of commercial and aesthetic values. The consumption of *Pamela*—and the establishment of this community of consumers— revolved around making the novel compatible with French taste and *moeurs*. The translator (at times incorrectly identified as Prévost but unnamed on the title page) made some minor accommodations to French taste but unlike Prévost in his translation of *Clarissa* left the text almost unmodified.[10] Despite French readers' complaints about Richardson's low style and "revolting prolixity,"[11] the novel was seen as sufficiently close to French writings that rumors arose that it was not in fact of English origin.[12] The lack of certainty about the novel's origins reflects the difficulty of essentializing what exactly is English within the text, suggesting the instability and malleability of national identity in the eighteenth century. The text's reception is similarly difficult to pin down. Any argument about the community forged by the novel must take into account not just the factions of pro- and anti-Pamelists (indeed, the two often share the same values, with the poles reversed) but also the dazzling variety of genres spawned by this singular piece. The novel was rapidly supplanted by a series of adaptations, ranging from Boissy's 1742 "comédie en vers," *Pamela en France*, to Nivelle de La Chaussée's 1742 "comédie larmoyante" or Voltaire's 1749 *Nanine*. As a commodity, *Pamela* would seem to defy generic categorization; by following and setting its own fashion, it circulated among a diverse readership both within and outside of national boundaries.[13]

The diffuseness of what William Warner calls "the *Pamela* media event" creates a methodological problem: how can one claim cultural agency and power for this particular "sentimental novel," given the difficulties of clustering "it" together generically, let alone as a kind of unified social force? The question posed about the Englishness of *Pamela*, that is, may be likewise posed about the unity of the text: what threshold of identity is necessary for an object to be recognizably "itself"? How much of the singularity of an object lingers after passage through the crucible of translation and historical context? As John Plotz has argued, issues of textual portability and fungibility call the essential identity of a literary object into question. Given the inchoate forms of national identity and the alchemical transformations worked upon *Pamela* by numerous adaptations and imitations, how much of a coherent object was there at the start? Is it possible to insist, as does Pamela, that "I am *Pamela*, indeed I am: Indeed I am *Pamela, her own self*?"[14]

Most of the population, literate and illiterate, probably knew *Pamela* not through "her own self" but through the numerous theatrical adaptations. Indeed, it seems likely that more readers consumed the by-products of the novel than consumed the original: Carlo Goldoni's Italian play was more successful than the novel and was translated into more languages than Richardson's original; it was not the English original but the French translation of *Pamela* that was placed on the Roman Index of forbidden books in 1744.[15] Mass-market *Pamela* outstripped *Pamela* the novel, suggesting that the elevated functions of moral improvement or social realism that currently claim *Pamela* for high culture are not reflected in the historical circumstances of the text's reception. What the history of *Pamela*'s consumption reveals is the ease with which texts can be dislodged from their cherished position as carriers of "culture," bastions against the inroads of mass consumption. The sacred singularity of the work of art cannot be dissevered from the myriad mass-produced profane commodities it spawns.

The artifact eighteenth-century readers consumed came to be less the text itself, the words Richardson produced, than a succession of textual and nontextual surrogates for *Pamela*. The history of *Pamela* reveals the degree to which the novel itself fragmented and disintegrated as it was marketed, consumed, and appropriated. The text's impact is not exclusively a function of its literary effects (its impact on the rise of the novel), its reception history (how it was read and by whom), or its mode of production (the author, the genius, from whom the text issued). Instead, a literary history focused on the cultural as well as literary meaning of texts must address the multifarious effects of *Pamela* as a disunified conglomerate of material artifacts. Texts are not always incorporated into culture in the ways conventional literary histories acknowledge: the *improper* use of texts, the ways texts are *not* read, can be as significant as the ways they are read. Eighteenth-century novels subsisted less in the autonomous produced texts than in their marketing surrogates, the disparate imitations, sequels, parodies, and consumer by-products that gave the novel an afterlife long after the original disappeared from the scene. The name and meaning of *Pamela* circulated independent of the text, detached from the novel that was its original signified; an eighteenth-century reader could fill in the substance of the story without reading the words of the novel. *Pamela* in its extratextual afterlife possessed as much cultural authority as its earlier Richardsonian incarnation.

The artifacts spawned by *Pamela*, then, furnish a cautionary tale about how the unity imposed upon texts in order to produce literary histories (we treat *Pamela* as if it were the single and singular text written by Richardson) is belied by the material and historical conditions of their reception.[16] The idea of the text as a stable entity or even as a discrete vessel for the contesting heteroglossic languages of the novel collapses beneath the intrusive labors of so many hands. *Pamela* is less a single work than a cluster of marketable elements. Transnational literary exchanges should be seen less as the discrete transactions of self-contained works than as a frenzied scrabbling marketplace, as in Trochereau's description of English texts as "stores packed with goods crammed confusedly on top of each other."[17] Not only is the novel itself a commodity but its text becomes an overflowing storefront chockfull of saleable items, to be pillaged by a reading public made up of avid consumers.

*Pamela* the original "model of Virtue" was transformed into a cheap, mass-produced imitation: the private meditations of the novel, written in the seclusion of Pamela's closet, were exposed in the theater to the public gaze, opening the virtuous heroine to additional accusations of manipulative duplicity and market-driven calculation of the rewards to be gleaned from virtue. Godard d'Aucour's 1744 burlesque *La Déroute des Paméla* satirized the proliferation of *Pamela*s as the original novel ("la Paméla Anglaise") comes to France in search of her two unhappy daughters: "la Paméla Française," Nivelle de La Chaussée's disastrous *Pamela*, performed at the Comédie Française, and "la Paméla Italienne," Boissy's more successful *Pamela en France*, staged by the Comédie Italienne, allegedly with Mme de Riccoboni as Pamela. So debased are these adaptations that the English Paméla barely recognizes her "daughters" and chastises them for assuming her name, indeed, taking it in vain: "You dishonor me in France; you cover me and my whole family with shame by assuming the name of my daughter."[18] Using an *ad feminam* argument that conflates "Pamela" the woman and the play, *La Déroute des Paméla* collapses the public circulation of the text into a female loss of chastity and reputation: the play on the market becomes a kind of prostitution (on the part of the author, the character, and the original text) in which the original title lends credence to upstarts.[19] Indeed, the adaptations are so detached from the original text that the Italian Pamela confesses that her name and origins were changed to Pamela by the playwright, "convinced that under that name, I would instantly be adored by the Public."[20] Rather than punishing the cheap imitations, the English Pamela hands them over to the tender mercies of "La Mère Bleue," the publisher of the cheap "Bibliothèque Bleue" editions, who prostitutes them to the public in turn.

Pamela, in short, was not always used as directed. Apart from the potential for prurient interest in Pamela's virtue, the novel was not necessarily read. Instead it was ostentatiously displayed—carried in the park, left on a side table—a portable signifier of the virtue, or at least of the fashionability, of reader and character alike. "One cannot enter a house without finding a Pamela," noted the Lettre sur Paméla, "it's the fashionable piece of furniture."[21] Pamela becomes a placeholder in a fashionable literary market, an interchangeable item to be supplanted in turn. "It's the thing to have a Pamela; it has eclipsed Le Sopha," observed Aubert de la Chesnaye-Desbois. "I am impatient for something else to evict it from the dressing tables of the Ladies, to go occupy the antechambers, and perhaps to serve as the curlpaper for the hairdresser of some petit Maître or of some young lady in a hurry to get to the theater."[22] The novel's downward mobility follows a trajectory from fashionable prop to marker of the class aspirations of the servants in antechambers, until the materiality of the book overtakes its content and the pages serve for curlers to a frivolous young lady en route to yet another entertainment. The novel's collapse from readable text to fashionable but empty sign is followed by the reassertion of its material origins as crushed pulp. Pamela will ultimately "have the ordinary fate of Novels, that is, to be buried in the dust."[23]

In 1821 Byron describes a murder case that featured, among the items of evidence, the discovery of "a leaf of Pamela wrapt round the bacon" by a grocer "which he was tearing for waste paper." Byron cannot help but wonder "what he [Richardson] would have said, could he have traced his pages from their place on the French prince's toilets . . . to the grocer's counter and the gipsy-murderess's bacon!!! . . . What can anybody say, save what Solomon said long before us? After all, it is but passing from one counter to another, from the bookseller's to the other tradesman's—grocer or pastry-cook."[24] The material fate of the text becomes a vehicle for anxieties about novelty and the novel, figuring the recognition that the buying and selling of cultural objects is no different from the getting and spending of other kinds of commodities: culture is something to be consumed in ways that are both liberating and terrifying.

The market for Pamela paraphernalia suggests that the community brought into being by the novel was derived less from sentiment than from the marketplace, a community forged not out of reciprocity of feeling but out of a shared love of an object coveted by another. The book's value arises less from any intrinsic merit than from its triangulated position in a consumer market driven by competitive covetousness: "So true is it that it is less the true merit of things which captures us, than the idea that others attach to them; there are in the world those things which have no other price than the one placed on them by fashion."[25] Value arises from the interested gaze of another, a triangular structure of desire that runs directly counter to the celebration of spontaneous sentiment with its suggestion of symmetrical emotions reciprocally exchanged. *Pamela* almost drops out of the equation; the novel fosters unity not out of its inherent power as fiction but because of the value attributed to it by others. On these terms, the community of consumers is not an imagined collective bound through shared sentiment but an imagined relation to an abstraction, an abstraction, moreover, whose value derives from others' relation to it.

This tricornered figure of consumer interest in a shared object is echoed in eighteenth-century descriptions of sentimental reading. The impact of the sentimental scene at times seems to stem less from the reader's reaction to the text than from the reader's consciousness of the reaction incited in *other* readers. Thus the "editor" of the English *Pamela* is convinced that his narrative will convert the reader because "he can Appeal from *his own* Passions, (which have been uncommonly *moved* in perusing these engaging Scenes) to the Passions of *Every one* who shall read them with the least Attention."[26] The sympathetic and involuntary movements of the various subjects conjoin the particular reader and his or her body to the bodies of all readers so moved. In his *Éloge de Richardson* Diderot describes the ideal workings of the sentimental text upon the reader as inspiring a homogenized community of crying witnesses: "Men, come, we will weep together over the unhappy characters in Richardson's fictions, and we will say: 'If fate overwhelms us, at least the good people [*les honnêtes gens*] will weep over us too.' "[27] The structure of being moved by Richardson involves a shared object ("the unhappy characters") witnessed by a collective readership ("*we* will weep together") who simultaneously precipitate themselves into the position of victim ("if fate overwhelms us") being bemoaned by yet another group of weeping "honnêtes gens." Identification with the suffering other lapses into the subject's assuming the position of the suffering object to be apprehended. The focus on the individual response to the text, on the emotions incited in the reader's own self, trains the many in the "proper" reactions, becoming the means by which to create (and potentially to dominate) the collective.

Although Diderot describes a reading process that creates a community of similarly weeping spectators, it is not exactly a symmetrical exchange. The reader does not simply identify with the suffering characters in the text but constructs a third position from which to apprehend his or her response to the sentimental text. Simultaneously observer of another and observed by others, the reader is addressed by Diderot ("Men, come") not simply to feel and cry but to model himself, from the position of the sufferer, after an ideal spectator of suffering. Even as the value of *Pamela* arises from the novel's being prized by others, here the meaning of the affect is derived from identification, not with the suffering object, but with a third position as a spectator observing that suffering. The ability to be pleasurably moved by suffering emerges from the reader's being at a remove from that suffering; the projected woes of the reader are left to a conditional anticipated state: "*if* fate overwhelms us." The elaborate relays of Diderot's model of identification substantiate Michelle Burnham's suggestion that the sentimental representations with which readers purportedly identify rarely resemble readers or their lives. Identification based on likeness, Burnham contends, is too simple a model; sentimental narrative employs "a model of identification that emphasizes disjunction and disavowal rather than resemblance and imitation." The relation of identification is never completely symmetrical: the precipitation of the self into the role of the other is not a reciprocal and balanced exchange. Some dangling remainder always subsists to unsettle the neatness of the balance sheet. Although momentarily arrested by the same spectacle of suffering, the community imagined through sentimental identification in Diderot is not consolidated into a homogeneous whole. As Burnham puts it, "What is sentimental about the imagined communities that novels create is the obscured fact that they are not based on likeness."[28]

Indeed, the political efficacy of the sentimental novel in part arises from this *lack* of sameness. For it is in part the absence of likeness, the fact that the novel does *not* mirror reality, that makes the novel the vehicle for fantasies of social mobility and, as I will discuss below, the agent of social change. In privileging identification as the contact point between text and reader, critics reinforce a single "correct" perspective on the novel, disallowing perspectives that attend to generic elements that do not fit into the "rise of the novel" thesis. The diversity of public responses to *Pamela* suggests that the text was unable to impose a fixed or uniform interpretation, and yet the sentimental ideal of a community to be forged from the novel writes over this absence of likeness or homogeneity. For Diderot, to participate in the community of *Pamela*'s readers involves a provisional acceptance of the roles and ideals it celebrates—and an implicit refusal of what it excludes or repudiates. In using Richardson as a "touchstone" to appraise others, Diderot banishes from his community those who dissent from his judgment: "[T]hose who find [Richardson's novels] displeasing," he announces, "are judged for me."[29] If another's position vis-à-vis Richardson cannot be spliced with his own, Diderot is obliged "by an effort of reason" to insulate himself from repudiating the other in a reprehensible "species of intolerance" (44).

Likeness would, however, seem to create the most fecund soil for sentimental identification, and sentimental novels often feature small clusters of individuals who share rank, birth, and wealth. Only by creating restrictive definitions of community, social affiliation, and value can the sentimental novel negotiate the contradictions between existing social and economic hierarchies and the universalized ideals of the self that the novel ostensibly seeks to promote. While this is most apparent in, for example, an enclosed sphere such as Clarens in Rousseau's *La Nouvelle Héloïse*, it is also evident in the imperative to elevate Pamela's rank in order to render her marriage acceptable to the tastes of the French reading public.[30] Readers of the novel were torn between the desire to revel in the pleasures of sentimental identification and the need to banish the "low" from this communion of feeling. If sentimentality fosters the peculiar pleasures of identification of the self with another, what bothered many eighteenth-century readers of *Pamela* was the breakdown of that delicious feeling by the impingement of class.[31] The public might be united in their taste for sentimental literature, but what they culled from these works might well differ depending on the rank of the reader. Thus Mary Wortley Montague remarked on *Pamela*'s "very extraordinary (and I think undeserved) success. It has been translated into French and Italian; it was all the fashion at Paris and Versailles, and is still the joy of the Chambermaids of all nations."[32] *Pamela*'s readers sought to find their likeness in the text, but what was construed as like varied dramatically. Noting the rank-stratified responses to Voltaire's adaptation of *Pamela, Nanine*, the abbé de La Porte remarked on the differences between the appalled aristocratic ladies in the loges and the delighted "grisettes" in the third tier of the theater, who saw themselves "metamorphosed into Countesses."

> I saw in the first tier of the theater several Ladies of rank who did not look with a kindly eye on the old Countess, and who, had they been in her place, would neither have been so indulgent toward their son, nor consented to such an unequal mar-

riage. By contrast, all the shopgirls in the third tier bestowed a million blessings on that good Lady, convinced that, should the fashion for this kind of marriage be established among us, they would soon find themselves metamorphosed into Countesses. . . . Pernicious sentiments among the common people, who, as long as they wallow in such fantasies, will neglect to become good workers—a thing a thousand times more useful and more necessary to a State, than all these imaginary Countesses.[33]

For the abbé, the danger of *Paméla* and its bastardized and bowdlerized adaptations is that the novel may stimulate hopes of social ambition, nurturing a class of unproductive individuals useless to the state. The passage comes dangerously close to being a commentary on the uselessness of the aristocracy, hinting at the incendiary potential of the novel's plot. And yet it is the fantasy that all people, even a common servant, have a right to the rewards of sentiment and virtue that constitutes *Pamela*'s most revolutionary labor.

For the extension of humanity to one individual implies a synecdochal image of the whole: the minute particular contains the universal. What makes Pamela's ascent pose such a threat to an aristocratic order, as the abbé de La Porte suggests above, is the implicit recognition that in one servant is contained the seething, socially climbing masses. Thus Desfontaines's suggestion that "so much virtue and resistance on the part of a person of high rank" would have lacked "verisimilitude"[34] sparked a vigorous protest about such generalizations: "You place no restriction on this odious maxim; you extend it to all women of all Nations and of all Climates. Can you reflect for an instant on such an excessive statement without blushing?"[35] The work done by the sentimental model of reading is politicized by the way the (affective, at times identificatory) extension of humanity to hitherto disenfranchised subjects comes to imply the inclusiveness of the claim to political and legal rights: *Pamela* is an invitation to women "of all Nations and of all Climates" to consider themselves entitled to belong to the sentimental world. The possibility that other women will take themselves for the singular Pamela constructs an interchangeable subject position of virtue and entitlement, implying that anyone can assume the role of the subject endowed with rights. The fact that everyone, prince or peasant, has a soul enlarges the moral and even the social sphere of the sentimental republic but does not reverse the political order.[36] Such an enlargement of the sentimental world to embrace high and low is itself a function of the marketplace with which we began. As the abbé Prévost writes in *Le Pour et le contre*: "Why would I prefer one reader over another? In making a work public does one not proclaim that one writes for everyone?"[37] Substitution paves the way for universality, even as the "nobody" of the market becomes the political "anybody" of Revolutionary ideals.

The sentimental novel works to reshape a perception of the community to which people were entitled to belong, as the novel's plots and formulas gained the status of cultural maxims. "Without *Pamela*," as Crébillon wrote to Chesterfield, "we would know neither what to read nor what to say."[38] The genre's stock characters, recurrent themes, and predictable situations help elaborate a collective vocabulary of feeling to channel readerly response. The repetition and rehearsal of emotions in the sentimental novel is the genre's contribution to the cultural labor involved in engineering a perceptual shift that, as Philip Fisher has argued in a different context, comes to be perceived as "fact."[39] The sentimental novel works to reshape perceptions of the community to which people were entitled to belong, be it nation, family, or rank. In order to flesh out the community to embrace other classes of individuals as part of the great category of humankind, sentimentality sought to create an acknowledgment of individual worth through recognition of the similitude of a particular individual; this recognition might then be imaginatively expanded to embrace *all* like individuals. Once Pamela's value is recognized (which is, after all, the *work* of the novel), one must authorize its reward. As Margaret Cohen has argued, the content of the sentimental novel—its depiction of the struggle between the individual's right to affect, virtue, personal freedom, and the opposing set of social or familial values and imperatives—echoes the performative aspect of the sentimental form, as the interior struggles of the sentimental hero or heroine *create* as well as exemplify sentimental virtue.[40]

But it is precisely this labor that must be disguised. As Fisher notes, in order to consummate a change in moral perception, a culture must also accomplish, "as a last step, the forgetting of its own strenuous work so that what are newly learned habits are only remembered as facts."[41] As the community represented in the novel becomes absorbed as a cultural fact, the perceived gap between the ideology propagated in the text and historical reality narrows. The work of cultural transformation and of forgetting are intertwined: what must be forgotten is both the previous form (e.g., Pamela abject, as servant), now perceived to be wrong, and the labor of constructing and maintaining the new, "correct" perception (Pamela virtuous and rewarded, entitled to belong to the community). Once absorbed as common sense, the stock figures or stereotypes of sentimental literature, which are meant to create change in the larger field of culture, come to seem exaggerated, trite, ossified, offensive, not (or not only) because they are crudely drawn, overly simplified, but because they betray the effort put into creating the convention. And it is in part the revelation of this labor that opens *Pamela* to accusations of "Shamela-ism." In the absence of any conventional or causal attributes of virtue (rank, wealth, birth), Pamela can only be allowed to be virtuous by her insistence in language on being so. She has to *work* to be virtuous, and because of her rank, she also has to *work* to be seen as virtuous. Because this labor is both part of a larger cultural agenda and a product of interior narrative (Pamela's letters and her work on herself), not only the novel but also its heroine is exposed to accusations of artificiality. Although Pamela's efforts to maintain her virtue in fact constitute her virtue, the marks of that labor are what expose her to accusations of duplicity. This doubleness is realized in Shamela's manner of speaking of her "Vartue" as a separate possession, a detachable object, rather than a constitutive aspect of the self. Once virtue ceases to be produced and performative and becomes an object of representation, it becomes artificial, ossified, a duplicitous mask.

The English debate between pro- and anti-Pamelists, which pitted the purity and simple authenticity of Richardson's Pamela against the duplicitous and manipulative Shamela, was recast, in France, in terms of nationalities. What Shamela was to Pamela, French stylized prose was to English authenticity. As the Reverend William Webster wrote in a prefatory "puff" to Richardson's novel, *Pamela* must be left in "its own native Simplicity": to add oratory or rhetorical ornamentation would be to "reduce our Sterling Substance into an empty Shadow, or rather *frenchify* our *English* Solidity into Froth and Whip-Syllabub."[42] If, as William Warner has recently argued, the moral respectability of Richardson's *Pamela* was intended to cut prosperous female writers like Haywood, Manley, and Behn out of the English market, it was intended to supplant the whole tribe of libertine writers in France.[43] From its first edition, Richardson's *Pamela* was implicated in a cross-Channel literary feud since in addition to Webster's "puff" Richardson affixed to the prefatory material a congratulatory, not to say unctuous, letter from Jean Baptiste de Freval, a minor French writer and translator living in London. *Pamela*, Freval announced, was a model that would reform the scandalously corrupt and frivolously immoral literature of France:

> Little Book, charming *Pamela!* face the World, and never doubt of finding Friends and Admirers, not only in thine own Country, but far from Home; where thou mayst give an Example

of Purity to the Writers of a neighbouring Nation; which now shall have an Opportunity to receive *English* Bullion in Exchange for its own dross, which has so long passed current among us in Pieces abounding with all the Levities of its volatile Inhabitants.[44]

Explicitly pitting English writing against the libertine novels of the French, the prefatory advertisement figures itself as a form of authentic currency that will circulate in lieu of the false coin of the French. Bullion, if not virtue, is to be extracted from the novel. The passage figures an extraordinary number of exchanges: between the falsity of the French "dross" and the authenticity of the English "Bullion," between the immoral dreck purveyed by French libertine writers like Crébillon and even Marivaux and the moral correctives of a Richardson, but also between the French money that purchases the English book and, presumably, the English coin (mis)spent on French novels. Freval advocates a kind of literary mercantilism, correcting the balance of trade between the two nations both by pitting a superior English product against an inferior French product and by exposing the "Pieces" (of literature, of coin) purveyed by the French as evacuated representations of an inflated currency. Freval's image of the novel as English Bullion invites anti-Pamelist comparisons between the marketing of the book and the heroine's artful manipulations of her own value, suggesting the fiscal rewards of the virtues of *Pamela* the book as well as its eponymous heroine.

The letter hardly seems calculated to endear Richardson's work to the French, and indeed it did not pass unremarked. In 1740 the English had just sided with Marie-Thérèse in the War of the Austrian Succession; on these grounds the *Lettre à Monsieur l'abbé Des Fontaines sur "Paméla"* took the abbé to task for his support of the novel. The *Journal de Barbier* likewise declared that it was "outraged by the author of the *Observations* for defending *Pamela*, and quite surprised that a *privilège* was conferred to print a work whose preface sings the praises of the English and is an insult to the whole of this nation."[45] The *Bibliothèque Raisonnée* pointed out the absurdity of the model of readerly response upon which the preface's notion of novelistic reform was based: "What good is it to insult so many great writers, who have in a large number of works of the same genre elaborated on the detours, ruses, and strategies of vice and libertinage? . . . They did not claim to propose these models for imitation. They contented themselves with marking the reefs upon which virtue often is shipwrecked."[46] If Richardson's novel ostensibly avoids presenting any transgressions for the reader to imitate, the French libertine tradition offers a series of cautionary tales for those who wish to avoid being snared by the transgressors.

And yet underlying the polish of the French and the bluntness of the English is the unifying stratum of the human heart.[47] The conflicts between individuals and institutions depicted in a sentimental text may arise from a particular confluence of historical circumstances, but the outpouring of feeling transcends local affiliations and origins. Certainly, Marquet concedes in the *Lettre sur Paméla*, "I admit that every people has its own habits; the exterior, ceremonial politeness of Paris is different from that of London. But the politeness of the heart, that delicate sentiment that arises from an unofficial and complaisant soul . . . that sweet and inestimable harmony of society, is, I think, of all countries, and does not belong more to one nation than to another; it must exist everywhere there are men."[48] The malleability of the sentimental plot—its geographical and historical mobility, the way it can be transplanted across state lines—is possible because of the purported universality of the human heart. "Love brings everyone together," writes the 1742 reviewer of *Pamela* in the *Bibliothèque Raisonnée*, "and spreads an amiable and just equality everywhere. It is thus that one finds amended the disorder of the Laws and rampant passions that introduced the inequality of rank and estates into the world."[49] The essence of the novel of sensibility is "sentiment, that universal and invariable language."[50] "The works of Richardson," writes Diderot, "will please more or less every man, in all times and all places." He qualifies this universalized community with the small caveat that "the number of readers who will sense the price will never be great."[51] The community readers imagine themselves to be joining in this celebration of love varies dramatically depending upon the reader doing the imagining. Part of what the sentimental novel does is produce a consensus on what the abstract idea or ideal of that community ought to be—who it should include, who should be banished, on what principles admission to or exclusion from the republic of virtue should be based.

The sense of community created by the sentimental novel had contradictory implications for eighteenth-century notions of national identity. Sentimentality, which represented intense shared and reciprocated emotions among novelistic characters in order to incite similar responses in its readers, orchestrated a communion of feeling that conjoined the reader to a larger "imagined community" not unlike the "imagined communities" Benedict Anderson has described as constituting the modern nation. The novel's claim to offer a detailed and verisimilitudinous representation of daily life—one of the technical innovations for which Richardson was both praised and reviled—echoes Anderson's notion that readers imagine the community of the nation as a set of separate characters simultaneously performing similar actions in "homogeneous empty time."[52] Based on the terms of Anderson's argument, affect, the individual felt experience of sympathy and simultaneity with the multitude, shapes nationality; as Michelle Burnham has compellingly argued, this makes the nation "a community constructed and maintained on the basis of resemblance or likeness."[53] Such arguments suggest a structural alignment of national sentiment and the conventions and premises of sentimental reader response, although they produce a disturbingly homogeneous end product: a nation constituted out of the reproduction of sameness. Burnham's timely reminder that sentimentality does not in fact produce a community of like persons functions as an important caveat in any easy fusion of sentimental identification and the formation of nationhood.

Sentimentality would seem to furnish some of the identificatory tools for imagining the horizontal arrangement of persons associated with the nation, while its own premises could not conceive the nation as a limited or bounded entity. If, as Anderson observes, "no nation imagines itself coterminous with mankind," then why should sentimental feeling stop at the border while a customs officer rummages through each consumer's literary baggage? For sentimentality to be harnessed to national feeling, something must arrest its effect, restricting its objects only to those who fall within national bounds. But sentimentality, as the thriving cross-Channel market suggests, perforce spills over national borders. National identity assumes shape and local habitation over and against the universality of these felt bonds of sentimental likeness; the admission of all alike into the shared community of sentimental reciprocity extends humanity to the disenfranchised and dilates the notion of human rights to embrace those often placed outside of its purview. Lying at the heart of the sentimental genre is a tension between the particular and the universal that would assume dire political significance in the Revolutionary reading of *Pamela* as a work of English sentimentality.

Even before the Revolution, however, the reformatory thrust of the sentimental novel was construed by some contemporaries as the guise under which pernicious notions were smuggled into France: the English moral redemption of French letters implied not merely a sad lack of patriotism on the part of its enthusiasts but also potentially subversive motives.[54] As Louis Philippe, comte de Ségur, wrote in his *Mémoires*, the rage for things English might cover up more pernicious and political effects. Under the guise of Anglomania, covetousness of the political freedom of the English was smuggled into France. "Hence I have always been surprised that our government and our statesmen, instead of rebuking as frivolous, foolish, and not quite French the craze that abruptly overtook France for English fashions, did not perceive therein the desire for an imitation of an entirely different genre and the germs of a great revolution in people's minds. . . . Surely they did not intend to limit their desires at such superficial imitations."[55] *Pamela*'s English origins, as well as its revolutionary interest in the language and thoughts of a servant, were seen as subversive of the larger social order. The affectation of English modes destroyed the distinction of rank and birth until "no one is in his place."[56] Anglomania fomented revolutionary sentiment. As a reporter wrote in 1788, "One cannot disguise the fact that Anglomania has for a long time paved the way for the revolution which seems about to occur. It has fixed our eyes upon a constitution that produces free men: circumstances and discontents have pushed our desire to enjoy the same advantages to a degree of violence that is alarming to despotic ministers."[57]

English sentimentality was not, however, the exclusive province of the Anglophile philosophes interested in the universalist, progressive ideals of cosmopolitanism. It was also appropriated by conservative writers who represented Anglomania as the harbinger of moral (not political) values in order to harness the sentimental concern for others to the interests of the nation. Patriotism was depicted as a sentimental virtue. As the 1767 sentimental novel *Les Amis rivaux* contended, "The 'Patrie' is always dear to great souls. To adopt the whole world for one's homeland [*patrie*] is to recognize none; it is to impose upon oneself a thousand imaginary duties, to free oneself from the most sacred duty of all. Woe to those insensible hearts, whose false tenderness embraces the whole human race, but never fixes on any one individual."[58] In thus depicting local loyalties as universal values practiced in miniature, the conservatives forged a connection between the sentimental and the national. Sentimentality encouraged a reading practice that oscillates between individual and universal, between isolated monad and the sociable collective of like-minded readers. The ability to move between particular and general took on heightened political significance during the French Revolution. As Michael Rapport notes, Robespierre and other Revolutionary politicians adroitly shifted between the revolutionary principles of cosmopolitanism and the localized interests of the nation. Far from being mutually exclusive, the two apparently antithetical ideologies of French Revolutionary nationalism and Revolutionary cosmopolitanism shared "the common foundations of the rights of man, contract theory and national self-determination. It was this common source of both nationalism and cosmopolitanism which was at the root of the ambiguities of the Revolution's ideology of the rights of man."[59]

The sentimental celebration of what Diderot calls "the human heart, which has been, is, and will always be the same" carved out a space of abstract humanity that anticipated the ideal of universality upon which Revolutionary doctrine was ideally or theoretically based.[60] This capacity for abstraction not only forged a sense of collective readership (the imagined community) but also cultivated the kind of reading practices that enabled individuals to grasp the abstract form of an appeal to universality upon which a document like the Declaration of the Rights of Man and the Citizen was based. The interchangeable subject positions implied by sentimental equality might logically be extended to suggest that anyone could assume the role of a subject endowed with rights.[61] As Keith Michael Baker has shown, one of the distinguishing marks of the French declaration (as opposed to the American model) is a universal language that contains only compressed and fleeting references to the French people, the nation, or the society. "The collectivity from which the document is held to derive," he argues, "is virtually effaced by the abstract form of its appeals to universality."[62] Sentimentality likewise established a community without referents, a community in which local references to "the French people" or to the "nation" became superfluous, absorbed into the great family of humankind. The universalized sensibility of Revolutionary cosmopolitanism is suggested in proclamations like the Constituent Assembly's Declaration of Peace to the World or its notions of the brotherhood of peoples embodied in the Fête de la Fédération of 14 July 1790, to which Anacharsis Cloots, the self-titled "Ambassador of Humankind," brought a deputation of the human races.[63] But in 1793–94, with the intensification of the war, laws were passed against foreigners, particularly the English. It was in the context of this conflict between universalism and national, patriotic identity that *Pamela* came under the scrutiny of the Revolutionary government.

In less than a century *Pamela* went from upsetting the aristocracy with its celebration of a servant's ascent through superior virtue to scandalizing revolutionaries. In August 1793, in the midst of the Terror, *Pamela* (or more accurately, yet another theatrical adaptation of *Pamela* based on Goldoni's version) was censured by the Committee of Public Safety. The playwright, a former deputy to the Convention, François de Neufchâteau, rewrote the play, excising certain objectionable lines, adding several perorations on patriotic topics like the decadence of English aristocratic dress, and most crucially, lowering the rank of Pamela's father from Scottish count to peasant.[64] The script was read and approved by Robespierre and Bertrand Barère de Vieuzac.[65] During the ninth performance, however, an aide-de-camp in the Army of the Pyrénées who was also an envoy to the Committee of Public Safety grew incensed at seeing "in a republic, the triumph of nobility over equality"[66] and the public's enthusiastic reception of what he saw as "praise of the aristocratic government of England."[67] He hurled invective at the actors and audience alike, sparking a small riot, and then raced to the Jacobin Club, where he reported the evils of the play.[68] Robespierre brought the captain's charges to the Committee of Public Safety, and the actors and actresses affiliated with this "Theater of the Nation, which was nothing less than national," were imprisoned, as was the play's author.[69] The *Feuille du Salut Public* rejoiced at this "Burial of *Pamela*," crowing that "that proud daughter of the citizen François . . . just died a virgin."[70]

This was by no means a cataclysmic event; its results were fairly self-contained. The Comédie Française was closed for the first time since its opening in 1680, and the scandal seized the headlines for a few days. The actors and the playwright were soon released from prison, although not before the author, François de Neufchâteau, had addressed the Convention Nationale with a fifty-five-page memorandum protesting his innocence and the destruction "of a moral and political work."[71] At least briefly, *Pamela* took center stage in an overtly political medium. The scandal furnishes us with an overt consideration of the hazards of misinterpretation and the potentially lethal consequences of misprision. François's apology to the Convention Nationale is nothing less than a reading lesson on topics ranging from quoting out of context and the tractability of the audience's response to the distinctions between text and performance and the difference between the sentiments of a character and those of the author. It was not merely the performer and producers but also the audience that was targeted by the Committee of Public Safety: the theaters, the reports contended, were overflowing with aristocrats and conspirators against the nation.[72]

Even as the sentimental genre found itself torn between the universal and its embodiment in a local particular, the Revolution wavered uneasily between patriotism as fidelity to the universal principles of the Declaration and patriotism as unequivocal loyalty to the nation. The suppression of *Pamela* was conjoined to national issues. The Committee of Public Safety was appalled by the British aristocratic scenery, costumes, and language: "The style announced the formal intention of casting a hateful veneer over the salutary revolution brought about by the French people;

the English government is praised with condemnable show, which could not be done except with the intent of misleading the people about the abuses of that monstrous government, to make them desire one like it."[73] François's *Pamela* was criticized for insisting on the commonality of all, "that man is the same under all governments."[74] This tenet, seemingly fundamental to sentimental ideals of natural and spontaneous virtues and natural-rights theories of universal humanity and self-determination, was said to undermine the Revolutionary order by suggesting that the nature of the government did not matter. The phrase was construed as an indication of the play's English origins, giving rise to citizen Barère's accusations that "the play *Pamela* has ... [troubled] public tranquillity. One saw not virtue rewarded, but nobility; the aristocrats, the moderates, the Feuillants, gathered together to applaud the maxims proffered by these Mylords; one heard the praises of the English government sung, and that at a moment when the Duke of York is laying waste to our territory."[75] Enthusiasm for the play was seen as a proclamation of identity, a declaration of one's affiliation with Royalist counterrevolutionaries. The model of reading proposed by the *Républicain Français* involved a direct application of the lesson presented on stage: the spectator would swallow the play's aristocratic maxims uncritically, crediting the praise of the enemy; by identifying with the characters, the spectator would desire what was praised on stage. The movement of human sympathy represented by sentimental identification could have lethal consequences, for to identify too closely was potentially to suffer the other's fate, particularly in the context of the Terror. In the whirligig implied by reciprocal identification the reader could get stuck in the movement of the trope.

What the Revolutionary debates reveal about *Pamela* is the incapacity of sentimental tropes to control what readers identified with in the text. The plurality of the possible sentimental responses described above gave way to the necessity to undo the genre. *Pamela* needed to be knocked into line with the ideology of the Revolution; the promise of subjective interchange, of pleasurable readerly identification, here became subversive because readers identified with the wrong party. Thus the *Feuille du Salut Public* described the play's slipperiness as follows: "In the same play one spouts this maxim: 'The party that triumphs is the only legitimate one.' Which means that the only thing despotism and aristocracy lack to be legitimate is to have triumphed. One knows that it should not be a crime for an author to make the characters of his play speak in keeping with their character; but one also knows that the character of the author often shows itself in that which he lends to his personages."[76] Collapsing the relation of character to author from representation to *porte-parole*, the journal makes the author liable for the language of his texts, rendering him that prosecutable entity that Foucault associates with the author function. François protests being quoted out of context, arguing that an individual author cannot control readerly responses within an open marketplace. Consumers of literary and theatrical products buy into what they please. "One knows," he writes, "that no play is safe from these absurd and unreasonable applications, which could not have entered the author's spirit, and all the venom of which exists in the imagination which makes them depraved."[77] The plurality of interpretation available to a range of readers turns deadly as the revolutionaries insist upon a single correct interpretation of François de Neufchâteau's words.

The risk of such misinterpretation and the dangerous relation of text to author led François de Neufchâteau to produce a superabundance of supplementary explanation as well as an authoritative version of the play to combat the pirated versions published by "those who wish to misuse the fame events have conferred on the work, in order to disfigure it and compromise the author."[78] The possibility of misinterpretation in the immediacy of a public representation obliged François to attempt a written corrective for the literate public. Crucially, the printed version, unlike the theatrical production, was allowed to circulate, suggesting a division between the literate elite and the people, between the dangers posed by (or to) a reader and those posed by (or to) a collective public audience.[79] Sentimentality, with its immediacy of affect, invites a powerful physical and emotional response to the representation; in the theater, this effect is meant to be public and collective, rather than the by-product of Diderot's isolated reading experience. If the *Pamela* vogue was driven by the desire to see Pamela embodied on fans and paintings as well as on stage, the revolutionary interest in *Pamela* involved the immediate physical presence, not of Pamela, but of the spectators. François described his dilemma as follows, claiming that his accusers repeatedly cited

> this verse, "The party that triumphs is the only legitimate one," as having been left in the September 2 performance, despite having been excised by the Committee. But this is a horrible lie, and that much worse, since one knows the effect that the citation of this verse might have presented by itself, deliberately stripped of what follows or what comes before, and without saying whether it is uttered in the play as a laudable sentiment or as a chance or uncertain maxim, appropriate for a particular role, etc. With this

artifice, it would be easy to corrupt even what is most sacred. In fact, if one detaches this phrase from the Psalmist *The fool says in his heart; there is no God* (Psalms 9:1) and then one drops the beginning of the phrase, *The fool says in his heart*, and only cites as an axiom the second half of the phrase: *there is no God*, then all the good souls will exclaim in horror, and it will be said that the gospel teaches atheism.[80]

In his insistence that the context of a particular phrase and its site of enunciation be considered in any interpretive act, François makes a compelling plea that words not circulate unmoored from their historical context, which is precisely the paradox of the circulation of *Pamela*. Detached from its original form, mangled in translation, mingled with or supplanted by other texts, *Pamela* becomes countless mirrors of a possibly duplicitous original. The original from whom a statement issues is not always as telling as "the fool says in his heart"; indeed, the promise of transparency held out by sentimentality is countered by a certain opacity, if not duplicity, at the heart of a character like Pamela.

Michelle Burnham's notion that sentimental readers identify with a community that is not a mirror image of themselves must be supplemented with machinery that allows the process of sentimental identification to be interrupted or forestalled. The audience must not identify with the wrong parties. The community *Pamela*'s consumers sought to join— or the community with which they wished to identify themselves—was not the community the Committee of Public Safety wished to reproduce.[81] Sentimental communion faltered before the injunction to see only what the committee wished to have seen. The sentimental text ultimately betrayed the failure of the Revolution to produce the collective community, as the Terror revealed the failure of the Revolution's initial dream of reconciling liberty and patriotic power. The ideal "human heart" that allows sensibility to flow unchecked across borders proved to contain a venomous streak: "Since the people conquered the rest of the rights disputed them by the new aristocracy, one no longer stages in our theaters those plays in which crowned vice triumphed over suffering virtue; in which the degraded people groveled before insolent masters; but have we weeded out the last root of those venomous plants which make their subtle poison infiltrate even to the heart of man? . . . It is imperative that all plays be patriotic or moral."[82] In order for all representations to be made patriotic or moral, all ambiguity must be eradicated: "In a moment of revolution, all that is not *strongly* pronounced *for* is *against*."[83] The revolutionary character of *Pamela* must be rewritten. *Pamela* could no longer be torn between two incompatible but equally just moral stances, between the imperatives of personal liberty and the needs of the larger social order, between the rights of man and the rights of the citizen (the curious doubling of the human as man and citizen in the title of the Declaration).

Instead, the model of reading desired by the Committee of Public Safety sought to legislate the absolute symmetry of sentimental identification with which we began: a model that would allow for a total congruence to be formed between the subject in the text and the reader/subject of the text. But it is the asymmetry between the individual and the world, between the desires and impulses of the character and the imperatives of the social order, that drives the sentimental plot. In endeavoring to use the theater to reconcile the gap between the moral subject and the patriot, the man and the citizen, the committee eradicates the tension that generates the text. If, as I discussed above, the overt moral or political labor performed by the sentimental text becomes too obvious, sentimentality turns into a grim rictus of the spontaneous outpouring of feeling the text was meant to inspire, leaving little of the sentimental social agenda beyond an overtly coercive pedagogy: "the theaters are the primary schools of enlightened men and a supplement to public education."[84] And indeed, the playwright's plea to the Convention Nationale ends with a proposal to reform the Comédie Française into a pedagogical institution. *Pamela* is to be supplanted by "a kind of history course in tableau and in action," so that "history which slept, mute in books, will be brought to life by us." Social advancement through virtue and an advantageous marriage is replaced by "the benefit of this new genre of national instruction," as the marketplace for the likes of *Pamela* is supplanted by efforts to sell the public on a particular set of principles.[85] In divining that sentimental reading involves the construction of an ideal collective unlike the community that already exists, in recognizing that the sentimental must contain within it a check on indiscriminate identification, the revolutionaries are simultaneously the least sentimental and the most perspicacious of readers of *Pamela*.

---

## Notes

I would like to thank Peter Stallybrass for the original references to *Pamela* in the Revolution and Margaret Cohen, Carolyn Dever, Mary Helen McMurran, and Joan DeJean for their comments and suggestions.

1. Horace Walpole, quoted in Bernard Kreissman, *Pamela-Shamela: A Study of the Criticisms, Burlesques, Parodies, and Adaptations of Richardson's "Pamela"* (Lincoln: University of Nebraska, 1960), 4. *Pamela* is the novel that most frequently appears in the 392 post-1760 library catalogs collated by Daniel Mornet (see his "Les Enseignements des bibliothèques privées [1750–1780]," *Revue d'Histoire Littéraire de la France* 17 [1910]: 461). Although there had been twenty editions of both *Pamela* and *Clarissa* in France by 1790, *Clarissa*'s 1778–89 print run at Rouen was 750 to *Pamela*'s 1200 (Thomas Beebee, *"Clarissa" on the Continent: Translation and Seduction* [University Park: Pennsylvania State University Press, 1990], 189 n. 5; see also Georges May, *Le Dilemme du roman au dix-huitième siècle* [Paris: Presses Universitaires de France; New Haven: Yale University Press, 1963], 164, 176).

2. Horace Walpole, *The Yale Edition of Horace Walpole's Correspondence*, ed. W. S. Lewis, 48 vols. (New Haven: Yale University Press, 1937–83), 10:172.

3. *Daily Advertiser*, 23 April 1745, quoted in *Samuel Richardson: A Biography*, by T. C. Duncan Eaves and Ben D. Kimpel (Oxford: Clarendon, 1971), 127.

4. On the reception of *Pamela*, see Kreissman, *Pamela-Shamela*; James Grantham Turner, "Novel Panic: Picture and Performance in the Reception of *Pamela*," *Representations* 48 (fall 1994): 70–96; Terri Nickel, "*Pamela* as Fetish: Masculine Anxiety in Henry Fielding's *Shamela* and James Parry's *The True Anti-Pamela*," *Studies in Eighteenth-Century Culture* 22 (1992): 37–50; and Morris Golden, "Public Context and Imagining Self in *Pamela* and *Shamela*," *ELH* 53, no. 2 (1986): 311–29.

5. Nancy Armstrong and Leonard Tennenhouse, *The Imaginary Puritan* (Berkeley and Los Angeles: University of California Press, 1992), 198. In challenging the notion of an originary metropolitan community and a derivative pool of colonial readers, their argument allows the origins of the novel to be sought outside of a narrowly delineated notion of nation based on the insularity of England.

6. Jean Antoine Rigoley de Juvigny, *Discours sur le progrès des lettres en France* (Paris: Saillant & Nyon, 1772), 184–87.

7. *Journal Étranger*, February 1757. For a list of novels "from," "by," and about the English, see the appendix to Josephine Grieder, *Anglomania in France, 1740–1789: Fact, Fiction, and Political Discourse* (Geneva: Droz, 1985), 151–62.

8. On this debate, see Harold Wade Streeter, *The Eighteenth-Century English Novel in French Translation: A Bibliographical Study* (1936; reprint, New York: Benjamin Blom, 1970); Joseph Texte, *Jean-Jacques Rousseau et les origines du cosmopolitisme littéraire: Etude sur les relations de la France et de l'Angleterre au XVIIIe siècle* (Paris: Hachette, 1909); Daniel Mornet, introduction to *La Nouvelle Héloïse*, by Jean-Jacques Rousseau, Grands écrivains de la France, 1 (Paris: Hachette, 1925); Lawrence Lynch, "Richardson's Influence on the Concept of the Novel in Eighteenth-Century France," *Comparative Literature Studies* 14, no. 3 (1977): 233–43; and Henry Seidel Canby, "*Pamela* Abroad," *Modern Language Notes* 18, no. 7 (1903): 206–13.

9. On the Rousseau craze, see Robert Darnton, "Readers Respond to Rousseau: The Fabrication of Romantic Sensitivity," in *The Great Cat Massacre* (New York: Basic Books, 1984). In their combination of moralism and realism, Georges May has

argued, Richardson's novels paved the way for Diderot and Rousseau to do their innovative work in this now somewhat respectable genre. Critics alternately advance and dismiss the notion that Marivaux was the originator copied by Richardson. The degree of influence granted to Richardson in France depends upon which French novels are taken into consideration: if one includes less canonical writers like Riccoboni or Baculard d'Arnaud, who produced an abundance of *histoires anglaises* and borrowed many tropes from the sentimental novel, one gets a very different picture (Georges May, "The Influence of English Fiction on the French Mid-Eighteenth-Century Novel," in *Aspects of the Eighteenth Century*, ed. Earl R. Wasserman [Baltimore: Johns Hopkins Press, 1965]).

10. Two volumes of the French translation were first published in London in 1741 with neither the author nor the translator identified; the complete translation in four volumes appeared in 1742 under an Amsterdam imprint. The first French translation claims to have been done with Richardson's assistance, and the sketches of the "fine" ladies who visit Pamela appear in the French before they do in the English (François Jost, "Prévost Traducteur de Richardson," in *Expression, Communication, and Experience in Literature and Language*, ed. Ronald Popperwell [London: Modern Humanities Research Association, 1973]. See also Frank Wilcox, *Prévost's Translations of Richardson*, University of California Publications in Modern Philology, 12 [Berkeley: University of California Press, 1927], 352, 360–62). *Pamela* appeared in Dutch in 1742, in German in 1743, in Italian in 1744–45, and in Danish in 1743–46 (See E. Purdie, "Some Adventures of Pamela on the European Stage," in *German Studies Presented to Professor H. G. Fiedler* [Oxford: Clarendon, 1938], 356–57).

11. Jean-François de La Harpe, "Des Romans," in *Oeuvres*, 6 vols. (Paris, 1778), 3:367.

12. "What is *Pamela*, Madame? According to some, they are monotonous letters that, composed with all the coldness with which one reproaches your fellow islanders, were born on the banks of the *Seine* and only owe their origin to some French 'Anglico,' who, in the desire to copy the manners of your nation made a ridiculous assortment of them. According to others, it is the translation of a History written and arrived thirty years ago on the banks of the *Thames*" (François Alexandre Aubert de la Chesnaye-Desbois, *Lettres amusantes et critiques sur les romans en général, anglais et francois, tant anciens que moderns* [Paris: Gissey, Bordelet, David, 1743], 43). Pierre Coste, John Locke's French translator, believed the author to be a French clergyman living in London, M. Bernard (See Charles Bastide, *Anglais et français du XVIIe siècle* [Paris: Alcan, 1912], 290). I thank Mary Helen McMurran for these references.

13. Adaptations like Boissy's *Pamela en France* show her virtue "mieux éprouvée" by having a marquis, disguised as a woman, kidnap her from Mr B. He takes her to France, where she has much more trouble resisting his refined blandishments than she does the crude and abusive overtures of the Englishman. The adaptation narrowly avoids representing Pamela's virtue as poorly defended by trans-

forming Pamela into "Wisdom" and the marquis into "Pleasure" and allowing the allegory to do the dirty work. As Prévost remarks, "The virtuous Englishwoman finds herself metamorphosed into an adventuress . . . as coquettish in France as she is represented as sensible in England" (Abbé Prévost, *Journal Étranger*, January 1755, 179–80).

14. John Plotz, "Portable Properties" (paper delivered at "National or Transnational? Britain, France, and the 'Rise' of the Novel," conference held at New York University, December 1999); Samuel Richardson, *Pamela, Or Virtue Rewarded*, ed. T. C. Duncan Eaves and Ben D. Kimpel (Boston: Houghton Mifflin, 1971), 61.

15. Translations of Goldoni's play appeared in German (1756 and 1768), English (1756), French (1759), and Spanish (1796). Goldoni's sequel was likewise translated numerous times. See *Index Librorum Prohibitorum* (Vatican, 1940), 407; Only in 1900 was the prohibition changed to the English original. (See Florian Schleck, "Richardson on the Index," *Times Literary Supplement*, 25 April 1935, 272; and Richard Thornton, "English Authors, placed on the Roman Index [1600–1750]," *Notes and Queries* 12 [1915]: 33). Why it was placed on the index is unknown: though Eaves and Kimpel hazard that it was its "popularity combined with its dubious moral" (*Samuel Richardson*, 126).

16. One of the more shocking "imports" requested by the duc de Chartres at the height of his "Anglomania" is Pamela, not the novel, but a six-year-old girl, of whom he writes, "above all, let the nose not be too long" (Grieder, *Anglomania in France*, 15).

17. Jean-Arnold Trochereau, *Choix de différents morceaux de poésie traduits de l'anglais* [1749], xix, cited in Streeter, *Eighteenth-Century English Novel in French Translation*, 29.

18. Claude Godard d'Aucour, *La Déroute des Paméla* (Paris: Veuve Pissot, 1744), 12.

19. That the name *Pamela* functioned as a marketing device is made evident by the tendentious relation of numerous Pamelas and anti-Pamelas to the original novel. While disparaging the use of the title *Anti-Pamela* in the *Mémoires de M.D.*, the reviewer in the *Bibliothèque Britannique* conceded that the *Mémoires* do "recount adventures that are opposed to those of the supposed *Pamela*." He added, however, that "three quarters of the bad little novels with which the public has been burdened for some time, could for the same reason carry the same title, because they contain nothing but little tales as insipid as they are scandalous" (*Bibliothèque Britannique* 12 (January–March 1744): 366, 367).

20. Godard d'Aucour, *La Déroute des Paméla*, 12.

21. Abbé Marquet, *Lettre sur Paméla* (London, 1742), 3. Or again, "All ladies, to make sure the author of the *Confessions du Comte de \*\*\** knows that they love virtue, all ladies have *Pamela* on their dressing table and make it a glory to themselves to give her their approbation, perhaps as much from propriety [*bienséance*] as from inclination" (Aubert de la Chesnaye-Desbois, *Lettres amusantes*, 47).

22. Aubert de la Chesnaye-Desbois, *Lettres amusantes*, 73.

23. Ibid., 125. Or, as the abbé Jacquin wrote, "Was I then wrong to predict that the novel *Pamela* would soon be forgotten? You idolized it at the time, and yet, without your little lapdog that you call by that name, would any thought of it remain to you? It was the same three years ago with *Tom Jones* and *Clarissa*" (Jacquin, *Entretiens sur les romans, ouvrage moral et critique* [Paris: Duchesne, 1755], 101). James Grantham Turner argues that the consumer frenzy over the novel is driven by a desire to see Pamela embodied for both Pamelists and anti-Pamelists. The public covets something they can grasp. "Internalists like Diderot continue to value the 'invisible' epistolary mode," Turner writes, "but the public demands a Pamela more objectified and artifactual, embalmed in waxwork or fluttering on the fan." Turner argues that the story thrives in media "that express or draw forth the private, inward *sentiment* of the character (in blushing paint, thrilling aria, throbbing violins) but do so in spectatorial forms that place the consumer securely in control, in the audience or in perspective, observing and taking pleasure in Pamela's emotions through the frame of the paintings or the proscenium of the theater" (Turner, "Novel Panic," 90–91). That the story flourished when thus bodied forth would seem to be belied, at least in France, by the failure of the various theatrical productions. So interminable was Nivelle de la Chaussée's production, according to Mme de Graffigny, that the audience shrieked with laughter at the line, "Take my coach so you can go faster." These tales of Pamela's imminent demise suggest another trajectory for the dive toward embodiment, not toward the concrete one can seize but toward objects' eventual decay (and the way the solidity of an object seems to stand against that decay).

24. George Gordon, Lord Byron, Ravenna Diary, 4 January 1821, in *Byron's Letters and Journals*, ed. Leslie A. Marchand, 12 vols. (Cambridge: Harvard University Press, 1973–82), 8:11–12. My thanks to Mary Helen McMurran for this reference.

25. Marquet, *Lettre sur Paméla*, 38.

26. Richardson, *Pamela*, 3.

27. Denis Diderot, "Éloge de Richardson," in *Oeuvres esthétiques de Diderot*, ed. Paul Vernière (Paris: Classiques Garnier, 1994), 33. First published in 1762 in the January *Journal Étranger*, the "Éloge" appeared as a pamphlet shortly afterwards and was subsequently reprinted with later editions of Richardson translations. One need only think of Lady Louisa Stuart's secret fear, in reading *The Man of Feeling*, that she "should not cry enough to gain the credit of proper sensibility" (Brian Vickers, introduction to Henry Mackenzie, *The Man of Feeling*, ed. Vickers [London: Oxford University Press, 1967], viii).

28. Michelle Burnham, "Between England and America: Captivity, Sympathy, and the Sentimental Novel," in *Cultural Institutions of the Novel*, ed. Deidre Lynch and William Warner (Durham, N.C.: Duke University Press, 1996), 53. Using a Lacanian version of "identification" as a perception of similitude "performed on behalf of a gaze from the perspective of which that image is seen as likable," Burnham notes that the pleasurable similitude one detects and "identifies" with is itself the product of the act of identification; it constructs the object with which one identifies

and retrospectively names it as coherent (and as like oneself), thereby obscuring any identification with difference.

29. Diderot, "Éloge de Richardson," 41.

30. The rewritings of the novel reflect not only changing attitudes toward social hierarchy (what justified it, what sustains it) but also convictions about national tolerance for elisions of rank. Thus Carlo Goldoni explained his elevation of Pamela's rank as imperative in any adaptation for the Italian stage: "In London, a Lord does not lose rank or title in marrying a peasant; in Venice, a patrician who marries a plebian woman deprives his children of his patrician nobility, and they lose their rights to sovereignty. Comedy, which is or ought to be the school for manners, should only expose human failings in order to correct them, and one ought not to risk sacrificing an unhappy posterity under the pretext of rewarding virtue" (Goldoni, *Mémoires de M. Goldoni, pour servir à l'histoire de sa vie, et à celle de son Théâtre*, 3 vols. [Paris, 1787], 2:63).

31. Whether Pamela is nobly born or common, however, the revolutionary implications of the plot can be displaced onto the love affair, which allows class mobility to be absorbed into the man's name in marriage. That Pamela in a number of the adaptations turns out to be from a noble family after all merely reasserts that nobility will have out: the goods of the gently born will always return to those who rightfully own them. If Pamela is common, her marriage shows that the social order is elastic enough to recognize and absorb true merit (see David Denby's analysis of Baculard d'Arnaud's version of *Pamela, Fanny, histoire anglaise*, in *Sentimental Narrative and the Social Order in France, 1760–1820* [New York: Cambridge University Press, 1994], 16–18).

32. Lady Mary Wortley Montagu to Lady Bute, 17, 25 October 1750, in Mary Wortley Montagu, *Complete Letters of Lady Mary Wortley Montagu*, ed. Robert Halsband, 3 vols. (Oxford: Clarendon, 1965–67), 2:470.

33. Abbé de La Porte, *Observations sur la littérature moderne* (La Haye, 1749), 60–61.

34. Pierre F. G. Desfontaines, *Observations sur les Écrits Modernes* 29 (June 1742): 211. The *Bibliothèque Françoise* defends the humble rank of Pamela, noting, "If he [the author] had placed so much virtue to the account of a person of high rank, I would not say *where is the verisimilitude?* But where is the honor of resisting?" *Bibliothèque Françoise, ou Histoire Littéraire de la France* 35, pt. 1 (1742): 323. Desfontaines was seen to be attacking not merely French noblewomen but the very sources of personality in his insistence that what anchored virtue was not rank or even education: "Would you not confess, Monsieur, that the manner in which children are raised consolidates virtue in their hearts? Are you not also obliged to admit that education usually follows birth? Then you must recognize that it is the greatest injustice to assert that it was more verisimilitudinous that a girl such as Pamela must be more firmly attached to her duty, than a person of distinguished birth" (*Lettre à Monsieur l'abbé Des Fontaines sur "Paméla"* [Amiens, 1742], 14–15).

35. *Lettre à Monsieur l'abbé Des Fontaine sur "Paméla,"* 11–12.

36. See Daniel Gordon, *Citizens without Sovereignty: Equality and Sociability in French Thought, 1670–1789* (Princeton: Princeton University Press, 1994).

37. Abbé Prévost, *Le Pour et le contre*, 2:30, quoted in Texte, *Jean-Jacques Rousseau*, 64.

38. Claude Prosper Jolyot de Crébillon to Philip Dorner Stanhope, earl of Chesterfield, 26 July 1742, quoted in Texte, *Jean-Jacques Rousseau*, 257.

39. Philip Fisher, *Hard Facts: Setting and Form in the American Novel* (New York: Oxford University Press, 1985), 4.

40. Margaret Cohen, *The Sentimental Education of the Novel* (Princeton: Princeton University Press, 1999).

41. Fisher, *Hard Facts*, 4.

42. Richardson, *Pamela*, 7. This observation prompted an acerbic rebuttal from Aubert de la Chesnaye-Desbois: "There is an art to embellishing *facts* without *disguising* them. . . . English solidity, without being turned into whipped cream, is susceptible to all the charms of diction" (*Lettres amusantes*, 73).

43. William Beatty Warner, *Licensing Entertainment: The Elevation of Novel Reading in Britain, 1684–1750* (Berkeley and Los Angeles: University of California Press, 1998). The debate about the moral efficacy of the novel existed in France as in England. Pamela's letters are riddled with incidents "which cannot fail to excite, in all the young people who read it, sentiments quite different from those of virtue" (*Bibliothèque Françoise, ou Histoire Littéraire de la France* 35, pt. 1 [1742]: 320). In *Adèle et Théodore*, Mme de Genlis advocates Richardson's works as pedagogically sound, morally upright novels for young ladies and Richardson is the sole exception to the no-novel rule laid down in Mme Elie de Beaumont, *Lettres du Marquis de Roselle* (London: Louis Cellot, 1764), 2:54.

44. Richardson, *Pamela*, 5.

45. Edmond Jean François Barbier, *Chronique de la régence et du règne de Louis XV, ou Journal de Barbier*, 8 vols. (Paris: Charpentier, 1857–85), 8:158. Barbier also praised the *Lettre à Monsieur l'abbé* for its critique of Desfontaines.

46. *Bibliothèque Raisonée des Ouvrages des Savans de l'Europe* 28, pt. 2 (April–June 1742): 421. The 1742 *Lettre à Monsieur l'abbé* protests against the "cruel satire" of this invitation to reform. Notwithstanding the anonymous author's presentation of himself as "a Frenchman jealous of the glory of his country [*Patrie*]," he insists that "a writer must be impartial; personal considerations, the love even of country, will not allow him to disguise the truth" (5–6).

47. As Baculard d'Arnaud put it, "The novel is the book of humanity. It insinuates in our soul that sensibility, that tenderness, the principle of true virtues; it tames the ferocity of our pride, it inspires compassion, it returns man to nature, entertains it in his heart. Sentiments are like the body; they grow feeble, exhaust themselves, and die when one does not feed them. Of all the genres of books, the novel is that which gives birth to sentiments, supports and strengthens them even more" (quoted in May, *Le Dilemme du roman au dix-huitième siècle*, 150).

48. Marquet, *Lettre sur Paméla*, 10–11.

49. *Bibliothèque Raisonée des Ouvrages des Savans de l'Europe* 28, pt. 2 (April–June 1742), 422.

50. Joseph de Laporte and Louis Mayeul Chaudron, *Nouvelle bibliothèque d'un homme de goût*, 4 vols. (Paris, 1777), 4:82, 103.

51. Diderot, "Éloge de Richardson," 39.

52. "Nationality," as Ernest Renan observed, "has a sentimental side to it" (Ernest Renan, "What Is a Nation?" in *Nation and Narration*, ed. Homi K. Bhabha [New York: Routledge, 1990], 18).

53. Burnham, "Between England and America," 50.

54. The *Lettres d'un François*, 3 vols. (La Haye: Jean Neaulme, 1745), 1:279–80, believes *Pamela* to be propaganda for the Society for the Reformation of Manners.

55. Ségur, *Mémoires ou souvenirs*, 3 vols. (Paris, 1826), 1:150–54, quoted in Arnaud de Maurepas and Florent Brayard, *Les Français vus par eux-mêmes: Le XVIIIe siècle* (Paris: Robert Laffont, 1996), 565–66.

56. Rigoley de Juvigny, *De la décadence des lettres et des moeurs* (Paris: Mérigot le jeune, 1787), 468.

57. Letter dated 25 March 1788, in *Correspondance secrète inédite sur Louis XVI, Marie-Antoinette, la cour et la ville de 1777 à 1792 publiée d'après les manuscrits de la Bibliothèque impériale de Saint-Pétersbourg*, ed. Mathurin François Adolphe de Lescure (Paris: Plon, 1866), 2:243, quoted in Grieder, *Anglomania in France*, 29.

58. Claude Louis Michel de Sacy, *Les Amis rivaux* (1767), 128, quoted in Grieder, *Anglomania in France*, 106.

59. Michael Rapport, "Robespierre and the Universal Rights of Man, 1789–1794," *French History* 10, no. 3 (1997): 306. On the formation of national identities in eighteenth-century France, see also David Bell, "Jumonville's Death: Nation and Race in Eighteenth-Century France," in *La Recherche dix-huitièmiste: Raison universelle et culture nationale au siècle des Lumières/Eighteenth-Century Research: Universal Reason and National Culture during the Enlightenment*, ed. David A. Bell, Ludmila Pimenova, and Stéphane Pujol (Paris: Champion, 1999), 227–51.

60. Diderot, "Éloge de Richardson," 40.

61. On this point, see esp. David Denby: "I concluded, at a much higher level of generalisation and abstraction, that sentimentalism belongs to the Revolutionary project by virtue of the manner in which it envisages the relationship between the individual and the universal" (Denby, *Sentimental Narrative and the Social Order in France*, 139). Although the bait-and-switch of one *Pamela* for another might seem to undermine the particularity of the individual as stand-in for the universal, the mobility of the original text requires the reader to impose unity upon the figure in the face of all these transformations while recognizing that the original example can be reproduced.

62. Keith Michael Baker, "The Idea of a Declaration of Rights," in *The French Idea of Freedom: The Old Regime and the Declaration of Rights of 1789*, ed. Dale Van Kley (Stanford: Stanford University Press, 1994), 160.

63. Anacharsis Cloots's dream was of a world without nations: "I propose an absolute leveling, a total reversal of all the barriers that cut across the human family. . . . I defy anyone to show me one sole article of our Declaration of Rights which is not applicable to all men, in all climates" (quoted in Albert Mathiez, *La Révolution et les étrangers: Cosmopolitisme et défense national* [Paris: La Renaissance du Livre, 1918], 55–56).

64. Only one year earlier François de Neufchâteau had been named minister of justice and had declined the post due to ill health; the previous month, his memoir on the "establishment of a granary of plenty" had been printed by order of the Convention Nationale (see the legislative records of the Revolutionary assemblies, the *Archives parlementaires de 1787 à 1860: Recueil complet des débats législatifs et politiques des chambres françaises* 52 (21 September 1792): 68, 74; (6 October 1792): 376; (7 October 1792): 384. François would bounce back and twice be named minister of the interior in the years VI and VII (1797–99) (see his *Recueil des lettres circulaires, instructions, programmes, discours, et autres actes public de François de Neufchâteau* [Paris: Imprimerie de la République, an VII (1798–99]; François employs a certain sentimental rhetoric in this self-vindicating compilation [see esp. 5]).

65. The *Journal des Spectacles* praised François's revisions, noting that "the Venetian lawyer was writing in Italy, where he could never have said, without exposing himself, that *the priests and the kings divide up the world*; that the principle of the equality of man is the great law of nature; and finally that Papistry, Protestantism and all religions are equally good for good people [*honnêtes gens*]" (no. 34 [3 August 1793]: 271).

66. *Feuille du Salut Public*, 4 September 1793. The paper parodied François's own comparison of the death of the play to that of a young girl. When the Committee of Public Safety demanded his papers, he offered Barère "the sacrifice of my play," saying, "Bury her in a box, on which you will write: here lies PAMELA" (François de Neufchâteau, *N. François [de Neufchâteau], auteur de Pamela, à la Convention nationale* [Paris, 1793], 24. The text was also reprinted in the *Archives parlementaires* 74 [12–22 September 1793]: 622–29).

67. *Gazette Nationale*, no. 248 (5 September 1793): 1054.

68. See Arthur Pougin, *La Comédie-française et la Révolution* (Paris: Gaultier, Magnier & Cie, 1902). For a transcript of the captain's testimony, see *Histoire parlementaire de la Révolution Française, ou Journal des Assemblées Nationales*, ed. P. J. B. Buchez and P. C. Roux, 40 vols. (Paris: Paulin, 1836), 29:18–23. See also the accounts in the *Feuille du Salut Public*, 4, 5 September 1793; the *Gazette Nationale, ou Moniteur Universel*, no. 248 (4 September 1793): 1054; *Le Républicain Français*, 5 September 1793, 1184, 1192; and the *Journal des Spectacles*, 5 September 1793, 525–26.

69. It seems likely that Robespierre had been hunting around for an excuse to clap the actors into jail; among the charges brought against them was the "sustained evidence of uncivic-minded spirit characteristic since the revolution and represented in anti-patriotic plays" (*Gazette Nationale*, no. 248 [5 September 1793]).

70. *Feuille du Salut Public*, 4 September 1793.

71. *Journal des Spectacles*, 24 September 1793, 670. In a neat turn, François transformed the fate of *Pamela* into a sentimental drama unto itself. "It is the fate of virtue," he wrote of the play. "She suffers, one offers her insults, but she triumphs" (ibid., 30 September 1793, 718).

72. *Histoire parlementaire de la Révolution Française*, 21. See also the *Courrier Français*, 4 September 1793, 5.

73. *Le Républicain Français*, no. 294 (6 September 1793).

74. *Feuille du Salut Public*, 21 August 1793, 3.

75. *Gazette Nationale*, no. 248 (5 September 1793): 1054. The same verdict, with a few deviations, is quoted in Louis-Sébastien Mercier's *Annales Patriotiques et Littéraires de la France et Affaires Politiques de l'Europe*, no. 244 (2 September 1793): 1134.

76. *Feuille du Salut Public*, no. 67 (5 September 1793): 3.

77. François de Neufchâteau, *N. François (de Neufchâteau), auteur de Pamela, à la Convention nationale*, 20; *Archives parlementaires* 74:624.

78. *Journal des Spectacles*, 30 September 1793, 717–18.

79. Susan Maslan, "Resisting Representation: Theater and Democracy in Revolutionary France," *Representations* 52 (1995): 27–51. As Maslan notes, the separation of print and theater, direct and indirect representation, has been perpetuated in Habermas and Chartier's theories of a public sphere that inheres in a virtual community of print culture that occludes the participation of the body of the people.

80. François de Neufchâteau, *N. François (de Neufchâteau), auteur de Pamela, à la Convention nationale*, 28–29; *Archives parlementaires* 74:625.

81. On the Revolution's use of sentimentality, see Denby, *Sentimental Narrative and the Social Order in France*, ch. 4.

82. *Feuille du Salut Public*, 27 November 1793, 3.

83. Ibid., 26 April 1794, 3.

84. *Archives parlementaires* 73 (3 September 1793): 364.

85. François de Neufchâteau, *N. François (de Neufchâteau), auteur de Pamela, à la Convention nationale*, 40–43; *Archives parlementaires* 74:627–28. See also *Journal des Spectacles*, 6 October 1793, 764–66; and *Archives parlementaires* 74:627.

MARGARET COHEN

## CHAPTER FOUR

# Sentimental Communities

No notion has been more important to materialist work on the novel in recent years than Benedict Anderson's "imagined community."[1] This importance is an instance of the tautological relation between object and method that characterizes the most successful criticism: the notion of distanced individuals joined by their common investment in an imaginary representation has been so invigorating to studies of the modern novel because it owes its existence to the genre. That is to say, it is not just that novels helped crystallize imagined communities—the notion of an imagined community was put into place by the modern novel and is foundational to its cultural work. The imagined community was, in fact, the product of a specific subgenre of the novel that dominated the literary landscape from the mid-eighteenth to the mid-nineteenth century. This subgenre is sentimental fiction, though sentimentality does not appear in Anderson's account that equates the representational forms catalyzing secular imagined communities with the codes of realism.[2]

During a century that ran from Richardson's *Pamela* (1740) to Harriet Beecher Stowe's *Uncle Tom's Cabin* (1852) sentimental novels were in the vanguard of formulating the notion of an affectively charged association among distanced readers. Sentimental discourse and its imagined communities, moreover, extended beyond the novel to figure prominently in political, moral, and aesthetic theory, drama, poetry, medical and humanitarian writings, historiography, nascent anthropology and ethnography, history painting, genre paintings of daily life, and images of children. The sentimental production of imagined communities was not limited to the years when sentimentality was a high cultural form. Though sentimental discourse fell from prestige around the middle of the nineteenth century, it has had an active afterlife in mass culture, where it has been used in a range of media genres popular with vast audiences, such as sensation novels, movies, television soap operas, talk shows, and news spectacles like the O. J. Simpson trial and the life of Lady Di.

The imagined communities of sentimentality were both sociological and textual; they existed among historical readers, and they were produced by the figures of speech and thought found in cultural artifacts. In this chapter I speculate on how these imagined communities were constituted through rhetorical strategies, how they were implied as text-effect. Given the tawdry aura that now hovers around sentimentality, it cannot be stressed enough that I offer my speculations not to unfold virtual possibilities contained in sentimental novels but rather to respond to the astonishing—indeed to many readers today almost scandalous—appeal these novels once had. "*Uncle Tom's Cabin* sold more copies than any book in the world except the Bible,"[3] and a similar popularity characterized the most prominent works of sentimental fiction in their time, from *Pamela* and *Clarissa*, *La Nouvelle Héloïse* and *Die Leiden des jungen Werthers*, to Staël's *Corinne*, Eugène Sue's *Les Mystères de Paris*, and G. W. Reynolds's *Mysteries of London*.[4]

The international significance of these works, however, points to a thought-provoking distinction between the *national scale* of the communities theorized by Anderson and the first modern imagined communities catalyzed by sentimental texts. The sentimental subgenre was a *transnational* literary form during the century of sentimentality's prestige, and sentimental novels were the most translated of all literary fiction.[5] Certainly, sentimental novels exhibit their transnational appeal in the Anglo-French invention of the novel. In contradistinction to many subgenres important to this process that were marked as national within the Enlightenment republic of letters (the French novel of worldliness, the British Gothic and domestic novel), sentimental fiction was the subgenre practiced with most equal enthusiasm by authors on both sides of the Channel, taking shape as a genuinely cross-Channel form.[6] As such, it served as a privileged site for the exchange of literary codes and observations concerning national character and difference, along with reflection on the process of exchange and translation itself. In her chapter in this volume, April Alliston, moreover, makes clear that sentimental fiction was the privileged Channel site for examining the complexities of the relation of national to trans- and subnational communities, along with the uses and abuses of the nation as the unit of collective identification.[7]

In describing the implied communities constructed by sentimental texts, I am interested in what features might account for their transnational appeal. But the fact that these features can travel does not mean that
they always signify the same way. And in conclusion I ask how a form's
international portability interacts with specific national context, describing
distinct national differences in the way sentimentality took root in England
and in France. At the horizon of my discussion is what might seem a rather
perplexing asymmetrical feature of the subsequent history of the novel in
the two countries, namely, that one international subgenre, sentimentality,
could end up with a completely opposing relation to realism, the form that
was to succeed sentimentality as the generic dominant of the novel in an
international republic of letters. In France, as I suggest in *The Sentimental
Education of the Novel*, sentimentality reigned pretty much intact until the
end of the Empire, and Balzacian realism emerged as a hostile takeover of
sentimental codes.[8] In Britain, sentimentality mutated in the later eighteenth and early nineteenth centuries into a range of subgenres (the Gothic
novel, the domestic novel and the related novel of manners, the national
tale and the historical novel) that writers then unified in the emergence
of a nineteenth-century Victorian realism.[9] Although a mix of specifically
literary and broadly social factors inform this asymmetry, I want to emphasize its beginnings in the practice of sentimentality preferred on each side
of the Channel.

The codes of sentimentality are first and foremost codes of narration. There is, in particular, one narrative situation that defines the subgenre (as well as the discourse more generally). This situation, what might
be called sentimentality's primal scene, is a spectacle of suffering that solicits the spectator's sympathy.[10] "Sentimentalism," Patricia Spacks quite
rightly declares, "implies a set of ethical principles," and she emphasizes
that "[p]olitical implications ... are always latent in sentimentalism."[11]
Philip Fisher, writing on the nineteenth-century American context, accurately observes these ethical and political implications when he proposes
that sentimental novels are engaged in creating the free subjects of liberal
democracy.[12] What Fisher does not sufficiently elaborate, however, is that
this is no easy feat, since liberal freedom is in fact fraught with contradictions and tensions from its Enlightenment inception. In sentimental suffering, the protagonist painfully plays out the practical ramifications of these
contradictions. Sympathy with this suffering is the beginning of spectators'
interpellation into sentimentality's cultural work.

The suffering of sentimental protagonists results above all from
one tension deeply troubling to Enlightenment political thinkers, and that,

according to Etienne Balibar, is "*the* political problem par excellence": how to construct a social form that is "both egalitarian and libertarian," or, as Enlightenment thinkers generally posed the problem, how individuals might fully exercise their private freedom without impinging on the equal freedom of their fellows.[13] Most artifacts represent this question through a conflict between what we might call, using the language of political theory, negative and positive rights. By *negative rights* is meant the private rights to life, liberty, and property. *Positive rights* designates the foundation of political rights, the public freedom to participate in the workings of the collective.

In many novels of sensibility this conflict emerges in a plot that stages what Henry Mackenzie called "that war of duties." Evincing ambivalence about the form that had made his fame, Mackenzie wrote: "The principal danger of novels, as forming a mistaken and pernicious system of morality, seems to me to arise from that contrast between one virtue or excellence and another, that war of duties which is to be found in many of them, particularly in that species called the *Sentimental*." In this war, "[t]he duty to parents is contrasted with the ties of friendship and of love, the virtues of justice, of prudence, of economy, are put in competition with the exertion of generosity, of benevolence, and of compassion."[14] If we look at the range of sentimental plots, it turns out that among the possibilities offered by Mackenzie the first conflict, that between duty to the family and love, is the conflict most frequently used by sentimental authors. In this conflict, the rights to participate in the collective epitomized by family obligation express positive freedom, and they conflict with the negative freedom to dispose of one's own person, epitomized by the rights of the heart.

The conflict between negative and positive rights structures many of the most celebrated eighteenth-century sentimental novels, such as Richardson's *Clarissa*, Rousseau's *La Nouvelle Héloïse*, and Goethe's *Sorrows of Young Werther*. In all these novels the conflict results from the impossibility of according more value to one of the duties in the conflict than to the other. Although the terms *virtue* and *duty* are most often used to characterize positive rights, it would be a mistake to understand sentimental conflict as transgression versus the law. As I argue in *The Sentimental Education of the Novel*, the pathos of the protagonists' situation is that right is on both sides; how is one to choose between conflicting duties, asks Rousseau's Julie, who is torn between a lover and a father. I propose that we call narratives built around this conflict *tragic sentimentality* in recognition of Hegel's proposition that tragedy stages the encounter of two valid ethical imperatives that meet in a situation of mutual contradiction.[15]

Mackenzie ascribes the plot of two conflicting duties to "our neighbors the French" (though of course the plot fully crystallizes for the first time in Richardson's *Clarissa*), and his comments are suggestive. François Furet and Mona Ozouf have proposed French liberalism as far more troubled by the problem of how to design a form of government promoting both negative and positive rights than Anglo-American liberalism, with its primary emphasis on negative rights. Certainly, this problem is central to Rousseau's theory of the social contract.[16] For Rousseau, the state of nature is characterized by freedom but no rights beyond what Rousseau called man's pre-moral "absolute right to anything that tempts him and that he can take."[17] The social contract creates both negative and positive rights, and the brilliance of this institutionalization, as well as the difficulty of realizing it in practice, is that to safeguard one form of rights, one must safeguard the other, even if they enter into flagrant contradiction.[18]

But tragic sentimentality is not the only way sentimental fiction plays out the difficulties of modern freedom; some works employ an alternative scenario of suffering also put into place by Richardson, who was a virtuoso in the modulations of Enlightenment pathos. In the novel bearing her name Pamela solicits sympathy from her mistreatment by Mr. B, who embodies negative freedom, but Mr. B's negative freedom takes the form of his natural freedom to do as he pleases. Against this negative freedom, Pamela asserts her virtue, the positive freedom to uphold community that the text grants full ethical sanction. When Spacks characterizes "the problem of self-love versus social" as defining British sentimental fiction in the 1760s and 1770s, it is this conflict between a negative natural freedom (self-love) and a positive social freedom (social) that is, I believe, at issue.[19]

As Spacks's terminology suggests, negative freedom is represented in much more ambivalent fashion in this version of sentimental conflict than in the tragic plot. The protagonist espousing negative freedom is an amoral figure, even a libertine, whose exercise of freedom is more strongly bound up in the desire for sheer possession, whether sexual or economic, than in the tragic version. Nonetheless, it would be an oversimplification to understand this freedom to be devoid of value, as the attractions of Mr. B and his redemption at the end of *Pamela* make clear. Positive freedom impedes the abuses of private natural freedom, placing salutary limits on it and channeling it for the public good.

In this version of sentimental plot, natural and social freedom are typically made concrete by being embodied in two opposing characters, in contrast with the tragic typology, in which one protagonist anguishes over the impossibility of choice. It is as if natural and social freedoms need to be delineated as so distinct that they cannot be espoused in a single voice; the distribution of roles emphasizes that these freedoms place their proponents in two different realms.[20] I will call narratives structured around this alternative primal scene *melodramatic sentimentality*, in recognition of the way melodrama pits characters embodying opposing forces against each other, specifically a character embodying the natural urge for possession against a character upholding virtue. This is, of course, anticipation, for melodrama is an inheritor of this strand of sentimental narrative via the Gothic.

That Spacks seizes the essence of this conflict in examining English novels from the 1760s and 1770s and that the Gothic was an English invention are not coincidental, for the melodramatic plot articulates freedom in a fashion that resonates with a celebrated Anglo-American lineage of liberal theory. In this lineage, as Thomas Paine declared, "natural rights are the foundation of all . . . civil rights": the state of nature comports freedoms that contain in embryo the freedoms promoted by the social contract.[21] These freedoms are negative; the most basic negative freedom in nature, as well as in society, is the freedom to possess property.[22] In this lineage of liberalism, positive freedom is instituted to check the abuses possible if each individual pursues negative natural freedom without concern for others. In contrast to the Rousseauvean version of the social contract, the character of positive freedom here is secondary and limiting rather than constitutive of the notion of freedom as an ethical right.[23] Joseph Priestly offers one of the most succinct formulations of such a view in his *Essay on the First Principles of Government*: "If I be asked what is meant by *liberty*, I should chuse for the sake of greater clearness to divide it into two kinds, *political* and *civil* . . . It is a man's civil liberty, which is originally in its full force, and part of which he sacrifices when he enters into a state of society."[24]

Nowhere is the melodramatic version of sentimental conflict more starkly played out than in the pathetic scenes of illness and death crucial to many nonfictional as well as fictional instances of sentimental discourse. In these scenes natural freedom takes its most ruthless and antisocial form. It becomes the freedom of nature to destroy and is pitted against the moral independence of sufferer or spectator in the face of death. In the deathbed scene that produced more tears than any other scene in all of sentimental fiction, indeed perhaps in all of literature, the fact that a child, little Eva, is its subject only redoubles the intensity of the melodramatic conflict. For the child already instigates pathos from the way she occupies the boundary space between the negative freedom of nature and a freedom to participate in the collective aligned with her induction into the moral order.[25]

The deathbed scene occurs before a group of spectators who dramatize for the reader the sympathy it solicits. As Jay Caplan, notably, has argued, the group of sympathetic spectators is fundamental to the workings of sentimental narrative; it is what the entire pathetic spectacle works to produce. When readers' sympathies are aroused, they sympathize not only with the sufferings represented but with one another, and through this sympathy they come together into a kind of community. "[N]o sympathy is stronger than the sympathy we feel with sympathy," wrote Schiller.[26] Diderot ascribes this reaction to the way in which the sympathetic response activates the spectator's imagination when he declares, "[C]ome, we shall weep together over the unfortunates in his stories, and we will say: 'If fate casts us down, at least honest [*honnêtes*] folk will also weep over us.' "[27]

The sympathetic community is, that is to say, a community that is constitutively imagined, even if its spectators are present to one another—it takes shape through the spectator's ability to picture himself or herself occupying the place of the victim. Tears are the bodily indication that the display of sympathy has bonded spectators or readers together; indeed, in her *Histoire des larmes* Anne-Vincent Buffault, inspired by Marcel Mauss, suggests sentimental communities as catalyzed and maintained by their exchange. Tears are so suggestive as the synecdoche of sentimental community because they are a universal human response and thus signify the universality of this community's potential membership, comprising the same formally equal individuals that are the citizens of emerging liberal society. The sympathetic response is available to anyone regardless of rank, social status, age, gender, or nationality; all that is required is the taste to be moved.

Showing spectators at a deathbed is one version of a common sentimental procedure to underline the importance of community, which is to include these communities as characters within the narrative.[28] Alliston analyzes novels of sensibility, where the formation of sympathetic communities is indeed a central thematic preoccupation. Even where this preoccupation is muted, sympathetic communities figure as peripheral spectators of the main action. They frequently appear, for example, in the framing devices common in eighteenth-century novels. In the opening to *Manon Lescaut* Des Grieux offers his tale to the man of quality and perhaps his aristocratic student, and he offers it to members of the community of New Orleans, including his adversary, Synnelet, as well as to his friend, Tiberge, at the novel's end. Richardson's editor introduces the letters comprising the "history" of *Clarissa* with mention of several "judicious friends" as he discusses his cogitations concerning whether to publish these "documents" in their complete but lengthy form.[29]

As David Marshall has stressed, sentimental communities owe much to notions of theatrical spectatorship; indeed, sentimentality's key codes for soliciting pathos historically took shape in the cross-fertilization between dramatic and novelistic forms.[30] That this process was an exchange between a genre that depends on spectatorial presence and one that works through distance is telling, for sentimental community extends the affective bonds of presence to define bonds of absence.[31] Accordingly, peripheral spectators may witness a living scene, hear an oral narrative, or read a written text, but they respond to all three forms of representation with the same warm, living tears. The importance of the continuum from presence to absence explains the availability of sentimental texts to deconstructive interpretations. But this continuum is invoked with specific historical significance: it is in fact central to liberal-democratic notions of citizenship and representation, a point that not only Anderson but Habermas has made when he links the modern novel to the emergence of the modern political formation in his *Structural Transformation of the Public Sphere.*

The play of presence and absence is, moreover, constitutive of the sympathy provoked by sentimental pathos, whether this sympathy is offered by spectators who are present at the spectacle of suffering or by spectators who witness it in mediated form. Sentimentality is, as Nietzsche charged in *The Genealogy of Morals,* pity at a distance. In *La Souffrance à distance* Luc Boltanski rightly observes that such distance invites the political objections brought against sentimentality throughout its history, but it is also crucial to the discourse's cultural work.[32] As a result of the spectator's distance from sentimental conflict, he or she not only is engrossed in its outcome but can debate its construction and significance.

Today, we are used to thinking of pity as narcotic if not totalitarian, shutting down the critical faculties, which is the legacy of an avant-garde Marxist lineage epitomized by Brecht. But when Richardson invoked his community of gentlemen friends in the preface to *Clarissa,* they turned out to disagree completely, a response that led him to solicit "others" to give their opinions, "but no two . . . [were] of the same mind."[33] Diderot too viewed diversity of opinion as constitutive of sentimental communities, pointing out that Richardson's works provoked debates concerning morals and taste as lively if not as heated "as if it has been a question of the most serious affair."[34] When Schiller theorized pathos as a figure devoted to vindicating freedom, he gave a rather Newtonian view of the matter: the more powerful the pathos that aroused feeling, the greater the freedom the spectator asserted in overcoming his initial response with reason. Schiller wrote that "the principle of freedom within us makes itself known only by the resistance it exerts against the power of feelings, while the resistance can be measured only by the strength of the onslaught of feelings. Thus, in order for human *intelligence* to reveal itself as a force independent of nature, it is necessary for nature first to demonstrate all its might before our eyes. The *sensuous being* must *suffer* deeply and vehemently, the pathos must be present, so that the rational being can testify to its independence, and, *by acting*, can present itself."[35]

Sentimental communities are thus situated squarely within the Enlightenment public sphere. As I argue in *The Sentimental Education of the Novel*, they are idealized instances of the liberal public sphere, offering an occasion for both the performance of community and the enjoyment of free debate. In doing so, they respond to Enlightenment difficulties by devising a form of political organization that enables modern freedom to be successfully performed.[36] In the imagined communities of sentimentality, individuals may exercise their own freedom without impinging on the freedom of their fellows. This freedom takes the form of judgments on what Diderot called morals and taste.[37] While an individual's aesthetico-moral judgments may run directly counter to the judgments of others, this diversity is in no way limiting; rather, it is an affirmation of the nature of the aesthetic collective constituted through discussion and debate. What better instantiation of Rousseau's idea of liberal citizenship, where, according to Rousseau, "every individual may, as a *man*, have a particular will contrary to, or divergent from, the general will which he has as a *citizen*."[38] Against those readings that would want to see sentimentality purely as false consciousness, it cannot be stressed enough that the public sphere is not simply a retreat from political activity but rather spans the distance from aesthetics to politics.

Sentimentality's preoccupation with the problem of how individuals can exercise their freedom without impinging on the freedom of their fellows also, I would suggest, explains the puzzling affinity of sensibility with irony from its inception. Boltanski observes this affinity and comments that not only did sentimental novels invite parody, as least as far back the publication of parodic novels immediately following the appearance of *Pamela*, but, "more remarkable," there is "the progressive appearance of works that mix, as was already sketched out in Sterne's *A Sentimental Journey*, 'sensibility and comedy' . . . sentimentality, the spectator who is moved in response to sufferings . . . and its ironic unveiling."[39] Such a mixture of sentimentality and irony may well reach its disturbing apogee with Sade's *Justine.*

How are we to make sense of such proximity? For Boltanski, the unstable boundary between sympathy and irony reveals the fragility of sentimental claims to sincerity; it reveals that, as Marshall observes, its theater of affect is predicated on a transparency that the spectator, dangerously, has no way to distinguish from artifice. I think, however, that this unstable boundary confirms sentimentality's engagement with the paradoxes of a community joined by the bonds of freedom. As Linda Hutcheon points out, irony is deeply engaged with the production of community; in order for irony to work, recipients must belong to what Hutcheon calls "discursive" communities; there must be agreement between writer and readers if they are to understand by certain discursive markers that a text means other than it says.[40] At the same time, ironic communities recall sentimentality in acutely problematizing the individual's situation vis-à-vis the collective. After all, ironic communities comprise individuals joined together on the basis of their difference from and, usually, resistance to the more naive communities that read ironic statements literally. Ironic readers both secede from literal communities and enter into an alternative community made up of readers attuned to figuration (and often represented as an elite—smart enough not to succumb to literal readings). Though irony expressed the individual's troubled relation to community long before Enlightenment liberalism, it makes sense that the figure would be of particular interest to this project. There is, moreover, a specific Enlightenment inflection of irony to explore contradictory aspects in the practice of modern freedom that finds its characteristic expression in the worldly knowledge of libertinage.

Let me offer one more speculation: sentimentality's ability to catalyze a community resolving the tensions in modern freedom helps explain the spectacular ability of the discourse to travel. To stick with sentimental novels, the subgenre is a wild success in emerging liberal societies, which is to say, precisely the societies where the constitution of modern freedom is a pressing political issue, whether in theory and/or in practice. Think, futhermore, of the affinity of sentimentality with political experiments in liberalism. Sentimental rhetoric permeated the debates of the French Revolution and the utopian socialisms of the first half of the nineteenth century, such as Chartism and the movements instigated by Owen, Saint-Simon, and Fourier, along with the theory and practice of revolutionary movements across Europe in 1848. And sentimental rhetoric, together with sentimental novels, played a prominent role in the institution of new Latin

American societies experimenting with "liberalism adapted from examples in Great Britain, . . . the United States, and also France."[41] Indeed, the prominence of sentimental rhetoric in the institution of nationally scaled liberal societies may well be the missing link between Enlightenment sentimental communities, with their universal aspirations, and the nationally based imagined communities discussed by Anderson. At the moment of their inception sentimental community was for the first time mapped onto a political rather than a cultural geography, and this geography was the modern nation.

Why political agents should invoke sentimental rhetoric is a thought-provoking question. This gesture might seem to be self-defeating, given that the success of sentimental community depends precisely on the autonomy of the aesthetic, on its distance from the questions of expediency governing political decision making. The case of the French Revolution suggests that such appeal is both to move the audience and also to underline the importance of freedom when its practice encounters impediments at the level of practice; thus, no moment of the French Revolution made greater use of sentimental figures than the Terror. The invocation of sentimentality, I am suggesting, implies that liberal democratic freedom is at issue but that it is in some way problematic, that there is an aspect of the political formation that is not working to fulfill the liberal promise. We could, I think, trace such a political use of sentimental rhetoric from the French Revolution and nineteenth-century abolitionism to a range of current American movements that have emerged at the faultlines of the liberal-democratic project, from left-wing identity politics to the Christian right's emphasis on the family.

But to assert that the preoccupations with modern freedom shared by Enlightenment societies explains the transnational appeal of the sentimental novel is not to oversimplify that this appeal was also rooted in local context. The specific national concerns informing the local implantation of this international subgenre are, I think, vividly illustrated by distinct national differences that emerged in the way the sentimental novel was practiced on either side of the Channel. I return here to the melodramatic and tragic conflicts structuring sentimental fiction.

Now, while I linked these conflicts to nationally based liberal lineages to heighten their political specificity, it cannot be stressed enough that both took shape in a transnational cultural field.[42] As I have pointed out, an English author, Richardson, first gives both conflicts their fully developed articulation, and the melodramatic conflict is the undoing of Prévôt's Des Grieux, who erratically praises virtue austerely codified by

Tiberge while savoring Manon's negative natural freedom, even as it crowns Richardson's Pamela. Meanwhile, tragic anguish over negative and positive freedom treated as fully constituted ethical duties destroys Frances Sheridan's Sidney Bidulph as well as Rousseau's Julie. But sentimentality's internationalism should not obscure the fact that by the 1760s a distinct national preference for each of these typologies had developed in keeping with the political articulation of freedom dominating each national context. Mackenzie was stating a truth about contemporary practice if not origins when he characterized tragic sentimental fiction as "borrowed from our neighbors, the French."[43] The tragic situation was not only preferred by French authors but became marked as a French import in the Channel literary field, and the melodramatic situation fared similarly in relation to England.[44]

Novelists give evidence that they recognize the link between narrative conflict and national preference when they employ the conflict that dominates across the Channel and map it onto the appropriate national geography. When Mackenzie pens his own novel about a tragic conflict between duty to the heart and duty to collective obligation, *Julia de Roubigné* (1777), he offers it as his translation from the French of actual letters. In *The History of Emily Montague* (1769), written by Frances Brooke (who was also Riccoboni's translator), Emily Montague and her beloved, Colonel Rivers, suffer from the tragic conflict in the form of Emily Montague's previously contracted engagement to another. At this same time, this novel terminates in the happy ending more characteristic of the melodramatic sentimental novel preferred in England, and it makes quite clear that the form of freedom at issue in its marriage plot is the negative freedom that has primacy in the English liberal lineage. Comparing the political freedom of the Hurons to the civil freedom of the English, one of Emily's friends remarks, "Dear England! . . . There is no true freedom anywhere else. They may talk of the privilege of chusing a chief; but what is that to the dear English privilege of chusing a husband?"[45] Fittingly, this sentimental novel joining tragic conflict with melodramatic outcome is played out in Canada, which is to say a setting evocative of Anglo-French political struggle in the wake of the recent Seven Years' War (1756–1763), and that offers the occasion for commentary on differences between England and France.[46] This commentary is not only hostile but seeks ways to represent Anglo-French interaction as mutually beneficial. Thus, the English hero remarks of the heroine that "her manner is irresistible: she has all the smiling graces of France, all the blushing delicacy and native softness of England."[47]

What we might call a similar channeling, though in reverse, characterizes those French novels that borrow codes from melodramatic sentimental fiction. The novels of Marie-Jeanne Riccoboni are frequently set in England, and this invocation must have been convincing, for I have found her classified as an English writer in an early-nineteenth-century French bookseller's catalog.[48] Riccoboni's literary geography is in keeping with her poetics: her novels set in England borrow the melodramatic narrative situation, though they confuse its terms in a way reminiscent of tragic sentimentality. In *Lettres de Milady Juliette Catesby* and *Lettres de Mistriss Fanni Butlerd* the jilted heroines transform melodramatic virtue in a fashion informed by the representation of negative freedom characterizing the tragic sentimental typology. The virtue upholding the community is the ethical grandeur of erotic love that embodies an individual's freely contracted obligations to another. This version of virtue is opposed to the betrayal of an absent protagonist who asserts his natural freedom to do as he pleases by engaging in a marriage of convenience on the grounds of self-interest. The marriage plot, that is to say, becomes a manifestation of excessive natural freedom rather than its containment, which is usual in melodramatic sentimental texts.

*Lettres de Milady Juliette Catesby*, moreover, explicitly veers in the tragic direction when we discover that Milady Catesby's lover has jilted her out of a sense of obligation to a woman he slept with in a moment of thoughtless passion, Miss Jenny, who subsequently found herself dishonored. Milord Ossery proves, that is to say, to be caught between his love for Juliette and his sense of duty toward another even though this other individual is not, as is typical, a member of his family but rather his sexual conquest. Jenny dies, however, and the two protagonists, paralyzed unhappily in the conflict of duties, receive the melodramatic ending of "virtue rewarded," as the alternative title to *Pamela* puts it.

Another example of a French, or, more properly speaking, Francophone, novel set in England that is a hybrid of melodramatic and tragic sentimental conflict is the Swiss-Dutch (though very much identified with French culture) Isabelle de Charrière's *Lettres de Mistriss Henley publiées par son amie* (1784). Like Riccoboni, Charrière cites the terms of the melodramatic conflict to twist them from their classic articulation. In Charrière's transformation, too, full ethical sanction is on the side of negative rights, in this case Mistriss Henley's rights to self-determination. The transformation continues in the person of the character who abuses her, a perfectly virtuous and devoted husband whose virtue is, however, ambiguously mixed up with his own negative rights to live as he pleases. For her husband's pursuit of virtue is in keeping with his retiring, upright disposition, which stifles Mistriss Henley's own yearning for worldly society.[49]

The English preference for melodramatic sentimentality and the French preference for tragic sentimentality were at the beginning of two highly specific national trajectories of the sentimental subgenre that, eighty years later, took the form of the distance separating prosentimental Victorian realism from antisentimental Balzacian realism. What I want to emphasize in concluding this article is aspects of the melodramatic sentimental conflict absent in tragic sentimentality that not only can be accommodated to the realist episteme but, more than that, help produce it in a lineage that leads from melodramatic sentimentality to realism via the domestic Bildungsroman, the Gothic, and the historical novel.[50] These aspects are bound up in the specific articulation of modern freedom characteristic of British liberalism, but they are its poetic manifestations, situated at the intersection of poetics and ideology. The crucial difference relevant for the history of sentimentality's relation to realism is the importance in melodramatic sentimentality of negotiation, both as narrative principle and as ethical stance.[51]

The plots of melodramatic sentimental novels are built on a narrative dynamic in which negotiation is paramount. This emphasis derives from the nature of the conflict between negative and positive freedoms. While the conflict is posed as a symmetrical one, this symmetry is illusory, for the primacy of negative freedom is never at issue, so the plot does not face an insoluble task (and hence, perhaps, the frequency of happy endings in this version of the subgenre).[52] Rather than trying to reconcile two contradictory imperatives, the challenge is how to check, channel, and limit negative freedom so that it will not be socially destructive; the plot dynamic is one of excess and corrective.

In the tragic conflict, in contrast, both negative and positive freedoms are equally valid, full-fledged ethical principles that cannot be transformed without diluting their power. It is thus not surprising that the most frequent outcome of this conflict is impasse, if not death. Since to act on one term is to negate the other, the characters are in a closed universe from the plot's inception; they are caught in a paradigmatic situation of double bind.[53] The tragic conflict hence contains no possibility for narrative negotiations—in tragic sentimentality, as I have argued, the impasse can only be played out with incremental, ineluctable force. True, Rousseau's Julie, like many other sentimental protagonists, does search for a way to shift the terms of her dilemma, and she thinks she has found it in trying a formula made celebrated by the Rousseauvean social contract, that is, in choosing freely to be unfree and marry Wolmar. But duty to the heart cannot be so easily cheated, and her love for Saint-Preux reasserts itself despite her best efforts. The non-negotiability of the principles coming into conflict finds its ultimate confirmation in the inevitability of the novel's ending, which only reiterates what *Julie*'s hero, Saint-Preux, already recognized from the first sentence: "I must flee you, young lady . . . or rather, I should never have seen you."[54]

Pamela's efforts to set the appropriate limits on Mr. B's excesses are called virtue. J. G. A. Pocock makes clear the ideological content of Pamela's activities when he describes how virtue was framed by eighteenth-century British liberalism. Pocock writes that "virtue was redefined . . . with the aid of the concept of 'manners.' . . . [T]he individual . . . entered an increasingly transactional universe of 'commerce and the arts' . . . if he could no longer engage directly in the activity and equality of ruling and being ruled . . . he was more than compensated for his loss of antique virtue by an indefinite and perhaps infinite enrichment of his personality, the product of the multiplying relationships, with both things and persons, in which he became progressively involved. Since these new relationships were social and not political in character, the capacities which they led the individual to develop were not called virtues but 'manners.' " Pocock's observation that the desire for possession is crucial to the process is illuminating concerning the importance of Mr. B's desire in Pamela's ability to bring him to heel. "The social psychology of the age declared that encounter with things and persons evoked passions and refined them into manners; it was preeminently the function of commerce to refine the passions and polish the manners; and the social ethos of the age of enlightenment was built upon the concept of close encounters of the third kind."[55] Pocock's notion of virtue as commerce also permits us to highlight what is slightly misleading in the novel's emphasis on Pamela's virtue as upholding her duty to the collective, for Pamela's commerce not only improves Mr. B but catalyzes an exponential "enrichment" of her own manners. The assertion of positive freedom, that is to say, turns out to be only a particular (and socially useful) individual choice about how to pursue negative freedom.[56] What could be more appropriate as a reward for such virtue than the private property that is the foundation of negative freedom in British liberalism? When Fielding points a finger at Pamela as Shamela, objecting that her virtue is hypocrisy because it makes her rich rather than upholding morals, he is not wrong about her actions, but he is wrong about the split between ethics and profit within the framework of British liberal ideology.

Now, it is certainly true that the melodramatic conflict elaborating virtue as commerce developed in a cross-Channel literary field. In drafting *Pamela* (1740), Richardson learned much from the negotiations of Marivaux's *La Vie de Marianne*, published across the 1730s, which was a great success in England as well as in France. But while Marianne's commerce remains resolutely self-interested and bound up in the power plays of *le monde*, the miracle of Pamela's negotiations is that such commerce is ethically forceful. A second difference between the commerces in virtue in the two subgenres, crucial for the nationally specific trajectories of realism, is that melodramatic commerce ultimately vindicates, as I have pointed out, the ethical force of *negative freedom*. In the novel of worldliness, in contrast, the commerce in virtue confirms, not freedom, but the inescapable weight of the collective.

The inescapable weight of the collective is also confirmed by the constitution of virtue characterizing the tragic sentimental conflict. When asked what virtue is, the protagonist of a celebrated early-nineteenth-century French tragic sentimental novel declares: "It is strength . . . it is the courage to carry out rigorously everything we feel to be good, whatever pain it may cause us."[57] Virtue, that is to say, is not a negotiation between negative and positive freedoms but an uncompromising sacrifice of private freedom. Diderot was codifying tragic virtue when he defined it as the reader's imaginary "sacrifice of oneself" in sympathy with the protagonist. The paradigmatic case of such sacrifice is the protagonist's painful abandonment of erotic love in a desperate though ultimately unsuccessful effort to preserve the integrity of the collective.

Such a notion of virtue as sacrifice contains precisely the hybrid fusion of republicanism and Anglo-American liberalism that I have suggested characterizes tragic sentimentality, like contemporary French liberalism, more generally. The notion of virtue as sacrifice owes much to the classical republican tradition, in which the citizen sacrifices the personal sphere for the good of the collective, though, as Alliston's work on the passivity of sentimental heroines makes clear, the sacrifice is not undertaken with the military, politically empowered agency of *virtus romana*.[58] Rather, it is performed in the private, social sphere of manners that is the site of virtue as commerce, and in requiring a sacrifice it produces interior struggle that develops the protagonist's personality. But this enrichment is not infinite. Its limits are the res publica, which cannot be reduced to commerce however hard protagonists try.

The melodramatic negotiations of virtue, however, also solicit a readerly response that is distinct from the sympathy founding sentimental community. This activity is the reader's speculation concerning the validity of the choices made to check negative freedom. At each juncture in *Pamela*, for example, the reader evaluates her perils and speculates on what course of action she should take. Such speculation is both ethical (what is the right thing for her to do?) and hermeneutic (what is the result of her choice? will it have the desired effect?). Readers thus not only sympathize with suffering represented and debate its ethical and aesthetic contours; as they read, they also pose the hermeneutic questions that Iser suggests are central to eighteenth-century English fiction more generally and that according to Barthes are certainly central to nineteenth-century Balzacian realism.[59] And hermeneutic speculation resolves the question of the relation between negative and positive freedoms rather differently from sympathy. In such speculation individual readers dialogue with a text that gives them their answer; that is, readers test their private readerly freedom against immutable objective conditions (the text) rather than elaborating them as part of the consensus-building process of aesthetic community.

The subsequent development of the Gothic and the domestic novel, two genres fusing hermeneutic and sympathetic ways of reading, makes clear that hermeneutic ways of reading need not conflict with the reader's participation in the aesthetico-moral judgments of sentimental community. But when the private dimension of the process is highlighted, it can disrupt sympathetic consensus and thus the solution sentimentality brings to the conflict between negative and positive freedom. Balzac made much of such disruption in his polemic against sentimentality, as I argue in *The Sentimental Education of the Novel*.

As I also argue there, hermeneutic questions, in contrast, are only of minor importance in tragic sentimentality. This is because the sentimental conflict highlights the impossibility of choice rather than testing its outcome. Another way to put this difference is that in tragic sentimentality the question what would be the right action—the ethical question—is only barely diluted by hermeneutic questions, since readers rapidly become aware that they witness an impasse repeated with increasing force from episode to episode. "All should be clear to the spectator," Diderot wrote of the narrative dynamic best suited to inspire disinterested sentimental "interest": "What a difference in interest between the situation where I am not in on the secret, and that where I know everything."[60]

The poetic legacy of melodramatic sentimentality to both Victorian and Balzacian realism is, in short, the commerce of virtue and its attendant confirmation of the primacy of negative freedom, both for the protagonists within the plot and in the processes of reading shaping the implied reader. In the case of realism, however, the emphasis is on *commerce* rather than *virtue*, since it occurs in a universe where rights and duties have become problematic (hence the "real" of the realist demystification of the ideal).[61] But rights and duties do not stop working in the same fashion on each side of the Channel; to isolate the contribution of melodramatic sentimentality to both Balzacian and Victorian realism is also to take an archaeological route into their differences. In Victorian realism, while ethical principles are not implemented in society, they are nonetheless preserved as an ideal; hence those numerous endings in which characters retreat into their private spheres to practice their ethically sanctioned negative freedoms. In French realism, in contrast, virtue cannot be parsed, to cite *Le Père Goriot*. The tragic conflict persists, but it has become a de facto description of contemporary society utterly devoid of ethical force. Individuals who are successful short-circuit its terms by asserting their negative freedom as the amoral right to anything that tempts them and that they can take.

## Notes

1. This chapter was conceived in conversations with April Alliston concerning the need to rethink Benedict Anderson's notion of the imagined community in light of what were in fact the first modern imagined communities: the transnational communities catalyzed by sensibility.

2. It is more accurate to speak of realisms than realism since Anderson allies the imagined community with a range of literary practices for representing objective social reality: eighteenth-century formal realism, nineteenth-century Balzacian and Victorian realisms, the realism of the mass daily, and a modernist realism of montage. The sentimental dimension to the imagined community is missing in recent work inspired by Anderson that pursues the details of the relation between novels and the consolidation and/or complication of national identity in a range of global contexts. See for example, Homi Bhabha, ed., *Nation and Narration* (New York: Routledge, 1990); or, more tellingly, Doris Sommer's *Foundational Fictions: The National Romances of Latin America* (Berkeley and Los Angeles: University of California Press, 1991), so important for understanding the way in which sentimental fiction is implicated in the emergence of the modern nation-state. Sommer has only the not quite accurate alternative of romance to name what are in fact sentimental codes, so denigrated has sentimentality become in the materialist theorizations informing her analysis, though sentimental discourse was once the lingua franca of transatlantic as well as European cultural modernity.

3. Elizabeth Ammons, introduction to *Uncle Tom's Cabin*, by Harriet Beecher Stowe (New York: Norton, 1994), viii.

4. According to Anne Humpherys, *The Mysteries of London* was "the biggest bestseller of the nineteenth century in England" ("Generic Strands and Urban Twists: The Victorian Mysteries Novel," *Victorian Studies* 34 [1991]), 456.

5. James Turner writes of *Pamela*: "If we said Europe was 'touched,' the pun would be appropriate, conveying an enthusiasm that supporters viewed as sentimental identification and skeptics diagnosed as a contagious madness" (James Grantham Turner, "Novel Panic: Picture and Performance in the Reception of Richardson's *Pamela*," *Representations* 48 [fall 1994]: 70). I quote at length from his description to emphasize the international appeal of the novel, whose cross-Channel contours are extensively discussed by Lynn Festa in chapter 3 of this volume. In England during the 1740s, when the vogue for the novel was at its height,

> a keen Pamela hunter . . . could buy the novel in large or small format, with or without Francis Hayman's engravings and Richardson's sequel plus *The Life of Pamela, The Celebrated Pamela, Pamela in High Life, Pamela or Virtue Triumphant, Shamela Andrews, Pamela Censured, Joseph Andrews, Pamela, or the Fair Impostor, The True Anti-Pamela,* and *Anti-Pamela, or Feigned Innocence Detected*, the last by Eliza Haywood, who also published her own translation of the Chevalier de Mouhy's *Paysanne parvenue* (Richardson's most striking antecedent and rival). She could visit two Pamela waxworks, drop in on Joseph Highmore's studio to see his twelve Pamela paintings, and buy the set of his engravings, then see David Garrick in *Pamela, a Comedy*. (With luck she could avoid the Newcastle ballad-opera version, with its grueling emotional climax "I'm sad if my *Pammy's* not there"). The day would end in Vauxhall Gardens, sitting in front of Hayman's Pamela murals, cooling herself with the Pamela fan, and opening a magazine to read "Remarks on Pamela, by a Prude." The next day she would slip across the Channel, picking up for the journey *Pamela, ou La vertu récompensé, traduit de l'Anglois* (rumored to be by Prévost), the Abbé Marquet's *Lettre sur Paméla*, the French translation of Haywood's *Antipamela*, and a different novel called *Antipamela, ou Mémoires de M.D.* In Paris she would take in the pathetic comedy *Pamela*, the burlesque *Déroute de Paméla*, Voltaire's *Nanine, ou le Préjugé vaincu* (also available in two different editions and an English translation) and Louis de Boissy's *Paméla en France, ou La vertu mieux éprouvée*, a comedy that miraculously turns into an opera in the last act, [which was] reissued . . . with a score for home performance. (71)

He says further that "*Pamela* was translated into Dutch, Danish, German, and Welsh; 'acomodada a nuestras costumbres' in Madrid; and adapted to the Venetian taste by Carlo Goldoni, who squeezed at least two plays and two libretti out of this story," and so on (71). A similar international enthusiasm surrounded the publication of all the great sentimental bestsellers, from *Clarissa, La Nouvelle Héloïse, Die Leiden des jungen Werthers, Corinne,* to *Les Mystères de Paris,* whose international resonance can be gauged by the number of direct imitations produced in Europe and the United States that were enormously popular in their own right. Only a small fraction of these rewritings are mentioned in the introduction to this volume.

6. Robert L. Dawson credits "truncated translations" of *Pamela* and *Clarissa Harlowe,* specifically, with promoting a boom in the French interest in British books that was crucial to the vitality of Anglo-French cultural exchange during a time of political tensions ("Books Printed in France: The English Connection," in *The Channel in the Eighteenth Century: Bridge, Barrier, and Gateway,* ed. John Falvey and William Brooks, Studies on Voltaire and the Eighteenth Century, 292 [Oxford: Voltaire Foundation, 1991], 139).

7. No work makes sentimental fiction's ability to facilitate reflection on international and inter-cultural interaction more explicit than Laurence Sterne's *A Sentimental Journey,* which opens by framing its hero, Yorick, as an unreflected mouthpiece of national clichés: "they order, said I, this matter better in France" (Laurence Sterne, *A Sentimental Journey* [1768; reprint, New York: Penguin, 1967], 3). Propelled across the Channel in only one sentence by his curiosity, Yorick goes on to demonstrate sympathy as a medium of cross-cultural, indeed universal, human exchange; suggests that sympathetic intercourse to be founded on an atomistic notion of isolated individuals whose alienation is so radical that even fellow countrymen meet one another through "translation" (79); recovers an eroticized sympathy offering refuge from alienation; pursues this mixture of the erotic and the sentimental via a freedom of circulation that eventually rouses the notice of repressive French authority; uses sympathetic bonds between Enlightenment intellectuals to escape French abuses of freedom; then represents these bonds as facilitating a conversation that perpetuates nationalistic clichés, and so on until Yorick irreverently dumps his reader midsentence with a vulgar pun as he gropes in a darkened hotel room for a woman met traveling, only to catch "hold of the [interloping] fille de chambre's—. / END" (148).

8. Margaret Cohen, *The Sentimental Education of the Novel* (Princeton: Princeton University Press, 1999).

9. As Katie Trumpener has suggested in *Bardic Nationalism: The Romantic Novel and the British Empire* (Princeton: Princeton University Press, 1997), the geneses of the national tale, the Gothic novel, and the historical novel are all implicated in the emerging nationalisms of Britain's internal colonies. If this chapter focuses on the relation of the imagined sentimental community to hegemonic notions of England and Englishness, it is not to deny the importance of sentimental fiction in offering alternatives to hegemonic cultural formations (on this subject, see chapter 5, Alliston's "Transnational Sympathies, Imaginary Communities"). Indeed, I think we can better understand the form's appeal to writers seeking to found a distinctively Irish and Scottish tradition of the novel if we understand its ability to catalyze imagined communities.

10. Here I concentrate on this narrative situation since it is the foundation of the sentimental aesthetic; all other codes help the sentimental primal scene to

emerge with maximum clarity. The sentimental primal scene is, moreover, a code that remains constant across a range of genres. The codes that help it to emerge with clarity, in contrast, vary more from genre to genre, for they depend on the specific techniques used in different genres to render vividly the affecting narratives being presented. I discuss some of the accompanying codes found in sentimental fiction in *The Sentimental Education of the Novel*.

11. Patricia Spacks, *Desire and Truth* (Chicago: University of Chicago Press, 1990), 130, 131.

12. See Philip Fisher's chapter on Stowe, "Making a Thing into a Man: The Sentimental Novel and Slavery," in *Hard Facts: Setting and Form in the American Novel* (New York: Oxford University Press, 1985).

13. Etienne Balibar, *Masses, Classes, Ideas*, trans. James Swenson (New York: Routledge, 1994), 212. Locke emphasizes that private freedom is foundational when he describes both the state of nature and life in society. Locke also, however, emphasizes that this private freedom is not unlimited but rather must be checked by individuals' need to respect the freedom of others. In the state of nature, "being all equal and independent, no one ought to harm another in his life, health, liberty or possessions". Similarly, Locke defines freedom in society as "[a] liberty to follow my own will in all things where that rule prescribes not" and "not to be subject to the inconstant, uncertain, unknown, arbitrary will of another man" (John Locke, *Two Treatises of Government* [1690; reprint, New York: Dutton, 1955, 119, 127). Rousseau formulates "the fundamental problem to which the social contract holds the solution" as how "to find a form of association which will defend and protect the person and goods of each member with the collective force of all, and under which each individual, while uniting himself with the others, obeys no one but himself, and remains as free as before" (Jean-Jacques Rousseau, *The Social Contract*, trans. Maurice Cranston [1761; reprint, New York: Pocket Books, 1987], 17–18).

14. Henry Mackenzie, *The Lounger* 20 (1785), quoted in Ioan Williams, *Novel and Romance, 1700–1800* (London: Routledge & Kegan Paul, 1970), 329–30. I thank Brian Norton for drawing my attention to this article.

15. See my use of Hegel in *The Sentimental Education of the Novel*. In a suggestive comment, Antonio Gramsci describes catharsis as "the passage from the purely economic (or egoistical-passional) to the ethico-political moment. . . . This also means the passage from . . . 'necessity to freedom' " (*Prison Notebooks* [New York: International Publishers, 1971], 366–67). My attention was drawn to this citation by the work of Ethel Brooks.

16. See François Furet and Mona Ozouf's preface to *Le Siècle de l'avènement républicain*, ed. Furet and Ozouf (Paris: Gallimard, 1993), as well as the chapter in that volume by J. Kent Wright, "Les Sources républicaines de la Déclaration des droits." See also *The French Idea of Freedom: The Old Regime and the Declaration of Rights of 1789*, ed. Dale Van Kley (Stanford: Stanford University Press, 1994), and, notably, Keith Michael Baker's "The Idea of a Declaration of Rights" included in the volume. Summarizing national distinctions among models of modern freedom in his in-

troduction, Van Kley writes, "Anglo-Saxon 'liberty'—English and American—has specialized in the defensive protection of the concrete rights of individuals, groups and regions from public authority." Van Kley contrasts this notion of freedom with a "uniquely French kind of republicanism that . . . saw the individual's freedom from the state as compatible enough with the state's collective freedom from each individual. . . . French freedom, moreover, not only alternated these freedoms cyclically but juggled them simultaneously" (19).

17. Rousseau, *Social Contract*, 65.

18. Nietzsche was in fact giving sentimentality its full political due when he inveighed in *The Genealogy of Morals* against "that sentimentalism which would have . . . ["the state"] begin with a contract" (1887; reprint, New York: Vintage Books, 1969), 86.

19. Spacks, *Desire and Truth*, 132.

20. That the two freedoms are personified in distinct characters explains, I think, the fact that, as Spacks observes, some protagonists, particularly those upholding virtue, are "unrendered as personalities" (ibid., 119). Being the embodiment of forces, these characters do not need to struggle with them and hence may never encounter the interior conflict that produces psychic complexity.

21. Thomas Paine, *The Rights of Man* (1791; reprint, New York: Penguin, 1984), 68.

22. Locke called natural freedom men's "*State of perfect Freedom* to order their Actions and dispose of their Possessions, and Persons as they think fit." Similarly, for Locke, "the great and chief end, therefore, of men uniting into commonwealths, and putting themselves under government, is the preservation of their property" (Locke, *Two Treatises of Government*, 118, 180).

23. Thus Locke's *Two Treatises*: "The great end of men's entering into society being the enjoyment of their properties in peace and safety, and the great instrument and means of that being the laws established in that society, the first and fundamental positive law of all commonwealths is the establishing of the legislative power." (183). Locke is emphatic that the establishment and maintenance of legislative power is through consent and participation of free and equal citizens, but it is important that Locke does not detail how this participation occurs, that is, how citizens are to perform their positive freedom.

24. Priestly continued, "[P]olitical liberty is that which he may or may not acquire in the compensation he receives for it. For he may either stipulate to have a voice in the publick determinations, or . . . he may submit to be governed wholly by others," though, Priestly emphasizes, "every man retains, and can never be deprived of his natural right" (Joseph Priestly, *Essay on the First Principles of Government*, quoted in Robert Eccleshall, *British Liberalism* [New York: Longman, 1986], 106–7).

25. Anne Higonnet calls this sentimental vision of the child the "Romantic child" in *Pictures of Innocence* (London: Thames & Hudson, 1998).

26. Friedrich Schiller, "On the Pathetic" (1793), in *Essays*, trans. Daniel Dahlstrom (New York: Continuum, 1993), 58.

27. Denis Diderot, "In Praise of Richardson" (1762), in *Denis Diderot: Selected Writings on Art and Literature*, trans. Geoffrey Bremner (New York: Penguin, 1994), 85. Similarly, Adam Smith cast the spectator's ability to imagine himself in the place of the sufferer as basic to sympathy in the first pages of his 1759 *Theory of Moral Sentiments* (Oxford: Clarendon, 1976). It is thought-provoking that this process makes persons fungible, though it occurs in the disinterested imaginary economy of sympathy. J. G. A. Pocock's writings on virtue as commerce provide the key to the relation between sympathy and liberal exchange, as I discuss below.

28. The death of little Eva shows how these communities open beyond the confines of the text to solicit its readers. The spectators at Eva's death are the protagonists Uncle Tom and St. Clare, secondary characters like Miss Ophelia and Marie, and nameless servants, who are represented as a passive bustle perceptible to anyone who wants to assume the position of spectator: "[T]he house was soon roused,—lights were seen, footsteps heard, anxious faces thronged round the verandah" (Stowe, *Uncle Tom's Cabin*, 256).

29. Samuel Richardson, preface to *Clarissa* (1747–48; reprint, New York: Penguin, 1985), 35.

30. See David Marshall's *The Surprising Effects of Sympathy: Marivaux, Diderot, Rousseau, and Mary Shelley* (Chicago: University of Chicago Press, 1988), and Michael Fried's *Theatricality and Absorption: Painting and Beholder in the Age of Diderot* (Berkeley and Los Angeles: University of California Press, 1980), for a discussion of the theatricality of sympathy. On the contribution of the *drame bourgeois*, specifically, to sentimental discourse, see Peter Szondi's "Tableau et coup de théâtre," *New Literary History* 11, no. 2 (1980).

31. Note that the play of distance and absence crucial to the imagined communities catalyzed by sentimental novels also characterizes the communities mobilized by theater once plays are reviewed and disseminated through the press.

32. Luc Boltanski, *La Souffrance à distance* (Paris: Editions Métailié, 1993).

33. Richardson, preface to *Clarissa*, 36.

34. Denis Diderot, "In Praise of Richardson," 88–89. I have here modified the English translation. The French runs: "que s'il eût été question de l'affaire la plus sérieuse" (Diderot, "Éloge de Richardson," in *Oeuvres esthétiques* [Paris: Garnier, 1959], 38).

35. Schiller, "On the Pathetic," 45.

36. Habermas writes, "The privatized individuals coming together to form a public also reflected critically and in public on what they had read, thus contributing to the process of enlightenment which they together promoted. Two years after *Pamela* appeared on the literary scene the first public library was founded; book clubs, readings circles and subscription libraries shot up" (Jürgen Habermas, *The Structural Transformation of the Public Sphere*, trans. Thomas Burger [Cambridge: MIT Press, 1989], 51). Whether or not Habermas's claim concerning *Pamela* is historically accurate, it underscores the important role Habermas accords sentimentality in catalyzing structures that define the liberal public sphere. For Habermas, the key to sentimentali-

ty's importance is its production of interiority; in my view, it is crucial that this interiority takes shape in a struggle with the problems inhering in the practice of modern freedom. Sentimental subjectivity thus thoroughly implicates the production of interiority in the emergence of the liberal citizen.

37. The freedom of such reaction marks a crucial distinction between the Enlightenment use of pathos and an earlier Christian solicitation of compassion. As Jauss remarks, Christian suffering is exemplary, and compassion provokes imitation. "The true *compassio* . . . must prove itself as readiness for *imitatio*," Jauss writes of Augustine on the dangers of the theater. Such imitation is at the farthest reach from the aesthetic freedom provoked by sentimental community (see Hans-Robert Jauss, *Aesthetic Experience and Literary Hermeneutics*, trans. Michael Shaw [Minneapolis: University of Minnesota Press, 1982], 104).

38. Rousseau, *Social Contract*, 63.

39. Boltanski, *La Souffrance à distance*, 143, my translation. This fact makes clear that it is a mistake to periodize the history of sentimentality into a moment of enthusiasm followed by a moment of disenchantment: both occur together from the very first.

40. Linda Hutcheon, *Irony's Edge* (New York: Routledge, 1995), 91–92.

41. Sommer, *Foundational Fictions*, 13. On the use of sentimentality in the French Revolution, see David Denby, *Sentimental Narrative and the Social Order in France, 1760–1820* (New York: Cambridge University Press, 1994).

42. Liberal political theory, too, of course, took shape in a transnational Enlightenment republic of letters, though it was simultaneously decisively informed by the political practices dominating in each national context.

43. Mackenzie continued by saying that their "style of manners, and the very powers of [their] language give them [the French] a great advantage in the delineation of that nicety, that subtlety of feeling, those entanglements of delicacy, which are so much interwoven with the characters and conduct of the chief personages in many of their most celebrated novels" (Mackenzie, *The Lounger* 20 [1785], quoted in Williams, *Novel and Romance*, 330).

44. It would, I think, be possible to read sentimentality in the eighteenth-century German context as honing a specifically German version of the tensions fissuring modern freedom. If, as Leonard Krieger has argued in *The German Idea of Freedom: History of a Tradition* (Boston: Beacon, 1957), German freedom emphasizes the moral autonomy of the individual against a strong state, *Werther* is a text that uses tragic sentimental conflict but inflects its terms in a fashion resonating with Krieger's analysis. Think, for example, of Werther's overwhelming subjectivity and his failure to find satisfaction in a political performance of his duty to the collective when he flees Lotte to accept a position at the court. I thank Andreas Huyssen for drawing my attention to the political specificity of Goethe's text.

45. Frances Brooke, *The History of Emily Montague*, 4 vols. (1769; reprint, 4 vols. in 2, New York: Garland, 1974), 1:116. Lady Sydney Morgan's novel *The Wild Irish Girl* (1806) is also based on the tragic narrative situation and gives it a happy

ending. Here, generic hybridity is mapped onto a third term, Ireland, a political formation geographically positioned between England and France. Moreover, Morgan interweaves the sentimental conflict with lengthy sections on Irish culture, history, and folklore and thus transforms the sentimental subgenre in a fashion both reminiscent of and diverging from the appropriation of sentimentality in domestic fiction. Description is not subordinated to the sentimental conflict here; it is not used as a tool to heighten the conflict's power. Rather, it is valued for its social specificity, but in contrast to domestic realism this specificity is pointedly historical and political rather than offering a window onto contemporary manners.

46. Mackenzie's novel, too, uses what might be called the "third" space of the colonial New World to facilitate Anglo-French interaction. Julia's beloved is not the somewhat austere nobleman chosen for her by her father but rather a childhood friend, Savillon, who has gone off to seek his fortune in Martinique. There, Savillon makes friends with an Englishman, Herbert, as national differences between the two are suspended in their common sympathy for each other's sufferings. The channeling effect intensifies as the novel draws to a close, for Savillon will narrate its tragic denouement in letters to Herbert.

47. Brooke, *History of Emily Montague*, 1:119.

48. The catalog is Antoine Marc's *Dictionnaire des romans* (1819).

49. Charrière's novel is itself a rewrite of a Swiss novel by Samuel de Constant entitled *Le Mari sentimental* (1783) that transforms the usual distribution of gender roles characterizing the melodramatic schema. In Constant's novel the character pursuing negative freedom is not a male rake but rather an abusive wife in love with worldly pleasures, while the character upholding virtuous duty to the collective is the sentimental husband. Riccoboni's novel *Histoire d'Ernestine* (1765) also invokes cultural foreignness in a plot containing elements from the sentimental conflict dominant across the Channel. Riccoboni's novel is shaped around the tragic conflict: the heroine, Ernestine, stifles her love because it runs counter to her sense of collective obligation to her beloved's higher rank and superior wealth until her virtue earns a melodramatic happy ending. Riccoboni, however, makes Ernestine German, not English, and her story is set in France. Montolieu's *Caroline de Lichtfield* (1786) is another tragic sentimental fiction with a melodramatic happy ending that takes place in Germany, more specifically Prussia.

50. Peter Brooks was the first to suggest the link between melodrama and realism, in *The Melodramatic Imagination: Balzac, Henry James, Melodrama, and the Mode of Excess* (New Haven: Yale University Press, 1976), and it is indeed accurate that in the French case, Balzacian realism takes a great deal from melodrama, minus the sentimentality. In Britain, however, Victorian realism is quite sentimental.

51. See Franco Moretti, *The Way of the World* (London: Verso, 1987), on compromise as distinctive to realism.

52. The predilection for a happy ending in the English context and the disastrous ending in the French context had, interestingly, already been noticed before the genesis of the sentimental form, as Richardson makes clear when he cites Joseph Ad-

dison to explain why he used a tragic ending for *Clarissa*: "The English writers of tragedy, *says Mr. Addison*, are possessed with a notion that when they represent a virtuous or innocent person in distress, they ought not to leave him till they have delivered him out of his troubles, or made him triumph over his enemies. This *error* they have been led into by a *ridiculous* doctrine in *modern criticism*, that they are obliged to an *equal distribution* of *rewards* and *punishments* and an impartial execution of *poetical justice*" (Richardson, *Clarissa*, 1495, citing Addison in the *Spectator*, no. 40). While the English think that morality should receive its just desserts, Richardson continues, the French, in contrast, recognize that poetical justice corresponds more to life in the world than to the judgments of a court. Thus, Richardson cites "a celebrated critic of a neighboring nation," René Rapin, on the nature and design of tragedy according to Aristotle: "[T]ragedy . . . makes man *modest*, by presenting the great masters of the earth humbled; and it makes him tender and merciful, by showing him the *strange accidents of life*, and the *unforeseen disgraces* to which the most important persons are subject" (1497). It remains to explore the full significance of Richardson's observation by contextualizing it in relation to seventeenth- and eighteenth-century dramatic as well as novelistic practice. Georges May, for example, gives evidence that French critics called for "the practice of the *happy ending* [in English in May's original French]" at the time of Corneille and Racine, though these dramatists had the "good taste to hold [it] in low esteem." (Georges May, *Le Dilemme du roman au dix-huitième siècle* [Paris: Presses Universitaires de France; New Haven: Yale University Press, 1963], 123, my translation). That May identifies a positive outcome with an English phrase is suggestive.

53. *Huis clos* would be Sartre's term. In the twentieth century the most powerful high cultural manifestation of this closure was existentialism, with its emphasis on freedom as the anguish of choice in situations of ethical double bind.

54. Jean-Jacques Rousseau, *Julie, ou la nouvelle Héloïse* (1762; reprint, Paris: Garnier, 1960), 5, my translation.

55. J. G. A. Pocock, *Virtue, Commerce, and History* (New York: Cambridge University Press, 1985), 48–49.

56. Pocock's theorization of virtue as commerce makes the link between Adam Smith's account of morality as founded on sympathy (*Theory of Moral Sentiments*, 1759) and his economic liberalism developed in the *Wealth of Nations* (1776). In enriching all whom it touches, melodramatic virtue is the "interested" (in the sentimental sense of disinterested), ethical manifestation of the happy "trucking" of liberalism's economic agents, benefiting society and individuals alike.

57. Sophie Cottin, *Claire d'Albe* (1799), in *Romans de femme du XVIIIe siècle*, ed. Raymond Trousson (Paris; Robert Laffont, 1996), 734, my translation. I discuss *Claire d'Albe* at length in *The Sentimental Education of the Novel*.

58. See April Alliston, *Virtue's Faults: Correspondences in Eighteenth-Century British and French Women's Fiction* (Stanford: Stanford University Press, 1996). The tragic notion of virtue as sacrifice is crucial to French history painting contemporary with the reign of sentimentality, from David to Delacroix.

59. Wolfgang Iser's notion of the process of reading as *Bildung*, as the "continual interplay between modified expectations and transformed memories," works beautifully for the eighteenth-century English novels that he discusses, as well as for the French novel of worldliness, but is less applicable to the tragic sentimental paradigm (Wolfgang Iser, *The Act of Reading* [Baltimore: Johns Hopkins University Press, 1978], 111. On the importance of learning to make choices for the *Bildungsroman*, see Moretti, *Way of the World*.

60. Denis Diderot, "De la poésie dramatique" (1758), in *Oeuvres esthétiques*, 227, my translation. Such clarity is epitomized in the most pathetic setpiece of the sentimental repertory, the deathbed scene, which involves, as Fisher observes, "action that occurs once a fate is inevitable but has not yet come to pass" (Fisher, *Hard Facts*, 109).

61. See Prendergast, in *The Order of Mimesis: Balzac, Stendhal, Nerval, Flaubert* (Cambridge: Cambridge University Press, 1986), on virtue as commerce in Balzac.

APRIL ALLISTON

## CHAPTER FIVE

# Transnational Sympathies, Imaginary Communities

One of the general goals of this collection is to propose ways of figuring cultural interaction as existing in tension with conceptions of national identity.[1] I would like to propose here that the eighteenth-century idea of *sympathy* often worked in exactly this way, even in novels written well into the nineteenth century. From its beginnings, the notion of sympathy allows for the imagining of an idealized interpersonal bond by offering a form of emotional communication that transcends the pitfalls and lapses of ordinary human interaction. Sympathy always transcends both the inevitable slippages of linguistic communication and the limits placed on interpersonal relationships by the laws and customs that divide people into separate groups (such as nations, classes, and legitimate, i.e., patriarchal, families) and then define individual identities and relationships strictly in terms of those legitimized groupings. Some of the most influential novelists in both France and England, from Rousseau to Brontë, employed this idealized interpersonal bond of sympathy, drawn from the literary code of sensibility that predominated in their time, in order to represent utopian imaginary communities that transgress the limits defining nations, along with national languages, class distinctions, kinship relations, and legitimate sexuality. These imaginary communities of sympathy, far from aligning "the novel" with the "imagined community" of the nation-state, mark the novels in which they appear as significant points of resistance to such an alignment, both generally and specifically in terms of the aspects to which Benedict Anderson points as the defining characteristics of the nation as imagined community.

133

*Sympathy* is a key term in the literature of sensibility, which is generally agreed to have predominated in literature written in English (and in French as well, although possibly to a lesser extent) for at least the second half of the eighteenth century. These conventions were still prevalent in the works of French women novelists in particular through the 1840s, in competition with the then emerging realist novel more familiar to the traditional canon.[2] I would propose that it also thrives through the Romantic and Victorian periods in England, primarily, although not exclusively, in the novel's Gothic mode.[3] Thus, I am focusing here on the century that stretches from Richardson and Rousseau to Brontë and Sand. Throughout that period *sensibility* meant a physiological and emotional sensitivity that was supposed to endow a character or reader with *sympathy*, as it was then called in both English and French, or *empathy*, as we now call it in English following the German Romantics: a capacity to participate in an almost unmediated way in the feelings and experiences, especially sufferings, of others as if they were one's own. Sympathy allowed a large number of novelists writing in French and English from the 1740s to the 1840s, at least, to imagine communities that were figured as utopian alternatives both to the nation and to its domestic core, the family.

During the first half of this period (and earlier, although to a lesser extent) these alternative social groups tended to be imagined as homosocial communities of women, usually "romantic friendships" but sometimes larger utopian, all-female communities, as in Sarah Scott's *Millenium Hall* and *The History of Sir George Ellison*. This form of sympathetic community predominates in the eighteenth century, even though one of the meanings of *sympathy* all along is related to the idea now referred to as "love at first sight," and has this sense as well even in fiction about female sympathetic communities.[4] After 1800, fictional communities are still established on the basis of sympathy and imagined as alternatives to both family and nation, but these "sympathetic communities" come to be constituted more often as heterosexual couples.[5] The romantic couple united through sympathy still substitutes for the kinship alliance represented by marriage and in fact is usually posed more violently in opposition to it than ever the female romantic friendships were. Whether such "imagined communities" are homosocial or heterosexual, though, sympathy continues to work to establish bonds that *specifically transgress and replace those of kinship and nation.*

Both romantic friendships and heterosexual couples bonded by sympathy are repeatedly represented as transgressing national boundaries as well as familial ones, and especially as linking individuals separated by the English Channel. In the eighteenth-century fiction just described, female characters in particular, exiled from their native country, are regularly united in sympathy with newly encountered foreign friends or maintain the bonds of sympathy with a compatriot from a position of foreign exile.[6] Later, heterosexual couples, from Staël's Corinne and Oswald to Sand's Indiana and Sir Ralph, also cross the English Channel in their sympathetic bonds at the same time that they defy the laws of family and kinship. These later novels also abandon the strictly epistolary form (although its traces remain strong) as they turn toward the representation of actual communities—people present to each other—rather than resigning themselves, as the earlier women's fiction had mostly done, to the abstraction of "communities" existing mainly as epistolary communications. Such epistolary relationships, marking the inevitability of female friends' separation in heterosexual marriages, convents, and patriarchal families, were nearly as abstract as Benedict Anderson's "imagined communities," or nations imagined through print.[7]

Even in the era of bourgeois print culture, which, Anderson argues, allowed for the imagining of a vernacular, national community independent of aristocratic kinship alliances, both bourgeois nation and bourgeois family continued to privilege a sense of identity based on kinship and lineage rather than on the freely chosen "elective affinities" of sympathy. Franco Moretti speaks of Austen's England as divided in the conflict between the rural central counties and the port cities, between Land and Money, and claims that in Austen it is Land that wins, "(preferably, with plenty of Money)." He also speaks of the importance of the marriage market in establishing a British sense of national identity, one that demanded a new mobility of women in order to link the central counties with one another while allowing the exchanged women nevertheless to feel at home, having moved only from one to another part of their own nation.[8] But the mobility of women in the marriage market was, in Austen (and Richardson) and in reality, not just a geographical mobility, but also, and perhaps even more importantly, a class mobility. The world in which the novel and the nation-state came to full flowering was not one in which Money triumphed over or became divorced from Land, but one in which Money married Land, as the bourgeoisie sought the land and titles that would give them aristocratic pretensions, while the aristocracy sought the money to support their ancestral estates and privileges. This is not to say anything new, of course, but it needs to be repeated in order to avoid the traps of oversimplification that can arise from Anderson's narrow focus on bourgeois national communities, as if they represented a point of clear opposition to aristocratic kinship groups, or Moretti's on a geographic mobility, which, it must be remembered, significantly entailed social mobility.

Communities based on concepts either of nationality or of kinship are traditionally conceived as grounded in lineage or inheritance, while sensibility is paradoxically figured as a heritable character trait that makes possible the sympathetic bonds through which communities can be imagined that transgress and substitute for those of family or nation. Sensibility as a character trait is inflected by the pan-European vernacular of "national character," and within that code it tends to be used in eighteenth-century novels as a kind of inheritance that can be transmitted outside, beyond, and across lineages either of family or of nation. Like any aspect of character, sensibility is imagined during the Enlightenment and Romantic periods as "heritable," sometimes through birth and sometimes through education. Elsewhere I have treated in detail the preoccupation in epistolary fiction by women with sympathy and sensibility as central aspects of an education in feminine virtue that constitutes a very literal kind of inheritance (one often contained in letters), which can be passed down from one *unrelated* female generation to the next, outside of kinship relationships and in compensation for the legal exclusions of women from passing on patriline inheritances of family name and real property.[9] What I would like to dwell on for a moment here, rather, is the way in which sensibility as a trait heritable by birth (as opposed to education) tends to be figured in novels as a mark of lineage that crosses national boundaries.

It may seem paradoxical, then, that sensibility is strongly associated with British national character. Just as Frenchmen are stereotypically courteous and superficial, while Italians are passionate, in the western European literary and cultural code of "national character" Great Britain is the home of sensibility. Richardson in *Grandison* and Sterne in *A Sentimental Journey* identify it thus, as do many women writers, from Frances Brooke and Elizabeth Griffith to Marie Riccoboni and Isabelle de Charrière. Still, this identification of sensibility with Britishness tends to be made in the context of constructing individual characters and imagining communities that themselves cross the very boundaries designated by the national character types invoked.

If sensibility is a British national characteristic, it is so in a way that is as complex as the very notion of a British nation. It comes increasingly to be identified with the Celtic Fringe, or with some even more vaguely defined border region that is Britain, but is decidedly not what Austen calls "the midland counties of England." Although the sensibility of Richardson's heroines of the 1740s is centrally English, the twin heroines of Sophia

Lee's *The Recess*, an early Gothic novel published in 1783, inherit their marked sensibility from their mother, the exiled queen of Scotland. It is no accident that the estate of Oswald in *Corinne* is in a place called both *Ecosse* and *Angleterre*, while that of Milord Edouard in *La Nouvelle Héloïse* is in Yorkshire—neither in the midland counties of England nor quite in a center of separatist nationalism. (I discuss Emily Brontë's return to the Yorkshire setting in *Wuthering Heights* in detail below.) Sympathy in this context might appear to be related to what Katie Trumpener has called "bardic" nationalism in its deployment in novels that imagine communities resistant to the nation as imperial state.[10] Yet if sympathy resembles a nationalism, it is more like one that insists on its own "hybridization," as that term is developed in David Lloyd's analysis of Irish nationalism.[11] Sympathy frequently marks a crossing between imperial nation-states, particularly the British and the French, as well as within them—between the metropolitan centers and the resistant margins of each, whether Yorkshire or Scotland or a French island colony.

Sensibility can be passed on by birth, as if it were a racial characteristic, but when it is so inherited, it tends to mark a hybridization of national character. Heroines like Corinne and Sophie von La Roche's Fräulein von Sternheim inherit it through the British side of their respective families. Staël's Oswald is the typical British "man of feeling," and while Corinne inherits a vivifying and convention-defying passion from her Italian mother, she inherits a morbid sensibility from the British side of her family that fatally complements Oswald's. A similar national hybridization is mapped geographically in these and related novels.

In Rousseau's *La Nouvelle Héloïse*, Milord Edouard Bomston attempts to seduce Julie and her Saint-Preux by imagining a community they might establish on Bomston's estate in Yorkshire, one where the bonds of sympathy would legitimate, rather than violate, the construction of a social order. In Rousseau's novel, this tempting alternative vision must be rejected in favor of the community he imagines at Clarens, where the same heterosexual sympathy is a powerfully disruptive force that must be contained in order to maintain the idealized patriarchal family as Swiss nationalist city-state. (The homosocial community of Julie and Claire is less threatening to the family-state at Clarens.) By contrast, in La Roche's *Geschichte des Fräuleins von Sternheim*, a German heroine who inherits the trait of sensibility from her English grandmother wanders in exile, establishing a utopian female community along the way in Belgium and ultimately marrying an English man of feeling, whose wealth allows her to create a duplicate of her father's German estate on her husband's property in England. There she, her husband, and his brother form a Clarens-like community in which, rather than dying like Julie, the heroine gets to live, keep both her lovers, and run both her husband's and her father's estates, while the community of female friendship remains purely epistolary. In La Roche's version the heroine marries the younger man with whom she falls in love at the beginning of the novel, while the role of Saint-Preux at Clarens as frustrated lover and educator of his rival's children is taken instead by the older man, who is wiser but not desired sexually by the heroine. The doubling of Sophie's father's continental estate on her husband's British property spatially maps the plot of La Roche's final revision of Rousseau, in which Sophie von Sternheim gets to live at once in the British paradise that Julie had to reject and also in the Continental one where Julie had to die in order for the disruptively sexual forces of sympathy to be contained. Sand's Indiana escapes at once from her loveless marriage and from her heartless French lover with her cousin, Sir Ralph— another British man of sensibility—with whom she is allowed to live happily ever after in a colonial island paradise of sensibility. This island utopia resembles the one imagined by Bernardin de Saint-Pierre in his Rousseau-inspired *Paul et Virginie*, but like La Roche's version, it is much less fatal to its heroine than is its more faithfully Rousseauvean model. All of these authors imagine communities that are utopian in their various refusals of the prevailing models of nation or family, but they locate them in very specific spots on the map of the real world that are significant in plotting the crossing of national boundaries.

## Utopias of Sympathy

In the wake of global exploration, according to Anderson, "it became possible to think of Europe as only one among many civilizations, and not necessarily the Chosen or the best."[12] Surely one could by the same logic substitute "the nation" for "Europe" and "imagined communities" for "civilizations," producing the statement, "It became possible to think of the Nation as only one among many imagined communities, and not necessarily the Chosen or best." If a strain of sentimental fiction after 1800 sought to imagine alternative communities based on presence but transgressing the boundaries of family and nation, that presence, by virtue of its very transgressiveness, had to occur elsewhere: neither in England nor in France, but in utopia. Yet these utopias, ideal and mythical as they may be, are never imaginary places like the original Utopia. They are always located on the map of the real world in ways that diagram spatially their complex relationships to the nation-state, in ways that attempt, indeed, to map the real geographical complexity of the nation-state, far beyond the "central part of England" to which Austen symbolically reduces the British nation.[13]

That "elsewhere" is represented in *Corinne* as an idealized map of Italy, a country that is neither a city-state nor a nation, but begins the novel as a sunny land of female freedom. It is transformed, as it becomes a place of absence rather than presence over the course of the novel, into a double of Oswald's estate in the border country between England and Scotland, a haunted land of exile from within the "empire of death."[14] There is also a French tradition, much older than *Corinne*, of locating such utopias on that nation's own colonial map.[15] Bernardin de Saint-Pierre's bestseller, *Paul et Virginie*, draws upon the eighteenth-century tradition of colonial utopias and merges it with the literature of sensibility's tradition of imagining communities in opposition to the nation and family in order to respond to the uneasy resolution offered by Rousseau in *La Nouvelle Héloïse* of the problematic relationship between nation and domestic sphere in the terms of sensibility. Attempting to domesticate the earlier women's tradition of female communities, while resisting, as had his predecessors, the containment of France's national boundaries, Bernardin transforms the bond of sympathy from the earlier model of female homosocial friendship into a heterosexual coupling within the first few pages of his novel: two mothers in exile form a sympathetic community crossing the boundaries of class and family honor (one woman is in exile because she has fallen from the path of feminine virtue and should be treated as socially untouchable by the other), as well as the internal regional boundaries within the French homeland (the aristocrat is Parisian, the peasant Breton—a denizen of the French "Celtic Fringe").[16] Bernardin undoubtedly chose the island of Ile de France (now Mauritius) as the scene for his utopia of sympathy partly because he had been there, but it is clear, too, that in a novel in which all place-names are loaded with significance the name also distinguished it from the many other French colonial islands, allowing this particular "île sauvage" the more readily to suggest the colonial synecdoche by which a distant colony could stand for the metropole, replacing the imperialist European nation-state of France (and, by another metonymy, its "central part," Île-de-France, Paris and the surrounding provinces) with a France in a utopian, Rousseauesque state of nature.

Utopian sympathetic communities thus lie somewhere between Anderson's account of More's, Bacon's, and Swift's "tongue-in-cheek uto-pias, 'modelled' on real discoveries," on the one hand, and the "barrage of subversive writings directed against current European social and political institutions" produced by Montesquieu, Voltaire, and Rousseau by "exploiting a 'real' non-Europe," on the other.[17] The later novels written by Bernardin, Staël, Brontë, and Sand represent neither newly "discovered" dystopias reflecting the ills of the metropole nor orientalist Others ventriloquizing internal political criticisms of the strongest European nation-states. Rather, they map their utopian sympathetic communities onto real colonies or borderlands—the very places only nervously gestured toward by Austen. They populate her Celtic Fringe and her Antigua, spaces that are liminal to the nation-states, both culturally and geographically, yet (uneasily) contained within them.

## Literary Channel-Crossing

The colony in the French tradition provides an "outside" from within the nation as family—always distant, and progressively freer, from stifling bourgeois marriages and country estates. Unlike Staël and earlier women writers, Bernardin does not imagine the English Channel as one of the significant borders crossed by the sympathetic bonds that construct his community, although he does draw on a literary tradition, as did his model Rousseau, built by novelists writing in English as well as French. The readership of his novel crossed the Channel, as does Bernardin's own intertextual "reading" in Paul et Virginie, leading to at least as many literary responses, not to mention mass sales of buttons, buckles, and lampshades bearing images from the novel, in Britain as in France. Two of the most famous English literary responses (which, however, as far as I know have never been identified as such) are Austen's Northanger Abbey and Emily Brontë's Wuthering Heights.[18] Unlike Sand, who, following the example of numerous English novelists (such as Maria Edgeworth in Belinda), draws attention to the fact that Indiana is a rewriting of Paul et Virginie, Austen and Brontë rewrite Bernardin without naming his novel or its characters, thus fostering an illusion that their writings are nationally self-contained while nevertheless, in the case of Wuthering Heights in particular, vigorously rewriting the French tradition of utopian sympathetic communities stretching back to La Nouvelle Héloïse through Indiana and Paul et Virginie.

Emily Brontë's choice of setting, like Bernardin's, has not only the usually emphasized biographical associations, but also literary and symbolic ones, which were more inescapably pervasive in their times than in ours.[19] In *Wuthering Heights* she revisits the very same spot on the map where Julie and Saint-Preux are allowed in one brief letter to imagine a heterosexual utopia of sympathetic community. Milord Edouard's estate in Yorkshire is the only place in which they might imagine escaping the patriarchal family to realize and live out their love. As mentioned above, Rousseau's lovers, and Julie in particular, must renounce this imaginary community in order to demonstrate a virtuous obedience to the law of the bourgeois paterfamilias, which Rousseau firmly instates in his preferred utopia at Clarens as the core, the deity, indeed the very identity of the ideal nation as Swiss village-state. Rousseau's disciple Bernardin envisions another pair of lovers, who, born far from Europe and far from any fathers, are at least able to attempt to live the utopia of sympathy renounced by Julie and Saint-Preux without losing their requisite virtue. That attempt too is doomed, not by the law of the father and the nation, but by the very feminine lineage that makes the attempt possible. Bernardin's novel takes up a whole tradition of earlier fiction in which a foster-mother's legacy of virtue through education enables life for heroines excluded from patrimony and patrilineage. His initial community based on feminine sympathy and romantic friendship makes the childhood idyll of Paul and Virginie possible in the first place, but in Bernardin's Rousseauesque terms the foster-mother's inheritance of virtue through (an inevitably European) education, now linked with rather than divorced from the filthy lucre of a material inheritance, and combined with Virginie's naturally dangerous female sexuality, is what requires it to end before adult sexuality can enter to sully the virtuous picture. Sand rejects all these Rousseauvean values to rehabilitate Bernardin's pair of child-lovers in the tropics and allow them, in the ending of *Indiana*, to live out the fantasy of adult sexual sympathetic community in the French island colony. This intertextual web woven by Rousseau, Bernardin, and Sand around naive quasi-sibling lovers in utopias of sympathy forms the rich material worked by Brontë.

Like Staël, Emily Brontë returns to the Yorkshire estate imagined as a false alternative to Rousseau's patriarchal nation. She places Bernardin's class-defying child-lovers on Rousseau's original site of utopian sympathetic community. Like Sand, Brontë complicates Bernardin's device of the frame narrative, in which the story of the lovers is related by a local observer to the novel's narrator, who in all three versions is a young and naive male visitor. Perhaps because she was really there, however, Brontë does not allow Yorkshire to be imagined in the end as a place where lovers might escape the rule of fathers, the bourgeois family, or the corruptions of European civilization and imperialism in order to live in a sympathetic utopia. Rather, she imagines the child-lovers' attempt to live out the French idyll of sympathetic community in a wild British borderland where the oppressive power of fathers is unrestrained by the European civilization they nevertheless well know how to abuse. The word *sympathy* is among the most frequently used in *Wuthering Heights* because this novel is above all an anguished exploration of the multifarious deformations, betrayals, and abuses of sympathy as a basis for imagined community.

## Imaginary Communities

Anderson emphasizes his distinction between the "creole nations" of the Americas and the fragmented European nationalisms that arose simultaneously during the nineteenth century, the former sharing a language with the metropolitan nation-states from which they claimed political independence, setting themselves up in the image of the mother-nation without challenging the hegemony of European print language, the latter breaking up ancient, multilingual empires in favor of regional vernaculars. Both the American creole nationalists and the European regional nationalists resisted imperialism, ironically, by imitating politically the strong nation-states at the core of the resisted empires (this holds true, for example, for both the United States, a "creole nation," and Ireland, a European regional vernacular-based nation, in relation to the United Kingdom). While Anderson's historical nationalist "imagined communities" sought independence from the European imperial powers by modelling themselves upon Europe's strongest nation-states, the imaginary communities represented in the novels of Bernardin, Staël, Sand, and Brontë resist the two strongest European imperialist nation-states of the eighteenth and nineteenth centuries neither by imagining political independence from them nor by imitating their structure or characteristics. Rather, they express resistances to and critiques of their own nation-states by legibly mapping the inescapable containment within their empires of even the most remote areas and most utopian communities.[20] Furthermore, they construct imaginary communities that cannot possibly be mistaken for an "imagined community" as nation because they specifically avoid the very features that Anderson and his intellectual heirs have identified as those by which an imagined community can be recognized as a nation.

First, as already mentioned, these novelistic sympathetic communities *decentralize the nation-state geographically*. They are specifically located on the margins of the nation-state, contained, but uneasily so, by its political boundaries, and distant in every sense from Paris or the "central counties of England." In this respect the French colonial islands of Bernardin and Sand resemble the Yorkshire borderland that recurs in Rousseau, Staël, and Brontë. Second, these novels of sensibility *decentralize the vernacular language shared with the resisted nation-state*. Bernardin develops a complex tree language, a Rousseauesque "natural" vernacular indigenous to his island setting and to a community in a state of nature—a language to which Sand refers directly in her revision of Bernardin.[21] Brontë makes use of Yorkshire dialect, a regional language that is emphatically *not* a print language or a national vernacular in Anderson's sense. All, drawing on a tradition that stretches back well into the seventeenth century and undoubtedly earlier, invoke sympathy itself as a nonverbal language of the eyes (and other bodily signs of emotion), an immediate form of communication that allows precisely for the formation of bonds across linguistic, as well as national and class, boundaries.

Third, sympathetic communities are miscegenated; unlike classic nation-forming communities, they deliberately imagine the crossing of racial boundaries. In Sand's self-conscious rewriting of *La Nouvelle Héloïse* via *Paul et Virginie*, the creole Indiana (whose racial impurity is heavily hinted at, although identified openly only in her double, Noun) and her English lover, Ralph, pass through a false tragic ending that echoes Virginie's virtual suicide by water (and Saint-Preux's contemplated one) to live out the happy ending denied to Bernardin's (and Rousseau's) purely European couple on another colonial island.[22] Virginie, like Paul, is racially pure European, but the European education entailed by her racial and class inheritance becomes her downfall. Indiana's mixed race and creole upbringing seem to help make the envisioned utopian sympathetic community of two more realizable.

David Lloyd argues in "Adulteration and the Nation" that imagining racial hybridization is an important way of resisting nationalism.[23] Much has been written on Heathcliff as a hybrid of racial Others, a "gypsy" figured as black who is also imagined as the son of "the Emperor of China and an Indian queen."[24] This hybridization takes on new significance when *Wuthering Heights* is recognized as a rewriting of the French tradition of sympathetic utopias. In that context, Heathcliff is surprisingly revealed as a masculine avatar of the French creole heroines Virginie and Indiana/ Noun. If the two Cathys are also avatars of those heroines, that ambiguity is accounted for by Catherine Earnshaw's most famous utterance, that Heathcliff is "more myself than I am."[25] It is Heathcliff who, like Indiana/ Noun, has the whiff of miscegenation about him, and it is Heathcliff who, like Virginie, crosses the sea, not to a corrupt Europe, but in the opposite direction, to dim colonial destinations, for his similarly gentrifying and equally tragic "education." Cathy's poisonous European bourgeois education, meanwhile—the cause of her loss of innocence and her death, just as Virginie's is the cause of hers—is to be found right at home, even though it is no more "native" to Yorkshire than to the island of Ile de France. Despite their inhabiting, in Brontë's Gothic vision, a patriarchal dystopia whose whole energy is directed toward the deformation of sympathetic as well as of kinship bonds, however, the potent miscegenation of Heathcliff with Catherine Earnshaw triumphs in a sympathetic community that cannot be contained by boundaries of class, race, nation, the domestic sphere, or even those that supposedly separate human and animal, life and death. Breaking every window, every coffin, every constraining domestic containment, they leave their descendants, the new child-couple of Catherine Linton and Hareton Earnshaw, to inherit the house and live out a tame version of the idyll made possible by the second Cathy's domestication of Hareton. It is no accident that Hareton's domestication is achieved precisely through the latest Virginie's teaching him to read proper English, the national print vernacular, by means of "costly" books that are as much an imported luxury in Yorkshire as in any colony. This ending gestures toward a consoling reinstatement of Austen's England in the "northern extremity" that Austen herself had yielded up to the undomesticated Gothic, but of course this doubling of the primary pair remains only a pale shadow of the imaginary community that eternally haunts the moors.

The fourth, final, and perhaps most fundamental way in which novels imagine sympathetic communities as *alternatives* to nations is by resisting the connection between the domestic and public spheres upon which the idea of the bourgeois nation is founded.[26] They resist the plot of the "national marriage market," whether by imagining homosocial communities based on women's romantic friendships or by imagining adulterous heterosexual unions.[27] Sympathy is repeatedly invoked in eighteenth- and nineteenth-century novels as a way of imagining alternatives to the type of group identity based on kinship or patrilineage by which even local, "hybrid," "bardic," or anti-imperial nationalisms generally define themselves. As I have shown, Bernardin, Staël, Sand, and Brontë employ the eighteenth-century code of sympathy to imagine utopian alternatives to the nation-state in part by legibly mapping out its fragmentation both from within and from without, and also by representing alternatives to the family at its heart, the private sphere that anchors and images the public nation.

## Notes

1. This chapter was conceived in conversations with Margaret Cohen concerning the need to rethink Benedict Anderson's notion of the imagined community in light of what were in fact the first modern imagined communities, the transnational communities catalyzed by sensibility.

2. See Margaret Cohen, *The Sentimental Education of the Novel* (Princeton: Princeton University Press, 1999).

3. I have argued elsewhere that the Gothic is a specific mode of literature of sensibility in which its typical emotional states are literalized (see April Alliston, *Virtue's Faults: Correspondences in Eighteenth-Century British and French Women's Fiction* [Stanford: Stanford University Press, 1996], chs. 4 and 5).

4. In *Virtue's Faults* I identified a subgenre of novels published by women in English and French that I called "novels of women's correspondence," which often used the epistolary form to enact and establish such homosocial communities of women (see esp. chs. 1 and 3).

5. Fictions of female community became prevalent later in the United States. The model that predominated in British and French fiction during the second half of the eighteenth century was adapted in American fiction primarily in the nineteenth century. On female communities in American fiction, see Nina Auerbach, *Communities of Women: An Idea in Fiction* (Cambridge: Harvard University Press, 1978); and Nina Baym, *Woman's Fiction: A Guide to Novels By and About Women in America, 1820–1870*, 2nd ed. (Urbana: University of Illinois Press, 1993).

6. A few examples include Sophia Lee, *The Recess; or, A Tale of Other Times* (1783–85); Marie Gacon-Dufour, *Le Préjugé vaincu, ou Lettres de madame la comtesse de \*\*\* et de madame de \*\*\* refugiée en Angleterre* (1787); and many novels of Marie Riccoboni (see Alliston, *Virtue's Faults*).

7. Benedict Anderson, *Imagined Communities: Reflections on the Origin and Spread of Nationalism*, 2nd ed. (1991; reprint, New York: Verso, 1998), esp. 9–82.

8. Franco Moretti, *Atlas of the European Novel, 1800–1900* (London: Verso, 1998), 14–20.

9. See Alliston, *Virtue's Faults*.

10. Katie Trumpener, *Bardic Nationalism: The Romantic Novel and the British Empire* (Princeton: Princeton University Press, 1997), e.g., 22–23.

11. David Lloyd, *Anomalous States: Irish Writing and the Post-Colonial Moment* (Dublin: Lilliput, 1993), 88–114.

12. Anderson, *Imagined Communities*, 70.

13. Moretti, *Atlas of the European Novel*, 15.

14. See April Alliston, "Of Haunted Highlands: Mapping a Geography of Gender in the Margins of Europe," in *Cultural Interactions in the Romantic Age: Critical Essays in Comparative Literature*, ed. Gregory Maertz (Albany: State University of New York Press, 1998), 55–78.

15. See, e.g., Julia V. Douthwaite, *Exotic Women: Literary Heroines and Cultural Strategies in Ancien Régime France* (Philadelphia: University of Pennsylvania Press, 1992); and Alliston, *Virtue's Faults*, ch. 4.

16. Bernardin figures his literary inheritance from earlier women novelists in the generational narrative of his novel: the original sympathetic community on the island is a female friendship between two women exiled from their nation and their families in which sympathy overcomes differences of class. The lovers of the novel's title are born into an ideal world constructed out of their mothers' homosocial sympathetic community, from which fathers are absent (Jacques-Henri Bernardin Saint-Pierre, *Paul et Virginie*, ed. Robert Mauzi [Paris: Garnier-Flammarion, 1966], 82–89).

17. Anderson, *Imagined Communities*, 69.

18. I discussed *Northanger Abbey* as a revision of *Paul et Virginie* in some detail in the epilogue to Alliston, *Virtue's Faults*.

19. On the pervasive influence of Rousseau's novel on British Romantic women novelists, see Annette Wheeler Cafarelli, "Rousseau and British Romanticism: Women and the Legacy of Male Radicalism," in Maertz, *Cultural Interactions in the Romantic Age*, 125–55: "The two key texts for women were Rousseau's novel *Julie, ou la Nouvelle Héloïse* (1761) and his educational treatise *Emile, ou de l'éducation* (1762). The plot of Julie succumbing to a liaison with her tutor Saint-Preux, and afterwards settling into an exemplary marriage amid sub-alpine scenery with the older Wolmar in perfect amity with her former lover, to whom she professes her enduring passion before expiring, *gave rise to a wide variety of novelistic sentimental duos and triads set amid inspirational scenery. . . .* Rousseau's *Héloïse* swept England in the 1760s, and its immense vogue generated plot and scenic elements throughout the late eighteenth-century British novel. Its popularity is evident in . . . the abundance of Rousseauvean landscapes, whether Alpine fantasies *or domesticated* as English Lake or Irish countryside, as in the works of Ann Radcliffe, Charlotte Smith, and Sydney Owenson Morgan. *More daring were the various triads that were modeled on the threesome of Saint-Preux, Julie, and Wolmar*" (126, 128, emphasis mine). Authors mentioned as reworking or referring to *Julie* include Jane Austen, Hannah More, Clara Reeve, Frances Brooke, Helen Maria Williams, Mary Hays, Mary Wollstonecraft, Elizabeth Hamilton, and others (128–33).

20. I include Staël in this group even though *Corinne* imagines the failure rather than the utopian success of a resistance to empire and nation attempted

through the establishment of a heterosexual sympathetic community. On the details of that failure, see my *Virtue's Faults* and "Of Haunted Highlands."

21. George Sand, *Indiana* (Paris: Gallimard, 1984), e.g., 319, first published in 1832.

22. Ibid., 330–44.

23. Lloyd, *Anomalous States*, 114–15.

24. Emily Brontë, *Wuthering Heights* (New York: Bantam Books, 1974), 51, first published in 1847. See also, for example, Susan Meyer, *Imperialism at Home: Race and Victorian Women's Fiction* (Ithaca: Cornell University Press, 1996); and Howard L. Malchow, *Gothic Images of Race in Nineteenth-Century Britain* (Stanford: Stanford University Press, 1996).

25. Brontë, *Wuthering Heights*, 73.

26. Although it may be a commonplace to say that the bourgeois nation is founded upon an ideology of the *separation* between public and private spheres, the very articulation of this separation establishes an interdependency between the two spheres, to which I refer here as a most significant "connection." One writer of the period in question who most clearly articulates the *connectedness* inherent in this separation of spheres is Mary Wollstonecraft, for example, in her argument that women become the guarantors of the public sphere by remaining sequestered in the private sphere and devoting themselves to the moral education of the children who will become future citizens and public actors: "Public education, of every denomination, should be directed to form citizens, but if you wish to make good citizens, you must first exercise the affections of a son and a brother. This is the only way to expand the heart; for public affections, as well as public virtues, must ever grow out of the private character, or they are merely meteors that shoot athwart a dark sky, and disappear as they are gazed at and admired. Few, I believe, have had much affection for mankind, who did not first love their parents, their brothers, sisters, and even the domestic brutes, whom they first played with. . . . A man has been termed a microcosm; and *every family might also be called a state*. States, it is true, have mostly been governed by arts that disgrace the character of man; and the want of a just constitution, and equal laws, have so perplexed the notions of the worldly wise, that they more than question the reasonableness of contending for the rights of humanity. Thus morality, polluted in the national reservoir, sends off streams of vice to corrupt the constituent parts of the body politic; but should more noble, or rather, more just principles regulate the laws, which ought to be the government of society, and not those who execute them, duty might become the rule of private conduct. . . .—The conclusion I wish to draw, is obvious; make women rational creatures, and free citizens, and they will quickly become good wives, and mothers; that is—if men do not neglect the duties of husbands and fathers" (Mary Wollstonecraft, *A Vindication of the Rights of Woman*, ed. Carol H. Poston, 2nd ed. [New York: Norton, 1988], 162, 177, first published in 1792). Since Wollstonecraft, like the many other British women writers documented by Cafarelli (see above, n. 19), is responding in this work primarily to Rous-

seau, the idea that "every family might also be called a state" may well derive partly from *La Nouvelle Héloïse*, in which the family of Wolmar almost literally becomes a state (as described in a more theoretical way in *The Social Contract*). The influence of Rousseau might help explain why this ancient patriarchal model of family-as-state, against which John Locke had argued a century earlier, might be revived by Wollstonecraft and other writers of her time.

27. Cf. Moretti, *Atlas of the European Novel*, 14–18.

# PART II

# Imagining the "Othered" Nation

RICHARD MAXWELL

## CHAPTER SIX

# Phantom States: *Cleveland, The Recess,* and the Origins of Historical Fiction

Unrecognized monarchs are often the least welcome of exiles. Typically forced to travel abroad owing to persistent official hostility at home, they tend to become superfluous; sooner or later, almost everybody, including their putative political allies, loses interest in their claims. The dethroned or the ineffectively aspiring sovereign—the *pretender*, in a useful eighteenth-century coinage—is thus doubly cursed: a would-be leader not only lacking an appropriate seat of power but also socially unacceptable. In this pathetic figure the displaced quality that accompanies so many kings and queens (who often, even at the best of times, retain their foreign accents or betray their alien cultural origins) acquires its most humiliating form.[1] However, despite their political and personal loneliness, pretenders over the last few centuries have retained the support of one ardent, insatiable faction. Even the defiant Redgauntlet (in the novel of that name, 1824) gave up on Bonnie Prince Charles. But his ingenious creator, Walter Scott, did not. The example may be generalized. Though they may be *persona non grata* in everyday life, pretenders have long remained a godsend to novelists.

Elsewhere I have traced a sustained line of pretender novels, beginning in the France of Louis XIV and extending, for all practical purposes, up to the present day.[2] Here I turn to one remarkable and little-noted side of this tradition. As the pretender fiction of post-Renaissance Europe suggests, the nation-state is most vividly conceptualized from a viewpoint outside, around, or—literally—underneath it. Such books are therefore crucial not only to the student of seventeenth- or eighteenth-century literature but to readers thinking in a much longer time frame; they created habits of interpretation or reception that could be drawn on well through the nineteenth-century heyday of the historical novel and often after that. A formative dilemma—that of the disenchanted heir who cannot return home but must keep moving—made possible intricately precise mixtures of history with fiction. By the same token, stories about displaced pretenders also encouraged an interestingly subtle approach to questions of nationhood and nationalism; far from remaining a hard-and-fast category, the nation was defined by nuance, degree, and—speaking dynastically—the persistent, unsettling pull of family resemblance.

Such developments are at their most compelling in two eighteenth-century treatments of the wandering pretender, both Stuart-related and both taking the form of novels: the abbé Prévost's *Le Philosophe anglais ou Histoire de Monsieur Cleveland* (1731–39) and Sophia Lee's *The Recess: A Tale of Other Times* (1785). *The Recess* works as a free imitation of and commentary upon *Cleveland*, allowing a demonstration of how and why French novels could seem so useful to English writers. Additionally, there is a second level of interest in the juxtaposition: not only is each work directly shaped by a series of cultural transfers between France and England but each helps define the shifting connections between nationalism, history, and fiction. As James Collins has argued, a royal dynasty can constitute an early version of nationalism. Nations tend to be based on four political arrangements, first a dynastic "family corporation" whose continuing existence is ensured by laws of succession[3] and subsequently a "polyglot empire" (culturally distinct territories only partly assimilated by a conquering country); a group of bureaucratic institutions increasingly controlled by a central state apparatus; and a widely shared consciousness of identity in common ("we are all French").[4] *Cleveland* and *The Recess* filter national history through tales of pretenders; by this means they suggest something of the piecemeal way in which the latter three elements emerged alongside the "family corporation," relegating it, finally, to a shadowy, semifictional but also foundational status.[5] The lost dynasty of the pretender creates a distinctive sense of historical time, linking the dynamics of royal succession with the (presumably) continuous history of a nation. Simultaneously, the pretender can be understood as a metaphor embodying, even justifying, history-fiction combinations. Thus, in its eighteenth-century versions this theme defines both a political and a literary agenda.

An epilogue to the discussion of Prévost and Lee will allow a view of the same process several generations later. During the nineteenth century the historical novel provided myths of origin and identity for a wide range of nations, but these myths were often accompanied by countermyths about the fragility or even the ghostliness of large-scale, collective identities. Paradoxically, then, it is not only the pretender but the nation from which he or she is exiled that seems to exist in an indeterminate phantom state. This turn of events is perhaps most memorably described in Walter Scott's early Waverley novels, in which Scottish history is defined through a range of Stuart political failures. Existing in an odd international triangle with England on the one hand and France on the other, Scotland became the perfect place from which to reconceive the eighteenth-century tradition of pretender lore. In contrast, the French reclamation of Scott— by novelists like Alexandre Dumas and Gérard de Nerval—enabled yet another treatment of the traditional pretender story, showing how it could become the repository of secret utopian desires. These Scottish and French versions of historical fiction are very different: what they have in common is an ability to adapt narratives about doomed dynasties to more recent developments in the evolution of the nation and more recent versions of nationalism. A genre intent on mingling facts with inventions finds its meaning in an archaic story about monarchs who recede into myth (or at least into a sort of glamorous, cursed irrelevance), only to reemerge, transformed, as avatars of modern life.

## Cromwell's Prévostian Bastard

Although Prévost's *Cleveland* is something of a cult favorite, at least among professional students of French, it is also enormous, largely unavailable despite an excellent scholarly edition, and, in our own time, largely unread despite its considerable eighteenth-century fame. Furthermore, no one has ever translated the whole thing into English. Under these circumstances, a few lines of preliminary description might be welcome. *Cleveland*'s eponymous hero is one of several illegitimate sons of Oliver Cromwell. His hypocritical father, wishing to suppress all evidence of his shamefully unbridled lust, plots to sell him into New World slavery. Learning of this plot, Cleveland's long-suffering but amazingly self-sufficient mother hides him in a remote cave, where she brings him up philosophically. After her death he emerges gradually into European society and history, aligning himself repeatedly with the Royalist, Stuart cause against which his male parent so notoriously fought. Linked, in turn, with the future Charles II, Henrietta, Charles's sister (herself a major player in the diplomatic interchange between England and France), and Charles's bastard son the duke of Monmouth, Cleveland becomes first a New World adventurer, at one point ruling a native tribe, and then an Old World intriguer. Surviving many sorrows—and many volumes—he confronts one personal disaster after another: the assassination of his half-brother Bridge (another Cromwellian bastard, whose adventures run parallel to Cleveland's before the two of them finally meet and swap stories), the apparent betrayal of Fanny, his wife, and the incestuous, ultimately suicidal behavior of Cécile, his daughter. Throughout these ordeals he continues to meditate on happiness and human existence. Counseled by Charles II's deposed minister Clarendon (whose history of the English civil wars was one of Prévost's important inspirations), he finds, in the end, a provisional repose recalling his mother's stoic stance but somewhat more fully Christianized.

It is Cleveland's claim to exist that becomes the dominating issue of the novel. Since he is Cromwell's bastard, the question whether he will be allowed to appear publicly—to appear *in history*—can be raised from the very beginning of this narrative. So can the related question of his fictionality. (Is he just a character in a novel, or was there someone named Cleveland who actually wrote the memoirs that we are reading? For reasons both philosophical and pecuniary, Prévost begins by encouraging the latter belief.) He is a pretender so far as his rights within a genealogical line remain at issue, at least until Cromwell's death. However, only after his father's demise does the problem of pretendancy come into its own. In the later books of *Cleveland*, when the hero first inadvertently courts his own daughter, then tries to marry her off to Monmouth—like himself, the illegitimate son of a ruler—Prévost discovers, chapter by chapter, how all the contrarieties of historical fiction can be inextricably woven together. The mixture of fact and invention, the obsession with succession, genealogy, and the nature of time in a nation suffering through a great public crisis, the identification with aspiring kings who have failed in advance, who can only pretend to what they will never attain, the desire to enter history (as though one had any choice, as though there were sanctuaries which could really protect people from it)—a distinctive mixture of these features establish the atmosphere and logic of *Cleveland*.

A playful preface sets the tone. Here we learn how Cleveland's son brought Prévost (that is to say, the author of the *Mémoires d'un homme de qualité*)—the autobiography in manuscript of the deceased bastard himself; later, they came to an agreement that Prévost would ready the manuscript for publication, translating it into French since his English was not quite up to the task. Prévost then proceeds to the main business of his preface, which is to determine whether the memoirs he has "translated" are accurate. He points out that the times in which Cleveland lived were near enough to the present that many living persons knew them. By the same token, history this recent (the period of the Commonwealth and Restoration, at most eighty years before) is generally familiar: reading the recollections of M. Cleveland, we cannot fear that we have been transported into the region of fables.

The novelist wants his story to look like a literal recitation of facts, at least to those readers contemplating its purchase; he hoped to sell *Cleveland* as a work of history. However, Prévost's kind of slipperiness suggests a very different sense than Defoe's, for instance, of how and why history might be mixed with fiction. It is not so much, or not only, that the fictional hero will be seen as factual by association with publicly recognized characters and happenings as it is that the history of England will be implicated more and more closely with make-believe. Cleveland's historicity is apparently confirmed by his status as bastard of Cromwell. On the other hand, we will find no repetition of the events of Cromwell's public life but will learn instead of those moments when the Protector lurked among half-lights, a penumbra that mixes the factual and the counterfactual as though they were light and darkness.[6] Prévost privately assured his publisher that in a book such as *Cleveland* history could be endlessly supplemented by fiction; therefore the novel could be as long or short as its author wanted to make it. The interesting assumption in this claim is that *Cleveland* treats the twilit kind of history that thrives on vacancies, blanks, and gaps.

Prévost's impatience with the French taste for making romance out of history is amply vented in *Le Pour et contre*, where he enthusiastically lambasts the protohistorical romances of Mme de Scudéry, which fictionalized the Fronde from a loser's perspective.[7] On the other hand, he seems to have been fully conscious of the ways in which his own novels were *like* hers. One sign of this is his interest in the problematic question of length. The French, as he observes in *Le Pour et contre*, had largely lost interest in the interminable romances of yesteryear. They now preferred short books, including such genres as the *historiette* of Tallemant de Réaux and the *nouvelle historique*, most eminently represented in the works of Mme de Lafayette. They wanted to get to the end of the story quickly; perhaps endings were all they enjoyed anymore. Prévost implies that this was a problem with Gallic reading habits without directly proposing a solution to it. His own response, however, is evident. He often wrote huge works of fiction whose endings sometimes were postponed for years or decades of the reader's life and whose plots ranged around the known world expansively. It is as though Prévost hoped to marry the extravagant length and scope of

Scudéry to the soberness of Lafayette, bringing them both down to the level of quotidian reality. Prévost's ambitions were those of the realist who hoped to absorb the energies of romance. Such maneuverings as he attempted in his penumbral world of incertitudes were ways of using fiction almost invisibly to get a perspective on historical conflict and change.

After the antics of the preface, the body of *Cleveland* proper begins as follows: "The reputation of my father will excuse me from taking many pains to enlarge upon my origins. No one can fail to be acquainted with the character of that celebrated man, who, during a number of years, held all Europe in admiration of his virtues and his crimes."[8] Cleveland is the unknown son of a famous father. Since everybody already knows about Cromwell, his own origin will not need much discussion. Nonetheless, the son acquaints us at some length with the history of his mother, Elizabeth Cleveland, a mistress to Charles I and then, after being dropped by Charles, a mistress to Cromwell. The story of Elizabeth Cleveland is that of a woman who lost her desire for power and place. If ambition begins as "the dominant passion of her soul" (4:4), it does not survive the successive rejections of Charles; her father, who refuses her "the asylum she had expected to find in her paternal home" (4:4); the court; and finally Cromwell. Pregnant with the latter's child, she willingly retires to Hammersmith: "She renounced not only ambition and love but even the most innocent pastimes which generally occupy women" (4:7). Elizabeth Cleveland brings up her son in a spirit of stoic refusal and abnegation.

While they live this "solitary and diligent" life (4:11), Cromwell emerges as a leader of the Puritan revolution. Cleveland is not told about his father until the traumatic moment of Charles I's beheading. "Although our retreat was deeper than the noise of war, which scarcely reached us, it was impossible to remain in ignorance of the detestable catastrophe" (4:12). Now, for the last time in her life, Elizabeth loses her self-command: she cries out to her son that the king is dead on a scaffold and that *his* father put him there. Her unprecedented agitation—Cleveland has lived his life thus far without the least trouble—and the hitherto unpronounced name of his father, "le nom de père que je n'avois jamais entendu prononcer" [the name of father, which I had never heard pronounced] (4:12), overwhelm him so thoroughly that he falls senseless to the ground.

*Cleveland* is a book of much fainting and much weeping, but this first manifestation of Cleveland's highly wrought sensibility has a special significance: he confronts at once the depredations of family and history. Prévost has perhaps overloaded the moment. Our hero learns of the death of a man who might have been his father while learning simultaneously that the party responsible for this death is his actual father. The news is broken by his mother, the victim of both men. Cleveland loses his innocence to history, which is revealed as a complicated tangle of genealogical claims and counterclaims punctuated by murder and overshadowed by Oedipal conflicts that will follow him through life. Far from banishing these horrors, stoic retirement and the austere rejection of ambition only intensify his vulnerability to them; no retreat, it seems, is so obscure that it can shield him from such shocks. Voltaire's *Candide* (1759) stands as both a pastiche and a critique of *Cleveland*,[9] but the earlier hero can hardly resolve his search for happiness and wisdom with a dictum like "Il faut cultiver notre jardin." Cleveland's parentage figures a connection with violence and war, with the depredations of ambition (so obvious in both his parents) that he cannot, finally, deny, no matter how cunning his retreats. There is no garden that is not littered with bones. It is this condition of Cleveland's life that the novel's first faint establishes. His abrupt entrance into the public realm—from which his mother's flight has thus far shielded him—suggests the linkage of historical and personal time under the aegis of a great, inescapable death's head. This is the juncture at which a term like *dynasty* comes to have its full meaning.

Even in these opening pages the novel suggests that we cannot escape from history, that the quest for happiness and wisdom must be accomplished within its limits or replaced by a different kind of quest. This discovery is reenacted a number of times, until it can be acknowledged by the traumatized discoverer; at the same time, it is gradually enriched by intervening complications. Cleveland is never identified with that great Tudor rebel, Perkin Warbeck (as were the later Stuarts during the decades of Prévost's writing career); nonetheless, he will, despite himself, approach the condition of a royal pretender, until he is finally linked to the hapless, vicious Monmouth. Prévost does not seem to have precisely this culmination in mind when he begins *Cleveland*, which makes it all the more fascinating to watch him—and his mournful hero—work toward it, through a mélange of international adventures, inside and outside history as it is publicly known.

Cleveland reenters the cruelties of historical time. Prévost evokes the crossing of this border by persistently readjusting the fit between fact and fiction. Elizabeth Cleveland introduces her young son to his father after he has become Lord Protector; Cromwell does not want to help, much less acknowledge, a bastard, so mother and child are forced to flee their retreat in Hammersmith for fear that the angry Protector will imprison or assassinate them. The turning point is their meeting with the resourceful

Mrs. Riding, who has already rescued, hidden, and raised a Cromwell bastard, after his mother, Mally Bridge, was killed by the Protector's agents. She was able to do so because her country house lies in an extraordinary situation. Near it there are "in the depths of a little valley which belongs to me, several openings which give subterranean access to the center of one of these mountains, so that besides the place being deserted, since nothing will grow there, it would be difficult to find a spot better designed to be an asylum against violence and persecution. I resolved to choose one of these obscure caverns in which to raise little Bridge" (4:44). With the help of a discreet servant, Mrs. Riding preserved her little Bridge to young manhood, after which he insisted on leaving the cave and seeking out his father, who promptly incarcerated him. The asylum of the distant cave remains undetected, however, and Cleveland and his mother are now conducted to it. The fictional mother and son enter this hidden sanctuary, where once again the narrative detaches itself from the exigencies of the English civil wars and their aftermath.

Cleveland and his mother live in their remote cavern for many years: her asylum becomes her tomb; his explorations of the cave's "recesses" are identified with early efforts at self-interrogation, inquiries into the "recesses" of his heart.[10] The identification of asylum with tomb and the emphasis on recesses of feeling would become omnipresent sentimental formulas of the eighteenth century; Rousseau himself was deeply influenced by the novel. Prévost gives us the sense of discovering them for the first time. Recess, asylum, and sanctuary are allegorized to suggest the novel's—and Cleveland's—discovery of a wounded subjectivity, of the way in which it can either consume itself fruitlessly or, by some miracle, find satisfactory expression, leading to that elusive Prévostian goal, happiness. (To write, Cleveland insists, is a way of transcending melancholy.) Prévost's heroes are equipped with capacities of feeling far above the average; as more than one reader has observed, it is their ability to *feel* that renders them heroic. This is never truer than in *Cleveland*, where the hero's early isolation does nothing to dampen his epic emotionality. His situation is compounded when, after a frightening expedition into the heart of the mountain, he discovers two other fugitives in the cave, also refugees from the civil wars. He learns to respect Lord Axminster and to love (in secret) Axminster's daughter, Fanny. Cleveland's sentimental education commences in earnest, far from the problematic world of his father. Within the asylum of the cave he has begun to think out the problematics of love, longing, class, secrecy, and despair. He is the Protector's son but also the Protector's bastard. He feels himself far below the aristocratic status of his companions even though his father controls England. It is only with painful difficulty that he finally articulates his feelings for Fanny. Cleveland and Fanny are thereafter ready to leave their hiding place to try to discover a place for themselves within the world outside it.

Although Cleveland subjects both himself and others to subtle, sometimes hair-splitting, analysis, his supposed memoirs are conceived in dramatically contrasted blocks, each, it often seems, a novel in itself. Because Prévost often situates these blocks as stories within stories, or even as stories within stories within stories, the reader can easily conceive them as nested commentaries on one another. The book's large-scale expressiveness emerges directly from this scheme. The nested tales of *Cleveland* are persistently focused on the contradictions of asylum and sanctuary; the fictional, typically fantastic tales enacted within the multifarious refuges of the book lead back to the threatening facts of history that they were originally designed to evade or conceal. Cleveland leaves his Devonshire retreat to attend at the court-in-exile of Charles II, where his Royalist grandfather forcibly packs him away to the New World (disturbingly enough, this had also been Cromwell's plan). Later, our hero meets up with Bridge (the long-lost half-brother mentioned above), who narrates the story of his sojourn in a secret island refuge settled by Protestant exiles from La Rochelle. This tale of a self-destructing utopian state—it founders on a scarcity of women and on a consequent difficulty in matching up marriage partners—is echoed in Cleveland's own colonial adventures: traveling in both hemispheres of the New World with Axminster and Fanny, he refuses asylum in Cuba, only, later on, to find himself lost among the indigenous tribal cultures of Appalachia. Here he becomes, perforce, a king and lawgiver. Upon his own return to England, Cleveland must come to terms with Fanny: rejected by him and apparently compromised, she retires to a nunnery, from which she should perhaps be rescued. Then again, Cleveland thinks seriously about abandoning her altogether and taking up with an attractive young woman named Cécile, whom he thinks he has met for the first time.

The question of what Cleveland's homecoming would mean must have been much on Prévost's mind when he finished volume 4, in 1731. By mentioning Captain Blood and the Rye House Plot, as well as Monmouth, the preface seems to anticipate that this return will be centered on intrigues of power from which the young Cleveland had necessarily fled. Apparently Cleveland himself will be involved in anti-Stuart plots. About this time, Prévost left off writing and took to other projects (outstanding among them *Manon Lescaut*, which concludes the *Mémoires d'un homme de qualité*). The first four volumes of *Cleveland* were published in 1731–32, initially in a French-language edition from Utrecht (chez Étienne Néaulme), then in the English version (a translation into English of a French book that presents itself as a translation from English into French), then, in a censored form, in a French-language edition from Paris. Prévost's novel was something of a pan-European event, albeit an incomplete one. In 1734, tired of waiting for the novel's completion, Prévost's publisher, Néaulme, commissioned a ghostwriter to finish *Cleveland*; all English editions of the complete *Cleveland* use the ghostwriter's volume 5. Prévost himself never published a volume numbered 5; instead he produced a continuation in volumes numbered 6 through 8 (published in 1738–39). It was the ghostwriter, therefore, who had the first word on how Cleveland's return to his homeland should be handled.

After he returns to England the Cleveland of the anonymous continuation is more prone to retirement than ever; made cynical by Clarendon's revelations about the workings of politics, he seeks to withdraw from the public life that he has almost inadvertently established for himself. At the same time, he continues to be drawn into high-level intrigues. Charles II demands his presence at court, so that refusal is either difficult or impossible. Billy, Cleveland's son by Fanny, is fatally mistaken for Charles, as anticipated in Prévost's own preface. (According to the anonymous continuation, if William of Orange ascended to the throne, "our dear son might make himself known to the new monarch," thus effecting a reparation of Cleveland's failed efforts with Cromwell—but William's triumph will occur long after Billy's inadvertent assassination.)[11] In light of such disasters as this one, it is hardly surprising that Cleveland wants to visit once more "the caves which had served [him] as an asylum" some thirty-five years before or that he should discover there one H——, Earl of R——, who of course has an instructive story to tell about his own failed engagement with the world.[12] The frequenting of "subterraneous places" as a possible solution for historical failures remains a theme of profound interest to the ghostwriter hired by Néaulme.[13]

Students of the anonymous continuation to *Cleveland* have suggested that it shaped Prévost's own artistic choices.[14] The pressures were indeed considerable. Not only did he wish to distance himself from his predecessor's rabidly anti-Jesuit opinions (he was attempting a reconciliation with the Jesuits) but he did not want to repeat his better and more faithful efforts. *Cleveland* would end as he, the original author, would have it end. However, since the anonymous writer took many hints from Prévost's own preface, he may in effect have compelled him to change his original plans. This apparently vicious circle often yields striking results. If Rumney Hole features largely in the anonymous continuation, it is neglected in Prévost's concluding volumes: Cleveland will have to find his place in the world without the option of a return to his beginnings. There will be no full circle implicit in his homecoming. Furthermore, if the spurious volume 5 highlights the tragic story of Billy's murder (anticipated, it will be remembered, in Prévost's original preface), then volumes 6 through 8 will focus upon the death of Cleveland's *daughter*, who turns out to be the young woman he is courting, the mysterious Cécile (this daughter supposedly had been eaten by cannibals in the New World but instead had been spirited away by Mrs. Riding). The story of Cécile, particularly her courtship by Monmouth, raises anew the problem of Cleveland's ambition, his confused and divided efforts to match or surpass the power of his father. The suppression of sanctuary corresponds to a new emphasis upon the implicit theme of pretension.

Even aside from the hints afforded by *Cleveland*'s preface, the inclusion of Monmouth in this scheme is hardly surprising. Prévost, it will be recalled, has already shown an interest in doubling the figure of the pretender. Cleveland's youthful travels must be set against those of his sibling Bridge: each brother's narration is the size of a substantial novel, so that the parallel is not only sustained but literally weighty. Bridge, however, is killed off in the course of *Cleveland*, treacherously slain by his supposed friend Gelin after they escape from their flawed Huguenot utopia; Monmouth then appears as a second doppelgänger of Cleveland, and a far more problematic one than the first.

According to Anthony Hamilton's immensely popular *Mémoires du comte de Gramont*, published in French in 1713 and, in English, translated by Walter Scott in 1811, the turning point of Monmouth's earlier career occurred when the king's chief mistress, the duchess of Cleveland, grew jealous of the treatment afforded this beautiful young man. Her own children by Charles were little more than "petit magots" [little baboons] compared with Monmouth, that young Adonis. They would never be legitimated, never get their moment in the limelight. The duchess took revenge by making love to Monmouth. According to Hamilton, the public behavior of his mistress, "cette prétendue belle-mère" [this supposed mother-in-law], made Charles uneasy. He quickly arranged Mr. Crofts's marriage to a great heiress, Anne Scott, already the countess of Buccleuch. It was thus that Mr. Crofts became duke of Monmouth and was given precedence over all dukes not of the blood royal.[15]

Apparently, Prévost had originally planned to involve Cleveland, as well as Monmouth, in the notorious Rye House Plot—by which the pretty little duke was implicated in an attempted assassination of Charles— and then to stage a falling out of some kind between the two bastards. The anonymous continuation takes a related tack, intertwining the story of Billy with controversies about Monmouth's legitimation, a crude but effective way of emphasizing father-son relations and questions of succession, the theme toward which Prévost himself would seem to have been working. By the time he came to write the last books of *Cleveland*, however, he hit on a third way of imagining parallels between Cleveland and Monmouth, both trickier and more scandalous than that of the competing sequel.

In Prévost's continuation the Cleveland-Monmouth parallel is articulated not through a doomed son but through a doomed daughter. Even after Cleveland identifies Cécile as his offspring, the tie between them remains subliminally amorous. He dotes on her; she loves him with a passion so consuming that no other man can ever be a plausible candidate for marriage. If our hero was too distant from his father, he is all too close to his daughter: either way, his position as a link between the generation that precedes him and the generation that follows seems to put an almost intolerable pressure on him, as though no form of succession, royal or familial, dynastic or biological, could ever be smooth. According to the perverse narratological conditions established by Prévost, Cleveland would be perfectly happy only with a woman whom he himself had engendered. His internal conflict over this impossible condition of bliss is suggested indirectly: Cleveland the narrator cannot, in this first-person case study, admit or even recognize all that he is feeling. But Monmouth too is caught between love for Fanny and love for Cécile. He courts first the one, then the other; it remains unclear throughout which one he desires more deeply.[16] He acts where Cleveland himself must repress action.

The doubling of Cleveland's erotic drives is unsettling, not only because of its incestuous aura but also because of its political implications. One might, of course, assume that the name Monmouth is used by Prévost as a sort of easy shorthand. It could well mean nothing more than a certain type of dashing and ruthless rascal, marked by "an incessant melange of vices and virtues" (7:315). The reputation of a historical figure well known among the French would lend a minimal solidity to a characterization otherwise somewhat thin. The allegory of desire would gain circumstantial plausibility. However, this statement of the case does *Cleveland* an injustice. If the triangle of Cécile, Cleveland, and Monmouth is memorable, the reason lies partly in a further dimension of the novel. Monmouth is analogous to Cleveland not only because he desires Cécile but also because of his problematic relations with a father who is a ruler. Monmouth is living proof that kings can love their bastards and even want to make them candidates for kingship. Monmouth represents not only what Cleveland might have been erotically, in some alternate version of history or this novel—an eligible suitor for Cécile, had she not been his daughter—but also what he might have been politically, a pretender in a public line of national dynastic succession.

Cleveland's intentions toward his potential son-in-law fluctuate. At first Monmouth's combination of violent rakishness and high rank make him seem an undesirable, implausible husband for Cécile. "What a sight, I answered without hesitation, that a girl so wise and so discreet should give herself over to feelings to whose fruition she can never, even so slightly, aspire [*prétendre*]" (7:227). Pretension to admission into the royal family seems far beyond Cleveland's dreams: he thinks of interceding with Monmouth's royal family to prevent the match. On the other hand, he is tempted. For Cécile's benefit, Cleveland lists the duke's many social qualifications. She denies that she ever felt anything for him. Warming to his theme, nonetheless, Cleveland presses her to accept Monmouth's hand: should she marry him, she will become "the first lady of England" (7:302). He confesses to himself that he on no account wishes "to lose all the hopes of grandeur that I had conceived for my daughter" (7:309–10). He takes the trouble to inventory his qualifications for admission to the royal family via his daughter's marriage: she is the unique heir of Lord Axminster; the stain of his own origin has been wiped out by his being knighted by Charles II; he is the son of a man who for a long time was, in effect, a king; and his grandfather rendered many services to the Stuarts (7:295). Philosopher that he is, however, he lapses soon after into aphoristic moralizing: "What good would it do to make such claims, and how would it make the heart happy?" (7:313). Nonetheless, happiness is not the only issue, a point that Cleveland recognizes. Son of two parents who were ambitious by nature, he finds himself—at this late juncture—prone to advance his own standing in the world, to come as close as possible to pretending, both in the French and in the recently developed English sense of the term. If Monmouth is a pretender according to the disastrous Stuart tradition (a tradition visible from the vantage point of 1738–39 though not from that of the Restoration), then so, by proxy, is his double, the melancholy father of Cécile.

None of this can come to any good. Prévost choreographs the doubling between Cleveland and Monmouth with skill and cruelty. As Cécile lies on her deathbed, Monmouth has disguised himself as a doctor. In this role he sees her naked. Dropping the disguise, he indulges in excited romantic hyperbole, and this last shock speeds her demise. Monmouth and Cleveland then mourn at the side of her bed, each echoing the other's physical and emotional position.[17] Prévost's identification of Cleveland as a figure akin to Monmouth seems to have left him nowhere to go. Prévost gives us ample reason to believe that the father, more than the lover, kills Cécile: kills her by monopolizing, however unintentionally, her erotic desires, becoming the object of a love that she can neither deny nor fulfill. The duchess of Cleveland, a figure at once absent and present, reminds us that Oedipal dramas, questions of succession, and problems of recognition can be so thoroughly connected as to produce fatal results. Getting from one generation to another—the kind of succession without which history cannot exist—comes to seem intrinsically a progress toward death.

Having presented this nightmare, the novel shifts to one further interpolated narrative. Throughout much of *Cleveland* the normative figure has been Clarendon. Immediately following Cécile's death, Cleveland and his family visit the great historian, who, having been forced "to seek asylum outside my native land" (7:48), is living in France. They find him in mourning for the death of *his* daughter, Anne, duchess of York (since 1660 the wife of the future James II). The tale of Anne Hyde, Cleveland writes, would have merited a full accounting in another part of his history but here, in this place, must be reduced to a small number of events. The offspring of a mere lawyer, she found herself almost a queen. As Clarendon puts it, "I saw the king without children, and the duchess of York my daughter two steps from the throne" (7:48)—two steps, presumably, because Clarendon anticipates that Monmouth will be declared legitimate, as mentioned at 7:56. This proximity to greatness proves a mixed blessing. Possibly, "the obscurity where I am condemned for the rest of my life could be turned someday to the advantage of the most precious part of my blood" (7:55), but when we hear how the current queen lives—the great courtier Buckingham offers to have her kidnapped and packed off to the Americas—greatness seems less desirable. Clarendon's tales of his daughter refer the reader back to Cleveland's predicament under Cromwell; both point up in a new context the problem of succession, especially for those indomitable persons who pretend to thrones.

In the last pages of *Cleveland* Prévost takes one particularly outrageous liberty with the facts: he makes the duchess of York childless, when she actually gave birth to two queens, Mary and Anne (see esp. 7:385ff.). In no time and place has historical fiction depended upon a strictly literal faithfulness to things as they are—fictiveness would otherwise be unobtainable—but this contradiction of an obvious genealogy, one with which everyone in early eighteenth-century England, including Prévost, was familiar, stands out for its brashness. Prévost is perhaps interested in heightening the pathos of Anne's death and Clarendon's loss; even more important is his thematic interest in making this line *come to an end*. The demands of living between everything and nothing—between royalty and fame, on the one hand, and anonymity or utter disappearance from historical process, on the other—governs *Cleveland* in all of its details. Anne's end must be absolute, as was Cécile's. Genealogical continuity is cut off; Cleveland (and his readers) can look into the dark. A fictional creation— as he obviously was, after the highly public dispute with Néaulme—this character is plagued by ontological as well as social insecurities. His inability to enter the historical record, to be recognized by his own father, much less to mix his blood with the blood of kings, is the fundamental condition underlying his narrative. He has left the caves of Devon but can neither return to them nor live wholly in the world. Despite his self-absorbed memoirs, he remains the man who is not there.

Prévost's hero has achieved a calm and apparently nondenominational Christian repose. He is reconciled even with the malevolent Gelin, who reappears as the one-eyed tutor of his sons. There remains only one figure still in unresolved action; naturally, this is Monmouth, who shows up at Cécile's funeral only to be lectured by Fanny (whom he is courting again, with obscene enthusiasm): "She took the occasion to give him a lecture . . . touching on the indecency of his feelings and on the vanity of his hopes" (7:447). The erotic and political pretender is the one part, the one side, of the narrator that remains unassimilable to any system of compromise. Chastised for his presumption, Monmouth leaves abruptly, blundering toward his own encounter with nothingness and fame, and on this note the novel ends. Prévost's prehistory of the duke has more than its share of sequels; by the end of the nineteenth century there would be roughly forty novels about the great rebellion in the west and the disaster of Sedgemoor. None offer so unforgettable a picture of Charles's most and least fortunate bastard.

Considered as a historical novel, *Cleveland* is memorable for its articulation of a paradox with a future. The pretender, not to mention his shadows and doppelgängers, is someone evermore about to be. This figure does not quite belong to the public record, certainly not in the way that an established monarch would belong. (It is in the interests of the winners to obscure the claims of the losers who dared challenge them; pretenders must seem never to have existed.) On the other hand, the pretender cannot be completely expunged from the record of national and dynastic history: some trace of a discarded or rejected monarch's existence always seems to survive, if only in the form of a rediscovered manuscript. Pretenders live in penumbras, close to the spotlight, seldom, if ever, under it directly. Written in a period when the Stuarts could be compared to Perkin Warbeck, when a genealogically authentic claim to royal power receded step by step into the realm of illusion and the fantastic, *Cleveland* offers an apt and original instance of what it means to mix history with fiction.

## In *The Recess*

The English historical novel derives from the French historical novel. One simple way of testing this claim is by opening the *Cambridge Bibliography of English Literature* to the list of miscellaneous or anonymous works of eighteenth-century fiction: an extraordinary number of the books in these columns, historical and otherwise, prove to be translations from works originally published across the Channel. The primacy of French models is hardly surprising: by the time that the English warmed up to historical fiction, in the mid-eighteenth-century, *roman* had given way to *nouvelle historique, nouvelle historique* to the faked memoirs of de Courtilz, and these to the ambitious hybrid narratives constructed by Prévost. These (often overlaid) models were richly suggestive, the more so because so frequently their subject was English, as well as French, history.

Under these circumstances, Sophia Lee's interest in French fiction is easy to understand. At perhaps the busiest moment of her literary career Lee published her translation of Baculard d'Arnaud's novel about Perkin Warbeck (*Varbeck*, 1786), which she allegorized in a preface as a warning to rebellious American colonists. J. M. S. Tompkins has argued that Lee's reading of d'Arnaud helped shape her writing of *The Recess*, published in 1783–85.[18] This observation needs to be supplemented by another point about influence. As first observed by her sister Harriet, Sophia Lee owes a deep debt to one of d'Arnaud's *own* sources, the abbé Prévost, who was also an important model for William Godwin and other late-eighteenth-century English novelists.[19]

The similarities between *Cleveland* and *The Recess* are matters of structure, theme, and tone. The narrative disposition of certain crucial materials announces an intimate connection between the two novels: doubled protagonists in hiding; tales-within-tales, allowing comparison and contrast between them; international adventure mixing romantic disaster with large-scale power politics; the second sibling's meeting a disastrous end; a shift of regime followed by a shift of spotlight to a new generation in which a return to royal status seems possible, only to prove a chimera. So, more generally, does the mournful philosophical sentimentality shared by Prévost and Lee, as well as their sharp interest in questions of duration, of historical change, and of succession within a great national dynasty. *Some* common characteristics of *Cleveland* and *The Recess* are to be found in many other eighteenth-century novels in the French line of historical fiction; no other novels that I know of share all, or even a majority, of them. It is in (and between) these two books that eighteenth-century pretender fiction achieves its distinctive and most fully realized form.

This is not to say that the reader of Prévost has nothing to learn from Lee. *The Recess* is one of those miraculous books that work closely from a distinguished model to a powerfully original effect. Most obviously, Lee chose to write about female pretenders rather than male ones. Salic law, which forbade the succession of women or of those descended in the female line, made the whole idea of a female claimant to a throne obscure or even incomprehensible to the French (even, one might suspect, to a Frenchman writing about England). Female regents, yes (Catherine de Medici achieved legendary status even in her own day); female monarchs, no. Lee takes advantage of a different legal situation and a different history to imagine her long-suffering heroines, Matilda and Ellinor, daughters of Mary, Queen of Scots, and inheritors by right of the English throne. Beyond this founding premise, several further innovations by Lee yield distinctive effects and deserve special attention.[20]

## Authenticity, Chasm, Recess

Prévost's preface seeks to show us obscure events authenticated by famous ones, thus justifying a scheme in which the fabulations of the novelist mingle with matters already part of the public record. At the same time, he locates a critical gap in Cleveland's original memoir—there is no mention of Richard Cromwell's failed government—thus anticipating the novel's interest in questions of generational and dynastic succession. Lee's shorter "Advertisement" follows a similar scheme. Lee accepts Prévost's version of the authentic, a quality that is confirmed by "a wonderful coincidence of events," stamping "the narration with probability," if not certainty.[21] The "coincidence," I take it, is a chronological one, by which actual and invented actions can be successfully integrated into a single, coherent time line: Lee's sisters live through well-known crises of history, such as the Babington plot to assassinate Elizabeth and the defeat of the Spanish Armada; we know that Matilda and Ellinor were real because, for instance, we believe that the Spanish Armada actually was defeated. (That Lee got the date of the Armada's attack wrong is irrelevant in this context.) Continuity and integration are not, however, the sole qualities of *The Recess*: "The depredations of time have left chasms in the story, which sometimes only heightens the pathos" (advertisement). These "chasms" are to be found in each sister's narrative; however, whereas the asterisked ellipses of Matilda's tale are used sparingly, those in Ellinor's are so frequent as to assume a major expressive function. This second sister's account is perused by the first in manuscript; as the ellipses, the "chasms," proliferate, madness overtakes the writer.[22]

Given the source of Ellinor's breakdown, the full force of her "chasms" becomes clear. Ellinor has been blackmailed into denying her parentage; only if she relinquishes her claim to be the legitimate daughter and heir of Mary will her mother's life be spared. "It was surely at this tremendous crisis in my life, my fermented blood first adopted and cherished those exuberances of passion which ever after warped the equality and merit of my character" (178). In other words, she begins her descent into insanity at the moment when she is threatened with either denying her own identity or (through her stubbornness) killing her mother. The connection between parent and child—ruler and possible heir—is shown to be both the point on which the narrative turns and the point that must, in public, remained unmentioned. "My intellects strangely blackened and confused, frequently realized scenes and objects that never existed, annihilating many which daily passed before my eyes" (182). (This incident recalls Cleveland's loss of consciousness on learning of the execution of Charles I; the crisis of one's relations with parents is also, for Lee and Prévost, the crisis of monarchy.) It is the desire for an impossible historical continuity, the link between Mary the pretender and two daughters who are rapidly acquiring their own pretensions, that produces gaps—in the written record, in that time line that is our touchstone of authenticity, and above all in human consciousness, so often and so easily slipping away.

Lee's version of this idea is at once a powerful reading of Prévost and a vivid variation on one of his great themes. Cleveland is a narrator of his own case history whose difficulty in facing his deepest desires and fears is a source of his errors in life. The same is true of Ellinor, but *her* gaps of knowledge and narration are integrated much more fully into the novel. The novelist does not need a mentor of Clarendon's kind to reveal them; the fragmentary condition of Ellinor's manuscript makes the point formally. The authenticity of faithfulness to an established time line is supplemented by the authenticity of a madness that proclaims itself in the breakdown of narrative coherence and the rise of a time-scarred "pathos." (Ellinor's madness, in its turn, prepares us to understand Matilda's quite different failures of understanding, a point to be developed below.)

The Recess not only presents the chasms of time, making their absence visible; it also inquires into how these chasms came about. Lee's project is appropriately centered on the Recess, which is itself a chasm of sorts, an unknown quantity in the geography of England and the timelines of European history. Not unlike Matilda and Ellinor, the Recess is imagined as a possible reality turned into a phantom by the great convulsions of the Reformation, the event that made Mary, Queen of Scots, theologically implausible as a successor to Elizabeth. Time also has its fainting fits. In the individual such fits take the form of unconsciousness or madness. In the larger schemes of national history they take the form of repressed collective memories, facts willed or decreed to be fictions and thus, necessarily, sent into exile. The Recess is thus the appropriate residence for a pair of sisters whose existence cannot be admitted on the record without bringing into question the movements of progress. It is the space of rejected tradition and also, equally, the space of novelistic invention. Invention, it appears, is the discovery of facts that have mysteriously become fictions.

## Traveling and Pretension

According to a widespread medieval standard, one who took sanctuary had to eventually abjure the realm, proceeding to the nearest port and leaving permanently for some other country. Similarly, one who sought political asylum had to quit his native soil in order to do so. Little wonder that tales focused on these institutions tend to take place within a generously conceived geography. Sanctuary and asylum are inherently claustrophobic: not many people would want to be cooped up permanently in a church courtyard or even in a backwater like the Pretender's court at St. Germain-en-Laye. At the same time, the fugitives who seek either form of refuge are likely, should they survive long enough, to end up seeing the world. By a sad but perhaps inevitable turn of fate the claustrophobe is given a chance to experience a new disease: agoraphobia.

Prévost was a committed travel writer and editor; his novels of exotic love and adventure are a substantial part of his oeuvre, as are his extensive editions of classic voyages. Of all his works, however, it is *Cleveland* that uses narratives of travel most artfully and elaborately. The story told by Cleveland's brother Bridge is particularly memorable in this respect, for when he reaches the hidden island kingdom of the Huguenots, he experiences a fulfillment seldom granted in stories of asylum: he encounters a retreat that is also a society in itself. Prévost seems to suggest that if one could only flee far enough, one could, just possibly, reconstitute society in an ideal form, a form characterized by security and justice alike. This virtually self-contained polity breaks down, throwing the evocatively named Bridge back upon his own resources, but here, as elsewhere in *Cleveland* (e.g., Cleveland's own adventures among the indigenous tribes of North America), the need for asylum and the need for a utopia are shown to be connected at their origins.

Lee works her own variation upon the Prévostian scheme. Leicester and Matilda seek asylum in France with a sympathetic relative, Lady Mortimer. By Lady Mortimer's treacherous orders Leicester is assassinated, and Matilda is packed off on an ocean trip to Jamaica, during which she is forced to marry Lady Mortimer's son (this is all part of a scheme to compel her conversion to Catholicism). When they arrive, Mortimer *fils* is killed in a slave rebellion, and Matilda is imprisoned;[23] her newly born daughter, Mary (offspring of Leicester), is raised sympathetically by former slaves, while Matilda watches from captivity. Ellinor follows Essex to Ireland, where he is in the midst of attempting to put down rebels against Elizabeth's rule. "Born and bred in the arms of luxury and prosperity, a distant war but faintly affects our minds; but oh, how tremendous does it appear when once we are driven into its tempestuous seat!—death, ghastly death, assumes a bloody variety of forms; while rapine, famine, sickness, and poverty, fearfully forerun him. . . . Beloved Matilda, born as you were to woe, you saw but one bounded prospect of the infinitude the globe presents to us; the horrors of this were unknown to you" (222). As the reader, though not Ellinor, must realize, Matilda has had the same kind of eye-opening adventures: born into that apparently changeless realm, the Recess, she too has traveled far and seen history made.

Though *asylum* remains an essential part of her heroines' sentimental vocabulary, Lee never lingers over the hope that a retreat like the Recess might be reconstructed in the open, that harmony and security might become the principles of an entire society. For this belief she substitutes the depiction of violent societies riven by self-seeking intrigue. As the court of England, so the globe: there is endless self-promotion at the top, with those beneath scuttling about in an effort to get their own share or to resist depredations from above. If neither novelist is finally willing to suppose that an ideal commonwealth could arise on earth, Prévost is at least willing to toy with this possibility: he has a serious intellectual interest, largely adapted from Fénélon, in imagining perfect systems, whether of ethical conduct or political power. Lee, on the other hand, is fascinated with imagining the rigors of a nightmarish queen's education. On the one hand, the book evokes a triumphalist national history tailored to glorify Elizabeth's reign and all that came from it; on the other, it follows the fortunes of two abandoned royal personages who wander at large among the world's horrors, learning and suffering until they expire in positions of frozen horror, both humbled and exalted by their losses.

## Recessive Narrative

The nature of these losses is traced through a labyrinthine narrative path. Prévost's intricate scheme by which Bridge and Cleveland grow up in the same cave, but separately and successively, and then follow parallel paths in life is reconceived. Lee's plot reaches one of its most illuminating crises in the final pages of part 2, when Matilda flees from the suspicions of Elizabeth I to Lady Arundell's house. Her previous life seems to have vanished from her memory until, in a sudden inspiration, her friend supplies the necessary clue. "How could it escape you," cries Lady Arundell, "that the Recess may still supply a sad and dear asylum till we can judge of circumstances?" (96). Separated from Ellinor, who must remain at court as a maid-in-waiting to Elizabeth, Matilda and Leicester hasten to the Abbey, searching out "that sad and dear asylum" recalled in such timely fashion. "At the well known prospect my heart dilated—my eyes wandered over the whole with sensations our first home only can excite. . . . 'Here,' cried I, checking my horse, 'here we shall be safe—ah, more than safe, here we may be happy!' " (97). When she enters the Recess, however, she finds herself "violently seized by several persons" (98); the asylum has become a prison, benevolent only in containing a secret trapdoor, through which flight fortunately proves possible for Matilda and Leicester.

Lee dwells twice on the Recess's transformation from asylum to prison, initially in Matilda's first-person narration and then, some hundred pages later, at the very center of the novel, in Ellinor's corresponding account. It turns out that Ellinor entered the Recess just a few minutes after Matilda had been captured there; Ellinor had arrived, she tells us, as a prisoner of "ruffians" who captured her without realizing her identity (172). It might seem that Lee is preparing to duplicate Matilda's earlier disillusionment, but this is not exactly the case. The effect she aims at is more devastating yet. Through Matilda we experience a return to the Recess, and then, through Ellinor's confessional letter, we experience a return to the return. The doubling of Lee's twinned stories culminates in the charged space of a childhood sanctuary, as if we were back in the time before history began for this novel's two heroines.

The moment when Lee's prototypical sanctuary fails to protect the sisters, to shelter their delicate position between fact and fiction, is sustained, elaborated, and extended by nested narrations. The novelist both exploits and negates the instantaneous revelation of those lightning flashes, the illumination by which Matilda last sees her "first home"; in the crossing of her own story with Ellinor's it is as though the flash has become a steady, blinding beam, a single moment an eternity. "Alas, my sister, call to mind your own feelings, and guess at mine when I once more opened my eyes in the great room of our Recess . . . that room where once the portraits of our parents smiled peace and security on their now desolate offspring—how hideous was the change!—its bare walls, grimed with a thousand uncouth and frightful images, presented only a faint picture of the present possessors, on whose hardened faces I dared not fix my fearful eyes" (173). Ellinor's disillusionment repeats and sustains Matilda's. By means of this ingenious formal arrangement, the Recess simultaneously gains a history and is forever destroyed as a possible retreat, a point of hope.

The double narration of the Recess's failure prepares a turn in the novel's tone, indeed in its direction. A new fear arises to haunt the sisters. Its first full expression is given to Ellinor, who is not only more unstable than Matilda but more sensitive as well. At court she soon realizes that she and her sister "were all an illusion" (157). Like other illusions, therefore, they could vanish without a trace. Imprisoned in St. Vincent's Abbey long after Matilda has quit its walls for good, Ellinor undergoes the sequence of blackmailing and bullying interrogations that will eventually precipitate her madness. "Impelled thus by tyranny down the precipice of fate, my swift course seemed ready to bury me in the gulph it overhangs" (180). Ellinor is on the verge of dropping off into an abyss; she is threatened with social annihilation, both because she is losing her mind and because she is being pressed to renounce her genealogical claims. Should she sign the documents thrust in front of her, her right to royal status will vanish. During their first period in the Recess the sisters had no formed aspirations beyond it; now they are pretenders par excellence, set on a path that leads to everything—or, as Ellinor increasingly sees, to nothing.

## Pretension, Tyranny, Eros

The perennial complaint about the French historical novel before Scott is that it attributed all public actions to the private fortunes of love. This formula—familiar in the present day in thirty or forty operas, many of them based on the novels in question—has often seemed reductive, but in the right hands it can yield considerable insight. Prévost's use of the connection between love and history contrasts illuminatingly with Lee's. Throughout Cleveland's life, eros and ambition are oddly intertwined, so that even when he courts Fanny in the caves of Devon (far removed from society, it would seem), he becomes aware of the pressures of social rank, dwelling on the paradox by which he is at once higher than her (son of the ruler of England) and lower (not an aristocrat at all, unlike his beloved). This peculiar bind also informs his relationship with Cécile, by whom he hopes to repair the break with public status and public power entailed by his father's rejection of him. Cécile will marry a bastard son of a powerful ruler, thus confirming the validity of Cleveland's life, his own social status, and uniting his own blood with that of the dynasty his father sought to eliminate. It is almost as though he is attempting to switch fathers, to claim descent from Charles I instead of from his rival and his murderer. Prévost thus links eros and pretension; pretending to a woman's hand and to a throne are analogous aspirations. For Cécile to marry Monmouth is for Cleveland to reappear definitely and irreversibly on the stage of history. Cécile, however, must die, turned in, erotically, on her own family tree, committed to the impossible dream of reinstituting a family by marrying her father. Her incestuous love for Cleveland is the sign of her inability—and therefore his—to assume a position on the stage of history. (Many real-life dynasties have died out for related though less sensational reasons—i.e., not enough exogamy.)

After Leicester's intrusion into the Recess, the shape of Lee's novel, and of her own fascination with pretension and eros, begins to reveal itself. Leicester is a favorite and almost a pretender; he hopes to use his position as a way to the throne of England. He might marry an aging queen, who would then die and leave him to rule as he saw fit. These motives are not stated quite so crudely, certainly not in Matilda's account of her own life, which occupies the first half of *The Recess*, but Leicester's actions can all be understood in terms of ambition. Even if his doting spouse is not inclined to do so, her sister is less reticent. Unburdened by the illusions of love for Leicester, Ellinor sees his manipulative side. His marriage to Matilda seems to her as calculated as his flirtations with Elizabeth, for if the one is queen in actuality, the other is well placed to succeed her. Thus emerges the Leicester familiar to a slightly later generation from Schiller's historical fantasia on the theme of Mary Stuart and Queen Elizabeth, *Maria Stuart* (1800).

This situation does not prevent Ellinor from falling into a similar trap. She secretly marries a schemer bolder and more blatant than Leicester: the earl of Essex, who also courts Elizabeth and is also pleased, for his own political reasons, to be affianced to a daughter of the Queen of the Scots. Essex counsels Ellinor, "Let us then adopt the views of Lord Leicester, who certainly meant by the most watchful policy, to pave the way for your sister's succession. . . . I will boldly present to the people of England another blooming Queen—they will with joy adopt you" (214–15). Not "every pretender" (83) who courts Matilda or Ellinor has his eye on the throne—"the pretensions of Sidney" (83) for Matilda's hand are in this sense disinterested—but no one who learns their true identity can afterwards ignore it. It is typical of this novel's distinctive perversity that when Leicester must conceal his marriage to Matilda from Elizabeth, he tells her that the sisters are actually the daughters of Lady Jane Grey, a genealogy almost as unacceptable as the one it conceals. (Jane Grey's sister Catherine was a leading pretender during the reign of Elizabeth; her secret marriage to a highly placed courtier led Elizabeth to imprison her, a circumstance that not only is mentioned by Matilda but, presumably, was one of the novelist's inspirations.) Even Leicester's lie reveals the fundamental truth about Matilda and Ellinor. To court one of these sisters is to declare that one seeks a throne.

## Generation and Succession

The throne remains unattainable. If only to keep going, however, a pretender story must sustain a spark of optimism, must discover untapped opportunities, as though one of the pretender's attempts to enter the historical record as a monarch might actually succeed, against all odds and

against the reader's knowledge of the most elementary history. Like Prévost, Lee focuses on succession—that great eighteenth-century problem,
as suggested by the names of several impenetrable wars[24]—as a pretender's
last and most tantalizing hope. Like Prévost, she traces the process by which
a beloved daughter fails to cooperate with a parent's aspirations, thus
bringing the parent to a crisis of self-understanding. Matilda has attempted
to link her daughter Mary's fortune with those of Prince Henry, son of
James I, himself the son of Mary, Queen of Scots. "With what secret transport," she exclaims, "did my soul welcome a Stuart worthy that name,
glorious for so many ages!" (284). Henry is her secret dream, the good heir
with whom her daughter could produce a triumphant dynasty and through
whom she herself would become an accepted figure of national history.
However, Mary is in love with the corrupt earl of Somerset rather than
with his great-souled rival. The prince soon dies, and his father, the ma-
leficent James, wipes out all evidence of Matilda's royal descent. After Mary
herself expires, poisoned, Matilda is cast out upon the world. She is not
even important enough to be held in prison any longer. She will finish her
days "in so narrow an asylum as an inn" and then, she assures us, find a
"nameless grave" (325–26).

This conclusion builds on Prévost, but not without changing a
fundamental point of *Cleveland*. After Cécile's death her father learns a
truth about himself that is meant to be more generally applicable. (In the
opening pages of the novel, history had been characterized by Cleveland
as the practical side of morality; the useful part of historical narrative is
therefore exemplary by definition. This point is emphasized by Cleveland's
last meeting with Clarendon, upon the death of *his* daughter.) Our hero
achieves wisdom by escaping his self-obsession, by ceasing to think of himself as a unique instance of misfortune. Retirement and rejection of ambition become, paradoxically, *sociable* acts, ways of sealing a reconciliation
with the world, not to mention deity itself. The pretender side of Cleveland
is given over to Monmouth, whose ungovernable energies are otherwise
set aside, expelled from the value system upheld by the novel. *The Recess*,
by contrast, dwells to the end upon its heroine's sorrows; that these sorrows
are doubled, twinned, is only a way of insisting more vividly upon their
uniqueness. Cécile's death brings Cleveland to an awareness of his humanity (at least it does so in theory; one might wonder whether he's fully
absorbed the lesson). Mary's death leaves Matilda alone with her singular
misfortunes, which can be understood at a remove (by a sympathizing
friend across the Channel, to whom her narration is ultimately addressed)
but without producing anything approaching a return to a grounded com-

munity. Not only will Matilda fail to found a dynasty but she will lose any place at all in the historical record—as opposed to the novelistic one.

Along the same lines, it is hard to imagine Prévost's novel being named something like *Le Souterrain*, which is the title of the contemporary French translation of *The Recess*. Even without the shifts forced by competition from the false continuation, the cave where Cleveland spends his youth could never have been so much the center of this book as the recess itself is of Lee's. Aside from obvious direct influences, her novel emerges from roughly the same generic cross as his; both works mix faux memoir, travel narrative, historical reconstruction, and sentimental meditation (further inflected, in Lee's case, by a powerfully Gothic bent). All the same, in the last analysis Prévost's *Cleveland* tells a tale of character formation based on the testing of theoretical philosophical premises; in his swerve from Cromwell to the Stuarts, the English Philosopher enacts dissonances and incoherences in national identity, but it is finally ethics—one might say, the state of his soul—with which he and his author are concerned. The lessons of the cave must be tested and to some extent found wanting in the real world outside it, a world, furthermore, where the Stuarts and their sympathizers are at least temporarily triumphant, a point that would qualify the attractions of even the most alluring underground hideaway. Lee's *Recess*, by contrast, dwells much more fully upon the dilemma of a haunted, only half-real place that persists as an influence on history and historical yearnings past anyone's expectations, even though, like the Stuarts whom it shields, it is always on the point of extinction. Up above that subterranean retreat of repressed Catholicism—and, given Mary's history, repressed Frenchness—England is ruled first by a woman strangely like a man and then by a man who is curiously effeminate. We are not meant to like this Elizabeth or this James, but we certainly perceive their undoubted success as rulers and, perhaps subliminally, connect it with gender ambiguity, itself the sign of a power to unite or embody opposites (sometimes a useful talent for a politician). Down in the Recess, conversely, an overwhelmingly maternal, female, and familial world is first invaded by those sharp male operators Leicester and Essex—as though we were in a kind of proto–National Tale, where courtship can articulate the relations of radically unequal states—then blotted out by the concerted efforts of a great propaganda machine, another kind of state creator.[25] I would not presume to sum up definitively this difficult and rather peculiar network of associations, in which heterosexual romance and a doomed ghost nation flirting with annihilation are memorably aligned against an emerging modern state. Lee has a knack for disrupting one's notions of what the marginal might be or how it would operate within the problematic realm of historical time; perhaps, read ambitiously enough, her book could perhaps make us start all over again in evaluating novelistic myths of state formation as they came to fruition during the eighteenth century.

At the very least, her *Recess* was rich enough to survive its own, immediate popularity, the sort of renown that spawns bad imitations. Over the space of more than half a century the territory opened up by Prévost and then given a yet fuller fantasy form by Lee would provide a starting point for a great onrush of (largely) historical fiction. A reader accustomed to ask of the public record, What has been left out? How was it made, or made up? How else could these events have happened? and, How do they define or undermine the official record, the public story of the nation? was prepared to discover new pretenders and new forms of pretension lurking in the hidden asylums of time. As an epilogue, I will glance at some of the books on which such readers could draw.

When Walter Scott published *Waverley* in 1814, both Prévost and Lee remained writers of strong current interest, outstanding figures in a vital and still current line of sentimental and historical novelists (including Madame de Genlis and Sophie Cottin, to cite two of Scott's widely read French contemporaries).[26] Though Scott himself did not typically produce their kind of book, he did write, often very self-consciously, for an audience used to reading it. The results are decisive. It is not just that many of the Waverley novels chart the decline of the Stuarts, through Mary, Queen of Scots, all the way to the hapless Charles Edward (the crucial historical figure in both *Waverley* and *Redgauntlet* [1824]) but that the pretender's diminishments, his or her tendency to become a lurking political specter, are identified with the fate of Scotland. Furthermore, though this kind of leap could perhaps have occurred elsewhere, Scott's choice of subject makes it especially apt. Politically speaking, "North Britain," as it was sometimes called, was not a nation at all: since the Act of Union in 1707 it had been ruled continuously from London. Scott's lifetime project was to glorify a half-existing political entity (the distinctiveness of whose legal system and currency he defended publicly and fiercely) while trying to ensure that its integration into the British empire would be complete even if it were accompanied by a certain inexpungeable nostalgia. In sum, Scotland itself, a country whose nationalism could not be identified with the power of a central state, took on the nature, the sinking, spiraling, and ultimately recessive charisma, of those characters who yearn to rule and are never quite able to do so, who maintain their regal quality while losing, or failing to gain, the power of monarchs.[27] This nationalism of the loser was partly a reversion to the earliest and most archaic form of national organization, James Collins's "family corporation"; it also became a means of compromising with a disputable though superficially firm imperial settlement. If the revolt of 1745 had succeeded, it might well have made Scotland (like England itself, under Charles II) into a French "client-state."[28] Under those circumstances the Stuarts would have assumed a different long-term significance for Scottish politics. In Scott, by contrast, the failed mystique of Charles Edward and his ancestors could be used as a general repository of cultural memory, while confirming the integration of a small country into a larger one. Thus, the political-literary dialogue embodied by *Cleveland* and *The Recess* found its appropriate home in a crucial "periphery": a century-long habit of reading about those memorable historical nonpersons, dynastic pretenders, had at once shifted to a new geographical position and assumed a new kind of relevance. Both Prévost's use of Stuart lore and Lee's adaptation of it found a new meaning under the Caledonian sun.

And not only there. The history of France—its progress under the Bourbons, and then under Napoleon, towards a centralized and hegemonic status among the nations of Europe—is drastically different from that of Scotland. All the same, whatever the author of *Waverley* may have taken from French models, he was able to give back with interest: a first wave of historical fiction à la Scott (in novels by de Vigny, Merimée, Balzac, and Hugo, among others) was succeeded by the amazing successes of Alexandre Dumas, especially during the 1840s, culminating in that richest, if also most miscellaneous, of pretender sagas, *Le Vicomte de Bragelonne* (1847–50), on the Man in the Iron Mask. From Dumas's perspective, the fall of the pretender was inextricably wrapped up with the fabrication of a powerful centralized bureaucracy by Colbert and Louis XIV; as the novelist well understood, such a bureaucracy can outlast and even replace the charisma of dynastic monarchy—which might be said to have collapsed when, at the accession of Louis-Philippe to the throne (1830), that last great Royalist, Chateaubriand, gave up on the Bourbons and went out to feed his chickens. In the three-musketeers cycle, to tell the tale of a great pretender is to chart the fall not just of a false king but of the *institution* of kingship, and of those heroes (like d'Artagnan) who devoted their lives to defending the French monarchy. What is left behind when the monarchy goes is an enormous apparatus of centralized government; here, in a somewhat ironic turn of events for worshipers of heroes and adventure, may lie France's future, its patriotic identity.

Around the same time, the work of Dumas's friend and sometime collaborator Gérard de Nerval attempted an even more drastic Gallicization of the theme of the wandering pretender that Prévost, then Lee, then Scott, had made so central to the genre of historical fiction. In 1839 Nerval had published his *Biographie singulière*, about Raoul Spifame, a contemporary of Henri II, who not only looks like his sovereign prince but comes to believe that he does in fact rule France. Accompanied by an equally deluded court poet, Spifame attains a purely literary kingship, enclosed in a fantasy to which Henri himself gives moral assent and financial support; on the other hand, this hermetic pretender also issues decrees proposing reforms that are adopted long after his time: secretly, the coddled, confused, and basically helpless imitation king embodies the future of enlightened government reform. *Les Faux Saulniers* (1850) takes this logic further yet. A *faux saulnier* is a dealer in contraband salt and thus a rebel against the great, much-hated tax monopoly of the *ancien régime*. Drawing from well-known experimental works by Laurence Sterne and Denis Diderot, Nerval's weird exercise in historical fiction—specifically designated as such by means of a perverse verbal game in which the author keeps denying that he is writing a historical novel[29]—zigzags between two stories. One centers on the abbé de Bucquoy, an eighteenth-century rebel who gets into trouble with the authorities for trying to make contact with salt smugglers. The bibliophile Nerval pursues a copy of a book by de Bucquoy while more or less simultaneously narrating his adventures, culminating first in the abbé's escape from the Bastille and then in his flight from France. Further, in an intercalated narrative, Nerval also follows the adventures of one of the abbé's ancestors, his great-aunt Angélique de Longueval, forced by an imprudent marriage into exile and constant, debilitating wandering. Angélique and the abbé both fall into the pretender's pattern of heroic, desolate, and generally exhausting cosmopolitanism: they are martyred nonpersons who cannot stop anywhere for long. Like pretenders, too, they threaten established authority, familial in Angélique's case, governmental in the abbé's—the private and public sides of the old dynastic dilemma, as though the saga of the Stuarts, or the later Bourbons, had been not only privatized but split in half. Finally, in *Les Illuminés* (1852) the tale of Raoul Spifame becomes a prelude to the tale of the abbé Bucquoy, lifted wholesale from *Les Faux Saulniers*, as well as to several other studies of eccentric protosocialists: prophets of a revived and enlightened public power difficult to conceptualize before the French Revolution except perhaps as a form of folly or delusion.[30] In this case, the phantom state of the wandering pretender corresponds, not to the ambiguous nationhood of a small, half-colonized state, but rather to a utopian prediction about the future of government—its removal *altogether* from the hands of kings.

That Nerval's pretender should finally become a protosocialist revolutionary will seem less odd if one recalls, yet again, Collins's formulation about the composite nature of the nation-state, a "quadrille" among four elements—the family corporation, the polyglot empire, the central state apparatus, and popular national consciousness. The first of these ingredients, on which most pretender stories turn, persists long after Prévost or Lee because of the ways in which it can be identified with, or shifted on to, one or more of the other three elements. In addition, this dizzying structural mobility is intensified by the thematic centrality of exile and wandering—an enforced cosmopolitanism—in all the books I have mentioned. Historically, England and Scotland have provided frequent avenues of escape for homeless Bourbons, and France has just as often returned the compliment, haboring, however grudgingly, a host of (doubly) deracinated Stuarts. These memorably hopeless flights back and forth across the Channel make visible both the decline of absolute monarchy and the rise of historical fiction, a genre obsessively concerned with following the fortunes of failed king or queens. Did fiction even, in some way, supplant the pretenders it chronicled? Around the middle of the seventeenth century a clever prophet might have suggested that where monarchs are, the novel shall be. However, without arguing for quite so drastic a symmetry, one can understand this most widespread and most elusive of genres not only as a creator and product of popular nationalism but also as an instrument for investigating the phantomlike aura that persists even in the most substantial modern states.

## Notes

1. This suggestion was made to me by Richard Sieburth.

2. Richard Maxwell, "Pretenders in Sanctuary," *Modern Language Quarterly* 61 (June 2000): 287–358.

3. To use Howard Bloch's phrases, not "the solidarity of brothers that included both agnatic and cognatic relations" but "the more vertically pitched consanguineal kin-group" (see Bloch, *Medieval Misognyny and the Invention of Western Romantic Love* [Chicago: University of Chicago Press, 1991], 191).

4. See James Collins, "State-Building in Early Modern Europe: The Case of France," in *Beyond Binary Histories: Re-Imagining Eurasia to C. 1830*, ed. Victor Lieberman (Ann Arbor: University of Michigan Press, 1999, 159–89; cf., in the same volume, Victor Lieberman's introductory comments, esp. 48–50.

5. In other words, while resurgences of dynastic feeling are always possible in later versions of nationalism and the nation-state, they are complicated by and filtered through the other three developments.

6. On Prévostian "penumbras," see Claire Eliane Engel, *Figures et aventures du XVIIIe siècle: Voyages et découvertes de l'abbé Prévost* (Paris: Editions "Je Sers," 1939), 61.

7. See the edition edited by Steve Larkin, Antoine Prévost, *Le Pour et contre*, Studies on Voltaire and the Eighteenth Century, no. 309 (Oxford: Voltaire Foundation, 1993), 1:223. The Fronde was the aristocratic and parliamentary rebellions against Cardinal Mazarin, 1648–53.

8. Antoine Prévost, *Histoire de M. Cleveland*, vols. 4–7 of *Oeuvres choisies de Prévost* (Paris: Leblanc, 1810), 4:1. Subsequent references to this edition appear in the text; the translations are my own.

9. On the connections between *Cleveland* and *Candide*, see R. A. Francis, "Prevost's *Cleveland* and Voltaire's *Candide*," Studies on Voltaire and the Eighteenth Century, no. 208 (Oxford: Voltaire Foundation, 1982), 295–303.

10. For a particularly good example, see the section of *Cleveland* in which, following his mother's death, the hero first lurks in his corner of Rumney Hole ("I neither grew weary of my recess, nor desir'd to quit it"), then, having encountered Fanny in her own separate chamber, experiences first love ("at last, by examining all the recesses of my Heart methoughts I discover'd that it was bashfulness had kept me from speaking") [Antoine Prévost and an anonymous author], *The Life and Entertaining Adventures of Mr. Cleveland, Natural Son of Oliver Cromwell, Written by Himself*, 2nd ed., 3 vols. (London: T. Astley: 1741), 1:41, 85.

11. Ibid., 3:225.

12. Ibid., 3:237.

13. Ibid., 3:255.

14. On the anonymous continuation of *Cleveland* and its relation to Prévost's own conclusion, see Philip Stewart, "Sur la conclusion du *Cleveland* de Prévost: L'Influence de la suite apocryphe," *Revue de Littérature Comparée* 51 (1977): 54–58; and R. A. Francis, "Prévost's *Cleveland* and Its Anonymous Continuation," *Nottingham French Studies* 23 (May 1984): 12–23.

15. Anthony Hamilton, *Mémoires du comte de Gramont* (Paris: Garnier Frères, n.d.), 385, 386.

16. This is the position worked out by Alan Singerman in *L'Abbé Prévost: L'Amour et la morale* (Geneva: Droz, 1987), 125–33.

17. See ibid., 131.

18. J. M. S. Tompkins, *The Popular Novel in England, 1770–1800* (Lincoln: University of Nebraska Press, 1961), 234–35. For a more skeptical view of Lee's possible debt to d'Arnaud, see April Alliston's introduction to her edition of *The Recess; or, A Tale of Other Times* (Lexington: University Press of Kentucky, 2000), xv.

19. On Harriet Lee's comment about *Cleveland*, see Alliston, introduction to *The Recess*, xxxix n. 15. Godwin appears to have been a suitor for the hand of Lee's sister Harriet at one point. His experiment with the Prévostian historical novel is

seen at its best in a book like *Mandeville* (1817). Other English imitators of Prévost included Charlotte Smith and Clara Reeve.

20. Among recent treatments of *The Recess*, see particularly April Alliston, *Virtue's Faults: Correspondences in Eighteenth-Century British and French Women's Fiction* (Stanford: Stanford University Press, 1996), on "secret communications" and the transmission of history in Lee; and Jayne Elizabeth Lewis, *Mary Queen of Scots: Romance and Nation* (London: Routledge, 1998), situating *The Recess* in the long line of literary and historical works centered on Mary, Queen of Scots.

21. Advertisement (unpaginated) to *The Recess* in Alliston's edition. Subsequent references to this edition appear in the text.

22. See Katie Trumpener, *Bardic Nationalism: The Romantic Novel and the British Empire* (Princeton: Princeton University Press, 1997), 112.

23. A serious effort to evoke this phase of Jamaican history might more plausibly concentrate on buccaneer raids or the extermination of the Arawak Indians.

24. Tom Nairn comments, "Popular recollection of the 18th century is clouded by Successions. Few can recall from their history classes why the War of the Spanish Succession or that of the Austrian Succession (1740–48) was so important, or remember much about the 1756–63 follow-up, the Seven Years War." Nairn goes on to suggest that "Charles Edward Stuart's attempt on the British throne would be better called the War of the British Succession (1745–6)" (see Nairn, "Diary," *London Review of Books*, 9 May 1996, 21).

25. On the origins of the National Tale, around the same time as *The Recess*, see Trumpener, *Bardic Nationalism*, esp. 128–57 and 328 n. 45.

26. On the sentimental side of this sentimental/historical matrix, see Margaret Cohen, *The Sentimental Education of the Novel* (Princeton: Princeton University Press, 1999). Scott's interest in Prévost is suggested by his decision to name the hero of *The Pirate* (1822) Cleveland; his interest in Lee by, among other things, his reappropriation of the famous festivities at Kenilworth in the novel of that title (1821).

27. The continuing use of Jacobite lore by Scottish nationalists well after Scott is chronicled in Murray Pittock, *The Invention of Scotland: The Stuart Myth and the Scottish Identity, 1638 to the Present* (London: Routledge, 1991).

28. See the comments of Nairn, "Diary," 21. Nairn reports sightings of bumper stickers in a parking lot at a reenactment of the battle of Culloden (where Charles Edward suffered a definitive defeat): "No doubt whatever as to the winner: Écosse." Here the identification with France is a way of saying "not English."

29. It is a running joke in *Les Faux Saulniers* that Nerval is *not* writing a historical novel; he could not possibly be doing so since under Napoleon III fictions in feuilleton form have become illegal. Of course, by making these denials so conspicuously, Nerval implies that *Les Faux Saulniers* does belong to the genre of historical fiction, constituting, indeed, a quintessential if highly unorthodox example of it. The author thus defies and perhaps triumphs over the sort of arbitrary power from which Angélique and the abbé once suffered.

30. The tale of Angélique, correspondingly, is reallotted to *Les Filles du Feu* (1854), replicating on a large scale the gender division of *Les Faux Saulniers*, with its male and female plots.

FRANÇOISE LIONNET

# Gender, Empire, and Epistolarity: From Jane Austen's *Mansfield Park* to Marie-Thérèse Humbert's *La Montagne des Signaux*

Jane Austen first published *Mansfield Park* in May 1814, the year the Treaty of Paris was signed by England and France, marking the end of the Napoleonic Wars. The publication of an innocuous novel of manners focused on the private lives of its characters and the signature in Paris by two imperial powers of a political treaty is a historic coincidence. These two events of seemingly incomparable scale are unrelated, yet they form part of the same discursive realm, and this telling coincidence highlights their connection. Together, these events mark the beginnings of the multilingual literary crossings that would become the hallmark of colonial and postcolonial Mauritian literature.

 *Mansfield Park* begins against a background of colonial history, even if this background is peripheral to the actual development of the plot and to the description of family mores. An exchange of letters between Lady Bertram and her sister Mrs. Price allows the reader to discover the existence of Sir Thomas's plantation in Antigua, in the British West Indies. Sir Thomas's imminent departure for the small island of Antigua and his long absence from Mansfield Park color the atmosphere at the great house, inscribing in filigree, within Austen's narrative, the conditions of possibility of Marie-Thérèse Humbert's 1994 autobiographical novel, *La Montagne des Signaux*. Mauritius is a small tropical island that survived on a plantation culture not unlike Antigua's in the eighteenth and early nineteenth centuries.

*La Montagne des Signaux* depicts everyday life in the 1950s, and woven into its narrative structure and thematic organization is a subtle engagement with problems of gender and representation, formal education and the act of writing. Humbert provides a contemporary articulation of issues that originated in the signature of the 1814 treaty and the changes it ratified in the faraway colony. Echoing Jane Austen's self-reflexive cultural and narrative transgressions of gender and power in *Mansfield Park*, Humbert's novel stages the circulation of written texts between center and periphery, foregrounding the importance of the written word and the ambiguous authority it bestows on those who share in a common history of cultural literacy. Together, *Mansfield Park* and *La Montagne des Signaux* demarcate what I would call a transcolonial zone, an inverted simulacrum of the literary Channel zone. This transcolonial zone reproduces, in an antipodal cultural context, the circulation of narrative traditions across the English Channel, adding a third pole, a virtual site of exchange between France and Britain, located in the Indian Ocean region and promulgated by the signing of this political treaty.

This 1814 treaty was a juridical act that had a considerable impact on the colonial holdings of Britain and France, since it sanctioned the consolidation of British imperial possessions at the expense of France's assets. If this political Channel-crossing signaled, as a result of Napoleon's mistakes, the decline of France in the colonies of the New World (in the Indian Ocean as well as in the Americas), it also changed the course of history for the inhabitants of these dominions. The Treaty of Paris can thus be viewed as one of the founding events of modern colonial history. As a written document, signed and sealed in Paris, it decreed the fate of many whose oral cultures bore no official or legitimate comparison to the literate and distant civilizations of Europe. It endorsed the transfer of the island of Mauritius from Napoleon's France to the British crown. It would thus seal the fate of this colony and its Francophone and Creolophone population for more than a century and half, until the declaration of Independence in 1968 and the accession to the status of republic in 1992. The British colonial system of education has molded the everyday lives and political institutions of Mauritians since 1814, and it continues to do so, even if the citizens of the island have also looked to other nations, such as France or India, for cultural guidance. Today the republic remains a member of the British Commonwealth.

The first half of the nineteenth century had a crucial impact on the colony: after the British parliamentary debates of 1806 and the official prohibition of the international slave trade in 1807, European public opinion was ignited against the existence of slavery. The abolitionist movement increased in numbers and intensity, leading up to formal emancipation in 1835, years before France, the United States, or Brazil would follow suit. It was during that period that the modern history of Mauritius became clearly defined. The slave trade continued clandestinely until 1824. English became (and still is) the official language of political documents, but French and Creole remained the principal vehicular languages, protected by the rhetoric of the 1814 treaty, which guaranteed the cultural autonomy of the former French colony. The landowners and planters, fearing the inevitability of abolition, encouraged the hiring of indentured laborers from India to work on the sugar plantations. The multiethnic character of the island today, powerfully present in the best of its literature, dates back to that unsettled period of its history. The status of that literature, its self-reflexive questionings of its legitimacy as literature, I argue, can be related back to nineteenth-century doubts and inquiries about power and literacy.

These questionings seem to me to have been propelled, on the political level, by the signature of the treaty and, on the cultural level, by what Ian Watt has termed "the rise of the novel" and Nancy Armstrong has called "the historical conditions that women have confronted as writers,"[1] which, Armstrong argues, Watt's explanations ignore. Literacy and representation are intimately bound up with these "historical conditions" that have marked the marginalized subjects of the European Republic of Letters. In her history of domestic fiction, Armstrong argues that "the modern individual was first and foremost a woman"[2] and that women's writing was the major force in the creation of the modern middle class.

Colonial and postcolonial women writers have played with and destabilized the historically gendered distinction between the public sphere of political events and the private arena of family life that male political activism has tended to reinforce at the expense of women's public roles in various independence struggles. From Austen to Humbert, women writers have skillfully deployed an acute awareness of the limits of this gendered distinction. Austen and Humbert display a similarly subtle understanding of the way questions of proximity and power were played out not just in public documents that legislated colonial rule but also in private correspondence that materialized issues of distance and periphery. Their novels call attention to the use of a form—the letter—that was used to marginalize this genre of women's writing. Despite many intertextual references to British literary texts, Humbert never actually alludes to Austen's work. However, she explores, through the trope of letters, the aesthetics and politics of language and representation and the subversive use of writing by women confined to marginal domestic or geographic spaces.

The role of epistolarity in both novels is key to understanding the constant tension between different forms of communication, as well as the function of education in the metropole and its colonies. Humbert's account of the forms of interaction available to her characters during the last decades of the colonial period reveals a melancholic desire for the impossibility of unmediated exchange, while mirroring her continued engagement with the political and literary past of her island. For Jane Austen, issues of authority and authorship are thematized in *Mansfield Park* through a contrasting use of different forms of communication: conversations, epistolary exchanges, and the staging of a play that reveals character flaws. For Humbert, texts within texts are a means of raising questions of literacy and identity, as well as an ambiguous expression of her distance from, and fascination by, both the British and the French metropoles.

These metropoles continue to cast a very long shadow on the educational institutions of the island. Like other authors who critique traditional institutions (colonial schools and canonical literature) and yet embark on aesthetic projects that clearly owe a great deal to the "classics" of Western and/or Francophone literature, Humbert exhibits the ambivalence (as theorized by Homi Bhabha) that resides at the heart of the postcolonial literary enterprise. In *La Montagne des Signaux* she underscores the social distinction granted by a prestigious scholarship (the "bourse d'Angleterre") and the cultural capital that is attached to the prospects of a formal European education for the colonial student:

> April Rouve, l'intellectuelle de la famille, le petit génie qui obtiendra forcément toutes les bourses—surtout, quand elle aura dix-huit ans, la plus convoitée de toutes: la "bourse d'Angleterre", la Grande Bourse comme dit Dolly avec emphase, celle qui vous paie le voyage en Angleterre et les études dans une université anglaise. . . . Etre "boursier d'Angleterre", à Maurice, n'est-ce pas mieux que de remporter la médaille d'or aux jeux Olympiques, mieux même, assurément, que d'être anobli par sa Très Gracieuse Majesté? Les noms des vainqueurs sont proclamés dans tous les journaux de l'île; ils sont interviewés, acclamés, portés en triomphe. . . . Des vedettes, je vous dis, de véritables monstres sacrés, les jeunes lauréats de la Bourse d'Angleterre.

> [April Rouve, the intellectual one, the wunderkind who will of course win all the awards—especially, at age eighteen, the most

sought after: the "scholarship from England," the Big Scholarship, as Dolly emphasizes, the one that pays for your trip to England and for studying in an English university. . . . Winning this scholarship in Mauritius, isn't it better than winning the gold medal at the Olympics, even better, surely, than being ennobled by Her Most Gracious Majesty? The names of the winners are announced in all the newspapers of the island; they are interviewed, cheered, carried in triumph. . . . Stars, I tell you, real sacred monsters, those winners of the Scholarship from England.][3]

Such a theme is a *locus classicus* of postcolonial literature in general and Francophone literature in particular. Many writers, notably Joseph Zobel in his Antillean novel *Rue Cases-Nègres*, have evoked, either romantically or ironically, the fate of the "good student" in colonial schools. Few have done so with as much thematic and structural originality as Humbert does in a novel that tracks the dialectics of representation and desire across gendered and colonial divides. Herself a winner of the fabled scholarship, Humbert derides the colonized mentality and its fascination for all things "foreign" while silently engaging with both the literary conventions she inherits from the European novel and *its* fascination for exotic locales. She questions the authority of "realist" representations of these locales and the way these representations are internalized by writers who have no choice but to engage with the fictional historical and geographical categories constituted by that tradition. Grounded in the liminal imaginative spaces created by Franco-British colonial encounters, she reimagines space through epistolary exchange and finds in Austen a precursor who successfully used this narrative convention to critique social hierarchies.

Epistolarity usually embodies a desire for exchange with a reader whose virtual presence authorizes the writer to find her voice, to express herself. Letter writing seems to have this function for Fanny Price in *Mansfield Park*. But in the first pages of the novel Austen begins by signaling the *negative* valence of letter writing. She informs her readers of the manner in which the "absolute breach" between Fanny's mother, Miss Frances, and her sister Mrs. Norris occurred: "Mrs Norris . . . had written a long and angry letter to point out the folly of her conduct" when Frances "married. . . , to disoblige her family, a Lieutenant of Marines, without education, fortune, or connections."[4] Similarly, *La Montagne des Signaux* opens on a scene of estrangement and conflict between two sisters who have not seen each other for twenty years. Their mother's death brings them together again, as the reader learns from the narrator, Cecilia, who explains that she has sent a "télégramme . . . impitoyable dans sa concision . . . pour exprimer ma colère" [concise and ruthless telegram . . . to express my anger] (7) at the fact that busy and successful April has never found time, in twenty years, to return "home" (7) to Mauritius from England and has seldom kept in touch. Generational conflict, silence, and inexpressibility figure prominently in the Rouve family, and Humbert exploits these conflicts to sharpen the autobiographical novel's articulation of the limits of language. In Jane Austen too, as James Thompson has noted, characters are often unable "to speak in the face of social and class pressures, as well as emotional and private strictures." And according to him, among Austen's novels, "inexpressibility figures most prominently in *Mansfield Park*," and "the awareness of the limits of language," which Austen shared with "many later eighteenth-century writers" (510–11), is a primary issue in this novel.[5] These limits are brought to the fore in the indeterminate space between unarticulated speech and actual letters that the reader will not see. The actual content of the exchange remains ambiguous, beyond language as it were. The virtual exchange of letters is thus the means by which the limits of language are played out.

The first indication that we have of the origin of the Bertrams' fortune comes from a letter that Fanny's mother writes to her sister to ask for help, wondering whether her ten-year-old son "might be useful to Sir Thomas in the concerns of his West Indian property" (6). This letter is sent despite the existing "breach between the sisters" (5). The first few pages of the novel allude to several other letters that underscore the fact that Mrs. Price had stopped corresponding with her family until then in order to "save herself from useless remonstrance" (6). A series of angry and disrespectful letters had "put an end to all intercourse between [the two sisters] for a considerable period," until "Mrs Price could no longer afford to cherish pride or resentment, or to lose one connection that might possibly assist her" (6). Thus, at the very beginning of the novel we are made aware that the written word can wreak havoc in an entire family, causing it to break apart and then allowing it to come together again.

A few pages later, her cousin Edmund finds Fanny "sitting crying on the attic stairs" because "she had not any paper" to write a letter to her brother William (13). Edmund then provides her with the necessary stationery, thus "authorizing" her to take up the pen: Edmund "has prepared her paper, and ruled the lines" (14). The link between the two cousins, which will become central to the plot, is initiated around this theme of writing, a theme that recurs, for example, when Edmund promises, "And *I* shall write to you, Fanny, when I have any thing worth writing about; any thing to say, that I think you will like to hear, and that you will not hear so soon from any other quarter" (253). Edmund's friendship and kindness alleviate Fanny's initial feelings of misery and marginality within Mansfield Park, giving her "better spirits with every body else. The place became less strange, and the people less formidable; . . . she began . . . to know their ways, and to catch the best manner of *conforming* to them. Her little rusticities and awkwardnesses . . . necessarily wore away" (15, emphasis mine).

Fanny's socialization into her role as a subordinate who needs to "conform" to the tradition and customs of her betters is thus mediated by a letter-writing episode that redeems her mother's willful subversion of the patriarchal family system and subsequent silence and estrangement. The reader is never shown the letter that Fanny writes on that day, but this episode sets in motion powerful social forces that, by the conclusion of the novel, will have Fanny installed at the empty center of the great house, marrying Edmund and becoming the lady of Mansfield Park. Letter writing and a ladylike education, Austen seems to suggest ironically, are the keys to social success, and to the "rise" of the poor cousin within the ranks of the landed gentry. Austen underlines the process by which the initially silent, marginal heroine is transformed into a conventional bourgeois lady.

Nina Auerbach has stressed that Fanny is the least "likable" of Austen's heroines, that her role often is that of "an omniscient outsider at family, excursion, wedding, play, or feast." Fanny's distance from others, and from the reader, reveals Austen's way of making and keeping her an unsympathetic character: "Fanny, like Mary Shelley's monster, becomes the solitary conqueror of a gutted family," says Auerbach. Geographic, moral, social, and psychological distance between the characters creates a sense of alienation that announce modernity and skepticism, as well as suspicion of appearances. Thus, Austen departs both "from the community and the conventions of realistic fiction toward a Romantic and dissonant perspective." Unlike the worldly Bertrams and Crawfords, Fanny accords far too much importance to the written word. Her (lower-class) earnestness is the cause of many misunderstandings, the source of her (and the novel's) "repelled fascination with acting, with education" as Auerbach concludes.[6] By foregrounding the circulation of the written word and then undermining its reliability, Austen signals to postcolonial readers her sophisticated awareness of the way power and communication are intertwined. Her understanding of the way language works and her "casual references to Antigua," as Edward Said puts it,[7] form part of a subtle gesture of denunciation that has not escaped Said's critical eye.

Like Austen, Humbert sets into circulation letters that create more confusion between characters on either side of the social or colonial divide. In *La Montagne des Signaux,* many of these epistolary messages fail to arrive at their proper destination. This failure of communication renders clearly visible the challenges and the risks associated with education and writing. Dolly, the romantic mother, sends long letters from Mauritius to her English aunt in Warwickshire. After the aunt's death the letters are appropriated by a cousin, Larry Bolton, who does not inform Dolly of her aunt's death: "Que voulez-vous, la tentation était trop forte! Ces lettres venues de si loin, ces timbres magnifiques . . . *Yes,* j'ai ouvert, j'ai lu. Je suis un mufle, *isn't it?*" [Well, the temptation was too strong! These letters from so far away, these beautiful stamps . . . Yes, I opened them, I read them. I am a lout, aren't I?] (257). These missives—or rather fables—have an unexpected effect. Seduced by Dolly's description of her exotic landscapes and by falsely upbeat tales of their comfortable tropical lives, Larry decides to embark on a journey to Mauritius, ostensibly to return the "guilty" correspondence to Dolly and make amends.

It is only after their mother's death that Cecilia, the narrator, discovers the letters "dans une boîte en carton, sur une étagère de son armoire" [in a cardboard box, on a shelf in her closet]. She is completely stunned by her mother's rhetoric: "Quelles lettres! De pitoyables morceaux de bravoure où Dolly, en anglais, rivalise de lyrisme avec la vieille Anglaise romantique à qui elle écrivait, vantant la beauté du pays, l'intelligence et la sagesse des enfants. . . . Et que de descriptions sirupeuses! On croirait lire des dépliants touristiques!" [What letters! Pitiful purple prose in which Dolly competes in English with the old romantic English aunt's own lyrical narratives, boasting of the beauty of the island, the intelligence and wisdom of the children. . . . And such syrupy descriptions! One would have thought these were tourist brochures!] (259). Cecilia's discovery of the mother's gentle mythomania, the secret "étalage d'exotisme de pacotille . . . ces pauvres lettres où elle se réinventait" [display of cheap exoticism . . . these abject letters in which she reinvented herself] (261), is crucial to Humbert's *mise en abyme* of the production and reception of writing. Humbert thus underscores that a text is as likely to be a lie, a fable or *fabula,* as it is to get into the wrong hands or to be misread—or might one say all too well read?—either by Larry, who is taken in by the writer's imagination, or by Cecilia, who happens upon her mother's secrets, becoming much too intimately aware of her devouring mother's imagination. It is this imagination and the nostalgic dissatisfaction it nourishes that forms the pernicious codependent bond between the mother and the other daughter, April, with whom she lives in a form of incestuous symbiosis. If Austen stresses distance and its pitfalls, Humbert insists on the snares of proximity and on the suffocating aspects of familial ties. Her characters enact the stifling colonial conditions that choke writers who internalize the narrative conventions of the metropole and deceive readers caught in its alluring rhetoric.

Larry Bolton is dazzled, seduced by Dolly's imaginary tales, ensnared by words that will cause his downfall. By going to Mauritius, Larry—much like nineteenth-century British figures such as Austen's Sir Thomas— will be burned and lose his fortune in this falsely represented "paradise." By reading what was meant for another pair of eyes, Larry becomes caught in a narrative trap, and Dolly's innocent fabrications produce his ruin. Her letters are like these historic *signaux de montagne* of the title. These used to transmit messages to passing ships outside of the island's capital; ships that did not understand the transmission codes would be lured toward dangerous reefs and then plundered by local pirates. Larry is taken in by a tropical, colonial "elsewhere," lured by the letters of a woman who raises her daughters within the temptation of another, equally destructive narrative. Dolly inspires in Cecilia and April the desire of another, European "elsewhere," hoping against all hope that she will be able to leave behind her colonial island, its Franco-British tensions, her status as a mixed-race "déclassée," and return to the land of her English ancestors. Her unappeased desire for this mythical Warwickshire poisons the life of her daughters. She is the phallic and dangerous mother who, like the sea (*mer/mère*), devours the beach:

> Bientôt des vagues étaient venues du large, petites et courtes d'abord, puis plus hautes, plus amples, de véritables houles enfin, lourdes et lisses comme celles de la pleine mer; elles se suivaient de plus en plus près, elles progressaient avec la silencieuse reptation de félins en chasse, avançant, avançant encore. . . . le lagon débordait d'une eau verte et bleue qui se renflait de partout, une masse, une épaisseur liquide inimaginable . . . on aurait juré que la mer allait accoucher d'une autre mer! De partout je pouvais voir et entendre cela; même si je m'étais bouché les oreilles . . . ce ruissellement énorme de la mer en travail . . . et le ronflement de forge des récifs.

> [Soon the waves were coming from the ocean, small and short at first, then higher and wider, finally big swells, heavy and smooth like the ones on the open sea; closer and closer together, they

progressed like silently crawling felines on a hunting trail, moving slowly forward. . . . the lagoon overflowed with green and blue water that bulged on all sides, an unimaginable mass of thick liquid . . . one could swear the sea was going to give birth to another sea! I could hear and see it from everywhere, even if I plugged up my ears . . . this enormous flow of the sea in labor . . . and the forge-like roar of the reefs.] (14)

Like this inescapable sea, the seductive stories Dolly tells penetrate her daughter's consciousness. When Cecilia discovers the epistolary lies of her mother, she becomes conscious of having violated a secret and of being in front of the uncanny heart of family life, the *unheimlichkeit* that propelled the mother's, and now her own, writing. She can then take some distance from her mother's castrating powers, reducing her to a mime or a ventriloquist, whose internalized colonial ideology can then be forestalled.

This negative portrayal of a pathetic mother allows Humbert to undo on a thematic level what her structural borrowings from the "mother-texts" of the Euro-canon construct on a narrative level. This canon, with its seductive texts and deceptive histories of exotic difference, constitutes the veritable matrix of the Indian Ocean colonial literary zone. In both Austen and Humbert the family system becomes a metaphor for larger social and political structures erected in conjunction with the colonial enterprise. By revealing that the authority the empire claimed for its written texts (such as peace treaties between England and France and the literary canon) is at best dubious and at worst a simulacrum, Humbert contributes to the postcolonial critique of political and literary representation. But this critique also raises another point. British debates over the desirability of a written constitution in Austen's time parallel the postcolonial dynamics of constitutional law in Mauritius in the 1970s. Although these larger political issues do not surface directly in the novels, the self-referential aspects of the narratives foreground the critical and interpretive moves that reading always requires. The letters or mere "epistles" that are the (private) texts within texts in these two novels can thus allow us to raise important (public) questions of political philosophy. These are the questions with which postcolonial democracies continue to struggle in their search for the best legal and political instruments to govern themselves. Literature remains one of the sites in which this struggle is indirectly played out.

# Notes

1. Ian Watt, *The Rise of the Novel* (Berkeley: University of California Press, 1957); Nancy Armstrong, *Desire and Domestic Fiction: A Political History of the Novel* (New York: Oxford University Press, 1987), 8.

2. Ibid.

3. Marie-Thérèse Humbert, *La Montagne des Signaux* (Paris: Stock, 1994), 67. Subsequent references appear parenthetically in the text.

4. Jane Austen, *Mansfield Park: A Norton Critical Edition* (New York: Norton, 1998), 5, 6, 5. Subsequent references appear parenthetically in the text.

5. James Thompson, "Jane Austen and the Limits of Language," *Journal of English and Germanic Philology* 85 (1986): 529, 510–11.

6. Nina Auerbach, "Jane Austen's Dangerous Charm: Feeling as One Ought about Fanny Price," in Austen, *Mansfield Park*, 449, 455, 445, 457.

7. Edward Said, *Culture and Imperialism* (New York: Knopf, 1993), 93.

## CHAPTER EIGHT

# The (Dis)locations of Romantic Nationalism: Shelley, Staël, and the Home-Schooling of Monsters

In 1829 and 1830 Mary Shelley wrote a number of letters to John Murray in which she proposed to write a life of Germaine de Staël for his publishing house's Family Library series. Murray did not grant Shelley the commission. It took ten more years for Shelley's interest in the woman writer whose Swiss salon had welcomed many English expatriates and Shelleyan associates to find belated but truncated expression: in 1839 Shelley included a short biography of Staël in the second volume of her *Lives of the Most Eminent French Writers*.[1] It is hard to imagine why Shelley assumed that Staël's story could be turned to edifying ends in British parlors. It was, in fact, a story distinctively short on home virtues "aux Anglais," chronicling, instead, a program of erotic cosmopolitanism that saw Staël bear five children (four out of wedlock) by four different fathers of three different nationalities. Contemplating the prospect of Staël's inclusion in his Family Library, Murray might well, one imagines, have echoed Mr. Edgermond, the character in Staël's *Corinne*, who, when befuddled by that heroine's ways of going public, queries her lover in the following terms: "[A]s lovable as [she] is, I think like Thomas Walpole: *what do you do with that at home?* [que fait-on de cela à la maison?] And as you know, home is everything in our country."[2]

That Shelley could be so oblivious to the peculiar tangle of family and literary values that dictated the relocation of culture in the Romantic period—that dictated, as I shall demonstrate, literature's simultaneous repatriation and domestication—is puzzling. And yet this chapter on Shelley and Staël, and on the ambivalent arguments that both novelists carry on with the nineteenth century's accelerating nationalization of culture, will take its cue from that obliviousness.

Shelley's misstep has something to teach us. In our postmodern era, when "internationalism" is "in distress," her category error might prompt us to reexamine the domestic framework literary history has used to normalize and naturalize a set of historically contingent arrangements for textual transmission.[3] It might prompt us to acknowledge the existence of alternative ways of imagining the genesis and the place of art than those writ large within the insular institution of the Family Library. In an essay entitled "A Home for Art," Mary A. Favret asks us to consider how contemporary academic practice perpetuates, Romantically, an identification of aesthetic and domestic space. I want to add the concept of the nation to Favret's list of the premises that we construct in order to keep "poetry away from the pressure of human bodies, locked in safe cabinets, at an imaginary distance from the noise of history."[4] If our current ways of, for instance, reading women's novels under the sign of "domestic fiction" reassert this isomorphism between place, culture, and nation, the way the novels of Staël and Shelley jointly disarticulate "mother" from "nature" and "mother" from "country" suggests, by contrast, that the lessons of Romanticism do not have to be those obtained through home schooling.[5]

Of course, Romantic ideas about the family and an accompanying determination to see works of literature as homegrown, domestic products set the terms on which Shelley, for one, is ushered into literary history.[6] As befits a national subject and a "proper lady" (Mary Poovey's term), Shelley is wont to figure even in revised Romanticist canons and curricula as somebody's wife and as, in her words, "the daughter of two persons of distinguished literary celebrity."[7] And indeed, making her novels into display cases (or reliquaries) for quotations from the works of Percy Shelley and the Lake Poets, mournfully advertising her Gothic indebtedness to the kin and compatriots who predecease her, Shelley can look as if she herself relishes her role as the curator of the family library and relishes this responsibility for the family heirlooms of the national literature.

And yet Shelley's misapprehension of the terms on which a woman writer might legitimately claim a place within the literary tradition has ample precedent in the novel that inaugurated her career. Cataloging the faults of *Frankenstein* in 1818, John Wilson Croker, a reviewer for the

*Quarterly Review,* laments the proofs this text tendered, most explicitly in its dedication, that "Mr. Godwin is patriarch of a literary family." When, however, he turns to the episode, at the midpoint of the novel, in which Shelley depicts the schooling both of Safie, "the fair Arabian," and of the monster, who eavesdrops on her language training, Croker abandons genealogical inquiry. In that episode in the De Laceys' cottage, the setting, or so it has appeared to many readers, for the novel's chief object lesson in what Percy Shelley's preface calls "the amiableness of domestic affection" (12), Croker is aghast to discover, not a family library, but instead, he sputters, "the Greco-Anglico-Germanico-Gallico-Arabic library of a Swabian hut."[8] To see *Frankenstein* as centered, literally, on a multilingual, transnational pedagogy—on acts of translation (those acts that must have transpired in order for the monolingual monster to be able to read his library of Plutarch, Goethe, and Milton) and of imitation (of the sort that ties *Ruins of Empires* to the "eastern authors" and renders it a suitable schoolbook for Safie's French lessons [116])—obliges us to reposition Shelley within the system of literary relations.

If, as my juxtaposition of these passages from Croker intimates, the introjection of the foreign into the domestic that transpires in this episode of *Frankenstein* subverts that book's relation to a paternal origin, then perhaps, conversely, it might also make it easier to envision atlases of the novel that bypass the national setting and paths of literary transmission that bypass bloodlines. Accounting for how *Frankenstein* comments on the language learning that ushers the citizen-subject into national communities—an acculturation that, in the creature's case, fails drastically—means, I shall propose here, attending to the pedagogic legacy of Staël's *Corinne* (1807) and *Delphine* (1802) within Shelley's text. This means, in turn, locating these two novelists within an alter-space for feminine solidarities and understanding their relations in terms that depend neither on received, patrilineal notions of literary influence nor on those concepts of a "women's tradition" in which to write as a woman entails thinking back through one's mother.[9] In my reading, significant relations *cannot* be blood relations. Indeed, I shall also propose that to read Staël and Shelley together, across borderlines and lines of descent, is to recognize in both a legacy that promotes artificial reproduction. *Frankenstein,* besides (famously) pitting "maternal nature" against the unhallowed arts that underestimate her claims (92), also (less famously) dissociates motherhood from concepts of an organic nature so as to relocate it within the technological domain.[10] While it writes back to and for *Corinne* and *Delphine, Frankenstein* aligns mothering with what, thinking of the fictive technologies that eighteenth- and nineteenth-century states used to create their subjects, we might call *letters of naturalization.*

---

Shelley learned a lesson in geopolitics from Staël, one also found within much of the queer theory that has remarked the imbrication of the (seemingly "natural") categories of national affiliation and sexual attachment. Staël was Shelley's model for a style of thought that could denature and disarticulate the bonds of blood, habitation, patriotism, companionship, and succor, as Eve Sedgwick puts it, "from the lockstep of their unanimity in the system called 'the family.' "[11] Let us begin, however, with the more celebrated lesson, familial and more familiar, that Staël taught to early-nineteenth-century culture. The fame of *De l'Allemagne* (1810), especially, rested on the protocols for literary legitimacy that it set into place when it argued, as a contemporary reviewer put it, that "poetry and eloquence may and in some measure must be national." Staël's recommendation in that work of Romanticism over classicism takes shape in some measure as a call for a reterritorializing of literature, a canonizing of that writing that was homegrown, "ayant ses racines dans notre propre sol" [with roots in our own soil].[12] Her metaphor, the word *propre* particularly, suggests how the new arrangement of the discursive field that brought into view a series of distinct, discrete, and, only on those terms, *expressive* national literatures had an equivalent within those Enlightenment and Revolutionary geographies and theories of government that emphasized in new ways the necessity of un-confounding national territories and so enclosing states "as a peasant would enclose its field."[13] Over the course of the eighteenth century national borders were "purified" and "rationalized." National affiliation became in unprecedented ways a matter of location. An older apparatus of political obligation that had emphasized not, as now, the territorial but rather the political bond between king and subject, a jurisdictional sovereignty that was affirmed in the oaths of allegiance taken by both individuals and corporate groups, fell into abeyance.

The meanings of *culture* underwent a related metamorphosis. Staël and the thinkers assembled at her salons—Chateaubriand, Humboldt, the Schlegels—contributed significantly to the shift that saw *culture* cease to designate in the first instance a process of cultivation typically thought to unfold through commercial and social exchange, a lateral diffusion of ideas and artifacts.[14] Reinvented, reoriented toward newly charismatic concepts of the mother tongue and the ancestral dead and toward the modes of self-authentication and remembrance those totems sponsor, *culture* came to signify a heritage that was transmitted in a vertical descent from each generation to its successors and that was, like the nation, localized in a particular plot of "classic ground" or of "literary landscape." And so in some ways culture, along with the nation (whose limits were, Continental advocates of the idea of "natural frontiers" asserted, prefigured in the very contours of the terrain), came to be assimilated to nature. The idea of the *state* of nature lost its leverage in accounts of the politically possible, Martin Thom writes in his account of the post-Revolutionary transformation of ideas of collective life, but, as the ultimate "repository of value," nature came then to be relocated *inside* the body politic. Earlier narratives of collective life, recounting the assembly of the people and their ratifying of the contract that would usher them from a state of nature and into civil society, were jettisoned in this era. (This involved, as Thom points out, extirpating, in turn, the escape routes that had once been open to individuals who wished to secede from the contract and cast off citizenship; instead, a confining principle of nationality blocked their access to that zone of natural, unconditional liberty that had once glimmered in the distance before and beyond civic life.) In the meantime, in conformity to the new conviction that the nation must extend back to prehistory, that the tribe always precedes the individual, and that there never was or could be a time before ethnic belonging, nature supplied each nation with its ontological guarantee.[15]

When in *De l'Allemagne* Staël calls for recognition to be extended to those works of imagination that both express and also, more problematically, help underwrite the new earthed identities of this age of national cultures, she furthers these redefinitions. This, as I have noted, was her chief legacy to a discipline of literary studies that in the nineteenth century was increasingly reordered along national lines. The "Romanticization" of literature that Staël's aesthetics commends took shape both as a naturalization of literature—a return to origins, "notre propre sol"—and a familialization. To be Romantic, according to the lessons offered in her aesthetic texts, was in part to see reading and writing as the occasions on which one rehearsed local attachments and practiced ancestor worship; occasions, that is, for a renewal of what Staël's English contemporary Coleridge would call, in his guise as a spokesman for an identity politics that naturalized the nation-state by casting it in the image of the family, "the true historical feeling, the feeling of being a historical people, generation linked to generation."[16]

*De l'Allemagne* argues in these terms for the centrality of romance to Romanticism. By engaging with medieval narratives of chivalry, modern literature would recover its status as the expression of what was native to this place and this culture. Through commemoration, paradoxically enough, it would recover its originality. Similarly, when Staël sets her heroine Corinne to her bardic work within a landscape of ruins and graves, she appears to be intent on literalizing what is figurative in these new axiologies of national cultures. If Italy is a privileged location for poetry in *Corinne*, it is because buildings crumbling into ruin may be seen as marking a reconciliation between human culture and the nature into which it devolves and because graves are where the land and the people belonging to it really do become one. At the same time that she transports her Scottish peer, Oswald Lord Nelvil, to Italy, there to fall in love with her heroine, Staël in *Corinne* also transports to the warm south the fantasies of a natural (oral) poetry and a natural landscape that might be a library that readers had earlier encountered in the Ossianic publications of the Scots James Macpherson (1760–) and in the novelist Lady Morgan's *The Wild Irish Girl* (1806). With this transfer, Staël perfects the modernized mode of presentation that was to remake the European nation as an "old country" and a body politic that granted the dead pride of place.[17]

However, Staël qualifies her allegiance to such organicism and nativism, and does so most within her fictions at those moments when she reminds us of the familial frame in which a national literature was, as such, meant to be (re)produced. The memories that enthrall the Highland bard Ossian are triggered in part by local associations. Nature, speaking in stones, provides the mnemonic; the bardic voice that "remains, like a blast, that roars, lonely, on a sea-surrounded rock" can, while it echoes nature, raise the ghosts of the family dead whom it commemorates on the very spots on which they died.[18] But the other trigger that sets Ossian remembering and reciting his tale of times of old is the presence of Malvina, the young woman who was left bereft years before by the death of her betrothed, Oscar, the warrior who was the bard's only son. Arranging for his readers to find their double in this female figure who has forsaken her own past and family in order to help Ossian remember his, Macpherson enlists the domestic affections in the cause of cultural transmission. Malvina, as her name suggests, plays Miranda to Ossian's Prospero, and as with Miranda, her charisma is that she both appears to have no life apart from the virtual one she obtains through listening to Ossian's tales and appears to have had no life prior to this filial one led at the site of bardic production. Images of Staël's Corinne, and of Staël *as* Corinne, that picture the improvisatrice with harp in hand, seated atop a rocky promontory, recycle this Ossianic iconography of the inspired and inspiring helpmate-student-muse. They capitalize on the fact that Corinne is a figure who combines Malvina and Ossian in one. To portray her in this mode not only ratifies the bardic collaboration between poet and place but also, albeit only via the *naturalization* that permits Malvina to view Ossian's ancestral dead as her own, works to align woman and place. Staël's novels, by contrast, exploit the paradoxes that at once structure and are concealed by such fantasies. They acknowledge that the kinship arrangement propping up the Romantic effort to make a national literature and a literary nation that will link "generation ... to generation" hinges on the *dis-placement* of women—on exogamous exchange. Her narratives use the exogamous storyline of daughterhood, the storyline of extradition and naturalization, to disestablish the bloodlines and the national tradition that the exchange of women is supposed to establish.

Writ large in the tableaux imaging Ossian's history lessons to Malvina is the pledge that a daughter, or even a daughter-in-law, might bear the word—might serve the culture as its vehicle for the transmission of home truths. But the figure who sustains the patrilineal order is not the daughter who is never, as Jane Austen's Emma aims never to be, "banished from home." It is the daughter who is. (Recast for the Revolutionary era, the version of the Sappho myth that, as a crucial subtext for *Corinne*, portrays the woman poet as a political exile merely extends to the geopolitical register the potential for banishment that defines the daughter's relation to both "her" father's house and fatherland.)[19] As Staël pursues the Romantic project of writing home, she everywhere betrays her awareness of how members of that gender most identified with home count as " 'stranger[s] [étrangère(s)] ... on paternal soil" (*Corinne* 353/499).

Accounts of Staël's contribution to Romantic nationalism—the very words *nationality* and *romanticism* make their first appearance in English in John Murray's 1813 translation of *De l'Allemagne*—cannot help but call attention to such entanglements of the domestic and the foreign. They do so each time they remark that ironic twist in intellectual history that sees the codes of cultural nationalism originate with a "foreign" woman.[20]

---

Staël's subtitle to her 1807 novel identifies woman and nation: Corinne *or* Italy. Yet a woman like Corinne (or, for that matter, like Staël herself, since she seems to have calculatedly fashioned her salon persona in her heroine's image) is ill suited to the requirements of that idiom of civic allegory that, after the late eighteenth century, made a generic national symbol out of the beautiful matron. Appearing on recruiting posters and postage stamps, this iconography was set up to mobilize for the nation the libidinal energies of citizens who would see in this "mother" the charismatic image of, to echo Staël's opening account of how Corinne appears to the poetry-loving audience that crowns her on the Capitol, their "common bond" (25).

However, for a woman to *be* Britannia, Kathleen ni Houlihan (personification of nationalist, Gaelic Ireland), or Italy, the fantasy that casts her as "the synecdoche of an unchanging cultural space" would in some sense have to be true.[21] Corinne's story line of loss makes a different point, as it adamantly dissociates fidelity to the father from fidelity to the nation. This heroine can become Italy only contingently, and only, in the first instance, by refusing an inheritance and betraying a family trust. For this fantasy to be true it would equally have to be the case that the girl-child had only one parent, that is, was possessed of a pedigree whose purity was guaranteed by its derivation from a unique, absolutely coherent and singular source. That fantasy of monogenesis, in which it would *not* take two to tango, is belied thoroughly by the genetic and geopolitical circumstances we confront with Corinne, the daughter of an Englishman and a Roman woman, and with Léonce, the hero of *Delphine*, born of a Spanish mother and a French father, as well as with Shelley's Elizabeth Lavenza. (In the 1831 edition of her novel Shelley supplies that bride of Frankenstein with a revised biography in which she figures as the offspring of a Milanese nobleman and a German woman; this miscegenated genealogy positions Elizabeth as the legitimate literary heir to the Staëlian protagonist.) *Corinne*, we should note as well, then, is also adamant about dissociating the nation from a matrilineal principle. Corinne cannot be both Italy and her father's daughter. But neither can she be both Italy and also her mother's daughter, for that fidelity to a maternal origin should entail reproducing her mother's mothering. Yet this heroine's family history—and especially the fate of her nameless Roman mother, who in her erotic life had been a poor observer of national boundaries—seems to suggest that expatriation, and perhaps not just from one's native land but also from the land of the living, is the inevitable correlative of the capacity to mother.[22]

The critics who found Staël's heroine loathsome proved blind to the monstrous aspects of those (Frankensteinian) fantasies of parthenogenesis that they faulted Corinne for betraying—those fantasies, shadowing nations' genealogical narratives, about the child who would be the clone of the father, about the intergenerational transmission of an unadulterated genetic capital and national character. These critics nevertheless did see monsters, but that was when they contemplated Staël's presentation of the contrasting situation of genetic hybridity. Hence one reviewer's vehement repudiation of Corinne on the quasi-eugenicist grounds that a heroine who unites "Italian and French voluptuousness with English virtue" represents "a physical impossibility."[23]

This complaint perhaps registers the suspicion that Staëlian genetic engineering makes a travesty of just that exogamy that it may on first glance seem to resemble. Of course, the complainant might also be responding to the crossbreeding of national literary traditions that structures Corinne—to the way this protagonist reincarnates, simultaneously, the heroines of Rousseau and Lafayette, on the one hand, and of Frances Burney, on the other[24]—as well as to the way Staël in this novel confers a strange portability on a poetics designed in the first instance to provide those Ossianic testimonies to the genius of the place and the locality of culture. And indeed there is something startling about the aplomb with which Staël, in so explicitly imitating Macpherson and Morgan, renders the bardic generic, as if it were a kind of tool kit that could be disassembled and reproduced anywhere. There is something startling, that is, about how she reinvents it as a medium that enacts its own iterability and proclaims its status as the currency of transcultural exchange.

Corinne is a "national heroine without a nation."[25] The figure standing behind such a heroine, as Staël's Delphine stands behind her Corinne, is the woman who, as Delphine puts it, remains outside "that chain of affection [that] from century to century, binds families together."[26] Delphine identifies her own self in this quotation from Staël's earlier novel of tragic love, as she outlines not just the affective but also what would soon be the legal condition of a woman without parents, husband, or children. In 1804 the Code Napoleon, institutionalizing the practices that preceded it, formally made women's nationality a function of their relationship to the men whose dependents they were. While nations were naturalized, and while histories were written that made nations seem, as they loomed out of a now immemorial past, inevitable, transcendent, and timeless, the nationality of women was made a contingent and unstable thing. Under the new civil code of France—and later, as other governments brought their conditions for national belonging into line with these conditions, under the civil codes of the European powers generally—a woman's nationality followed her husband's. The woman who married a foreigner became a foreigner. Those arrangements subordinated women's political relationship to the state to *private* relationships inside the family. The state in the meantime expanded its jurisdiction to include the future, a future requiring populating. Increasingly, it concerned itself with the erotic lives of its subjects, establishing the populationist policies and the institutions for the policing of families that would promote this new match between Eros and Polis.[27]

The coupling of exile with the renunciation of erotic satisfaction that structures Delphine's story line is mandated by these arrangements. *Delphine* begins as a novel about giving, about the anomalous power that this orphaned, childless, widowed heroine has to give herself in love and also, since her wealth enables her to supply the dowry for her cousin, Matilde, to give another woman away in marriage; it rapidly becomes a novel about giving up, as Delphine sacrifices everything to ensure Léonce, who has married Matilde despite his feelings for Delphine, "the happiness of domestic bonds" (199). In this heroine's homelessness—and namelessness—in the last two parts of her story, we read Staël's acknowledgment of the new felicific calculus that dictated that it was only by first belonging to a family that one could enjoy the happiness of belonging to the larger group called the nation and of participating in those shared commitments and loyalties that make individuals one another's fellow citizens.

Thus the disorientation we suffer as we read the epistolary novel's concluding sequence. Part 5 chronicles Delphine's flight from the Ile de France to the Swiss convent in which she means to mourn the loss of Léonce. She travels incognito and "at random" on "foreign soil" (347/ 1:735), crossing and recrossing the threshold of the Abbaye du Paradis and the boundaries that divide Switzerland both from France and from the Austrian Empire. Staël makes it hard for her readers too to get their bearings. Presenting us in this section and the next with a sequence of letters that have been sent from Madrid, Lausanne, Montpellier, and so forth, she asks us to infer the whereabouts of her hero, her heroine, and the latter's jealous persecutor, the royalist refugee M. Valorbe, and to do this while we are ourselves being wrenched from nation to nation by each new letter and each new superscription. It is 1792, and war is commencing. If, on the one hand, military aggression dictates that the differences between groups should harden, that the clarifying work of inclusion and exclusion enacted by concepts of the native and the foreign should be carried out with even greater energy than usual, on the other hand, over the course of this sequence those borders that Delphine is said to be crossing come to seem fortuitously, randomly positioned. In Staël's hands the map of Europe comes to seem vulnerable to perpetual, haphazard redesigning. In this last part of the novel, nature—natural frontiers—guarantees nothing. An asylum can transform itself, with phantasmagoric speed, into enemy territory. Delphine can traverse a border freely (as when she leaves the convent and goes to the aid of M. Valorbe, imprisoned for his debts in a German border town), only to find that same border nightmarishly impassible when she reverses the direction of her journey.

Staël inaugurates the plot of *Delphine* with the assault that interrupts Léonce's journey across the mountain frontier between Spain and France and that makes it seem for a while as though the border town of Bayonne will be this badly injured hero's final resting place. In symmetrical fashion, in the novel's concluding transmontane sequence it is as if Delphine finds herself in her native place by tarrying at or on borders, rather than traversing them. Thanks to the Gothic fictions of eighteenth-century Britain, the Pyrenees and the Alps were for readers of 1802 immediately recognizable as highly literary locations. (The Alps, of course, were of biographical as well as literary importance for Staël, who, Parisian-born, was in spite of her wishes and the law of the jus soli deemed Swiss.) But it is not only because, as has often been claimed, the Gothic romance collects examples of sublime landscapes that this novelistic tradition is preoccupied with the mountain ranges that were the period's prime examples of nations' natural frontiers, of the evidence that national divisions were providentially guaranteed. It is also because, one might venture, the Gothic romance is dedicated to tracing the ways that the fictions of law—the institution of coverture, for instance—and the writing of history jointly exile women to a "twilight zone of being," that "phantom state" and "enclave of fiction" that we visit with authors such as Sophia Lee, Ann Radcliffe, and Eliza Parsons, in which Gothic women literalize the association in English law of the marriage state and civil death and live on, inside haunted houses that aren't really their homes, and in spite of rumors of their decease, as ghosts of their former selves. For this reason, the Gothic works to expose the lack of fit between the borders that recorded history recognizes and the borders that it does not, namely, those borders that delimit a territory of female experience that is "the negative space of history's tableau." Certainly, the second half of *Delphine* cultivates the uncanny in recognizably Gothic ways, blurring the lines dividing the dead from the living.[28] In the language of self-abjection that Staël specializes in for this novel, Delphine describes herself as dead. She makes her final foray into a Parisian social world that is now intent on shunning her and reports that "it was my ghost strolling among the living; I could imagine the pleasures stirring them no better than if I had been contemplating the concerns of the earth from the realm of the dead" (342/1:727).

This is Corinne's language also. The female genius inherits the ghostliness that was the portion of the abandoned woman of the earlier novel.[29] More precisely, Staël's novel seems to suggest that to be a woman of genius is already to be a ghost: as we learn belatedly, it was only by dying to the world, by allowing her English stepmother to circulate a report of her death, and by renouncing the use of the patronym by which she was known by her contemporaries, that Corinne could devise a way to use her talents—to become a Corinne. When, late in the novel, Corinne travels, in quest of news of Oswald, back to the Britain she had abandoned years before, and when she acts out her exilic condition and wanders through the grounds of her father's Scottish estate without daring to announce herself, she unwittingly haunts her half-sister: "one would have thought ghosts were roaming"; Lucile Edgermond "was convinced that her sister's image had appeared walking toward their father's grave to reproach her for forgetting it" (354/499, 355/501).[30]

Corinne's return defies Lady Edgermond's effort to control the map of Europe, an effort that has Gothic precedent in that it makes Britain, the stepdaughter's fatherland but now for the expatriate Corinne a prohibited no-man's-land, into the equivalent of the locked chamber of the Gothic tyrant's castle. Her reappearance on the Edgermond estate in fact turns the topography of the fatherland inside out (and so it is that, as the narrator informs us, the ground gives way beneath her feet—"la terre manquait sous ses pas" [353/499]). The woman who should be within the home is outside, and the man whom she seeks, within. Corinne's haunting ungenders a conventional gendering of space, making her follow in the footsteps both of the demonic antagonist of a masculine tradition of "outsider Gothic" and, as Alliston observes, of Nemours from *La Princesse de Clèves*, "the male intruder whose desire leads him to trespass on another man's property." Ironically, in her guise as apparition, Corinne at the same time helps to authorize the paternal will (for Lucile, this "image" of the half-sister she presumes dead is a mnemonic for lessons in filiopiety she is in fact at little risk of forgetting).[31]

Shelley's creature reincarnates these Staëlian specters, transposing them from a figurative to a literal, and emphatically embodied, register. Victor Frankenstein's genetic engineering raises ghosts. When Victor assembles a conglomerate of the scraps of the dissecting room under one skin and thereby materializes his monstrous conception of laboratory-made new life, the dead walk. But unlike Corinne, who is complicitous with the transmission of paternal plots and properties, the ghost who stalks through Shelley's novel, and across borders—wantonly roaming, as Croker complained, "through Germany and France, to Scotland, Ireland, and England . . . [and] to the most inaccessible point of the earth"—is not exactly one (indeed, it is not *one*) who does the bidding of the forefathers.[32] On the one hand, the book has as its master discourse of interpretation the effort to reconnect the novel object to its source, an effort that the monster enacts as he brings a paternity suit against Victor on his own behalf and that novel readers enact as they respond to the invitation tendered by Shelley's 1831 preface and try to move back from the text to its author in order to speculate about how "a young girl" came to "think of and to dilate upon so very hideous an idea" (5). But such attempts to make a singular author, authority, or origin monopolize meaningfulness are, on the other hand, repeatedly countered by the revelation of how thoroughly plural that origin is, how thoroughly different from itself.

In *Frankenstein* the attempt to bring interpretation home by locating a source seems always to end in an encounter with foreignness. Commenting on how the creature appears to have too many selves under its skin, Pamela Clemit writes that "constructed out of arbitrary bits and pieces, fragmented relics of the past, it defeats the very idea of a coherent tradition." And, similarly, the farther we read in the 1831 preface and the more we know about the ghost-story contest at the Villa Diodati, the conversations between Lord Byron and Percy Shelley to which Mary was a "devout but nearly silent listener" (7), and the "volumes of ghost stories, translated from the German into the French" that "fell into [their] hands" (6), the more opaque authorial intent comes to seem and the less certain we are that we agree with Shelley's seeming truism (itself a quotation, "in Sanchean phrase") that "every thing must have *a* beginning" (8, emphasis mine).[33] Beginnings proliferate in the preface. The novel, like the body of the creature (so unlike what Victor intended it to be), is a composite that refracts authorial intent and mediates difference.[34]

This dissemination that renders the book and the creature no *one*'s offspring dictates how each will stand in relation to geopolitical boundaries, as well as to the institutions of authorship and paternal will. Identifying a flaw in the education he received while eavesdropping on and "imitating" the lessons that took place in the De Laceys' cottage, the monster admits, "I had a very confused idea of kingdoms, wide extents of country" (125). A failure when it comes to the geopolitical idiom proper to an age of nations, he has in these language lessons learned French while in Germany. If the center of *Frankenstein*, the monster's autobiographical narrative, has as its generative locale the Swabian hut, home to the Greco-An-glico-Germanico-Gallico-Arabic library that no doubt does nothing but exacerbate a reader's geographical confusion, England is first positioned, disconcertingly enough for an English audience, at the outer edge of the novel; it is the destination (never glimpsed by this audience) of the letters Walton sends to his sister, which compose the outermost frame in this series of frame tales. Indeed, there is a second sense in which the creature learns French in the novel's central episode, another way in which Shelley at this point breaks faith with her contemporaries' sense of national and literary origins. At this point the creature learns to be a Staëlian hero/ine. The monster's position outside the cottage—eavesdropping on the education given to Safie, listening to the music she and her sister-in-law provide for their menfolk, Felix and his blind father, looking in at all the sympathetic exchanges denied to him—seems to repeat that of Corinne when she haunts her father's estate. The domestic idyll that the monster stages for Victor Frankenstein when he recounts how he spied on this fam-ily circle (a circle the more tightly knit because the De Laceys were in collective exile from France) is, furthermore, a new version of a similar Staëlian object lesson in what it means to lead "life fixed in [one's] family's bosom" (*Delphine*, 229). When *Delphine* takes us to a cottage as full of music as Shelley's Swabian hut, we discover the original for the creature's envious account of a schoolroom-home. The letter at the center of Staël's novel, in which Léonce comes to recognize his own exile from the domestic affections, describes the visit that he and Delphine paid to the peasant's house—situated, he writes, in a "lost corner of the earth" (232)—where the blind M. Belmont and the wife who sacrificed her place in society for him together tutor their children.

As the product of Victor Frankenstein's experiment in imitating life and usurping the prerogatives that Victor himself ascribes to "maternal nature," the creature has begun his existence already alienated. Not to be born but to be made is, as the etymology of nation (from *natio*) suggests, native nowhere. A misfit of this sort strains against the system of familial, civic, and territorial categories that human beings have developed to iden-tify one another and to speak themselves. This is the point that the corre-spondences between Shelley's and Staël's texts bring home. Always some-thing less than a subject, the creature stalks through the landscape of Shelley's novel as a *figure* (on being sighted, he is described as "a figure of a man" [e.g., 95]). What Victor as scientist seems to have achieved in communicating life is (as Shelley's choice of the word *communicate* sug-gests) what a novelist achieves in animating a character: in this "figure" he has personified an effect of reading. Might the creature be seen as a personification of metaphor particularly, in its guise as the figure that ungrounds meaning, the figure of transport? In this case it would be fitting that Alpine borderlands (where, as Percy Shelley put it in remarks on *Frankenstein*, "the head turns giddy, and the ground seems to fail under our feet") are the sole approximation of a native habitat that the creature can claim. Victor notes that "he bounded over the crevices in the ice, among which I had walked with caution" (98).[35]

Since he lacks the means to insert himself into the patrilineal scheme (Delphine's "chain of affection," which reappears in *Frankenstein* as "the chain of existence and events" [143]), since he inherits and owns nothing that he could pass down, not even a name, what is the creature's relation to the apparatus of citizenship that organizes the nineteenth-century nation-state? Which nation? When the creature comes to him with his plea for fellowship, Mr. De Lacey senior, possibly pleased to be hearing a French without German accents, asks him whether he is his "countryman" (129). He gets no response. This conversational dead end could represent Shelley's quiet joke at the expense of the nostalgic émigré, a figure whose avidity for news from home is notorious. But it would be premature to propose that nationalisms' modes of organizing and delimiting communities (émigré nationalisms' ways of doing so included) are a laughing matter for her novel. Notably, although *Frankenstein* and the novels of Staël do allude to the happy freedom that the creature and his destined bride, Delphine and Léonce, and Corinne and Oswald might find should they escape Europe for what each text refers to as "the wilds" of the New World, and although through this allusion Shelley and Staël do keep in circulation the Enlightenment notions of the state of nature and of the legitimacy of political secession that were during their lives rapidly being eclipsed by "a confining principle of nationality," these visions of nontragic endings of course prove no more than visions.[36] *Frankenstein*, I hinted earlier, is less resigned than *Corinne* is to the idea that the dead who walk must walk *for* the father. It is less intent than the earlier novel on imagining even the "unhallowed arts" (Victor's phrase) of a woman who refuses the patronym as operating to restore the father's image.[37] (Corinne, of course, uses her artistic talent to repair Oswald's miniature of his father after it has been damaged. As others have noted, it is as if her retracing of the lines of the painting dictates that her lover will retrace his steps back to his fatherland and the wife his father had chosen for him.) But even while *Frankenstein* problematizes the authority of origins in the manner I describe above, it also in its own way inherits and in turn passes on the old Gothic plot of malign legacies and intergenerational resemblance and repetition, the plot about the sins of the fathers.

That the creature becomes the serial murderer of Victor Frankenstein's loved ones suggests, especially to him, the omnipotence of that plot: it suggests how he is *fated* to lose his innocence and, just like Victor before him, "sport . . . with life" (96). As much as a mournful, guilt-ridden Staëlian heroine, the creature ends up haunted by "his" dead—and by the end of the novel and his killing spree, there are dead who "belong" to him. Perhaps the guilt staves off what in a new nationalist, historicist age might by definition be a greater terror, that of *not* being haunted, of "ceasing to feel the weight of past generations in one's bones."[38]

---

As I have suggested, the monstrosity that puts the creature outside the common order of nature exiles him likewise from the categories of family and nation. In this way Shelley arranges for the creature to reiterate the question Staël's heroines pose as they plead for sympathy. What relations (in a double sense of that term)—that is, what kinds of *stories*, what provisions for an audience, what arrangements for recognition by others who are equals, and what sense of groundedness—are available to those outside the chain of affections? Rather than supplying the answer that this leading question demands ("none"), we might instead follow Bruce Robbins's lead and, altering the terms, envision models of coalition different from the inclusion-exclusion structures of the nation and family and ask why we assume that either structure represents affection's "natural home." Setting out to redeem cosmopolitanism, Robbins has us rethink the way we transfer to the nation the warmth, inevitability, and inviolability that we associate with the familial sphere. Robbins complicates that transfer—familiar since Edmund Burke attacked the Jacobins' universalist rhetoric with the claim that "to be attached to the subdivision, to love the little platoon, is the first principle . . . of public affections"—as he observes that feeling "extends no less naturally beyond the nation than up to the nation's borders." Robbins also speculates on whether it might be possible to find an alternative to the narrative of moral and affective development assumed by the Burkean account, that account in which the child begins by loving only its particular parents and moves on to its other relatives, then the local group, then the nation, and only then—but perhaps never—humanity in the abstract. Couldn't one develop a moral code in which it would be easier to couple love and *inter*nationalism if one acknowledged that individuals' affinities for the particular are as much the objects of social construction and social contest—and, especially when we remember the generational and other unhappinesses to which families are liable, are finally as unnatural—as those other forms of commitment that might at first strike us as abstract, estranged from everyday experience, and, in a word, bloodless? Why assume that for culture to count as authentic, as a plausible object of love, it must be transmitted vertically along bloodlines? Why subordinate the "other" relations that contribute to the formation of children's individual and cultural identities—those between, for instance, siblings and peers—to filial love?[39]

Indeed, for centuries states have, in Frankensteinian style, indulged in the genetic engineering that rescripts "natural" relations. One prerogative of the British Home Office has been to send and receive the "letters of naturalization" (in France these are *lettres de naturalité*) that by overwriting the principles of jus soli (citizenship by birthplace) and jus sanguinis (citizenship by family) work to transform aliens into natives, "children of the kingdom." And, as Benedict Anderson's work suggests, letters of naturalization in a broader sense of the term that would include such artifacts of print capitalism as the novel must be seen not simply as supplements to the identity of a nation "born out of the dark, unconscious continuities of inherited culture" but instead as that identity's source.[40] Nations in this account are paper bodies, imagined before they are experienced. The bonds of affiliation that make a nation are not found in nature but made by books. And the success of their post-Romantic efforts to monopolize natural feeling notwithstanding, nations are no more grounded in the realm of the particular and the palpable—and in this sense as well no more natural—than Frankenstein's footloose creature.

Furthermore, as Robbins asks while he engages Anderson's story of how print capitalism's combination of technological and social innovation made it possible to extend the scale on which community could be imagined, why follow the example of *Imagined Communities* and assume that such a process comes "to a halt once it has produced national culture"?[41] The most remarkable feature of *Frankenstein* may be its reluctance to heed that stop sign. The novel goes to great lengths to separate not only artificial reproduction (Victor's practice of unhallowed arts) but also sexual reproduction from inviolate national spaces. In the scenes of home life that Percy Shelley wanted readers to take to heart parenting repeatedly crosses national lines, especially after Mary's 1831 revisions. Bride of a Frenchman who is in exile in Germany, Safie begins her life as the product of another mixed marriage, contracted between her Turkish father and

Christian Arab mother (119–20). Adoption that is the result of international travel brings Elizabeth Lavenza, first encountered as the nursling of an Italian peasant, into the Frankenstein home, where Caroline Beaufort Frankenstein raises the orphan to be Victor's cousin-sister and her own substitute. The novel's stories of courtship and marriage, Frances Ferguson observes, make "the standard means through which a new family is created and continued," namely, the woman's departure from her father's household and her entry into her husband's, look "strangely monstrous." This is one way Shelley undermines from the outset any contrast we might wish to establish between the creature's natal alienation and human beings' capacity to call some place and some social circle home. If in fact Victor commences his autobiographical narrative by wielding his genealogical capital—"I am by birth a Genevese, and my family is one of the most distinguished of that republic. My ancestors had been for many years counsellors and syndics; and my father had filled several public situations with honour and reputation" (31)—the details of the story following this beginning belie this confidence about origins. Victor, it turns out, is born far outside Geneva's gates, at Naples, while his footloose parents take the Grand Tour (33); and Victor Frankenstein senior's retirement from public life, and the fact that the story casts such retirement as prerequisite for paternity, trouble models in which citizenship entails a distinctively public exercise of virtue.[42]

Because *Frankenstein* defines exile as the inevitable, primordial condition, the family affairs in the novel unfold as often as not through letters of naturalization. The novel demotes sexual reproduction, positioning it as one means of homemaking among others. Long before Victor sets up his workshop of filthy creation, the Frankensteins have set the transmission of a family resemblance at odds not just with the inheritance of nationality but also with the preservation of a bloodline.

If Victor's experimentation remakes fatherhood as an oddly literal and embodied business—if his flagrantly visible physical symptoms during the weeks leading up to the creature's animation controvert Freud's claim in *Moses and Monotheism* that the recognition of fatherhood depends on a faith in things unseen and represents the triumph of intellectuality over sensuality—by contrast, mothering, when Victor describes his home life, seems to entail abstraction, imagination, and metaphorical substitution.[43] It is apt that when he returns home after communicating life to his monster Victor's reintroduction to his family is inaugurated by the sight of two family pictures in his father's library. Over the mantelpiece is a full-scale portrait of Caroline Beaufort Frankenstein, imaged kneeling by the coffin of her dead father, and below it is a miniature of William, her murdered son (75). To acknowledge the scandalous suggestion that this arrangement of big and little family pictures in the family library conveys—to note how with this display of three generations of specimens of *nature morte* Shelley makes it seem as though a reproduction could reproduce, as if one artistic conception might generate the next—is to begin to enrich our sense of the central conflict in the novel. It is not straightforwardly between (maternal) nature and (masculine) technology. Instead, the novel stages a "rivalry of artificial seminations," "a contest between ways of reproducing nature [variously, the scientist's, the novelist's, and the artist's] which denies natural reproduction altogether."[44] To recognize this is also to rethink how Shelley figures women. In some measure, to be a mother in her novel is to be a beautiful image (artwork) and not a living woman. (A prime source of the novel's horrors, this of course is the logic that dictates that, with the monster's murderous assistance, Shelley's prose will exhibit a series of lovely corpses.) Caroline, tellingly, is painted twice. But while she lives, Caroline contrives to copy herself. At her instigation, the Frankenstein family procures its daughters by unnatural rather than sexual means. Caroline, as I have noted, selects Elizabeth, who first enters the novel *as* an image, as, in Victor's words, "a pictured cherub" and "apparition" (34), to be her substitute. She also creates another virtual image of herself when she connives to have Justine admitted into the family as servant-cum-daughter and sponsors that "imitat[ion]" of her own "phraseology and manners" that will be the short-lived Justine's life's work (64). (Subsequent to Caroline's death, Elizabeth describes Justine as if she were her foster mother's funeral effigy: "her mien and her expressions continually remind of my dear aunt" [64].)[45]

As others have observed, to note how Caroline makes nurture substitute for nature is to glimpse a precedent for her scientist son's determination to *imitate* life—for Victor's indulgence in what the creature, who is made up from secondhand parts and receives his education at second hand, describes as the unauthorized, derivative copying that makes him but a copy of a copy. "God, in pity, made man beautiful and alluring, after his own image; but my form is a filthy type of yours, more horrid even from the very resemblance" (126–27). The creature, in this account, does more than embody Victor's masculine presumption: his existence also testifies to the son's assimilation of lessons learned at the mother's knee. But I wish to think about Justine and Elizabeth as copies for a second reason, so as to reopen discussion of the allegory of authorship that *Frankenstein* offers and so as to install this model of a woman-to-woman transmission of culture, and attendant disruption of paternal privilege, at the center of that discussion.[46] What happens if, rather than focusing exclusively on Victor's creation of a monstrous progeny, one acknowledges that Shelley might likewise be discussing artistic inspiration and creation when she gives this account of Caroline's parenting—Caroline's way not just of making babies but also of, in effect, deploying letters of naturalization so as to make them *up*?

To acknowledge this, I wish to contend, is to re-see textual relations in ways that undermine the patrilineal structure and domestic framework of our literary histories because it is to see how Shelley casts her authorship as the consequence of her textual fostering by a foreign woman. Pointing to Shelley as a negative object lesson in the power of a patriarchal literary tradition, of an arrangement that gives women less than full citizenship in the republic of letters, feminist criticism has demonstrated brilliantly, if pessimistically, how the book-baby (the "monstrous progeny") that is *Frankenstein* "literalizes the literalization of male literature." (This is how Margaret Homans puts it as she considers how, given a normative account of women as the vessels for embodying and realizing male ideas, the monster, as he wanders about the woods of Germany carrying his male-authored library as well as the scientific journal Victor kept prior to his creation, must be seen as perversely enacting a female fate: he is quite precisely "bearing the words" that recount his origin.)[47] But while she re-scripts familial and national relations both *within* and *through* the novel, Shelley is also casting *Frankenstein* as the realization of Staël's alternative vision of how to probate a textual inheritance. For scenes in which Staël depicts the learning of foreign languages, scenes of home schooling that make home into a way of going outside, provide the script for Justine's imitation of Caroline's "phraseology and manners" as well as for the creature's imitation of Safie's French lessons, read out of the book that the abbé Volney wrote in "imitation of eastern authors."

It is to that script of "imitation" that Shelley imitates that I turn in concluding. Staël's writings on aesthetics, I noted above, provided one template for narratives identifying the Romantic movement with a rupture with the mimetic tradition. The turn from neoclassical practices of imitation that is at stake in Romanticism enables, according to this familiar story line, a (redemptive) return to origins and, since Romantic originality is easily harnessed to nationalist ends, the recovery of native, vernacular powers. *De l'Allemagne* may, with its talk of how Romantic literature is "chez nous indigène," be aligned with Edward Young's *Conjectures on Original Composition*, which had cautioned five decades earlier that "an Imitator is a transplanter of laurels, which sometimes die on removal, always languish in a foreign soil."[48] However, if we admit that *De l'Allemagne* advocates, in cosmopolitan fashion, literary change inside *France*, and if we consult the discussion of novel writing that occupies Staël's preface to *Delphine*, the originality that Staël values comes to seem an affair paradoxically dependent on cross-cultural exchanges and border violations. Each text proposes that it is through the emulation of foreign examples that a purely native literature may be acquired. For instance, the preface argues that only by transcending the prejudices that prevent them from studying any subject but themselves, only by reading novels that originate beyond the borders of the nation (especially English and German novels), will the French in the nineteenth century produce a literature possessed of "a character all its own" (6/1:85). And *Corinne*, when it allegorizes authorship, makes authorial self-expression, even by Shakespeare, Romantic uber-author and epitome of original genius, depend on the author's relocation to what one might punningly call the bilingual state. By translating *Romeo and Juliet* into Italian (and so providing herself with a star vehicle), Corinne, we are told, is repatriating a play written "with the southern imagination." She returns it to its "native tongue" [sa langue maternelle] (126/194).

As if complying with a logic that, in Staël's novel too, dictates a literalization of literature, art's imitation by nature, Corinne's half-sister Lucile names the daughter who is born to her and Oswald Juliette. Staëlian genetic engineering contrives it so that this British child is the living souvenir of Corinne's Shakespearean performance, the incarnation of her translation. With her dark eyes and hair, Juliette is made in Corinne's Italian image. And when she retraces the Italian journey her father took years before her birth and, arriving in Florence, begins language and music lessons with her aunt, the scene of schooling that follows is described in ekphrastic terms, that is, precisely *as* a scene. "[Juliette] was holding a lyre-shaped harp made for her size, in the same way that Corinne held it, and her little arms and pretty expression imitated Corinne perfectly. It was like seeing a beautiful painting in miniature" [la miniature d'un beau tableau] (411/575).

As this description suggests, Juliette also keeps alive the memory of that "binge of mimesis" that distinguishes the closing days of Corinne's career. This is when the novel complicates its initial staging of the *paragone* and so complicates the modeling of international relations and gender relations that such assessments of the rivalry between visual (representational) and verbal (rhetorical) arts had sponsored at least since the time of Lessing's *Laocoön*. (As W. J. T. Mitchell notes in his account of the language of eighteenth-century aesthetics, such efforts to determine the boundaries between poetry and pictures and between writing and speech customarily proceeded with reference to national borders, as if aesthetics functioned as a kind of European boundary commission. They also proceeded by way of claims about the masculinity and femininity of poems and images, as if the genres had to be segregated because the genders did.)[49]

One symptom of that complication is the way that Corinne the improvisatrice becomes, her bardic work and distaste for "cold letters" (268) notwithstanding, associated more and more as the novel unfolds with arts of imitation and with the visible, cases in point being her restoration of the miniature imaging old Lord Nelvil and her choice to write her life story for Oswald (who, for his part, despite his former habits of silence and reserve, manages to *tell* his). Pictures proliferate in the last part of *Corinne*, as, referring to *images, spectacles,* and *apparitions,* the language of Staël's narrator exhibits a growing propensity for a pictorialism that, as in the narratives of *Frankenstein,* with their references to these terms, has the effect of making originals appear as visions and so like reproductions themselves. The *tableau vivant* that the dying Corinne arranges from a distance, when by making Juliette her double she takes a Gothic revenge on Oswald and the paternal literary order, marks the culminating stage in this process. And, as others have argued, it is troubling how Corinne here replays the Gothic father's power of self-replication, by the book even: how she gets even with the imperatives of patrilineal inheritance and English nationalism by imitating what we would rather see her resist.[50] But what is also notable is how these mutations in the novel's ordering of the genres also entail a slide that makes the oral tradition with which the bardophilic *Corinne* is fascinated strangely different from itself. I am thinking of how the sound of language in this part of the novel becomes subject to the iteration, quotation, and dislocation that in the history of the novel are associated with *letters,* with novels of epistolary intrigue; how the improvised, unscripted speech of the bard—so important to cultural nationalism's memory work because its immediacy seemed to guarantee the locality and locatedness of the word and of communities mediated by words—becomes here deracinated and portable, a token of desire.

Let me refer to a language lesson that transpires in Staël's earlier, epistolary novel so as to suggest how the aural desire and oral imitation of this episode might trouble the linguistic nationalisms of an era obsessed with the locality of the mother tongue and intent on using nostalgic reconstructions of an originary speech as "a machine for re-creating context."[51] In the letter she writes on arriving in Switzerland and taking up residence in the Abbaye du Paradis, Delphine describes her fascination with the abbess, who, she has learned, is Léonce's maternal aunt. Her description of Mme de Ternan seems to reverse the orders of the generations as it insists on how the aunt takes after the nephew; it registers a significant challenge to patrilineal protocol in noting that the nephew was named for the aunt (christened Léontine); and, as Delphine outlines the educational program she will pursue in the convent, it denatures speech, making the mother tongue an object detachable from the maternal body. "When she speaks, she has the slight Spanish accent that, as you know, lends such grace and nobility to Léonce's speech. . . . As I live with her, I shall learn all the words she pronounces as Léonce does; all the impressions that reinforce the traces of her resemblance to him" (363/1:770). At home in England, Oswald makes a discovery about the imitability of speech that resembles Delphine's. "Occasionally, Oswald indulged in the pleasure of using Corinne's expressions to explain her ideas; he enjoyed listening to himself when he borrowed her language" (387/544). At the end of her life Corinne makes Oswald's discovery in reverse: her enjoyment of her language depends on her lending it out. As the narrator makes clear, it is not so much the plaintive content but the medium that is the message in what the novel calls, misleadingly in fact, "Corinne's Last Song"; when, at this point, Staël restages Corinne's laureate performance and so conducts the narrative, full circle, back to its euphoric opening, it is the "touching" discrepancy between the verses that Corinne has written out and the body of the young girl who has been recruited to speak them that gives this heroine pleasure (415). Self-expression depends in this instance on language's availability to others, the iterability that enables its passage across bodily boundaries.

I think that we are close here to the idiosyncratic style of language learning that is modeled by Shelley's monster, whose schooling at the De Lacey cottage elides the distinction between the phonetic and the alphabetic (as Maureen McLane notes, the monster does not acquire his first language, French, by purely oral means, but relies as well on a book): such an elision suggests that language is always already alphabetized, a denatured *combinatoire*, for it casts the native speech at the novel's center as reinvented transcription.[52] Another way to specify the nature of this schooling is to note that the monster learns his first language as if it were a second. If the ideas of the mother tongue embraced with such enthusiasm in the new Europe of nations are mobilized the better to bind people's affections to their country of origin, bilingualism (advocated in *De l'Allemagne* because "il est amusante de prononcer des mots étrangers: on écoute comme si c'était un autre qui parlât" [it is pleasing to pronounce foreign words:

one listens as if it were some one else who was speaking])[53] works altogether differently. It makes speech into something neither here nor there. The lessons in a second language that Juliette receives from Corinne, like the ones her mother before her received (lessons that for Lucile made her half-sister as much beloved as if she were her "second mother"), invent *relations* in all senses of that term ("Bilingual wit," Doris Sommer writes, "attest[s] to the kind of intelligence that invents relationships where there had been none").[54] They carve out an extraterritorial space for feminine solidarities. And what readings of the ending of *Corinne* as a revenge fantasy that merely reinstalls a Gothic law of fathers can underestimate is the extent to which first Lucile and then her daughter are active participants in their fostering by Corinne. Juliette, after all, resembles Corinne because during her confinement Lucile is "absorbed with memories of her sister" (386). By endowing Lucile with an unconfinable imagination, Staël locates the reproduction of culture outside nature and the confines of the nation-state, in the circulation of languages among women. To transgress the boundaries of nationalist literary histories, traverse the Channel, and reconstruct Shelley's ways of entering into this circuit is to realize that such artificial insemination represents both the content and the form of Staël's pedagogic legacy.

## Notes

Correspondence and conversation with Carolyn Dever, Logan Esdale, Ina Ferris, and Tom Keirstead helped me write this chapter: my thanks to them and to the anonymous readers for the Princeton University Press for their assistance.

1. Mary Shelley to John Murray, 18 November 1829, 5 March, 25 May, 9 August 1830, in *The Letters of Mary Wollstonecraft Shelley*, ed. Betty Bennett, 3 vols. (Baltimore: Johns Hopkins University Press, 1983), 2:89, 105, 110, 113. Bennett observes that Prosper Merimée cautioned Shelley about the difficulties that would get in the way of describing Staël's erotic life "*plainly* aux Anglais" (89 n. 3). See also Mrs. Shelley et al., *Lives of the Most Eminent French Writers*, 2 vols. (Philadelphia: Lea & Blanchard, 1840): a 45-page biography of Staël concludes vol. 2.

2. Madame [Anne-Louise-Germaine] de Staël, *Corinne, or Italy*, trans. and ed. Avriel Goldberger (New Brunswick, N.J.: Rutgers University Press, 1987), 133; and idem, *Corinne ou l'Italie*, ed. Simone Balayé (Paris: Gallimard, 1985), 204. Subsequent references are to these editions and appear parenthetically in the text.

3. Bruce Robbins, *Feeling Global: Internationalism in Distress* (New York: New York University Press, 1999).

4. Mary A. Favret, "A Home for Art: Painting, Poetry, and Domestic Interiors," in *At the Limits of Romanticism*, ed. Mary A. Favret and Nicola J. Watson (Bloomington: Indiana University Press, 1994), 78.

5. Indeed, each novelist contrives to pay homage to the previous century's epistolary fiction, a genre that, notwithstanding its reputation as a crucible for the invention of privacy, had a significant investment in the idea that literacy might bring into being new formations of intimacy, communities whose lingua franca would be sentiment and whose memberships would extend beyond the boundaries of home and of nation. The epistolarity that links *Delphine* and *Frankenstein* suggests, that is, that Staël and Shelley might with some justice be said to favor correspondence courses and distance learning.

6. Courses on "the Shelley Circle," for example, circumscribe those processes of literary exchange that we now call Romanticism, naturalizing a notion of Romantic intertextuality as a family affair.

7. Mary Poovey, *The Proper Lady and the Woman Writer: Ideology and Style in the Works of Mary Wollstonecraft, Mary Shelley, and Jane Austen* (Chicago: University of Chicago Press, 1984); Mary Shelley, "Author's Introduction to the Standard Novels Edition (1831)," in *Frankenstein, or the Modern Prometheus*, ed. Maurice Hindle (Harmondsworth: Penguin, 1992), 5. Subsequent references to *Frankenstein* are to this edition, based on the revised 1831 text of the novel, and appear parenthetically in the text.

8. [John Wilson Croker], review of *Frankenstein, or the Modern Prometheus*, *Quarterly Review* 18 (1818): 382, 380.

9. I receive assistance in this project from April Alliston's description of how critical attention to women's correspondences can unsettle customary ways of construing literary influence: "What I am plotting here is neither the map of a lost mother country nor the visible line of a tradition, but rather the readable lines of women's correspondence, which invite its readers, strange heirs—strangers and therefore heirs—to break the frames of maternal inheritance" (*Virtue's Faults: Correspondences in Eighteenth-Century British and French Women's Fiction* [Stanford: Stanford University Press, 1996], 17). See also Nanora Sweet's rereading of the salon in the Romantic period—Staël's salon at Coppet among others—as a site of language learning that provided nineteenth-century women with routes from the parlor to the international arena, bypassing the national altogether: " 'Lorenzo's' Liverpool and 'Corinne's' Coppet: The Italianate Salon and Romantic Education," in *Lessons of Romanticism: A Critical Companion*, ed. Thomas Pfau and Robert F. Gleckner (Durham, N.C.: Duke University Press, 1998), 244–60.

Previous discussions of Staël and Shelley have focused on the Englishwoman's later fictions: see Doris Y. Kadish, *Politicizing Gender: Narrative Strategies in the Aftermath of the French Revolution* (New Brunswick, N.J.: Rutgers University Press, 1991), 15–36 (on *The Last Man*); and Karri Lokke, "Sibylline Leaves: Mary Shelley's *Valperga* and the Legacy of *Corinne*," in *Cultural Interactions in the Romantic Age:*

*Critical Essays in Comparative Literature,* ed. Gregory Maertz (Albany: State University of New York Press, 1998), 157–73.

10. Mary A. Favret, "A Woman Writes the Fiction of Science: The Body in *Frankenstein,*" *Genders* 4 (1992): 61. Reading Favret's essay helped me immensely in composing my own.

11. Eve Kosofsky Sedgwick, *Tendencies* (Durham, N.C.: Duke University Press, 1993), 4. See also Andrew Parker et al., eds., *Nationalisms and Sexualities* (New York: Routledge, 1992).

12. James Mackintosh, review of *On Germany,* by Madame de Staël, *Edinburgh Review,* October 1813, quoted in Kurt Mueller-Vollmer, "Staël's *Germany* and the Beginnings of an American National Literature," in *Germaine de Staël: Crossing the Borders,* ed. Madelyn Gutwirth et al. (New Brunswick, N.J.: Rutgers University Press, 1991), 143–44; Germaine de Staël, *De l'Allemagne,* intro. Simone Balayé (Paris: Garnier-Flammarion, 1968), 214.

13. I quote Peter Sahlins, *Boundaries: The Making of France and Spain in the Pyrenees* (Berkeley and Los Angeles: University of California Press, 1989), 95. For a parallel account of how the nationalism of the Republic led the state to promote the teaching of French in the provinces, in an effort to assure "l'unité de l'idiome," see Michel de Certeau, Dominique Julia, and Jacques Revel, *Une Politique de la langue: La Révolution française et les patois* (Paris: Gallimard, 1975), esp. 160–68.

14. For much of the early modern period the *translatio imperii et studii,* for instance, had supplied a classic means of talking about that diffusion, providing a narrative framework that could be mobilized to tell the universal story of worldly refinement and material progress anytime and anywhere. On the shift from *cultivation* to *culture* see David Hill Radcliffe, "Ossian and the Genres of Culture," *Studies in Romanticism* 31, no. 2 (1992): 213–32; and for the role of the Coppet salon, Martin Thom, *Republics, Nations, and Tribes* (London: Verso, 1995), esp. pt. 3.

15. Thom, *Republics, Nations, and Tribes,* 33–34.

16. Samuel Taylor Coleridge, *The Friend,* quoted in David Simpson, *Romanticism, Nationalism, and the Revolt against Theory* (Chicago: University of Chicago Press, 1993), 62.

17. On how cultural nationalisms of this era were shaped around memories (authentic, false, or appropriated from others) of oral traditions and the bards who preserved them, see Katie Trumpener, *Bardic Nationalism: The Romantic Novel and the British Empire* (Princeton: Princeton University Press, 1997). Staël's ability to mobilize the glamour of the Celtic fringe and apply it to new ends in other climes makes her useful in her turn for novelists on the other side of the Channel. Thus, as George Eliot's Maggie Tulliver will recognize, in the episode of *The Mill on the Floss* in which Maggie proves an unpliable student and Philip Wakem, who provides those reading lessons, proves an untrustworthy teacher, the Staëlian heroine repeatedly reappears in Scott's fiction as that dark, passionate heroine whose various avatars, in one Waverley novel after another, must be renounced by the heroes. They instead marry the blonde

counterparts of those dark unhappy ones, sacrificing ardor to the claims of pruden-
tial morality and the security of real property (see George Eliot, *The Mill on the Floss*,
ed. George S. Haight [Oxford: Clarendon, 1980], 261–71, 285–96; and Alexander
Welsh, *The Hero of the Waverley Novels, with New Essays on Scott* [Princeton: Princeton University Press, 1992], 54–82).

18. The quotation is from James Macpherson's "The Songs of Selma," in
*The Poems of Ossian and Related Works*, ed. Howard Gaskill (Edinburgh: Edinburgh
University Press, 1996), 170.

19. On Sappho's transformation in this era see Joan DeJean, *Fictions of Sappho, 1546–1937* (Chicago: University of Chicago Press, 1989), 158–66. On expatriation and marriage in Staël, see Claire Garry-Boussel, "Les Conduites spatiales des per-
sonnages masculins dans les écrits fictionnels de Mme de Staël," *Eighteenth-Century
Fiction* 10, no. 4 (1998): 483–99.

20. See the discussion of this irony in John Claiborne Isbell, *The Birth of European Romanticism: Truth and Propaganda in Staël's* De l'Allemagne (Cambridge:
Cambridge University Press, 1994).

21. Trumpener, *Bardic Nationalism*, 142. See also Anne McClintock, "Family
Feuds: Gender, Nationalism, and the Family," *Feminist Review* 44 (summer 1993):
61–80; and Deidre Lynch, "Domesticating Fictions and Nationalizing Women: Edmund Burke, Property, and the Reproduction of Englishness," in *Romanticism, Race,
and Imperial Culture, 1780–1834*, ed. Alan Richardson and Sonia Hofkosh (Bloomington: Indiana University Press, 1996), 40–71.

22. See Alliston's discussion of *Corinne* in *Virtue's Faults*, esp. 195–205.

23. Anonymous review of *Corinne, or Italy*, by Madame de Staël, *Anti-Ja-
cobin Review* 32 (April 1809): 456. Compare the worries about interbreeding expressed in the *Gazette de France*, 27 May 1807, when it draws a parallel between Corinne, a woman "who has the talents and qualities of a man" and should therefore
"not be counted as a woman," and "a rose bush that bears laurel leaves" and should
therefore not "be counted as one of its kind" (quoted in Margaret Waller, *The Male
Malady: Fictions of Impotence in the French Romantic Novel* [New Brunswick, N.J.:
Rutgers University Press, 1993], 60; the translation is Waller's).

24. Another key text is Samuel Richardson's *Sir Charles Grandison* (1754),
whose plot *Corinne* retraces and whose truth it verifies. Corinne says to Oswald that
when he returns home his countrymen "will tell you . . . that every Englishman in
the world has loved Italian women in the course of his travels and forgotten them
when he got back" (310).

25. I owe the phrase "national heroine without a nation" to conversations
with Ina Ferris and the opportunity to see something of her forthcoming *Unsettled
Subjects: The Romantic National Tale and British Discourse on Ireland*.

26. The quotation from *Delphine* appears in Germaine de Staël, *Delphine*,
trans. Avriel H. Goldberger (DeKalb: Northern Illinois University Press, 1995), 379;
and in Madame de Staël, *Delphine*, ed. Simone Balayé and Lucia Omacini, 2 vols. (Ge-

neva: Droz, 1987), 1:802. Subsequent references to *Delphine* are to these editions and appear parenthetically in the text.

27. McClintock, "Family Feuds," 65. On populationist policies, see DeJean, *Fictions of Sappho*, 186–87; the essays in pt. 3 of Parker et al., *Nationalisms and Sexualities*; and Ruth Perry, "Colonizing the Breast: Sexuality and Maternity in Eighteenth-Century England," *Journal of the History of Sexuality* 2 (1991): 204–34. For an account of how French politicians in the Thermidorean and Directorial eras paved the way for the 1804 code by casting the family rather than the individual as the bedrock of the modern state, see Suzanne Desan, "Reconstituting the Social after the Terror: Family, Property, and the Law in Popular Politics," *Past and Present*, no. 164 (August 1999): 81–121. My thanks to Keith Luria for this reference, and I am grateful as well to his fellow French historians Jeremy Popkin and Rod Phillips for helping me to understand the implications of these legal transformations.

28. On Staël's engagement with Britain's Gothic tradition, see also Alliston, *Virtue's Faults*. The phrase "twilight zone of being" is E. J. Clery's; I borrow it from her discussion of how the female Gothic exposes the phantasmagoric dimensions of English property law (*The Rise of Supernatural Fiction, 1762–1800* [Cambridge: Cambridge University Press, 1995], 120). I also draw here on accounts Jayne Elizabeth Lewis and Richard Maxwell have offered of the tomblike, womblike space that Sophia Lee invented in her 1783–85 novel *The Recess*, which provides Lee with a site from which public history may be rewritten (see Lewis's *Mary Queen of Scots: Romance and Nation* [London: Routledge, 1998], 137–38; and Maxwell's chapter in this volume). Ann Radcliffe makes the perilous journey through the smuggler-infested mountain ranges that separate nations a trademark of her fiction (see *The Mysteries of Udolpho* [1794] particularly, but see also *The Romance of the Forest* [1791], in which the hero abandons his regiment just as it begins its duty at a frontier post in the Pyrenees and the heroine's escape route takes her across the Alpine border between France and the duchy of Savoy). On natural frontiers, see Denis Richet, "Natural Borders," in *A Critical Dictionary of the French Revolution*, ed. François Furet and Mona Ozouf (Cambridge: Harvard University Press, 1989); and Daniel Nordman, "Des limites d'état aux frontières nationales," in *Les Lieux de mémoire*, ed. Pierre Nora, 3 vols. (Paris: Gallimard, 1986), 2, pt. 2:35–61.

29. Corinne's talents are equivalent to the anomalous legal and fiscal independence that Delphine has as a widow.

30. On Scotland as "a state of haunting rather than a state of being on the [eighteenth-century] map of national character," see April Alliston, "Of Haunted Highlands: Mapping a Geography of Gender in the Margins of Europe," in Maertz, *Cultural Interactions in the Romantic Age*, 55–78, quotation on 73.

31. Alliston, *Virtue's Faults*, 205. On outsider versus insider Gothic, see Kate Ferguson Ellis, *The Contested Castle: Gothic Novels and the Subversion of Domestic Ideology* (Urbana: University of Illinois Press, 1989).

32. Croker, review of *Frankenstein*, 381.

33. Pamela Clemit, *The Godwinian Novel: The Rational Fictions of Godwin, Brockden Brown, Mary Shelley* (Oxford: Oxford University Press, 1993), 166. On the form of the novel, and for a compelling account of the status of "origins" according to Shelley's Introduction, see Mary A. Favret, "The Letters of *Frankenstein*," *Genre* 20 (spring 1987): 3–24.

34. Shelley anticipates Edward Said's *Beginnings: Intention and Method* (Baltimore: Johns Hopkins University Press, 1975) in understanding textuality as the displacement of relations linked by familial analogy. Where formerly one found "father and son, the image, the process of genesis, a story," modernism, Said asserts, foregrounds, not those dynastic or mimetic relations that privilege a paternal origin or a source, but instead discontinuities and processes of paragenesis (66). Said's discussion of novels' treatment of notions of origin and filiation would have been considerably enriched, and differently periodized, had he attended to novels by women.

35. Percy Bysshe Shelley, "Remarks on *Frankenstein*," quoted in Favret, "Letters of *Frankenstein*," 20. See Maureen Noelle McLane's "Literate Species: Populations, 'Humanities,' and *Frankenstein*" (*ELH* 63, no. 4 [1996]: 959–88) for a superb discussion of the creature as natally alienated, without a native place.

36. The quotation is from Thom, *Republics, Nations, and Tribes*, 34.

37. *Corinne*, by contrast, although it breaks out of the confines of the sentimental novel to include the entire European continent, invents a world that can seem merely to "replicat[e] the repressive constraints of the family circle" (Waller, *Male Malady*, 68; see also Margaret Cohen, "Melancholia, Mania, and the Reproduction of the Dead Father," in *The Novel's Seductions: Staël's "Corinne" in Critical Inquiry*, ed. Karyna Szmurlo [Lewisburg, Pa.: Bucknell University Press, 1999], 95–113).

38. I owe this insight to Patricia Yaeger's meditations on mourning in "Consuming Trauma; or, the Pleasures of Merely Circulating," *Journal X* 2 (1997): 236.

39. I draw here on Robbins, *Feeling Global*, 151, 19–20, 170; and Angelika Bammer, "Mother Tongues and Other Strangers: Writing 'Family' across Cultural Divides," in Bammer, ed., *Displacements: Cultural Identities in Question* (Bloomington: Indiana University Press, 1994), 90–109. The quotation is from Edmund Burke, *Reflections on the Revolution in France*, ed. Conor Cruise O'Brien (Harmondsworth: Penguin, 1968), 136.

40. Robbins, *Feeling Global*, 148–51, 21.

41. Ibid., 21. See also Benedict Anderson, *Imagined Communities: Reflections on the Origin and Spread of Nationalism*, rev. ed. (London: Verso, 1991).

42. Frances Ferguson, *Solitude and the Sublime: Romanticism and the Aesthetics of Individuation* (New York: Routledge, 1992), 109. At this point in my reading of Shelley I depart from Maureen McLane's account. Taking Victor's assertion about his secure natal relation to the state at face value, she assumes that there is a natural relation to the nation that the fact of the monster's existence violates ("Literate Species," 966–67).

43. Sigmund Freud, *Moses and Monotheism*, in *Standard Edition of the Complete Psychological Works of Sigmund Freud*, trans. and ed. James Strachey (London: Hogarth Press, 1964), 23:113.

44. Favret, "A Woman Writes the Fiction of Science," 51, 61. Importantly, Favret insists that when we redefine the terms of the novel's conflict in this way, we are not suspending the possibility of a feminist reading of *Frankenstein*: "by removing the debate from natural to only unnatural productions we intensify the issue of gender difference" (51).

45. See Johanna M. Smith's discussion of Frankensteinian parenting in her Case Studies in Contemporary Criticism edition of Shelley's novel, " 'Cooped Up' with 'Sad Trash': Domesticity and the Sciences in *Frankenstein*," in Mary Shelley, *Frankenstein*, ed. Smith (Boston: Bedford Books, 2000), 313–33; and Frances Ferguson, "The Nuclear Sublime," *diacritics* 14 (1981): 4–10.

46. For a representative sample of discussions of authorship in *Frankenstein* see Marie-Hélène Huet, *Monstrous Imagination* (Cambridge: Harvard University Press, 1993), 129–62; Margaret Homans, *Bearing the Word: Language and Female Experience in Nineteenth-Century Women's Writing* (Chicago: University of Chicago Press, 1986), 100–119; Favret, "Letters of *Frankenstein*"; Sandra M. Gilbert and Susan Gubar, *The Madwoman in the Attic: The Woman Writer and the Nineteenth-Century Literary Imagination* (New Haven: Yale University Press, 1979), 213–47; and David E. Musselwhite, *Partings Welded Together: Politics and Desire in the Nineteenth-Century English Novel* (London: Methuen, 1987), 43–74.

47. Homans, *Bearing the Word*, 117. See also ibid., 115: "Shelley's novel literalizes romantic imagination. . . . Shelley criticizes [texts such as *Alastor* and *Paradise Lost*] by enacting them, and because enactment or embodiment is both the desire and the fear of such texts, the mode of her criticism matters. . . . [I]n the ideology of postromantic culture, it is part of a woman's duty to transcribe and give form to men's words, just as it is her duty to give form to their desire, or birth to their seed, no matter how ambivalently men may view the results of such projects."

48. Edward Young, *Conjectures on Original Composition*, ed. Edith J. Morley (Manchester: Manchester University Press, 1918), 7.

49. On this "binge of mimesis," see Cohen, "Melancholia, Mania, and the Reproduction of the Dead Father," 112; and on the *paragone* as international competition as well as an occasion for reestablishing the boundaries between genders, see W. J. T. Mitchell, *Iconology: Image, Text, Ideology* (Chicago: University of Chicago Press, 1986), 105, 109. See also the description of the lovers' tour of the artistic masterpieces collected in Rome (*Corinne*, 146): "Oswald and Corinne disagreed, but their differences here as in everything else had to do with differences of nations, climates, and religions."

50. See Cohen, "Melancholia, Mania, and the Reproduction of the Dead Father"; Joan DeJean, "Staël's *Corinne*: The Novel's Other Dilemma," reprinted in Szmurlo, *The Novel's Seductions*, 126; and Alliston, *Virtue's Faults*, 213.

51. Susan Stewart, *Crimes of Writing: Problems in the Containment of Representation* (New York: Oxford University Press, 1991), 122.

52. McLane, "Literate Species," 973.

53. Staël, *De l'Allemagne*, 197, my translation.

54. Doris Sommer, "Be-longing and Bi-lingual States," *diacritics* 29 (1999): 95.

CAROLYN DEVER

# "An Occult and Immoral Tyranny": The Novel, the Police, and the Agent Provocateur

> The frequent appearance of the police in novels is too evident to need detecting.
>
> **D. A. Miller,** *The Novel and the Police*

> From a certain point of view we are here in the presence of a domestic drama.
>
> **Joseph Conrad,** *The Secret Agent*

On 29 September 1854 the *Times* of London published an article celebrating the constitution of a new Parisian police force, which it said was "avowedly made in imitation of the excellent body in existence among ourselves."[1] In Paris "sergents de ville" now walked a beat and wore blue frock coats and hats after the pattern of the London Metropolitan Police. The imitation originated with Louis Napoleon, who while living in London prior to the 1848 revolution had served as one of approximately 85,000 Metropolitan Police special constables deputized for a major Chartist meeting on Kennington Common on 10 April 1848. Despite anticipated violence, the Chartists had met peacefully that day. Their plan for a procession from Kennington to the Houses of Parliament was derailed, and Louis was sufficiently impressed by the massive government and police preparations for the event that he took the Metropolitan Police as a model several years later.[2]

Louis's gesture of imitation completes a circuit of exchange that had begun several decades earlier, for the London Metropolitan Police, constituted through Peel's Police Act of 1829, was itself patterned on a French original. Stanley H. Palmer writes that in the early nineteenth century "the police was not an institution familiar to Englishmen; in their minds, a strong police was associated with societies on the Continent, above all with France, the state that created the first powerful police system in the Western world."[3] There had been enormous resistance to the constitution of a civil police force in Britain, particularly in urban and working-class centers. This was because of the public perception that police served political ends, as the British press reported of the French police. Bernard Porter writes that "a political police needed to be, essentially, a detective police, one which discovered . . . conspiracies, or the perpetrators of them. The British tradition of policing had always been very different. For many years the creation of a police force of any kind had been obstructed by strong prejudices from all classes against what were taken to be the necessary implications of a detective system, for which the chief model was the French."[4] As Porter suggests, debates surrounding the organization and administration of policing agencies in Britain turned on the uneasy concept of detection, which provoked widespread public resistance to the government's appropriation of broad investigative privileges. Even while the protection of the private sphere, and specifically of property rights and personal safety, might be served by a local, visible police presence, the constitution of that police force as an investigative body opposed rights of privacy and personal opinion that were in theory endemic to British citizenship.

In the preface to his 1852 novel *The Recollections of a Policeman*, the popular novelist Thomas Waters expresses the terms of this distinction:

> The Detective Policeman is in some respects peculiar to England—one of the developments of the last twenty-five years. He differs as much from the informer and spy of the Continent of Europe, as the modern Protective Policeman does from the old-fashioned Watchman. In point of fact, he is a preventive as much as a detective. His occupation is as honorable as it is dangerous. Its difficulties and danger give it an odor of the romantic. The record of "hair-breadth scapes," which follow, is another verification of the old saying, "Truth is stranger than fiction."[5]

The English detective policeman is more preventive than detective; he is no spy, nor is he an informer. Waters borrows his descriptive language directly from the first *General Instructions* issued by the Metropolitan Police, in 1829.[6] For Waters, as for the Metropolitan Police, the preventive policeman's function—honorable, romantic, even glamorous—involves valiant efforts of public protection that ultimately contribute to the prevention of crime but leave intact the civil liberties threatened by the insidious practices of the Continental spy-police. In his emphasis on the preventive qualities of the police hero, Waters partakes of a conventional contrast of English virtue and Continental vice and suggests, implicitly, that the detective's function is in part to buttress English borders against the dangers of Continental infiltration.

This distinction is as concerned with the cross-Channel transmission of ideas, particularly those related to government access to domestic privacy, as it is with the export of actual criminals. Josephine Butler argues that domesticity itself is at stake when the politics of nation turn tyrannical:

> Everything is known, or supposed to be known, to the secret agents of the powerful police; private life is not secure against their prying observation, and the knowledge they accumulate of every flaw in the domestic relations or character of those in power or office is constantly held in reserve as a threat or check, not only to serve private ends in cases of personal rivalry, but for the suppression of any inconvenient protest against abuses, or of any attempt at social or political reform. . . . The records of private and family life, gathered by espionage and treasured up in the secret cabinets of the police, constitute the instruments of an occult and immoral tyranny.[7]

In Butler's larger analysis, France is a police state in which individual liberties have given way to the abusive prerogatives of a corrupt and centralized government. Police access to the domestic sphere—"[t]he records of private and family life," stashed in the interest of future blackmail—represents the first step on the slippery slope to "an occult and immoral tyranny." In mid-Victorian Britain such an insidious threat to domestic autonomy was consistently represented as French, and more specifically as the vestige of a French government obviously, conspicuously, disastrously crooked. Such attempts to define the terms by which British "private life" might preserve its autonomy borrowed from the discourse of xenophobia in order to construct domestic privacy as a national as well as a personal interest. Disavowing French corruption made it possible to construct the British police as a body dedicated to the preservation of uniquely British ideals of personal liberty symbolized in a fully autonomous domestic sphere, detached from corruption by French influence and from infiltration by the spy-police.

This emphatic disavowal was of course disingenuous; Bernard Porter has traced the long and colorful history of spies, agents provocateurs, and "domestic espionage" in late-eighteenth- and early-nineteenth-century Britain. But the very vocal public resistance to an investigative police force had powerful effects, and the machinery of the British spy-police was gradually sealed off for the period that Porter describes as a "vast mid-Victorian chasm of spylessness,"[8] which extended from the early 1840s to the 1880s, when the Special Branch was established in response to Fenian aggressions. If the police procedures of mid-Victorian England were in theory aboveboard, however, police-procedural novels of the period absolutely reveled in the imaginative possibilities afforded by plots of surveillance, subversion, and criminal transgression. Mid-Victorian literary and especially pulp fictions portray Britain as full of "French" detectives, spies, secret agents, and all manner of provocateurs, including home-grown officers schooled in the techniques of the Continental "spy-police."

In this chapter I pursue the figure of the French detective in the yellowback, or "below-stairs," police novels so popular in mid-Victorian Britain, especially among a growing working-class readership. As fervently as the British public resisted the constitution of a detective police force, British novelists embraced the ambiguities afforded by the detective plot, and the contrast is telling. Even as they gesture toward the popular repudiation of the French police, pulp detective novelists exploit the French connection, especially in their representation of the protean detective as agent provocateur. In the original, Napoleonic incarnation mythologized in Britain in the notorious figure of Eugène-François Vidocq (1775–1854) the agent provocateur was as much criminal as cop, a spy working not only to expose dens of sedition but also to entrap would-be innocent citizens into crime.[9]

The morally ambiguous, psychologically mobile agent provocateur serves a narrative and symbolic function in literary contexts ranging from Brontë's *Villette* (1853) to Conrad's *The Secret Agent* (1907). A cosmopolitan figure, the agent provocateur provides a complex model of agency that turns the apparently sanctified domestic sphere inside out, gesturing toward concepts of liberty and privacy but in the end working to subvert the presumption of their stability. In canonical literary texts, as in the yellowback police novels in which the figure first appears, the agent provocateur reveals the complex transactions through which moral virtue, and the domesticity for which it stands, is constituted. British fictional detectives abhor the corruption represented by the agent provocateur, but they don't hesitate to go under cover when justice calls. The resulting economy of ambivalence, paranoia, and normative bad faith hypothesizes a guilty underbelly for every seemingly innocent subject and suggests that even the oaken-hearted British cop might be on the take. My focus on the agent provocateur concerns the transnational production of British "domestic relations" and takes this figure as a symbol not simply of alterity but also of the possibility of subversion from within. For the agent provocateur gets under the skin of domestic ideology and exposes the ideal of autonomy as a structure of dependency, identification, and exchange.

——————

The 1854 *Times* report describes London's Metropolitan Police as a body "sufficiently strong to quell mere disturbance and riot, but . . . not powerful enough to overwhelm any general movement of the citizens. It is powerless against liberty—powerful against the disturbers of order." In the context of this description, the *Times* suggests that the reorganized Paris police force represented a renewed ideological commitment on the part of the French government. This involves a vision of "liberty," and an accompanying technology of social control, borrowed from the English, who have managed, the *Times* implies, tectonic social change without descent to "disturbance and riot" and the incivilities of revolution. Indeed, it suggests that a good English bobby on patrol would have done a great deal over the years to nip mob violence in the bud, in the process forestalling "little imitations of the original Parisian melodrama" that followed across Europe. The *Times* muses that "all this might have been prevented had there been present at the critical moment a stupid fellow in an oilskin cape, with a staff in his hand, at that spot near the Barrière d'Enfer where the Rue de Vésuve makes corner with the Rue de Satan-Polichinelle, just when the two original patriots from the cellar were engaged in rousing the civic feelings of the dozen of *gamins* who were there playing with their large double sous. 'Move on! can't ye?' would have saved Europe, had the words been spoken in time."

Revolution originated in France, and social order in Britain, and the *Times* is unmistakably self-congratulatory, even smug, in its presentation of this argument. The "stupid fellow" in his oilskin cape prevents revolution not by his political savvy nor by his infiltration of the patriots' cellar. Far from provoking rebellion, the bobby transplanted simply dissolves it at the source; "Move on! can't ye?" makes harmless excitement of potentially dangerous rabble-rousing. The stolid English cop speaking stolid English on a Paris street corner represents a politics of visibility that distinguishes the British police from the French, who are conventionally represented as the invisible and thus insidious "eyes and ears" of a repressive, centralized police state. "[T]he faceless gaze," writes D. A. Miller, "becomes an ideal of the power of regulation."[10] Stationed near the Barrière d'Enfer, the English policeman is effective because he is visible, conspicuous in his cape and truncheon, and indeed in his beefy stupidity—in contrast to the foxlike cunning of his native counterpart.

In theory, the British cop is a man on the street engaged in keeping the peace, protecting rather than prying into the private sphere. "If a man is prepared for all emergencies, he does not care to be listening at keyholes and playing the spy," the *Times* continues. "Who would hesitate between a system of anxiety and one of security?"[11] As Henry Wreford suggested in 1850, the English ideal of the "private sphere" obtains even in the most public of contexts and extends from the physical person to the more abstract concept of political opinion:

> We have no political police, no police over opinion. The most
> rabid demagogue can say in this free country what he chooses,
> provided it does not tend to incite others to do what is annoying
> to the lieges. He speaks not under the terror of the organised spy
> system. He dreads not to discuss the affairs of the nation at a tav-
> ern, lest the waiter should be a policeman in disguise; he can
> converse familiarly with his guests at his own table without sus-
> pecting that the interior of his own liveries consists of a spy;
> when travelling, he has not the slightest fear of perpetual impris-
> onment for declaring himself freely on the conduct of the pow-
> ers that be, because he knows that even if his fellow-passenger be
> a Sergeant Myth or an Inspector Wield, no harm will come to
> him. . . . It is not so across the Channel. There, while the crimi-
> nal police is very defective, the police of politics is all powerful.[12]

The presumption of privacy accompanies the British citizen from home to tavern to stagecoach, and it is fundamentally attached to the freedoms of speech and opinion. Unlike "across the Channel," Sergeant Myth and Inspector Wield distinguish between crime and politics, and unless the private citizen works "to incite others to do what is annoying to the lieges," he or she speaks with impunity.

As the massive police presence at the 1848 Kennington Common protest should suggest, however, the distinction between crime and politics expressed by Wreford was perhaps finer in practice than in theory. Not coincidentally, the citizen Wreford describes is quite solidly middle class: even a "rabid demagogue" moves unmolested from home to tavern to coach. In contrast, a working-class or poor demagogue would have been far likelier to attract the unwanted attentions of a Sergeant Myth or an Inspector Wield. "The police carried out their mission as 'domestic missionary,' " writes R. D. Storch, ". . . through the pressure of a constant surveillance of all the key institutions of working-class neighborhood and recreational life," including and especially taverns.[13] "Most obnoxious to the policed perhaps was the imposition of the 'move-on system,' " Storch reports. "The practice of breaking up congregations of men on the streets and in front of pubs was considered novel and humiliating. . . . The coming of the police produced what was perceived as an attack upon a traditionally sanctioned freedom—freedom of assembly in the streets—and a keenly felt sense of humiliation."[14] Storch cites a trade-unionist broadsheet from 1833 that further undermined the disinterested ideal of police protection, describing the police as " 'a political, not a protective force— . . . its object . . . not so much to prevent thieving as to watch political feeling, and give report to the Ministers of the political movements of the working classes.' "[15] The uniforming of police officers patrolling public streets was intended to produce the impression of ideological neutrality, of the machinelike functioning of a legal system that treated all citizens with equal consideration: "Selection, training and control were strictly exercised to make policemen models of civility and restraint," writes Robert Reiner. "These steps were all part of a deliberate strategy of presenting the policeman as the incarnation of impersonal authority, the agent of the *law* not a government or class." Reiner cites an 1850s journal that described the police officer as "stiff, calm, and inexorable . . . an *institution* rather than a man."[16] But Engels, writing in 1845, suggests not only that the institution was patterned after a man but that it was patterned after a particular kind of man: "Because the English Bourgeois finds himself reproduced in his law, as he does in his God, the policeman's truncheon . . . has for him a wonderfully soothing power. But for the workingman quite otherwise!" As a result, "every week in Manchester policemen are beaten."[17]

Popular yellowback detective fictions of the 1840s, 1850s, and 1860s intervened in this debate. Through their appropriation of the destabilizing social mobility of the detective figure, especially of the detective working under the influence of the French, they produced a critique of the bourgeois complacencies of police virtue even as they expanded the imaginative possibilities built into the mystery plot. Decades before Sherlock Holmes, railway fiction organized around the premise of crime detection flourished in Britain, and early British detective writers capitalized on the Francophilic roots of a genre invented in part by Poe in the marvelous figure of Dupin. They also invoked the French police tradition as a means of explaining the operations of a newly formalized police force to a British readership to whom police procedures were as new as police fictions. Yellowback detective novels conventionally begin with an explanation of the form and function of a police force and a focused introduction to the stalwart virtues of the particular detective narrating this volume.

In dozens of novels, including *The Experiences of a French Detective-Officer* (1861) and *Experiences of a Real Detective* (1862) by the pseudonymous Waters, Canler's *Autobiography of a French Detective* (1862), and the tawdry *The Dance of Death; Or The Hangman's Plot: A Thrilling Romance of Two Cities*, by Detective Brownlow and Monsieur Tuevoleur, Sergeant of the French Police (1866), the authors of British detective fictions marshal a series of moral, generic, and political cues through their invocation of the French. Indebted to, but also influencing, literary authors ranging from Poe to Sue and from Dickens to Hugo, himself a refugee from France whose *Les Misérables* (1860) was translated into English in 1862, popular detective fiction in England was a highly stylized form. Like Sue's *Les Mystéres du Paris* (1843), it focused on the dark and dangerous realities of urban life. British novels such as George W. M. Reynolds's *Mysteries of London* (1848), James M'Levy's *Curiosities of Crime in Edinburgh During the Last Thirty Years* (1867), and James M'Govan's *City Detective* series, published in Edinburgh during the 1880s, contributed to the sense of titillating glamour that urban danger would offer to Holmes and Watson in the years to come.[18] These texts are formula fiction set in urban contexts, generally narrated by a retired detective, focusing in each chapter on one of a number of standard plots featuring petty (and invariably victimless) crimes or phenomena such as somnambulism, mesmerism, or monomania. They partake of the narrative and psychological concept of "mystery" that also characterized more literary fictions of the mid-Victorian period.

Pulp detective novels, however, emerged in the 1840s, in an industrial economy made newly competitive by an influx of Irish immigrants, at a time of Chartist and trade-unionist activism.[19] Focusing on action and adventure, pulp detective novels present a contrast to the psychologically entangled narratives of middle-class identity crisis in the more familiar sensation novels of the 1860s. Privileging verisimilitude, pulp fictions present the "true-life" experiences of narrators who claim years of service as agents of justice, almost always working alone, in public, and at night.

The detective's vulnerability is twinned with extraordinary physical and psychological mobility.[20] The combination underscores the moral ambiguity as inherent in the detective as in his nemesis, the agent provocateur.

While critics credit William Godwin's *Things As They Are; or the Adventures of Caleb Williams* (1794) with originating the detective plot, a template for the pulp tradition was *Clement Lorimer; or, The Book with the Iron Clasps*, published by Angus Bethune Reach in 1848–49, with illustrations by George Cruikshank. "A tale of vendetta, murder, racehorse doping, slow poisoning and abduction,"[21] *Clement Lorimer* was a product of Reach's career as a journalist covering the Old Bailey for the *Morning Chronicle*. Its protagonist, the "sleuth-hound" Lorimer, sends a message to his criminal adversaries: "Tell them, that if they can burrow I can dig—if they can plot, I can unravel; and tell them, too, that not a peaceable night, nor a tranquil day, shall I enjoy, until I have unkennelled them, one and all!"[22] British critics were enthusiastic in their reception of this novel; stymied, however, by the challenge of describing its form, the critic for the *Atlas* reached across the English Channel for the appropriate term: " 'Mr. Reach excels in what we must call, for lack of a home comparison, the Dumas style of writing.' "[23]

Reach's Lorimer had a French precedent: in 1845 the notorious agent provocateur Vidocq had shared the Regent Street exhibition hall of London's popular Cosmorama, opening a prominent display of his own. Reach attended Vidocq's exhibition and afterward befriended the garrulous detective, who had a special reception room in which he spent hours regaling journalists with tales of his adventures. Vidocq's exhibition included selections from his private art gallery, as well as more than four thousand wax samples of tropical fruit and, what was most interesting to the general public, souvenirs of notorious crimes with which he had been associated as a criminal or as an investigator. The exhibition contributed to the British mythology of the detective as agent provocateur: at the door Vidocq distributed a brochure titled *Vidocq, Chef de la Police de Sûreté (Detective Force) de Paris, which was created by him, and which he directed for twenty-nine years with extraordinary success*. And following his regularly scheduled lectures, Vidocq appeared to his visitors in elaborate disguises—as a nun, a Jew, a sailor, a criminal—"before suddenly unmasking with a cry of 'I am Vidocq!' "[24] Romantic and exotic, Vidocq haunts the world of mid-Victorian pulp fiction: a dangerous Frenchman transplanted to English soil, a figure for the implicit moral instability of the detective police officer, and a double agent adept at teasing vice from apparent virtue, the Vidocq figure complicates boundaries of national and individual identity by undermining the moral virtues through which such identifications occur. It is the very instability of this figure that stocks the detective's plot with titillating, if unrealized, possibilities.

The French serve as a symbol for the failure of ethical coherence, all the more powerfully because they function as a site of identification as much as alterity. In English representations of the French criminal justice system, revolution follows upon revolution, cops are quite often robbers, and "detection," far from being preventive, is enacted through gestures of political espionage against private citizens. The English novelist Waters, for example, presents Duhamel, narrator of *The Experiences of a French Detective-Officer*, who escaped his native France to avoid imprisonment for political reasons. Duhamel writes: "The writ of Habeas Corpus is unknown in France, but under the quasi constitutional regime Authority availed itself of practically unlimited power, rarely and in exceptional instances. Now, every man and woman in France are, by express statute, placed at the discretion of Messieurs les Autorites—that is, of the Prefect, Procureur-General, and General-in-chief of the Department, by whose order any one, without a hearing, without knowing what they are accused or suspected of, may be packed off to Algeria or Cayenne!"[25] Duhamel flees to England to escape the arbitrary violence of the government for which he once served as an enforcer. "I did, and always should, chameleon-like, reflect, and truly, the particular line of politics ... which should happen to be in the ascendant for the time" (225). Although Duhamel now practices the art of detection in Britain, his "memoir" recalls a career in France in the context of such romanticized turbulence as the 1848 revolution, the "*Coup de canaille*, from which the fall of France, from her high place amongst free nations must always be dated" (238). As a refugee from the newly fallen French state, Duhamel represents an unswerving commitment to a better, purer England. But as an immigrant turned defender, he emblematizes the insidious potential of the secret agent seeking to colonize from within.[26]

As Duhamel's example suggests, French detectives have an enormous degree of individual power, and it is their flirtation with its abuse that makes these figures so compelling in mid-Victorian novels. Concern with the empowerment of individual police officers in the violence of revolution is still more central within Canler's *Autobiography of a French Detective*. Translated in 1862 by Sir F. C. L. Wraxall, himself a novelist, reviewer, and the translator of Hugo's *Les Misérables*, the novel's notoriety originated in its status as victim of an oppressive French police state. Wraxall reports in the translator's preface that in France the first three editions of the

*Autobiography* sold out in a fortnight, and then the French government reportedly "suppressed" the work. Wraxall speculates that the government was ashamed of revelations about the workings of its police system because of its criminal connotations.

*Autobiography of a French Detective* thus takes the trope of verisimilitude to a new extreme; indeed, whether this is a novel at all has been the matter of some dispute. The text follows exactly the central tropes popularized by English novelists such as Waters, including chapters on monomania, somnambulism, and that singular novelty, a female detective, and Waters's *Experiences of a French Detective-Officer*, to which it is strikingly similar, preceded Canler's text by a year.[27] On the other hand, some readers of Canler's *Autobiography* treat it as nonfiction; while in the introduction Wraxall describes the text as a memoir, he also dedicates an entire chapter to its relative merits in his book of literary criticism, *The Second Empire as Exhibited in French Literature, 1852–63*, which otherwise considers only novels.[28] As recently as 1992 the *Autobiography* appeared in Jean-Marc Berlière's historiography *La Police des moeurs sous la IIIe république*, as a source of information on the enforcement of French regulations similar to Britain's Contagious Diseases Acts.[29] Ambiguously positioned relative to English and French political, literary, and regulatory traditions, *Autobiography of a French Detective* suspends the question whether it is a French detective's French-detective memoir or an English novelist's French-detective novel. "Truth is stranger than fiction," writes Waters's detective-narrator, and in *Autobiography of a French Detective* "truth" and "fiction" are only two of a number of categories in symptomatic collapse.

Canler's *Autobiography* situates itself at the heart of the social unrest of Paris in the mid-nineteenth century and through its comparison of British and French systems of justice constructs an analogy that hits home in a British context. In a chapter titled "The French Detectives," Canler describes the origin of the French detective system in the work of Vidocq. In Canler's version of the story, Vidocq was a thief who made money in prison by acting as a stool pigeon; upon his release, he was hired to act as a double agent, a paid spy among criminals who, ever a criminal, soon resorted to the deployment of agents provocateurs to gain the bonuses that accompanied a high rate of arrest. Vidocq's career, which prompted the foundation of the first official French detective squad, was consistently characterized by the fraudulent provocation of public turmoil for the sake of financial gain in the name of "justice."

The philosophy "set a thief to catch a thief" described British critics' understanding of the French justice system.[30] The good Canler, in contrast, is in theory invested in justice for the sake of justice. A veteran of Antwerp, Quatrebras, and Waterloo, he was the son of the head of the military gaol at Namur: "And thus I spent my earliest years in a prison. The recollections of that period have made me understand what influence the impressions of youth have upon the ideas which are developed at a later date in the man. Brought up in principles of the strictest probity, I naturally felt a salutary terror of everything that might entail punishment" (10). Canler proposes childhood psychological traumas as the rationale for his fanatical commitment to justice. This is a notably negative model of "probity," constructed relative not to an abstract idea of the good or the virtuous but to the looming, aversive threat of prison punishment. Thus firmly establishing a negative basis for virtuous acts, and therefore the presumption of normative guilt, Canler offers a critique of a police system in which duties are political rather than magisterial, in which agents provocateurs are regularly deployed to embroil "innocent" citizens in incriminating antigovernment plots from which individual officers stand to profit. In rural areas, Canler reports in disgust, agents provocateurs were especially adept at flushing out the thoughts and desires of private citizens: agents disguised as itinerant salesmen were known to sell icons of the royal family, then secretly offer icons of the emperor, arresting all those who purchased emperor souvenirs. In Paris, agents disguised as workmen were known to get real workmen drunk, incite remarks against the government and in favor of revolution, and then arrest those workmen for political insurgency (14).

The success of agents provocateurs in France produces a blurring of the distinction between *gens d'armes* and criminals. The implication is that corruption lurks deep within even the most virtuous citizen, even unconsciously, and that it can be exposed for the purpose of punishment. This is every bit as true for the police, who never escape the insinuation of corruption despite Canler's gestures toward their heroic stability in a city devastated by violence:

> In fact, what is the soul of the policeman? Money: for he must have in his pay, first, skilful, active and intelligent agents by profession, who second his chief in his plans and wishes, accomplish his orders, follow his plans, in a word, realize the thought which he has conceived; and secondly, denouncers, contemptible beings, dragged out of crime by fear, and selling to the police, for a small fee, the secrets of their comrades. . . . Next, what are the means given to the head of the detective department to sim-

plify, facilitate, and foster his operations? The centralization of information which tells him every day what crimes have been committed, what convicts have broken their bans, what malefactors have entered the lodging-houses, and a thousand other not merely useful but indispensable facts and occurrences. (160–61)

Thus, the "soul" of the policeman is money, and money produces information, with paid informants feeding into a bureaucracy and into the comprehensive dossier of social exchange. The eyes and ears of the police are everywhere, and neither a right to nor a presumption of privacy survives. The heady combination of money and information constitutes police power: the bureaucratic, panoptical centrality of the Sûreté underscores the insidious threat to autonomy and personal privacy.

Corruption follows power. If the "soul of the policeman" is money, the flow of information is a means to a personal as well as a political end. The narrator of Waters's *Recollections of a Detective Police-Officer* (1856) typically attributes his employment to "the period when adverse circumstances—chiefly the result of my own reckless follies—compelled me to enter the ranks of the Metropolitan Police, as the sole means of procuring food and raiment."[31] In Canler's text the underemployed and underpaid cop is a bribable and corruptible cop, and Duhamel, in Waters's *Experiences of a French Detective-Officer*, informs us in no uncertain terms that an unconscionable degree of power accrues to the individual detective within the corrupt and political French system:

> Why is it that enrolment in the ranks of the gendarmerie is so eagerly sought after, especially in the rural communities? The pay is wretched, the fatigue and peril confronted by those brave, devoted men, immense. True, but as a great amends, they exercise vast personal and practically irresponsible authority and influence. The cultivator, and the village artisan, have always a welcome for the gendarme. The best wine, or cider, as the case may be, the whitest bread, the richest cheese, is always placed before him. Quite natural that it should be so! Is he not officially present at all their festivals—at saint-days, wedding day *fêtes*, at the Guinguettes, to see that the right tunes are played, the right songs sung, the right toasts given? And cannot he, in these monthly reports of his, designate this one as favourably, the other as unfavourably, disposed towards the Government! Sacred Blue! I should think so! (16)

In contrast to a French economy dependent on such fawning flattery and dissimulation, England has the opportunity to emerge in implicit contrast as a haven of egalitarian democracy. "My excuses for interweaving such comments with 'The Experiences of a French Detective Officer,'" writes Duhamel, "rests upon the fact, set forth in the first pages of my book—namely, that a French Detective Officer, is and must be, more or less, a political spy; and as a necessary consequence, that his vocation is not merely influenced, but governed by political exigencies" (168). For Duhamel as for Canler, "political exigencies" come to mean the cruel and arbitrary agendas of self-interested political regimes, vulnerable at all times to violent coups d'état fueled by the dissimulation encouraged among its citizens. The function of the spy-police, then, is to penetrate the ever-increasingly performative artifice of ostensibly honest citizens, to rupture the facade of that very moral virtue that is in theory beyond imitation. The dissimulation of the spy-police thus mimics the behavior, and perhaps the dissimulation, of the private citizens it monitors. The privacy of the domestic sphere is therefore turned inside out and revealed to be not only eminently permeable to police surveillance but a manipulatable, political trope.

Waters and Canler both labor to establish distinctions between French and British police systems, and Waters spends an entire introductory chapter defining and defending the relationship, which breaks down for his narrator Duhamel over the question of politics:

> It is true that they are alike agents of the public force, and that their common mission is to frustrate or detect offences against the person and against property. But there the resemblance ends. The English officer is not required to watch the political tendencies of the dwellers in his district—to report which newspaper citizen Gros-Ventre subscribes to, or whether the print-portrait purchased by Jacques Bonhomme for four sous was one of Napoleon, Henri, or Barbés. The city commissioner would stare if my lord mayor directed him to furnish an exact list of the names and pursuits of the individuals usually invited to Professor ————'s reunions, with a sketch of the under-current of conversation which prevailed thereat; and Sir Richard Mayne would conclude that Lord Palmerston had been suddenly smitten with insanity, if the noble premiere were to request him to ascertain how the account of a distinguished member of the parliamentary opposition stood at his bankers. And these are among the every-day duties of the French Detective Police! (13–14)

Duhamel's assessment of the distinction between British and French detectives illustrates the complex and potentially competing agendas of detective fiction. The defense of the British police as not only honest but honorable is facilitated through the example of a French system of totalitarian surveillance that simply goes too far. These novels, in their construction of this salient distinction, begin to articulate boundaries of public and private that define and protect the autonomy of the British citizen. French social unrest constitutes the symbolic negative of that autonomy, the contrast that enables its expression obliquely by means of what it is *not*: "the domestic warfare constantly waging between the agents and breakers of the law" (vi).

Thus novels such as Waters's walk a fine line in relation to the "domestic" nature of warfare. For the mission of the detective novel is, as Miller writes, "a penetration of social surfaces,"[32] making what is invisible, concealed, or transgressive not only visible but aligned with standards of behavior, justice, and morality; in their emphasis on a society's urgent need for police protection, police fictions display bourgeois moral ethics almost exclusively in terms of their failure. Victorian detective fictions succeed in presenting the transgression of crime as titillating because they do so within the containment structure imposed by resolution. Waters's defensiveness about both the police and the process of detection displays the practical advantages of a preoccupation with the French: through the display of what the English system is not, he makes clear not only what that system might be but also the terrific powers afforded a centralized, bureaucratic, and information-gathering government police aligned against the population it is meant to defend—and he wields this comparison like a truncheon. The superabundance of French detectives in British detective fiction, many of whom are themselves, like Duhamel, escaped political prisoners, exposes the fragility of the distinction between politics and protection, public and private spheres of agency and knowledge, and perhaps most significantly of all, the complex and multiple vulnerabilities of the private citizen.

The figure of the French detective on British soil enables a deterioration of the integrity of private and public spheres, and this implicates the sexual politics through which those spheres are differentiated. As Josephine Butler argues, the constitution of a spy-police in the streets and alleyways of Britain undermines the presumption of individual erotic autonomy: "In Paris and every bureaucratically-governed capital we have the fullest proofs that not only is a State police apt to fail in its duty of protecting the persons of the citizens, but that its agents become themselves the violators of personal liberties, the assailants of the modesty and chastity of women, and the cause, frequently, of public disorders." The spy-police signify corruption that extends even to their assault on "the modesty and chastity of women"; in the context of resistance to the Contagious Diseases Acts, Butler sought to reclaim women's right to habeas corpus—to their retention, in the public sphere, of an unassailable zone of personal privacy. The deterioration of "personal liberties" in Britain, after the model of the French, signifies, for Butler, the deterioration of chivalrous ideals of virility and chastity that symbolize the domestic discourse of the British nation: "Thus public spirit in France became emasculated," she writes, and should the French system take hold in London, "[t]he perpetuation of such a system of rule as that existing in the Metropolis is not only enervating to the manly independence of the Englishmen who reside there, but is fraught with danger to our constitutional freedom."[33] The "manly independence" Butler describes as so jeopardized in modern Britain involves the steady draining of the stuff of private life into public view. By presenting this in terms of threatened "emasculation," Butler suggests that the "personal liberties" of the British citizen are gendered liberties, anchored within heterosexual codes of chivalry and chastity. The introduction of a spy-police force undermines the sexual continence of each private citizen, male or female. The implication lingers: to this day a lingerie boutique in the West End of London bears the name Agent Provocateur, its blackened windows and pink neon sign belying, or perhaps just exposing another side to, its rather dignified upmarket neighbors.

What, then, of the agent provocateur in England? From the cover of *Revelations of a Lady Detective*, published in 1864, peers "Mrs. Paschal," smoking a cigarette, her crinoline sufficiently short to expose a pair of slender ankles, her skirt hiked up to reveal the red petticoat she wears beneath. Mrs. Paschal quite brazenly inhabits the public sphere, and the café table visible behind her locates the British detective imaginatively, once again, on a Parisian boulevard; although the novel's action is confined to England, the lady detective, mobile and by definition manipulative of the "cover story" provided by feminine virtue, is coded as French.

The provocative cover image belies the novel's presentation of Mrs. Paschal as an older widow at the same time that it underscores the unusually high level of physical exertion she brings to her job; in nearly every episode, as the cover suggests, her body is on the line. Midway through the novel a frustrated criminal exclaims, "Why, I should as soon have thought of seeing a flying fish or a sea-serpent with a ring in its nose" as a lady detective.[34] No mere peeler in petticoats, Mrs. Paschal practices

*Revelations of a Lady Detective.* Reproduced by permission of the
Fales Collection, Bobst Library, New York University.

the art of stealthy gliding at home in order to be prepared for action in
the underworlds of London. She crawls through subterranean tunnels—"I
sighed for a Colt's revolver" (26)—and apprehends Italian "Carbonari"
gangsters. She pursues bandits through a pneumatic mail-delivery tube,
landing squarely, and unexpectedly, in the midst of King's Cross Station,
and she enlists as a novitiate in a Catholic convent in order to save a misguided heiress. Mrs. Paschal practices an intensely physical ethic of justice.

Never hesitating to use her gender strategically as a means of infiltrating dens of moral turpitude, Mrs. Paschal's heart is as stout as her prose is purple. She succumbs only once, and then not too convincingly, to the impulses of nature: "When I found myself amongst friends and freed from the great danger which lately menaced me, I showed that I was a woman and swooned away" (88).

The criminal dread of female detectives originates in a built-in surprise factor: men are "thrown off their guards when they see a petticoat" (57). Constantly catching criminals, and men more generally, unawares, and implicitly versed in the ways of provocation, Mrs. Paschal suggests that all female detectives, indeed all detectives, are provocateurs. She reports that the employment of female detectives in England originated with the famous French investigator Fouché.[35] Mrs. Paschal writes of her superior, Colonel Warner:

> It was through his instigation that women were first of all employed as detectives. It must be confessed that the idea was not original, but it showed him to be a clever adapter, and not above imitating those whose talent led them to take the initiative in works of progress. Fouché, the great Frenchman, was constantly in the habit of employing women to assist him in discovering the various political intrigues which disturbed the peace of the first empire. His petticoated police were as successful as the most sanguine innovator could wish; and Colonel Warner, having this fact before his eyes, determined to imitate the example of a man who united the courage of a lion with the cunning of a fox, culminating his acquisitions with the sagacity of a dog. (2)

Fouché symbolizes a veritable menagerie of desirable qualities. In the process of imitation, Colonel Warner, successful deployer of female detectives, hopes to achieve the characteristics of courage, cunning, and sagacity emblematized in his French colleague. What remains implicit but unspoken is the suggestion that Warner has imitated Fouché not only in the deployment of female detectives but also in their deployment to political ends: the great Frenchman "was constantly in the habit of employing women to assist him in discovering the various political intrigues which disturbed the peace of the first empire." Again, the Victorian police novel exploits the qualities of ambiguity inherent in the detective who is always potentially agent provocateur. And what is acutely clear is the potential of the "petticoated police," lifting her skirt to expose a bit of red, to make the private public, to expose what lurks behind the facade of virtuous convention.

The female detective underscores the detective's more general investment not only in the performative qualities of undercover work but also in an overdetermined display of moral virtue, which is sharply contrasted to criminal vice. Mrs. Paschal is ostensibly more domestic missionary, less domestic "protective," than convention would dictate; thus, her narrative generates a much more explicit metalanguage of explanation and justification than the narratives of her brothers in moral rectitude. As Mrs. Paschal's exaggerated fainting spell suggests, this underscores a certain performative mode that attaches itself to moral virtue: "I showed that I was a woman and swooned away." Mrs. Paschal foregrounds that performative investment early and often:

> I was well born and well educated, so that, like an accomplished actress, I could play my part in any drama in which I was instructed to take a part. My dramas, however, were dramas of real life, not the mimetic representations which obtain on stage. For the parts I had to play, it was necessary to have nerve and strength, cunning and confidence, resources unlimited, and numerous other qualities of which actors are totally ignorant. They strut, and talk, and give expression to the thoughts of others, but it is such as I who really create the incidents upon which their dialogue is based and grounded. (3–4)

Like all ladies, she is an actress, only more so; like Macbeth, she is concerned with both the power and the futility of such theatrical display. Mrs. Paschal's identity is fluidly adaptable to the demands of any given crisis. Will she cheat, lie, deceive, bait her suspects in order to achieve justice? Certainly, and she will do so to even greater effect than most detectives, much less most actresses, because as a middle-aged widow she has seen a bit of the world. But will Mrs. Paschal overidentify, turn criminal herself to catch her prey? Certainly not, for she is working on behalf of a higher power: justice.

Stalking a lesser actress, the beautiful Lady Vervaine, to discover the source of her mysteriously plentiful cash, Mrs. Paschal reports:

> I envied this successful actress all the beautiful things she appeared to have in her possession, and wondered why she should be so much more fortunate than myself; but a moment afterwards, I congratulated myself that I was not, like her, an object

of suspicion and mistrust to the police, and that a female detective, like Nemesis, was not already upon my track. I vowed that all her splendour should be short-lived, and that in these gilded saloons and lofty halls, where now all was mirth and song and gladness, there should soon be nothing but weeping and gnashing of teeth. (9–10)

This is a moment in which pleasure turns to rage, a moment of one talented actress's identification with another, a moment of discrepancy, in which Mrs. Paschal envies "all the beautiful things" Lady Vervaine appeared to possess. The signifiers of femininity suggest, Mrs. Paschal recognizes, a class formation from which she is excluded, destined, like Heathcliff, to watch splendor unfold from the wrong side of the window. So Mrs. Paschal constructs a sharp distinction between the "beautiful things" that accrue to signify femininity and the virtue that in theory accompanies them. In other words, she takes the high road, congratulating herself "that I was not, like [Lady Vervaine], an object of suspicion and mistrust to the police." By disavowing the stuff of femininity, Mrs. Paschal claims its righteousness for her own. And in the name of the righteous, sanctioned context of official police business, she legalizes revenge as the domain of virtue: "I vowed that all her splendour should be short-lived, and that in these guilded saloons and lofty halls, where now all was mirth and song and gladness, there should soon be nothing but weeping and gnashing of teeth." In a moment of disavowal, Mrs. Paschal rechannels desire into rage, into revenge: she can't have it, so she will destroy it, quite viciously, in the name of virtue. In the encounter of the two actresses, though, for a moment the question arises how one can tell the difference between detective and criminal. Is there, ultimately, a difference at all? The detective, motivated by desire and righteousness, succeeds in proportion to his or her ability to successfully identify with the criminal mind. But it is the complete reversal of such identification that finally separates detective from criminal. Psychologically promiscuous, the protective detective dallies with vice but, in theory, at the end of the day sleeps the sleep of the just.

The success of agents provocateurs in France blurs the distinction between detectives and criminals. As a paradigm of remote control and a signifier of the erosion of individual autonomy, the agent provocateur is a figure of theoretical complexity who conceives of subjectivity within profoundly paranoid terms: power—police power, if you will—emerges not from direct action but from the successful displacement of action, and accordingly responsibility for its consequences, from subject to object. In other words, the agent makes himself or herself known, and indeed profitable, through the conduit of the other: Mrs. Paschal's righteousness is brought into being by means of contrast with Lady Vervaine, still more acutely because this contrast is grounded in the terms of identification and desire. In fictional contexts, the Victorian fascination with the agent provocateur is symptomatic. This figure represents an attempt to conceive of moral and ethical complexities that challenge the desiring but would-be virtuous subject. In detective fictions, engaged with questions of ethical stability, the police detective is a surrogate for that desiring subject, trying to be a good person in the face of an apparently intractable moral degeneracy. Facing a seductive intimacy with the underworlds of London, the preventive detective wields great power—for good or for evil.

The agent provocateur represents object-relations theory gone awry, taking as it does the relational constitution of the subject to its logical—or illogical—extreme: you think, therefore I am. Freud often described the psychoanalyst as a detective, but in his 1914 "Observations on Transference-Love," he contended that not the analyst but "resistance itself [acts] as an *agent provocateur*."[36] The resistance in question involves, for Freud, the tangled web of analytic transference: both doctor and patient are embroiled in a love-hate relationship, each trying to evoke from the other some kind of emotional response—desire, anger, love. Within the terms of this exchange even resistance assumes the role of provocateur: saying no only provokes the agent to further provocation in an increasingly high-stakes gambit. In the case study of Dora, Freud writes that "there is no such thing at all as an unconscious 'No.' "[37] This suggests the seductive passive aggression of the agent provocateur, in which disavowal is the ultimate statement of desire. There is no getting beyond the pleasure principle here, for in the economy of free-floating guilt that characterizes both detective fiction and the psychoanalytic transference, who is the criminal and who is the detective? Who is the agent behind the provocateur?

The mid-Victorian resistance to the French, and especially to the titillating spell of the agent provocateur, occurs in the name of intelligible distinctions between the best of times and the worst of times, between virtue and vice, cop and criminal, public and private. But Freud's use of the term suggests that the work of the "domestic missionary" might be more complicated than it initially seems; this concept is as seductive as it is dangerous, and narrative excitement emerges from the very possibility that the detective might go native. This gets at the heart of the paradox that constitutes the genre of police fiction: just as it is the work of the police to draw distinctions between virtue and vice, to distinguish cop from criminal in the sharpest terms possible, it is the task of the novelist to complicate such distinctions. The pervasive figure of the agent provocateur and, more generally, the counternarrative provided Victorian novelists by the example of social volatility across the Channel postulates a profound instability at the heart of bourgeois ideals of English domestic virtue—just barely in the subjunctive.

For centuries of shared history contribute to a sense of irreconcilable sibling rivalry between Britain and an "Other" only as different as the Channel is wide.[38] From the opening moments of *A Tale of Two Cities* (1859), Dickens constructs that rivalry in terms of mimetic identification: "There were a king with a large jaw and a queen with a plain face, on the throne of England; there were a king with a large jaw and a queen with a fair face, on the throne of France. In both countries it was clearer than crystal to the lords of the State preserves of loaves and fishes, that things in general were settled for ever."[39] Such mimesis encompasses not only the genetic and hegemonic structure of royalty but also an ill-fated complacency about social unrest; the notion that "things in general were settled for ever" in 1775 was belied more rapidly and more dramatically in France than in Britain, but Dickens goes to pains to undermine any lingering ethos of well-being on the British side of the Channel.

In the newly Darwinian world in which Dickens produced *A Tale of Two Cities*, the presence of French and Irish refugees on British soil brings to crisis an issue expressed through the racist terminologies of empire: the project of telling the difference between individuals of varied national identities, ethnicities, and races, when such distinctions remained invisible to the naked eye. Discourses of discrete national identity threatened by the infiltration of spies—and even by the infiltration of the *idea* of spies—are an attempt to fathom the implications of a newly porous social order in Britain. Discrepancies between the urgent disavowal of agents provocateurs and the French police and the parallel fascination with the Vidocq figure in contemporary fiction suggest the volatility inherent within cross-Channel cultural exchange in the mid-nineteenth century.

"All that's wanted now," declaims a police commissioner in Conrad's 1907 novel *The Secret Agent*, "is to do away with the *agent provocateur* to make everything safe."[40] Even in that novel, however, the agent provocateur is a hydra-headed figure. Conrad resurrects the familiar figure of Vidocq in Verloc, anarchist and agent provocateur. Verloc is killed for his activities, but by his wife rather than the police, and even after his death plots of provocation, secrecy, political intrigue, seduction, and revenge continue unabated. "From a certain point of view we are here in the presence of a domestic drama," writes Conrad. This is domesticity writ small, revealing the murderous frustrations and passions that constitute the "respectable bond" of husband and wife (221). It is also domesticity writ large and similarly in crisis, Britain infiltrated by anarchists and spies, by police and politicians working in their own private interest, rather than in the interest of abstract ideals of nation, virtue, and liberty that constitute the public good. At the novel's end Mrs. Verloc, murderer of husband and agent provocateur, kills herself by jumping overboard while crossing the Channel. "An impenetrable mystery seems destined to hang for ever over this act of madness and despair," reads the newspaper report of her suicide (307). Thus, in a very literal sense the "domestic drama" of Victorian fiction ends where it began, in the English Channel, in deceit, in mystery, in the ambivalent excitement of madness and despair through which conventions of moral virtue are, if only for a moment, secured.

## Notes

1. *Times* (London), 29 September 1854, 6, col. D. Subsequent references are to this article.

2. Stanley H. Palmer, *Police and Protest in England and Ireland, 1780–1850* (Cambridge: Cambridge University Press, 1988), 14; on the Kennington Common meeting, see 484–89. Palmer reports that contemporary newspaper reports estimated the number of special constables present to be as high as 125,000. See also Philip John Stead, *The Police of Paris* (London: Staples, 1957), 119. Stead reports that despite Napoleon III's affinity for a British constabulary "designed to ensure public tranquillity," political policing "took a new lease on life" during the Second Empire (118–19).

3. Palmer, *Police and Protest*, 11. The French *maréchaussée* was a highly centralized police force founded in 1544. It had more than 3,000 *gens d'armes* in the mid-eighteenth century, and by the mid-nineteenth century the number had increased to 25,000 (ibid., 11–12). See also Phillip Thurmond Smith, *Policing Victorian London: Political Policing, Public Order, and the London Metropolitan Police* (London: Greenwood, 1985). In 1856 further legislation required the establishment of local police forces in even the smallest towns in Britain, under the decentralized, relatively autonomous control of local authorities.

4. Bernard Porter, *The Origins of the Vigilant State: The London Metropolitan Police Special Branch before the First World War* (Woodbridge, N.J.: Boydell, 1987), 4.

5. Thomas Waters, *The Recollections of a Policeman* (London, 1852), preface.

6. Bernard Porter, *Plots and Paranoia: A History of Political Espionage in Britain, 1790–1988* (New York: Routledge, 1989), 71.

7. Josephine Butler, *Government By Police* (London, 1879), 22–23.

8. Porter, *Plots and Paranoia*, 81. Porter's theory of this dramatic change in police strategies involves the rise of a "chivalric ethos" of honor and decency that contrasted British social stability with the revolutionary fervor on the Continent, accompanied by Whiggish ideals of progress, openness, and fair play (see esp. chs. 4 and 5).

9. See Eugène-François Vidocq, *Vidocq, The French Detective: An Autobiography* (Philadelphia, 1881); and, more recently, idem, *Vidocq: The Personal Memoirs of the First Great Detective*, ed. and trans. Edwin Gile Rich (Cambridge, Mass.: Houghton Mifflin, 1935), Philip John Stead, *Vidocq: A Biography* (New York: Staples, 1953), and Samuel Edwards, *The Vidocq Dossier: The Story of the World's First Detective* (Boston: Houghton Mifflin, 1977).

10. D. A. Miller, *The Novel and the Police* (Berkeley and Los Angeles: University of California Press, 1988), 24.

11. The *Times* article is quite critical of the fact that even in reform the Parisian police force remains armed, often with swords or pistols, in marked contrast to the Metropolitan Police, who rely on their truncheons alone. Such "ostentatious display of offensive weapons," the *Times* argues, is a holdover from the system of provocation that has always characterized the French police and is bound to do more to cause crime than to prevent it: "In a street-row you can do nothing with a deadly implement but run the offender through the body, if it be a sword, or blow his brains out, if it be a pistol you hold in your hand. Now, this won't do. In the first place, the act may really be tantamount to murder; and in the second place, if the victim were at the time engaged in open resistance to the public authorities, it will never do to slaughter him on the spot. Public opinion will not tolerate results of this kind, unless satisfactory reasons be shown in each particular instance to justify the act."

12. Henry Wreford, "Spy Police," *Household Words* 1 (21 September 1850): 611–14, also quoted in Porter, *Origins of the Vigilant State*, 2, and idem, *Plots and Paranoia*, 89.

13. Robert D. Storch, "The Policeman as Domestic Missionary: Urban Discipline and Popular Culture in Northern England, 1850–1880," *Journal of Social History* 9 (1976): 487. See also E. P. Thompson, *The Making of the English Working Class* (New York: Vintage, 1966), 81–83.

14. Storch, "Policeman as Domestic Missionary," 482.

15. Robert D. Storch, "The Plague of the Blue Locusts: Police Reform and Popular Resistance in Northern England, 1840–57," *International Review of Social History* 20 (175): 66. Storch quotes from the union broadsheet titled "Destructive And Poor Man's Conservative," 2 November 1833.

16. Robert Reiner, "Political Conflict and the British Police Tradition," *Contemporary Review* 236 (1980): 194, emphasis in the original.

17. Friedrich Engels, *The Condition of the Working-Class in England, from Personal Observation and Authentic Sources* (Moscow: Progress Publishers, 1973), 264.

18. On urbanity, allegory, and mystery in mid-nineteenth-century British and French fiction, see Richard Maxwell, *The Mysteries of Paris and London* (Charlottesville: University Press of Virginia, 1992).

19. For a history of the infiltration of agents provocateurs within Luddite and other labor movements of the early nineteenth century, see Porter, *Plots and Paranoia*, 41–64.

20. John Carter writes: "Some of the many volumes which appeared in London from the 'fifties onwards, purporting to be reminiscences, may actually have been genuine; but the authors of most of them were literary hacks, and it is probably safe to label the whole class of 'Revelations' and 'Experiences' and 'Diaries' of 'Real Detectives' and 'Ex-detectives' as fiction, at any rate as far down as 1890" ("Detective Fiction," in *New Paths in Book Collecting: Essays By Various Hands*, ed. John Carter [London: Constable, 1934], 35).

21. Eric Quayle, *The Collector's Book of Detective Fiction* (London: Studio Vista, 1972), 35.

22. Angus Bethune Reach, *Clement Lorimer; or, The Book with the Iron Clasps* (London, 1849), 130.

23. The critic for the *Atlas* is quoted in Quayle, *Detective Fiction*, 37.

24. Quayle, *Detective Fiction*, 35. See also Stead, *Vidocq*, 213–17; and "Vidocq's Exhibition in Regent Street," *Times* (London), 9 June 1845, 6, col. b.

25. Waters [pseud.], *The Experiences of a French Detective-Officer, Adapted from the Mss. of Theodore Duhamel* (London, 1861), 228. The British Library catalogue lists an 1847 version of this book that credits Duhamel with its authorship. Subsequent references are to the 1861 edition.

26. On the doubleness of the political refugee in mid-Victorian Britain, see Porter, *Plots and Paranoia*, 76–78, 90–91.

27. There has been some confusion among bibliographers about the distinction between Waters's *Experiences of a French Detective-Officer*, published in 1861, and Canler's *Autobiography of a French Detective from 1818 to 1858*, published in 1862. Editions of the two texts were issued separately by the Parlour Library, but in the Fales Collection at New York University Canler's *Autobiography* is bound with a novel by Waters (*A Skeleton in Every House*), and the catalog gives Waters publication credit for the Canler text. Although frequently confused and quite similar both in form and in content, they are in fact two different texts; the proximity of their production and their contemporary popularity should underscore the symbolic significance of the "French detective" figure in mid-Victorian Britain.

28. F. C. L. Wraxall, *The Second Empire as Exhibited in French Literature, 1852–63*, 2 vols. (London, 1865); see vol. 2, ch. 8, "The French Police System."

29. Jean-Marc Berlière, *La Police des moeurs sous la IIIe république* (Paris: Éditions du Seuil, 1992); see esp. 198 n. 192 and 199 n. 206.

30. M. Canler, *Autobiography of a French Detective from 1818 to 1858, comprising the most curious revelations of the French Detective Police System* (London, 1862), 4. Subsequent references are to this edition.

31. Waters [pseud.], *Recollections of a Detective Police-Officer* (London, 1854), 9.

32. Miller, *The Novel and the Police*, 23.

33. Butler, *Government By Police*, 45–46, 21, 36. On the Contagious Diseases Acts, see Judith Walkowitz, *Prostitution and Victorian Society: Women, Class, and the State* (Cambridge: Cambridge University Press, 1980). On the interlocking discourses of nation and femininity, see Anne McClintock, *Imperial Leather: Race, Gender, and Sexuality in the Colonial Contest* (New York: Routledge, 1995).

34. *Revelations of a Lady Detective* (London, 1864), 160. Subsequent references are to this edition.

35. Through a reading of Balzac, Miller connects the operations of Fouché and the secret police with the disciplinary functions of the omniscient realist narrator (see Miller, *The Novel and the Police*, 21–26).

36. Sigmund Freud, "Observations on Transference-Love," in *The Standard Edition of the Complete Psychological Works of Sigmund Freud*, trans. and ed. James Strachey, 24 vols. (1953; reprint, London: Hogarth Press, 1966), 12:163. Italics in original.

37. Freud, "Fragment of An Analysis of a Case of Hysteria," in ibid., 7:57.

38. On the mutually constituted national histories of Britain and France, see Linda Colley, *Britons: Forging the Nation, 1707–1837* (New Haven: Yale University Press, 1992).

39. Charles Dickens, *A Tale of Two Cities*, ed. Andrew Sanders (New York: Oxford University Press, 1988), 1.

40. Joseph Conrad, *The Secret Agent* (New York: Oxford World's Classics, 1996), 228. Italics in original.

SHARON MARCUS

## CHAPTER TEN

# Comparative Sapphism

It is a truth universally acknowledged by readers of nineteenth-century literature possessing an interest in sapphism: they ordered this matter better in France. Odd women, romantic female friends, passionately devoted sisters and cousins may shadow British narratives of courtship and marriage; otherworldly female creatures drawn to women may occasionally creep into its supernatural fiction. In almost every case, however, those British texts refuse to define any relationship between women as explicitly sexual. For representations of women whose desire for women is unmistakably sexual—and it is that desire I am calling lesbian, and those representations I am calling sapphic—one must cross the literary channel from England to France.

Comparative studies of British and French literature have paid little attention to sapphism even though critics have long defined the difference between the two national literatures as sexual, particularly with respect to the novel. For most comparatists the sexual difference between nineteenth-century British and French literature is exclusively heterosexual: against the staid British novel of courtship throbs the French novel of adultery. But the lack of any British counterpart to the sapphism that thrived in France shows that the difference between the two literatures is also homosexual. With respect to heterosexuality, nineteenth-century French and British novels offer a contrast between two kinds of presence; with respect to sapphism, the contrast is between presence and absence. It would thus seem that the critic who compares nineteenth-century French and British sapphism is in the paradoxical position of comparing something to nothing.

One overlooked factor, however, complicates this opposition. Although nineteenth-century British writers did not produce an indigenous sapphism, French sapphism entered England through the mediation of the British periodical press. Throughout the Victorian era (1830–1900), British periodicals, whose readers often numbered in the tens of thousands, published numerous reviews of French literature that frequently discussed the work of Balzac, Gautier, Baudelaire, and Zola, including their sapphic texts.[1] While the British novel avoided sapphism, British criticism defined it as an element in the difference between national literatures, thus producing a domestic sapphism aimed at the general public—a British sapphism that alluded to lesbianism, but always and only as foreign.[2]

The British sapphism purveyed by articles in the periodical press was, as we will see, a discourse that applied to lesbianism the periphrasis and circumlocution that Ed Cohen and William Cohen have analyzed in Victorian accounts of men put on trial for sodomy and gross indecency.[3] Like knowledge of sex between men, knowledge of sex between women was expressed in language that disavowed both that knowledge and its object. When discussing French sapphic texts, reviewers used the now familiar rhetoric of the "open secret," in which, as D. A. Miller and Eve Sedgwick have argued, homosexuality can only be connoted, not denoted, and becomes visible only as a pattern of elision.[4] By the same token, a pattern of elision and circumlocution around sapphism becomes a sign of sapphism's visibility.

And a pattern there certainly was, one that prevailed over the heterogeneity of the authors who wrote the numerous articles about French literature that appeared in a wide array of British periodicals over a seventy-year period. Reviewers of French literature ranged from men and women obscure even in their own time to authors whose prestige as novelists and critics endures to this day. Some of the more famous reviewers of French literature were popular novelists, such as Eliza Lynn Linton, Margaret Oliphant, Vernon Lee, and George Moore. Others were polymaths whose areas of expertise included French literature, such as George Lewes, George Saintsbury, Leslie Stephen, and Andrew Lang. Lang, for example, was a folklorist and translator of Homer who also wrote many articles on French authors. George Saintsbury was a prolific critic of French literature who began publishing with an essay on Baudelaire for the *Fortnightly Review* in 1875, wrote numerous essays and books on French, British, and European literature, and in the 1890s edited a forty-volume translation of Balzac.[5]

The reviews cited here are drawn from periodicals representing diverse formats, prices, religious views, and political orientations. Reviews of French texts (translated and untranslated), French authors, and French literature appeared in the *Quarterly Review*, the *Fortnightly Review*, the *Westminster Review*, the *Saturday Review*, the *Contemporary Review*, and the *Edinburgh Review*, in *Cornhill*, *Blackwood's*, and *Pall Mall* magazines, and in the *Spectator*, the *Athenaeum*, *Temple Bar*, and *Belgravia*. Those periodicals differed significantly from one another with respect to format, audience, religious views, and political bent. Some were published weekly, some monthly; the *Edinburgh Review* was Whig, the *Quarterly Review* Tory, the *Fortnightly Review* freethinking under John Morley's editorship (1867–82). Some, such as *Blackwood's*, *Dark Blue*, and the *Westminster Review*, were directed at an intellectual readership, while others, such as *Cornhill*, were designed to be read by all members of middle-class families.[6] Varied as these publications were, when confronted with French sapphism their contributors displayed a remarkable unanimity in what they said and how they said it.

In what follows, I excavate Victorian critics' awareness of French sapphism; analyze those critics' rhetorical maneuvers, political intentions, and aesthetic commitments; and highlight some of the surprising findings about Victorian sexuality and Victorian literature that emerge from a reading of this archive. Let me signal my main claims at the outset. First, the visibility of French sapphism in the British periodical press indicates that the Victorian general public was aware of lesbianism and could be expected to understand even highly coded references to it. Many have argued that the Victorians produced so few sapphic texts because of a pervasive ignorance of lesbianism in Victorian England, pointing to the paucity of references to lesbians in juridical, legal, and medical records of deviance. British reviews of French sapphism suggest, however, that we have been looking in the wrong places for knowledge of sex between women and that such knowledge surfaced regularly in a genre focused on aesthetics and culture (the book review) and in a medium defined by middle-class respectability (the periodical). Second, British reviews of French sapphism reveal that Victorian critics often linked their condemnation of sapphism to a rejection of realism. This conjunction leads me to challenge the common assumption that realism was *the* dominant aesthetic in Victorian England and to question the received view of the relationship between lesbians and realism: that realism relegates lesbians to the status of the spectral, the apparitional, and the fantastic. Victorian critics perceived the lesbian not as a ghost but as a sign of the real, as the embodiment of a desire that could never transcend materialism and sensuality. For the many Victorian critics who considered realism to be a morally debased, empiricist aesthetic, realism was not antithetical to sapphism but the most plausible aesthetic in which to couch it.

## British Critics and the French Sapphic Canon

In order to introduce the sapphic canon, let me begin at the nineteenth century's end, with Havelock Ellis's "Sexual Inversion of Women," published in 1895. "Sexual Inversion in Women" is best known as one of the first sexological works to define lesbianism, but it also deserves a place in the history of literary criticism as one of the earliest formulations of a sapphic canon. Ellis's article is a model of cosmopolitanism, written by an Englishman for an American journal and replete with medical and anthropological evidence from England, Spain, Italy, Germany, and the United States. Ellis opens with a sweeping generalization: "Homosexuality has been observed in women from very early times, and in very wide-spread regions." The reader expects a similar expansiveness from the literary claim that immediately follows: the "passion of women for women has, also, formed a favorite subject with the novelist."[7] Yet the footnote to Ellis's comment about novelists has a very limited historical and national range: of the twelve authors Ellis cites—Diderot, Balzac, Gautier, Zola, Belot, de Maupassant, Bourget, Daudet, Mendès, Lamartine, Swinburne, and Verlaine—only Diderot wrote in the eighteenth century, and only Swinburne, albeit often identified by his compatriots as in effect a French writer, was English; the remaining ten sapphic authors wrote in nineteenth-century France (141–42).

   In his comments on one of the French novels he cites, Ellis refers to a "*liaison*" between two women, emphasizing the French origins of the term by italicizing it (142). In so doing, he underscores the common association of nineteenth-century France and French literature with lesbianism. The mark of France often accentuates the sapphic strain in Victorian stories of odd women: it is in France that Miss Havisham completes Estella's education and that Miss Wade transmits her "History of a Self-Tormentor"; it is in French, if not in France, that Brontë sets her eccentric Lucy Snowe, and Wilde his perverse Salomé.[8] In her study of lesbianism in literature, Terry Castle looks to France to restore the lesbian body to Anglo-American literature, arguing that "it was precisely by way of *Nana* that [Henry] James found an ingenious means of treating the subject of lesbianism"; that British lesbian couples signified their bond through imagined encounters with Marie Antoinette; and that what she calls the "counterplot of lesbian fiction" emerged in a twentieth-century British novel set in 1848 Paris.[9]

Critics who equate the literary history of lesbianism with nineteenth-century France display so much unanimity in their choice of texts that they have established what Elisabeth Ladenson calls a "canon of lesbianism in French literature."[10] Scholars repeatedly select the same works: Balzac's *La Fille aux yeux d'or* (1835), *Séraphita* (1834), and *La Cousine Bette* (1846); Gautier's *Mademoiselle de Maupin* (1835), which, according to Ellis, "made the adventures of a woman who was predisposed to homosexuality and slowly realizes the fact [its] central motive"; "Lesbos" and "Femmes damneés (Delphine et Hippolyte)," two of the condemned poems from Baudelaire's *Les Fleurs du mal* (1857); and Zola's *Nana* (1880), which, again according to Ellis, "described sexual inversion with characteristic frankness."[11] Although each of those texts represented lesbianism in complex, sometimes elliptical and equivocal ways, nineteenth-century critics and authors ignored those complications by citing them as signs of lesbianism. When the narrator of Adolphe Belot's *Mademoiselle Giraud, ma femme* (1870) tracks his errant wife to an apartment containing copies of *La Religieuse*, *La Fille aux yeux d'or*, and *Mademoiselle de Maupin*, the reader is meant to decode instantly what the misguided husband, who can only imagine a male rival, understands only in retrospect: that his wife and her female best friend are conducting a sexual affair. Within a text like *La Religieuse*, even within *Mademoiselle Giraud, ma femme* itself, lesbianism is never denoted, but once Belot uses Diderot's text to connote lesbianism, he concretizes its status as a lesbian sign.[12]

Havelock Ellis identified the French sapphic canon and discussed lesbian sexual practices as part of a controversial project to create a public discourse that characterized homosexuality neutrally, even positively. In so doing, Ellis broke with the rhetoric prevailing among British literary critics, who throughout the nineteenth century operated under and reinforced constraints on any explicit discussion of homosexuality. British critics were unable to condemn sapphism outright, as they did novels of adultery, because to do so would have required demonstrating and purveying knowledge of sexual practices and desires of which everyone, they believed, should be kept ignorant.[13] To resolve the conflicting demands of censure and censorship, British critics short-circuited meaning and made their discourse circular, repeatedly using negation, ellipsis, periphrasis, and metonymic allusion to indicate without actually explaining why *La Fille aux yeux d'or*, *Mademoiselle de Maupin*, and *Nana* made them so indignant.

Ellipsis often took the extreme form of refusing to name sapphic works by title. In one of the very few nineteenth-century British reviews of Baudelaire's work, George Saintsbury refers to Baudelaire's "Lesbian studies." Especially when capitalized, *Lesbian* could mean "from or of Lesbos" and not "female homosexual." Saintsbury, however, does not associate the term with the Greek island, nor even with Baudelaire's poem entitled "Lesbos," which itself links *Lesbian* to *lesbian* ("Lesbos, où les Phrynés l'une l'autre s'attirent"). Rather, he anchors the meaning of the term in female homosexuality by referring it to the "passion of Delphine" and thus to the sapphic poem "Femmes damnées (Delphine et Hippolyte)." Saintsbury thus signals his understanding that Baudelaire wrote sapphic poems and is so familiar with Baudelaire's "condemned pieces" that he knows how many lines they total, but not once does he quote from or name "Femmes damnées" or "Lesbos."[14]

Leslie Stephen used a similar strategy when, in an 1871 article titled "Balzac's Novels," he discussed Balzac's *La Fille aux yeux d'or* without giving its title. *La Fille aux yeux d'or* was first published in France in 1834 and 1835 in the *Scènes de la vie parisienne* as part of a series of three linked works collectively entitled *Histoire des treize*. Few British critics ever mentioned it, and as late as the 1890s George Saintsbury excluded it from an English translation of *The Thirteen*, noting in his preface that "[i]n its original form the *Histoire des Treize* consists . . . of three stories: *Ferragus* . . . *La Duchesse de Langeais* . . . and *La Fille aux Yeux d'Or*. The last, in some respects one of Balzac's most brilliant effects, does not appear here, as it contains things that are inconvenient."[15] British critics who read French were probably aware of *La Fille*, since their articles often referred to French editions of Balzac's complete works, as well as to *Ferragus* and *La Duchesse de Langeais*, the other two works that made up the *Histoire des treize* in the *Comédie humaine*. In 1896 Leonard Smithers, known as a publisher of both Decadent literature and expensive pornography, published a limited, illustrated edition of *La Fille aux yeux d'or* with a translator's preface by the poet Ernest Dowson. Given its reputation as a work about forbidden sexual practices, it is not surprising that until 1886 no review of Balzac's works referred to *La Fille aux yeux d'or* directly by name.[16]

Most of the critics who did not name *La Fille aux yeux d'or* also did not discuss it, a simple form of critical neglect that could have had multiple motives or none. Leslie Stephen's "Balzac's Novels," published in the *Fortnightly Review* in 1871, is more striking: Stephen devotes an entire paragraph to Balzac's "most outrageous story" without ever providing that story's title. Even more curiously, Stephen comments on the story by extensively paraphrasing but never directly quoting its opening pages.[17] As a result, only one who has already read the tale, can recall it, and has it to hand can identify that the "most outrageous story" is *La Fille aux yeux d'or*. Stephen's elision of *La Fille*'s title suggests that reading the story would be so dangerous that he can neither direct his readers to it nor even acknowledge that he himself has read it. In writing about a sapphic text, Stephen goes against the critical grain by concealing instead of demonstrating knowledge of his subject. At the same time, however, Stephen's choice of paraphrase over quotation means that instead of keeping Balzac's words separate from his own, he has put them into his own words, made them his own in the very process of disowning them. And in another of the paradoxical effects characteristic of censorship rhetoric, because only those who *have* read the forbidden *Fille* can understand what Stephen is talking about, his prose creates a community based on the very thing he intended to suppress: shared knowledge of *La Fille aux yeux d'or* and the lesbianism it represents.[18]

Critics who, unlike Stephen, were willing to name sapphic titles were no more willing than he to discuss the content of sapphic texts, even if only to condemn it. Instead, they reverted to ellipsis, negation, and circumlocution so consistently that a cumulative reading of their reviews establishes the blatant refusal to speak about sapphism as *the* way to speak about it. An 1866 *Saturday Review* tirade against Swinburne's *Poems and Ballads* excoriated the poems as "unspeakable foulnesses" that depicted "the unnamed lusts of sated wantons." The reviewer took as his "only comfort" the belief that "such a piece as 'Anactoria' will be unintelligible to a great many people, and so will the fevered folly of 'Hermaphroditus,' as well as much else that is nameless and abominable."[19] As poems that overtly depict sapphism and bisexuality, "Anactoria" and "Hermaphroditus" confer on the indeterminate terms "nameless" and "unspeakable" a specific and easily determined meaning. Although intended as synonyms, "nameless" and "unspeakable" register the contradictions of a rhetoric that simultaneously wants to stigmatize sapphism and make it invisible. The reviewer calls the poem's subjects "nameless" in order to enact his wish that they have no name, but he belies that namelessness with the term "unspeakable," which suggests that the poem's subjects do have names, but ones too awful for him to utter.[20] In an 1889 essay titled "Some of Balzac's Minor Pieces," George Moore, an admirer of Balzac and Zola, explained that he could only list the titles of Balzac's queerest hits: *La Fille aux yeux d'or*, *La Dernière Incarnation de Vautrin*, *Une Passion dans le désert*, *Séraphita*, and *Sarrasine*. Moore allies those texts with "the strange, the perverse, the abnormal" and suggests that he would like to write about them but can do no more than name them: "[I]t would be both interesting and instructive to analyse these strangest flowers of genius, but having regard for the susceptibilities of the public, I will turn at once to Massamilla [Doni]," a story of heterosexual intrigue whose plot he recounts at length. Moore's use of the word "susceptibilities" suggests a set of competing publics: a censorious one he cannot risk offending, a vulnerable one he cannot risk harming or infecting, and a queer one that he cannot risk arousing.[21]

Such hyperbolic ellipses, whose characteristic expression would be "I'm so shocked that I can't say why," had their corollary in the redundant understatement "It's so clear that I don't need to explain." Eliza Lynn Linton, a novelist and frequent contributor to the *Saturday Review*, wrote a series of articles in 1886, published in *Temple Bar*, entitled "The Novels of Balzac." Cannily relating lesbian characters to gay ones in order to avoid naming what they have in common, Linton writes that the "love of la cousine Bette . . . for Valerie is emphatically in all things of the same kind as that of Vautrin for Lucien."[22] What kind of love, one might ask, was the love of Vautrin for Lucien? Vautrin, Linton explains, "watches over [Lucien] as tenderly, if not so purely, as a mother."[23] But Linton offers no further explanation and praises Balzac for providing almost none himself. Linton approves of the "trenchant touch" with which Balzac depicts "the various corruptions of society": "A rapid hint—a side flash—one word— haply a mere gesture, photographs a whole moral tract which only the initiated see and of which the ignorant remain ignorant." She then specifies that Balzac's linguistic economy saves the ignorant reader from gaining knowledge of homosexuality: Balzac, Linton states, "shows us Vautrin's secret by a touch as rapid as a fencer's riposte—an allusion as obscure as a cypher —."[24] Linton's telegraphic, paratactic prose mimics the compactness and the inscrutability she praises and has the same ostensible purpose she ascribes to Balzac: to bleed explanation from representation, to show not only without telling but practically without showing. When her own discussion threatens to reveal too much about Vautrin's secret Linton replaces coded understatement with outright ellipsis: Vautrin's apparently selfless love for Lucien has, we are told, "a baser thread than appears on the surface in this double life—but with that we need not meddle."[25]

As a supplement to ellipsis, British critics of the French sapphic canon added two tropes of substitution: antonomasia and the pronominal adjective. In antonomasia a proper name supersedes a descriptive term; critics frequently used proper names to avoid using terms for women who had sex with women (*lesbian, invert, sapphist*, and *tribade* were among the several available at the time). Often the proper name was that of a contemporary or classical author associated with sapphism or homosexuality; sometimes an allusion to Sodom and Gomorrah or the name of a literary character served as the substitute.[26] The *Saturday Review* article on *Poems and Ballads* worried that if Swinburne published enough, "English readers will gradually acquire a truly delightful familiarity with . . . unspeakable foulnesses" that would allow them to grasp "the point of every allusion to Sappho . . . or the embodiment of anything else that is loathsome and horrible."[27] Arthur Waugh wrote that Swinburne "scrupled not to revel in sensations which for years had remained unmentioned on the printed page; he even chose for his subject refinements of lust, which the commonly healthy Englishman believed to have become extinct with the time of Juvenal."[28] As Terry Castle and Emma Donoghue have shown, the English had associated Juvenal with sapphism for centuries.[29] Intended as veils that would conceal sapphism, the proper names *Juvenal, Sappho, Catullus*, and *Swinburne* became instead veils that outlined it.

Antonomasia was potentially endless in its circularity. Baudelaire's sapphism was termed "Juvenal," Swinburne's sapphism "Juvenal," "Sappho," and "Baudelaire." Critics evoked the sapphism of Gautier's work by alluding to Catullus, Baudelaire, Swinburne, and the Plato of the *Phaedrus* and the *Symposium*; they designated Balzac an author of queer texts by comparing him to the Shakespeare of the *Sonnets*.[30] Every term in the antonomasiac series became interchangeable, so that just as Swinburne's sapphism was called "Juvenal" or "Baudelaire," Zola's sapphism was called "Swinburne."[31] In an article on Zola, Vernon Lee noted that "Nana . . . gradually extends her self-indulgence (not accompanied by shades of Swinburnian empresses, but, as she comfortably believes, of real ladies, of *femmes du monde*) to regions not usually included by those who seek merely a *good time*: sane and without bad intentions, she enters the happy hunting-grounds of monomania and crime."[32] The reader who has Zola's novel *Nana* to hand can determine that Lee's Swinburnian empresses are sapphic and that Lee is alluding to the episode in which Nana has an affair with another woman, Satin, because, like Leslie Stephen writing of *La Fille aux yeux d'or*, Lee is paraphrasing Zola's novel without acknowledging it. Lee's comment that Nana believes her actions to be the same as those of "real ladies, of *femmes du monde*," echoes the justification of Nana's lesbian affair with Satin in Zola's text: "Why, it was done everywhere! And she named her woman friends, and swore that society women did it too"; in the original French, the phrase for "society women" is "dames du monde."[33] The comparison is instructive: where Zola uses free indirect discourse ("Why, it was done everywhere!" is narration, not quotation) and thus merges his narrator's voice with Nana's, Lee separates her views from Nana's with the phrase "as she comfortably believes." By avoiding direct quotation of Zola's text, Lee refuses to confer on his words the denotative status that might then also extend to the lesbianism his text depicts. As recent critics and biographers have shown, Lee had an acute and negative awareness of lesbianism, whose overt sexuality she rejected in favor of romantic female friendships based on ideals of purity and beauty.[34] Since to attack lesbianism directly would reveal her intimate knowledge of it, Lee distances herself and the reader from lesbianism by displacing Nana's "crime" onto euphemism ("Nana's self-indulgence") and literary allusion ("Swinburnian empresses"). As if to compensate for the extent to which *Swinburne* had in effect become a synonym for *lesbian*, Lee then obscures the allusion to Swinburne through a double elision (Nana is "*not* accompanied by *shades* of Swinburnian empresses" [emphasis mine]).

In a second form of substitution, critics of sapphic texts replaced verbs and nouns with a cluster of recurring adjectives: *unnatural, artificial, morbid, obscene, immoral, perverse, impure,* and *diseased.* Those adjectives functioned as pronouns that syntactically modified words like *story* or *poetic imagination* but semantically replaced words like *invert, lesbian,* or *sapphist.* By using such adjectives, reviewers could substitute negative evaluations of sapphism for accounts of what prompted their disapproval. Leslie Stephen described Balzac's *La Fille aux yeux d'or,* we will recall, as his "most outrageous story," without giving the story's title or explaining what made it outrageous. George Moore associated *La Fille* with Baudelaire's *Les Fleurs du mal* when he included it in his roster of Balzac's "strangest flowers of genius" and then explained one adjective ("strangest") tautologically with a string of others that qualified the works listed as "abnormal," "bizarre," "strange," "perverse," and "exotic."[35] A commentator on *Mademoiselle de Maupin* wrote that Gautier puts "forward wanton evidences of abnormal disorders and unhealthy moods of passion"; his "morbid expressions" are themselves "the evidence of disease," and his heroine pursues knowledge of humanity "in a very unnatural manner."[36] Swinburne, we are told repeatedly, dwells on "morbid cravings and monstrous appetites," on "what is lowest, most perverted, and extreme in nature"; *Parallèlement,* Verlaine's collection of sapphic poems, exhibits "perversity, moral and artistic."[37] In citing these remarks, I have not separated them from explanations of what made the texts at hand perverse or morbid. The adjectives *perverse* and *morbid* did not modify exegeses of character and plot but substituted for them. In the amalgam of excess and lack typical of a rhetoric that cannot designate its subject, the lacunae of ellipsis were filled with the redundancies of tautology.

That sapphic texts so consistently elicited adjectives such as *morbid*, *perverse*, and *unnatural* suggests that reviewers replaced specific references to lesbianism and homosexuality with general terms of opprobrium, as did a host of Victorians writing in other domains. A concordance of a recent anthology titled *Nineteenth-Century Writings on Homosexuality*, which collates texts drawn from law, science, literature, and politics, would reveal that words like *morbid*, *degrading*, and *unnatural* are among those recurring most frequently throughout the volume, often in tandem with outright ellipsis.[38] John Symonds took for granted that terms such as *unnatural* and *perverted* were equivalents for what he called sexual inversion, and he alternately rejected and employed those adjectives to describe the sexuality for which he sought greater tolerance.[39] The same adjectives resurfaced in Havelock Ellis's essay "Sexual Inversion in Women," although Ellis used them to redefine lesbianism, not to condemn and elide it. Sexual inversion, wrote Ellis, is an "abnormal passion," but only in the numerical sense; and only in a few, not all instances, was lesbianism "morbid" and "vicious." Heterosexuality itself could be unnatural and perverse: for "the congenitally inverted person the normal instinct is just as unnatural and vicious as homosexuality is to the normal man or woman, so that in a truly congenital case 'cure' may simply mean perversion."[40]

As with other forms of substitution, the censorious adjectives that so consistently replaced references to sex between women finally stood for the signs they were meant to supersede. Yet the adjectival litany applied to sapphic texts also complicates what until now I have presented as a one-to-one relationship between sapphism and the British reception of Balzac's, Gautier's, and Zola's texts. While only in the case of homosexuality did British critics refuse to specify exactly what made them so indignant, their assessment of texts as "obscene," "morbid," "perverse," "eccentric," and "diseased" was in no way limited to sapphism. Reviewers of *Villette*, for example, used the same words when they consistently faulted its protagonist Lucy Snowe for being "eccentric," "morbid," deliberately "queer," and "perverse." In explaining those judgments, however, they never cited her theatrical cross-dressing, her flirtatious relationship with Ginevra Fanshawe, or her fascination with other women's bodies; they listed as the substance of those adjectives Lucy's "moodiness," "melancholy," and "sluggish despondency."[41] The English sensation novel was frequently indicted in terms similar to those used to describe sapphism; Margaret Oliphant, a novelist and frequent contributor to *Blackwood's*, criticized the sensation novel for being replete with "disgusting" stories of bigamy and seduction by authors possessing either "forbidden knowledge" or a "morbid imagination."[42]

The labels affixed to French sapphism were also attached to French literature that represented sexual transgressions other than lesbianism, in articles spanning decades by authors both hostile and sympathetic to French literature and thought, publishing in periodicals with diverse, even opposed political programs. An 1833 review of recent French novels attacked "scenes of licentious indulgence, or revolting atrocity" that depicted "adultery or incest."[43] W. R. Greg, a prolific contributor to the periodical press who is now known for his articles on prostitution and the redundancy of women, also wrote several articles on French literature. In an 1855 essay in the *Edinburgh Review* Greg described modern French literature as "diseased to its very core," an instance of "talent perverted," "morbid" and "dangerous," preaching a "tone of sexual morality . . . lax and low," catering to a "demand for what is unnatural, extravagant, and bad," and devoted to situations both "grotesque" and "improbable," exemplified in "monstrous, harrowing, unnatural conceptions."[44] George Lewes described the suggestions of incest in Balzac's *Père Goriot* as "revolting" in 1844, and as late as 1903 Lionel Strachey called the suggestions of incest in *La Curée* "monstrously grotesque."[45] Leslie Stephen characterized Balzac's entire oeuvre as "strange, hideous, grotesque," the work of an author with "morbid tendencies" and a "taste for impossible horrors," whose *Comédie humaine* was "a collection of monstrosities, whose vices are unnatural."[46]

When Hannah Lynch attacked Zola's detailed accounts of pregnancy and childbirth in *Fécondité*, she differed from critics writing about sapphism by documenting exactly what she reviled in Zola's work, using the lengthy citations typical of Victorian reviews. Her language converged with that of critics of sapphism, however, when she condemned this thoroughly heterosexual text for its "morbid uncleanliness," "nauseous abundance of obscenities," and its characters' "vices" and "perversities."[47] When British critics placed sapphic texts on a continuum with other French representations of sexual transgression, they replicated a move often made within sapphism itself, for *Mademoiselle de Maupin*, *La Fille aux yeux d'or*, and *Nana* also linked lesbianism to male and female cross-dressing, male masochism, prostitution, and adultery, all often qualified as exotic in the orientalist sense of the term. By using identical terms to evaluate representations of lesbianism, homosexuality, adultery, prostitution, and incest, critics created a broad category of sexual transgression associated with French literature.

How can the British reception of French sapphism in particular and French literature in general explain the comparative difference between French and British sapphism with which we began? Because British reviewers, male and female, writing across the social and political spectrum of the periodical press, used a rhetoric that clearly signaled their awareness of sapphism's lesbian content, we cannot adduce sheer ignorance of lesbianism to explain why there was no nineteenth-century British sapphism. And because Victorian critics responded to representations of heterosexual and homosexual infractions alike with similar expressions of outrage, hostility to homosexuality alone cannot explain the Victorian refusal to depict lesbianism in literature or its unwillingness to discuss such depictions explicitly. To explain the sapphic difference between nineteenth-century British and French literature we must instead place it in larger contexts, and several plausible ones present themselves. One such context would be the British mistrust of France as a site of political and sexual revolution. In 1850 a *Dublin University Magazine* critic conjoined sexual mores and French political forms when he accused George Sand of ministering to "the vicious appetites and dangerous ambition of a depraved democracy."[48] W. R. Greg related French literature's sexual content to the French people's political longing for a "universal liberation from all bonds."[49] In 1890 William Barry contended in the *Quarterly Review* that the "license of the eighteenth century culminated in '89 and '93" and led to "a literature which is read by hundred of thousands, and which inflames while it expresses their vilest fancies."[50]

The orientalism of Victorian critics could also explain the rejection of sapphism in particular and French literature in general. British reviewers associated French fiction with a notion of the East that indiscriminately included Islamic and Indian religions, Arab literature, Chinese society, and a Mediterranean culture historically linked to ancient Greece and Rome. Orientalist allusions accreted around Balzac's queer texts. Linton noted that Vautrin's story was "one of those impossible romances which hold us like an Arabian Nights' tale"; George Parsons located the source of *Séraphita* in "a mass of occult doctrine, the origins of which must be sought in the theosophy of India."[51] In her review of Zola's corpus, Emily Crawford, a journalist who wrote many articles about France, noted that Zola had not founded naturalism but "brought into it new blood from Italy and the Levant." Crawford identified that "new blood" with an ancient and Eastern brand of sexuality: "In the Mediterranean States south-east of the Alps, the Satyr has survived Jupiter, Apollo, and Minerva." Seeking to explain how France had come into contact with the East, Crawford pointed to Venice, which she claimed "was in more direct contact with the Levant than any other Italian city and picked up some survivals of the ancient cults of Syrian gods and goddesses that must remain nameless in this article." By means of Venice, Asia Minor's sexual corruption had converged on European literature, since "[t]hat Bride of the Adriatic [Venice] was the root and stem of the tree which has had for its fruits the books quoted in the Vizetelly prosecution" (Vizetelly was prosecuted for publishing English translations of Zola and other French authors).[52]

A third explanation that could encompass the British hostility to French representations of lesbianism *and* adultery would be opposition to any autonomous female sexuality. Literary critics and historians have documented the British animadversion to female sexuality outside the framework of marriage, along with the British fear of novels as incitements to female sexual fantasy.[53] During the eighteenth century, British fears about reading's effect on women were directed at novels in general, including British novels. In the nineteenth century, British reviewers began not only to differentiate between the more respectable British novel and its less respectable French counterpart but also to contrast and defend the reading practices of Englishwomen against those of Frenchwomen. With rare exceptions, British critics identified women's novel reading as more democratic in England, more restricted in France. In France, they argued, marriages were usually arranged, and because novels emphasized passion, French literature had to focus not on loveless marriages but on adulterous liaisons driven by desire. Because French novels so frequently depicted adultery, French parents forbade them to unmarried daughters, who, British critics asserted, were under strict family control.[54] Conversely, reviewers claimed that in England young, unmarried women enjoyed great liberty and were thus allowed both to read novels and to be heroines of novels. But because young women were allowed to act in and read them, British novels had to focus on lawful courtship and marriage so that they would be suitable for their audience.[55]

The scenarios of reading that nineteenth-century British critics elaborated for French women underscore once again the connections they made between heterosexuality and lesbianism. For British critics, the peculiarities of French marriage made novels a sexual commodity; their female readers thus formed an erotic community organized around a shared pleasure in novel reading. When they imagined what might happen when such reading took place, female encounters with the heterosexual transgressions within novels often led to visions of women using books to have group sex across class lines. In an article titled "French Novels and French Life," published in *Macmillan's* in 1877, Caroline Peyronnet, using the pseud- onym Honoré de Lagardie, wrote that in France "the chief consumers of novels are . . . shop-girls and ladies' maids, who devour them; then, alas! young married women, whose first use of their newly-acquired liberty is to seize on the forbidden fruit of their girlhood, novels and the minor theatres."[56] The word "devour" takes on a sexual cast when novels are de- scribed as "forbidden fruit," and the use of eating metaphors to describe the reading of working and middle-class women creates a bond of sexual appetite among them, a bond made even more cohesive when their desires converge on the same object. As the paragraph continues, the book's status as a token of sexual exchange among women intensifies:

> [T]he only customers publishers can reckon on . . . are the circu-
> lating libraries. The volumes which come from these pass from
> the grisette to the great lady but are never allowed to lie on the
> table of a well-ordered drawing-room. She who reads them
> hides them in her bedroom, or secretes them under the sofa
> cushion if a visitor is announced. There is a guilty joy in the in-
> dulgence, and the volume, moreover, is generally soiled and un-
> seemly in more than a figurative sense.[57]

This passage demonstrates a link between reading and autoeroticism whose pervasiveness has been noted by many scholars.[58] Peyronnet exhibits the female reader in her bedroom, emphasizes the privacy, secrecy, and guilty pleasure of her reading, and even suggests that the reader's aroused body makes direct contact with her book, which thus becomes "soiled and un- seemly in more than a figurative sense." Less familiar is the lesbian element of this scene: when the book passes from the working-class "grisette," known for her sexual freedom, to the lady liberated by marriage, sexual pleasure is transmitted as well. Although in this vision of sexual exchange, female readers do not make direct contact, the image of the same book passing from one masturbating woman to another suggests a mediated form of sex between women, brokered by the circulating library. Female reading is thus a problem because it both exposes women to (hetero)sexual content and enables (homo)sexual relations. Reading places those two ap- parently distinct forms of sexuality on a continuum of activities in which women wriggle free of male, familial, and marital control.

## Idealism, Realism, Sapphism

Hostility to revolutionary politics, to "the oriental," and to female sexual autonomy could each plausibly explain why British critics called French sapphism and French novels perverse, morbid, and unnatural—but each can account for only a portion of their responses. Hostility to French revolutionary politics cannot explain why critics rejected the British sensation novel. Many reviewers never linked France to the East. Nor can hostility to female sexual independence explain one of the knottiest puzzles of the British reception of French literature: the widespread critical appreciation of George Sand. Certainly, the British periodical press often attacked Sand as a novelist and as a person; how could they not, given her French nationality, her affiliation with revolutionary ideas, her frequent recourse to Byronic orientalism, her use of the novel to criticize marriage and justify adultery, and her reputation as a woman who dressed in men's clothes and had sex outside marriage with both women and men? More astonishing is the high number of reviewers, some friendly to French literature, some hostile to it, who from the 1830s on noted all these facts and nevertheless accorded Sand the highest place in French literature, well above Sue, de Kock, Dumas, Janin, and even—or especially—Balzac.[59] An 1833 *Edinburgh Review* article predominantly hostile to French fiction lamented Balzac's "cynicism" but praised Sand's *Indiana* and *Valentine*, novels that indicted marriage, as works "in a calmer, truer, and better spirit than those with which we have been occupied."[60] George Reynolds, who modeled his popular *Mysteries of London* on Eugène Sue's work and who translated French authors, including Paul de Kock and Victor Hugo, also wrote *The Modern Literature of France* (1839). A review of that work cited Reynolds's high opinion of Sand as "an *hermaphrodite* of intelligence, combining in her soul the masculine ideas and spirit of the lords of the creation with the delicacy and softness of her own sex." The anonymous reviewer concurred with Reynolds, writing appreciatively of Sand's "gallant effort to revolutionize the social position of her sex" and her "transcendent genius," which "scorned the vulgar trammels of matrimony." He also complimented her for being "more intellectual and less anatomical" than Balzac, as did George Lewes, who contrasted Sand's "earnest error" to Balzac's "immorality."[61] In 1855 W. R. Greg called French literature "diseased to its very core" but exempted Sand, noting that she had "gradually worked herself free from all the turbid and unlicensed sensuality which disfigured her earlier productions, and that a manlier tone, a better taste, and a higher morality have grown upon her year by year."[62] Nina Kennard's 1886 review of Sand's correspondence with Flaubert stated, with no negative comment, that Sand looked like she belonged to the "troisème sexe" and elected her to the literary pantheon because "she remained an enthusiast, a believer in good, a troubadour singing ideal art and love."[63] An 1892 review titled "The French Decadence" compared Sand favorably with de Maupassant: "It was said of George Sand that ... she 'always wrote like a gentleman.' M. Guy de Maupassant is a gentleman ... but he does not write like one."[64]

What is the common denominator of these statements? In stating that Sand followed the established code of a gallant gentleman, that she transcended the vulgar, the anatomical, and the sensual, and that she differed from realists and naturalists by expressing her belief in the good, the moral, and the ideal, British reviewers recognized and approved in Sand an aesthetic that has only recently received attention from twentieth-century critics: idealism.[65] Naomi Schor's *George Sand and Idealism* and Margaret Cohen's *Sentimental Education of the Novel* have shown that in nineteenth-century France the aesthetics and poetics they respectively call "idealism" and "sentimentalism" were influential predecessors of realism and remained prestigious alternatives to it throughout the nineteenth century.[66] The British response to George Sand suggests that Victorian critics also assigned pride of place to their own version of idealism, reserving their greatest praise for novels whose characters exhibited the ideal and idealizing qualities of faith, altruism, self-sacrifice, and love. Like their French counterparts, British critics were suspicious of detailed descriptions of material objects and bodies, as well as of plots that established self-interest, knowledge, and power as the engine of social life.[67] Naomi Schor has shown that French idealists emphasized political utopianism, Margaret Cohen that French sentimentalists appropriated the poetics of tragedy.[68] British idealists differed from their French counterparts in that they did not believe that novels should convey a utopian or tragic worldview but rather that literature should communicate a moral vision shaped by accepted religious and social values. Although British idealists insisted on the novel's moral purpose, they rejected romance, melodrama, and fable in favor of everyday life, unity of plot, developed characters, and plausibility; hence the ease with which scholars of British novel theory have portrayed Victorian idealists as realists only.

At the same time, however, British idealists saw no contradiction between plausibility and conformity to a moral code, "lifelike characterization and good ethical doctrine," because their notion of verisimilitude was saturated by social convention.[69] While French novelists and critics opposed realism to idealism, Victorian critics tended to *blend* the two. The ease with which Victorian criticism and novelists combined an interest in verisimilitude with an allegiance to moral norms has led twentieth-century critics who define realism in terms of French literature to deem the Victorian novel non-realist. Hence, for example, Erich Auerbach's exclusion of Victorian novelists from his magisterial literary history of realism, *Mimesis*, and hence the frequency with which critics concede that the Victorian exemplars of realism—Dickens, Gaskell, Trollope—fail to be fully and consistently realist.

A reading of *Victorian* literary criticism shows that Victorian critics called the aesthetic to which they subscribed "idealism" far more often than they called it or described it as "realism." In a philosophical context, *ideal* meant conceptual or imaginary, confined to the realm of thought. In Victorian literary criticism, however, *idealism* referred to the belief that *literary representations should be governed not by mimesis and fidelity to reality but by values, by adherence to ideas of the good.* As the Victorian author Edward Bulwer Lytton put it, "Art concerns itself only with the realm of ideals; it is not the imitation but the 'exaltation of nature.' "[70] Kenneth Graham, in *English Criticism of the Novel, 1865–1900*, has noted that "the moral ideal, or a specifically Christian ideal, or, most frequently, a belief in the absolute nature of the social code" dominated Victorian aesthetics.[71] Other major studies of Victorian theories of the novel (by Richard Stang, Edwin Eigner, George Worth, and David Skilton) have, however, overlooked the importance of idealism. Instead, they have focused on equating Victorian critics' rejection of the outlandish improbability associated with romance with a Victorian anticipation of realism as defined by Henry James, in which mimesis, verisimilitude, and objectivity are preferred to authorial intervention and poetic justice.[72] Yet for the many Victorian critics who distinguished romance from the ideal there was no conflict between verisimilitude and poetic justice, realism and idealism: for those critics the standard of verisimilitude in realism was not based on objective, empirical norms but on moral values. As Margaret Oliphant asserted in an article entitled simply "Novels," a "sublime respect for sentimental morality and poetic justice . . . distinguishes the English public. . . . The wicked people are punished and the good people are rewarded, as they always should be."[73]

Idealism was not only, as Richard Stang concedes, a coherent alternative to realism; for the majority of British critics writing in the periodical press, it was the preferred alternative. When Victorian critics referred to realism or to constitutive aspects of realist poetics, it was often to compare them unfavorably with idealism or to defend them as being alloyed with idealism. Even critics who supported realism had to acknowledge that idealism was the more highly valued approach. In the 1862 introduction to his novel *Basil* (1852) Wilkie Collins justified basing his story "on a fact within my own knowledge," on something "real and true," by explaining, "My idea was, that the more of the Actual I could garner up as a text to speak from, the more certain I might feel of the genuineness and value of the Ideal which was sure to spring out of it."[74] In an 1858 essay titled "Realism in Art" George Lewes asserted that "[r]ealism is . . . the basis of all Art" but had to clarify that "its antithesis is not Idealism, but Falsism."[75] Alfred Austin, a frequent contributor to the periodical press in the 1860s and 1870s who was appointed England's poet laureate in 1896, wrote an article titled "Our Novels" for *Temple Bar* in 1870 that seemed to adopt what we now call a realist position by objecting to lapses in verisimilitude. But even as he argued that fiction should be faithful to reality, he conceded that "the novelist is not bound to hold the mirror up to Nature"; rather, the novelist "has a perfect right to imagine [the world] better than it really is, and so to describe it. But his ideal must be loftier than the real he abandons for it. . . . The novelist . . . should describe life either as it is or as it ought to be; *the latter application and employment of art being, in our opinion, the higher of the two.*"[76] When he states that a novelist would be justified in abandoning empirical precision for a moral vision of life "as it ought to be," Austin is articulating the central principle of idealism.

So strong was the critical investment in idealism that British critics could only defend authors we now think of as incontrovertible realists by turning them into idealists. In 1880 W. S. Lilly argued that Balzac's "realistic power" was "united to and subserved a marvellous gift of idealization, whence resulted those colossal types, whose effect upon the mind is such as no servile copying of the living model, no direct imitation of the seen and actual can ever produce."[77] An 1861 article titled "French Fiction—Its Better Aspects" identified a striving for idealism as one of those better aspects. Beneath French literature's realist veneer and French authors' apparently "cynical creations," the reviewer detected "a yearning . . . for some other state than one of unaspiring indifference" and a shift away from "gross materialism" toward a "realism . . . vivified by the incarnate Ideal."[78] A realist would call the lack of a moral position objectivity; this critic, as an idealist, calls the lack of a moral position indifference and cynicism, not because he actively objects to representations based on verisimilitude but because he considers moral values to be integral to the definition of truth. Vernon Lee's article "The Moral Teaching of Zola" similarly makes clear that the only way she could justify Zola's novels was to contain their realism within a larger idealist project. She emphasizes that her thoughts about his work are "connected rather with right and wrong than with ugly or beautiful, accurate or inaccurate," and explains that her "desire" is "to suggest what moral lessons Zola may bring to his worthier readers, by showing what lessons he has conveyed to myself."[79]

Because idealists were committed to representations based on social norms endowed with the status of transcendental moral values, they responded with intense disapproval to descriptions and plots detached from those norms. For idealist critics, neutral physical descriptions of reality were immoral, cynical, and antisocial because they failed actively to promote correct social values. As late as 1899 Edouard Rod diagnosed Zola's problem as his membership in a generation devoted to the "materialistic and narrow; which believed itself justified in denying the existence of realities that do not fall under the senses," an aesthetic credo that Rod directly opposed to Sand's "idealism."[80] The faithful transcription of reality became the abandonment of moral values and the debasement of nature since idealists understood nature not as a set of empirical facts but either as a source of social conventions or as a state that needed to be morally overcome and perfected. An encyclopedic approach that recorded all social types became a refusal of literature's duty to inculcate models of virtue. An 1839 review of George Reynolds's *Modern Literature of France* singled out Balzac as exemplifying the demerits of the French writers who "profess to draw from life": "Wherever literature follows instead of leading, imitates instead of creating . . . wherever nature is treated like the magazine of a magic lantern, in which beings the most beautiful or grotesque . . . are all *equally admissible* . . . a cynical hardihood [is] generally the result."[81] Using a commonplace figure for realist techniques and effects (the magic lantern) as an epithet, the reviewer disparages Balzac's inclusive understanding of nature as antisocial ("a cynical hardihood") and a servile abdication of duty ("following instead of leading").

Some Victorian idealists explicitly called the aesthetic they opposed "realism" or identified it as a representational commitment to the "real" and "reality."[82] The author of an 1878 article in the *Gentleman's Magazine* linked the "minuteness with which [Balzac] describes places and objects until they are pictured to our eyes" to Balzac's dedication to a "realism so perfect that no flaw could be discovered in it"; and J. A. Symonds wrote that Zola's "realism consists in his careful attention to details . . . and his frank acceptance of all things human which present themselves to his observing brain."[83] An even larger number of critics, who did not use the term *realism*, disapproved of representations that depicted reality vividly but without respect to moral bounds because such representations lacked an ideal with which to delimit the material. What realists would call an objective and encyclopedic grasp of the world, idealists called "granting a bill of indemnity to all that is perverse and ungovernable in our nature."[84] Alexander Innes Shand, a prolific journalist who wrote an article on Balzac for *Blackwood's* in 1877, argued that Balzac's detailed descriptions "carr[y] the conscientiousness of his art to a morbid extravagance"; by calling Balzac's realism not only morbid but extravagant, Shand suggests that by the standards of idealism, which establishes reality ethically and not empirically, realism failed to be realistic.[85] Thus, William Barry, in his 1890 article "Realism and Decadence in French Fiction," similarly charged Balzac with using "materialist and physiological methods" in order to depict the "abnormal, *not* the ideal." Note that Barry's phrase opposes the abnormal not to its nominally *empirical* opposite, the norm, but to its *ethical* competitor, the ideal. Balzac's depictions are "abnormal" not because they lack statistical representativeness but because they lack decency. Indeed, Barry sees Balzac's fiction as all too real when he associates it with materiality; but for Barry that materiality lacks representational authority: "With him [Balzac] the spirit is but a more finely-woven flesh. The whole world is artificial . . . or it is monstrous, unhealthy, chaotic."[86] It would seem that nothing could be more natural and real than "flesh." But Balzac's materiality challenges the foundational supremacy of pure "spirit," of the transcendental values that Barry believes should underwrite representation. Balzac's fictional universe is "artificial," hence unreal, in the sense that it fails to match up to the *beliefs* that should govern reality. And since the idealist legitimates sexual desire only as an expression of spiritual values and moral norms, Barry also criticizes Balzac for according a fatal power to "physiology" that makes the "ideal . . . powerless," just as Linton disparaged Balzac for making "love . . . simply sexual . . . he pretends to nothing higher."[87] For the idealist, an exclusive commitment to materiality and empirical reality was not only an impoverished mode of representation but a morbid, depraved, and unnatural one.

"Morbid," "monstrous," "unhealthy," "unnatural": Victorian critics applied the same terms to realism and to sapphism, and the British response to sapphism becomes clearer once we recognize its connection to the aesthetic debates about realism. British critics labeled both sapphism and realist texts "morbid" and "unnatural" because they associated both with fleshliness, sensuality, and representations of material embodiment that bypassed moral values.[88] British reviewers considered sapphism morbid and perverse because they understood homosexuality as a carnal, utterly sensual form of desire that could never be idealized as love.[89] Because they deemed lesbianism irrevocably material, Victorian critics were attuned to how even the most nonrealist sapphic texts—those by Swinburne and Gautier—used detailed description to create reality effects. Henry Buxton Forman, for example, compared Swinburne's work to Dutch painting and police reports, two common figures for realism, then chastised Swinburne for "the falsity and impropriety of his ideal."[90] Forman considers Swinburne false not because he writes about the unreal—what could be more real than a police report?—but because he writes about the improper; his ideal, not his reality, is what Forman deems false. And lest we think that lesbianism would not be included in a Victorian list of improprieties, note that Swinburne himself linked lesbianism to the impropriety documented in police reports. In defense of Baudelaire's "Femmes damnées" Swinburne explained that the "side of . . . [Delphine and Hippolyte's] passion which would render them amenable to the notice of the nearest station is not what is kept before us throughout that condemned poem."[91]

To associate Swinburne and Gautier with realism now seems counterintuitive, given Swinburne's phantasmagoric poetry and Gautier's avowed relationship to aestheticism and French romanticism. The Victorian tendency to ascribe features of realism to sapphism is even more surprising because, as several scholars have shown, lesbianism has historically been deemed a spurious desire.[92] One would thus expect Victorian critics to have associated lesbianism with the unreal and sapphism with antirealism, and indeed a few reviewers did so. Writing for the *Fortnightly Review* in 1885, William Courtney, a philosopher who also contributed to and edited a number of periodicals, called Swinburne an "artificer of impotent emotions" and asked, "Is it experience, or morbid fancy, that dictates . . . poems . . . on an extinct type of Roman lust, or a love fragment of Sappho, or on the statue of the Hermaphrodite in the Louvre?"[93]

Far more frequently, however, critics associated Swinburne with an excessive and unseemly emphasis on physical characteristics, sensations, and desires that they considered unworthy of representation despite their registration as real, or rather because they referred to the real and nothing but the real. Swinburne's *Poems and Ballads* were excoriated for their preoccupation with "fleshly things" and their exhibition of a "feverish carnality."[94] Unlike Shakespeare, who portrayed "the exquisite innate purity and rich idealism . . . of the passion," Swinburne's emphasis on the "carnal details" and "material" aspects of love led him to depict "morbid cravings and monstrous appetites" and the "violent bodily pains and pleasures that terminate in the senses." For this critic, states of pain and suffering "are least of all fitted for poetical or artistic use" because a "shriek or a swoon is so purely physical as to exclude for the moment the ideal element altogether."[95] When this critic calls Swinburne's representations of lesbian and other deviant sexual desires "monstrous," he means not that such desires are fantastic but that they are unsanctified by moral norms because they derive from "the sensual appetite instead of . . . pure spiritual feeling."[96] Far from lauding Swinburne for achieving realism's impossible goal—creating a representation so vivid that it would attain the materiality of what it represents—this critic deploys materiality as a term of reproach because he does not consider mimesis to be the goal of representation. That a desire indubitably exists would thus be no justification for representing it; indeed, since the "purely physical" can only be impure, the more a desire exists in the register of reality alone, the less authority artists would have to depict it. "Monstrous appetites" should be absent from literature not because they do not exist but because they *should* not exist.

If it surprises us to discover that Victorian critics linked their rejection of sapphism to their condemnation of crucial features of realism, we are surprised both because we associate the Victorian novel with realism and because critics have persuasively argued that realism is inimical to lesbian representation. Terry Castle, Marilyn Farwell, and others have argued that realism's investment in the marriage plot, in narrative structures fueled by heterosexual desire, and in heteronormative notions of verisimilitude make it impossible for realist texts to represent women's desire for women as anything but a disruptive, excessive, and spectral remainder of the real.[97] Recent critics differ from Victorian ones in assigning a very high value to the real; indeed, one might say that contemporary critics idealize realism. When realism is deemed the most worthwhile aesthetic, to be excluded from representations of the real is to be denied social value. A crossing of the realist and idealist wires makes the values assigned to representation (as ideal or not ideal) come to stand for the fact of representation (as real or not real). Critics thus assert that representations that deny lesbians social value also deny lesbians that other supreme value, representation as real.

Victorian critics, who did *not* value the real in and of itself, believed that French sapphism, far from reducing lesbianism to a spectral state, rendered it as all too real. Contemporary critics, who do value the real, equate the valence of a representation with its degree of realism and thus assert that when writers generate what in another decade we called "negative images" of lesbians, they also relegate lesbianism to the realm of the illusory. Thus midway through *The Apparitional Lesbian* Terry Castle cites Gautier's *Mademoiselle de Maupin* as one of several "overt references to lesbian eroticism," an example of the "would-be salaciousness, shading at times into outright obscenity, so common in the nineteenth-century French literature of female-female desire."[98] With the words "overt references" Castle asserts that Gautier depicts lesbian sexuality as real. With the phrases "would-be salaciousness" and "outright obscenity" Castle also suggests that Gautier devalues lesbianism. Castle's sense that Gautier holds lesbianism in contempt explains why earlier in the same book she adduces *Mademoiselle de Maupin* not as an "overt reference to lesbian eroticism" but as a "derealization" of lesbianism that reduces it to "an essentially phantasmatic enterprise."[99] Castle contradicts herself when she writes that Gautier depicts lesbianism as unreal, but her contradiction has a syllogism's consistency: reality has a higher social value than spectrality; Gautier assigns lesbians a low social value; therefore Gautier does not depict lesbians as real.

That French sapphism gave lesbianism a realistic form does not negate contemporary critiques of French sapphism's negative portrayal of lesbianism. The nineteenth-century authors who produced the sapphic canon did not represent lesbianism because they valued it or promoted it as an ideal but because as realists they claimed to separate representation from social values. What better way to demonstrate that a representation was unconstrained by conventions and governed only by material reality than to depict desires whose ratification was not that they were good but that they existed? Because idealism represented the world as it should be, idealizations of lesbian sexuality could only be produced by writers who believed and were willing to assert publicly that sexual desire between women was a moral good. Because realism represented the world as it was, realists felt authorized to represent sexual desire between women despite its outlawed social status since the exaltation of social conventions was not their justification for writing.

The French sapphic texts that so outraged British critics often condemned the lesbian desire they depicted, yet British critics responded as though the French sapphic canon constituted a lesbian manifesto. The British critical misreading of French texts stemmed from a perception that to speak of homosexuality at all was to advocate it. British writers refused to advocate homosexuality because they were hostile to it in and of itself, but they shared that hostility with many of the French writers who wrote about homosexuality at length. What the authors of the sapphic canon did not share with British critics was an idealist aesthetic, in which to show things as they were was to argue that they should be. Idealists believed that disapproval of lesbianism could only be properly conveyed by refusing to represent it at all; realists saw no contradiction between portraying lesbian sexuality (this exists) and expressing narrative disapproval of it (this should not exist).

To conclude, let me return to the comparative gap between French and British sapphism with which I began and suggest that the absence of sapphism in England might be explained not by the dominance of realism in nineteenth-century British literature but by its relatively weak implantation. It has seemed obvious that realism was incompatible with sapphism because it has been so amply demonstrated that both British and French nineteenth-century realist novels have heterosexual, homosocial plots in which masculine desire works to contain female sexuality. That definition of realism, however, may be more true at the descriptive level (what realist novels did) than at the formal one (what realist novels must do). Nor does it explain why French nineteenth-century literature has so many dead and damned lesbians but Victorian literature has almost no lesbians at all.

British writers failed to produce a sapphic canon because as idealists they could not represent lesbian desire to a society that did not embrace it. Realists often asserted their difference from idealists by proclaiming that they wrote "for men, not for girls." An 1871 *Edinburgh Review* article cited Swinburne's self-defensive remark that the "purity" of art is "not that of the cloister or the harem"; cloisters and harems were often sapphic settings, but Swinburne invokes them here as metonymies for the female readers who lie outside the boundaries of "adult" art.[100] It may now strike us as ironic that realists excluded women by penning tales of girl-girl love. But in so doing, sapphic authors were making the realist point that the moral code embodied by the young female reader did not limit the content of their depictions, which would include even women outside the confines of normal femininity. A commitment to detailed portraits of a full range of social types, to representing what existed regardless of its social value, and to emphasizing matter and the body encouraged realists to represent sexual desire, especially desires marked as morally improper. In his translator's preface to a limited 1896 English edition of *La Fille aux yeux d'or* Ernest Dowson invoked those aspects of realism when he defended the story's "morbid ... to certain minds horrible" subject matter: "It was in the scheme of the *Comédie Humaine* to survey social life in its entirety by a minute analysis of its most diverse constituents. . . . [I]n the great mass of the *Comédie Humaine* with its largeness and reality of life, as in life itself, the figure of Paquita justifies its presence."[101] Dowson's comments exemplify why French realists so frequently represented lesbianism, and so frequently represented it as evil: not in order to derealize lesbianism but to appropriate it as a sign of the real.

Since French sapphism was fully compatible with anti-lesbian sentiment, and since Victorian England easily rivaled its neighbor across the Channel in its homophobia, we cannot explain the divergence between British and French literature solely in terms of the two nations' different attitudes to homosexuality. Rather, any explanation of their sapphic differences must also compare the two nations' aesthetic tendencies. Such a comparison suggests that there would have been more lesbianism in the British novel if there had been more realism and that British critics would have been more capable of commenting on French sapphism had they not been such thoroughgoing idealists.

## Notes

1. For an overview of the British response to Zola, see William C. Frierson, "The English Controversy over Realism in Fiction, 1885–1895," *PMLA* 43, no. 2 (1928): 533–50. On the reception of Baudelaire in England, see Patricia Clements, *Baudelaire and the English Tradition* (Princeton: Princeton University Press, 1985).

2. For example, an 1873 article in *Cornhill* magazine called Gautier's *Mademoiselle de Maupin* "so unashamed and profligate as to be to English ideas utterly intolerable" (Sidney Colvin, "Théophile Gautier," *Cornhill* 27 [February 1873]: 162–63).

3. See Ed Cohen, *Talk on the Wilde Side* (New York: Routledge, 1993), 143–56, 184, 195; and William Cohen, *Sex Scandal: The Private Parts of Victorian Fiction* (Durham, N.C.: Duke University Press, 1996), 75, 90–93.

4. D. A. Miller, "Anal *Rope*," in *Inside Out: Lesbian Theories, Gay Theories*, ed. Diana Fuss (New York: Routledge, 1991), 132, 125, 124; Eve Kosofsky Sedgwick, *Epistemology of the Closet* (Berkeley and Los Angeles: University of California Press, 1990); idem, "Privilege of Unknowing: Diderot's *The Nun*," in *Tendencies* (Durham, N.C.: Duke University Press, 1993), 23–51. See also Jeff Nunokawa, "The Disappearance of the Homosexual in *The Picture of Dorian Gray*," in *Professions of Desire: Lesbian and Gay Studies in Literature*, ed. George E. Haggerty and Bonnie Zimmerman (New York: Modern Language Association of America, 1995), 183–90; and Patricia White, *UnInvited: Classical Hollywood Cinema and Lesbian Representability* (Bloomington: Indiana University Press, 1999).

5. For more on these critics, see Harold Orel, *Victorian Literary Critics: George Henry Lewes, Walter Bagehot, Richard Holt Hutton, Leslie Stephen, Andrew Lang, George Saintsbury, and Edmund Gosse* (London: Macmillan, 1984); and Noel

Annan, *Leslie Stephen: The Godless Victorian* (London: Weidenfeld & Nicolson, 1984). On English literary criticism during this period, see Kenneth Graham, *English Criticism of the Novel, 1865–1900* (Oxford: Clarendon, 1965).

6. On the Victorian periodical press, see Joanne Shattock, *Politics and Reviewers: The "Edinburgh" and the "Quarterly" in the Early Victorian Age* (London: Leicester University Press, 1989); Joanne Shattock and Michael Wolff, eds., *The Victorian Periodical Press: Samplings and Soundings* (Leicester: Leicester University Press, 1982). On book reviewing in the periodical press, see David Skilton, ed., *The Early and Mid-Victorian Novel* (New York: Routledge, 1993); J. D. Jump, "Weekly Reviewing in the Eighteen-Sixties," *Review of English Studies* 3 (July 1952): 244–62; Laurel Brake, "Literary Criticism and the Victorian Periodicals," *Yearbook of English Studies* 16 (1986): 92–116; and Oscar Maurer, " 'My Squeamish Public': Some Problems of Victorian Magazine Publishers and Editors," *Studies in Bibliography* 12 (1955): 21–40.

7. Havelock Ellis, "Sexual Inversion in Women," *Alienist and Neurologist* 16 (1895): 141.

8. For a reading of Miss Wade in relation to the category of the lesbian, see Annamarie Jagose, "Remembering Miss Wade: *Little Dorrit* and the Historicizing of Female Perversity," *GLQ* 4, no. 3 (1998): 423–52; on *Villette*, see Ann Weinstone, "The Queerness of Lucy Snowe," *Nineteenth-Century Contexts* 18 (1995): 367–84.

9. Terry Castle, *The Apparitional Lesbian: Female Homosexuality and Modern Culture* (New York: Columbia University Press, 1993), 159, 107–49, 66. France also resurfaces as a site for the production of Anglo-American lesbianism in Castle's chapter on Janet Flanner, 186–99.

10. Elisabeth Ladenson, *Proust's Lesbianism* (Ithaca: Cornell University Press, 1999), 33.

11. Ellis, "Sexual Inversion in Women," 141, 142. See also Castle, *Apparitional Lesbian*, 156; Jeannette Howard Foster, *Sex Variant Women in Literature* (1956; reprint, Tallahassee: Naiad Press, 1985), 60–72, 76–78, 91–90; Henri Peyre, "On the Sapphic Motif in Modern French Literature," *Dalhousie French Studies* 1 (October 1979): 3–33; and Lillian Faderman, *Surpassing the Love of Men: Romantic Friendship and Love between Women from the Renaissance to the Present* (New York: Morrow, 1981), 254–94.

12. Adolphe Belot, *Mademoiselle Giraud, ma femme* (Paris: Dentu, 1870), 143.

13. For a discussion of this rhetoric in legal discourse, see Martha Vicinus, "Lesbian Perversity and Victorian Marriage: The 1864 Codrington Divorce Trial," *Journal of British Studies* 36 (January 1997): 70–98.

14. Charles Baudelaire, "Lesbos," *Oeuvres complètes* (Paris: Laffont, 1980), 102; George Saintsbury, "Charles Baudelaire," *Fortnightly Review* 24 (1875): 503, 501, 502.

15. George Saintsbury, preface to *The Thirteen*, trans. Ellen Marriage (London: J. M. Dent; Philadelphia: Gebbie, 1898), ix. When in 1900, Harper & Row published a U.S. version of Saintsbury's edition of Balzac's works, *La Fille* was included

in *The Thirteen*, and Saintsbury excised the line about inconvenient matters from a preface that was otherwise identical to the one in the British edition. Walter Kendrick mentions that Saintsbury also excluded *Sarrasine* and *Une Passion dans le désert* from the British edition of Balzac's work ("Balzac and British Realism: Mid-Victorian Theories of the Novel," *Victorian Studies* 20 [autumn 1976]: 9); as I discuss below, George Moore associated those stories with *La Fille aux yeux d'or*.

16. For examples of articles that name *Histoire des treize*, the *Duchesse de Langeais*, and *Ferragus* but not *La Fille aux yeux d'or*, see [Henry Sutherland Edwards], "Balzac and His Writings," *Westminster Review* 60 (July 1853): 199–200; [Alexander Innes Shand], "Balzac," *Blackwood's* 121 (March 1877): 302; and John Walter Sherer, "Balzac's Dreams," *Belgravia* 54 (1884): 439. Among the earliest articles I have found to cite *La Fille aux yeux d'or* by title are [T. E. Child], "Balzac," *Cornhill* 53 (May 1886): 476; and an American article by George Frederic Parsons, "Honoré de Balzac," *Atlantic Monthly* 57 (June 1886): 845.

17. Leslie Stephen, "Balzac's Novels," *Fortnightly Review* 15 (1871), 24.

18. Even in cases where critics eventually gave a sapphic text's title, they often began by establishing it as unfit to be spoken. For critics who did this with Gautier's *Mademoiselle de Maupin*, see W. S. Lilly, "The Age of Balzac," *Contemporary Review* 37 (1880): 1009; George Saintsbury, "Théophile Gautier," *Fortnightly Review* 29 (March 1878): 429, 431, 433; and Colvin, "Théophile Gautier," 162–63.

19. "Mr. Swinburne's New Poems," *Saturday Review*, 4 August 1866, 145.

20. Arthur Waugh similarly asserted that Swinburne "scrupled not to revel in sensations which for years had remained unmentioned upon the printed page," but as though to undo Swinburne's work of mentioning, he refused to specify what those sensations were ("Reticence in Literature," *Yellow Book* 1 [1894]: 213).

21. George Moore, "Some of Balzac's Minor Pieces," *Fortnightly Review*, n.s., 46 (October 1889): 498–99.

22. [Eliza Lynn Linton], "The Novels of Balzac, III," *Temple Bar* 78 (December 1886): 498.

23. [Eliza Lynn Linton], "The Novels of Balzac, II" *Temple Bar* 78 (November 1886): 389.

24. [Eliza Lynn Linton], "The Novels of Balzac, I" *Temple Bar* 78 (September 1886): 198, 199.

25. [Linton], "Novels of Balzac, II," 388. On Linton's engagement throughout her career with infractions of sex and gender norms, often in order to attack them, see Deborah T. Meem, "Eliza Lynn Linton and the Rise of Lesbian Consciousness," *Journal of the History of Sexuality* 7, no. 4 (1997): 537–60. Meem insists somewhat anachronistically on reading Linton as a repressed lesbian suffering from "internalized homophobia" (559). "Officially Linton abhorred homosexuality, both female and male. . . . Only by tortured indirection can Linton own her desire" (558–59). It would be more accurate to say that during the nineteenth century, to speak negatively of homosexuality was almost the only way to speak of it, and therefore homophobic remarks can prove little about their speakers' sexuality.

26. For examples of references to Sodom and Gomorrah, the Cities of the Plain, see William Barry, "Realism and Decadence in French Fiction," *Quarterly Review* 171 (July 1890): 83; and Lilly, "Age of Balzac," 1024, 1016, 1017.

27. "Mr. Swinburne's New Poems," 145.

28. Waugh, "Reticence in Literature," 213.

29. On Juvenal and allusions to sex between women, see Castle, *Apparitional Lesbian*, 102–3, 256 n. 9; and Emma Donoghue, *Passions between Women: British Lesbian Culture, 1668–1801* (New York: HarperCollins, 1995), 44, 52, 212–14, 257. Throughout the nineteenth century, British writers equated Juvenal and Catullus with obscene literature and with sapphism. When put on trial in 1888 for publishing an English translation of Zola's *La Terre*, Henry Vizetelly defended himself by citing Thomas Macaulay's comments earlier in the century that it was ridiculous to suppress an edition of Restoration drama when universities taught Juvenal's *Satire* 6 and the poems of Catullus (*Extracts, Principally from English Classics: showing that the legal suppression of M. Zola's novels would logically involve the bowdlerizing of some of the greatest works in English literature* [London: W. Vizetelly, 1888], 4).

30. For the comparison between Baudelaire and Juvenal, see "Baudelaire," *Belgravia* 15 (October 1871): 450; for the comparison between Gautier and Plato as author of *Phaedrus*, see Andrew Lang, "Théophile Gautier," *Dark Blue* 1 (March 1871): 31; for comparisons between Gautier and Baudelaire and between Gautier and Alcibiades, who overtly expresses his desire for Socrates in the *Symposium*, see Evelyn Jerrold, "Thoéphile [*sic*] Gautier," ibid. 4 (November 1872): 281; and for a comparison linking Gautier to Catullus and Swinburne, see "A Parisian Pagan," *Dublin University Magazine*, n.s., 92 (July 1878): 73, 81. In "Some of Balzac's Minor Pieces," George Moore wrote: "Shakespeare's genius was unquestionably healthier than that of any of his contemporaries, yet he wrote the sonnets; Balzac's genius was unquestionably saner than any of his contemporaries . . . and yet Balzac wrote *La Fille aux Yeux d'ors*, *La dernière Incarnation de Vautrien*, *Une Passion dans le Désert*, *Seraphita*, and *Sarrasene*" (498–99, the misspellings are Moore's). On queer readings of Shakespeare's sonnets in the 1880s and 1890s, see Cohen, *Sex Scandal*, 191–225; Andrew Elfenbein, *Romantic Genius: The Prehistory of a Homosexual Role* (New York: Columbia University Press, 1999), 66; and Chris White, ed., *Nineteenth-Century Writings on Homosexuality: A Sourcebook* (London: Routledge, 1999), 127 (excerpts from Edward Carpenter, *Homogenic Love and its Place in a Free Society* [1894]).

31. Swinburne himself both deployed and shrewdly exposed antonomasia when he said of Simeon Solomon, after the artist's arrest for having sexual contact with another man in public, that Solomon was "a Platonist, the term is at once accurate as a definition and unobjectionable as a euphemism" (H. Mongtomery Hyde, citing the second volume of Swinburne's letters, in *The Love That Dared Not Speak Its Name: A Candid History of Homosexuality in Britain* [Boston: Little, Brown, 1970], 115).

32. Vernon Lee, "The Moral Teaching of Zola," *Contemporary Review* 63 (1893): 209, emphases in the original.

33. Emile Zola, *Nana*, trans. George Holden (New York: Penguin, 1972), 329; for the phrase "dames du monde" in the original French, see Emile Zola, *Nana*, ed. Colette Becker (Paris: Classiques Garnier, 1994), 266.

34. See Kathy Psomiades, " 'Still Burning from this Strangling Embrace': Vernon Lee on Desire and Aesthetics," in *Victorian Sexual Dissidence*, ed. Richard Dellamora (Chicago: University of Chicago Press, 1999), 21–42.

35. Moore, "Some of Balzac's Minor Pieces," 499, 498. Moore signaled his debt to Baudelaire's *Fleurs du mal* when early in his literary career he published collections called *Flowers of Passion* (London: Provost, 1878) and *Pagan Poems* (London: Newman, 1881).

36. "Parisian Pagan," 82, 84.

37. Thomas Spencer Baynes, "Swinburne's Poems," *Edinburgh Review* 134 (July 1871): 82, 91; Arthur Symons, review of *Bonheur*, by Verlaine, *The Academy*, 18 April 1891, 362. Henry Spencer Ashbee defined "perversity" more precisely when he cited a description of Verlaine's *Les Amies*, included in *Parallèlement*, as six sonnets "en rimes feminines sur l'amour sapphique" (Pisanus Fraxi [Henry Spencer Ashbee], *Index librorum prohibitorum: bio-biblio-icono-graphical and critical notes on curious, uncommon and erotic books*, vol. 1 [1877; reprint, New York: Jack Brussel, 1962], 42. Arthur Symons was well versed in French literature and a frequent contributor to the *Fortnightly Review*, the *Athenaeum*, and the *Saturday Review*.

38. White, *Nineteenth-Century Writings on Homosexuality*, 20, 22, 32, 39, 42, 47, 48, 53, 60, 64, 73, 82, 85, 133, 213.

39. Ibid., 71–73, 82–85 (excerpts from John Addington Symonds, *A Problem in Modern Ethics* [1896]).

40. Ellis, "Sexual Inversion in Women," 142, 144, 158.

41. On Lucy Snowe as "morbid," "diseased," "eccentric," and "perverse," see the reviews in the *Nonconformist*, 16 March 1853, 224; *Littell's Living Age* 36 (1853): 589; and [Stopford Brooke], "Recent Novels," *Dublin University Magazine*, November 1853, 613.

42. [Margaret Oliphant], "Novels," in *Blackwood's* 102 (September 1867): 258, 260.

43. "French Literature—Recent Novelists," *Edinburgh Review* 57 (July 1833): 330, 337; the author is thought to be Thomas Moore.

44. [William Rathbone Greg], "Modern French Literature," *Edinburgh Review* 101 (January 1855): 115–16. For some of the numerous other instances in which French literature was qualified as "obscene," "perverted," and "morbid," see also [John Wilson Croker], "French Novels," *Quarterly Review* 56 (April 1836), which uses the term "pervert" to describe Raymond's seduction of Indiana in George Sand's *Indiana* (101) and calls the prostitutes in *Lélia* "monsters" (105); Croker, an expert on the French Revolution, contributed frequently to the *Quarterly Review*, including a notorious review of Keats's "Endymion" in 1818. See also [George Moir], "The Hundred and One," *Foreign Quarterly* 9 (May 1832): 349; and "Novels," *Monthly Review* 166 (December 1844), which argues that the distinctly French contribution to

the novel is "the inclination towards obscene scenes, the amalgamation of voluptuousness and cruelty," often in the form of "adulteries," "incest" (549, 550), and other
"wanton freaks of an overstrained imagination" (555). In his notorious article
"French Fiction: The Lowest Deep," W. R. Greg saw French fiction as a symptom of
"the hunger after the most diseased, unholy, and extravagant excitement," steeped in
"the voluptuous, the morbid, or the monstrous," catering to "the jaded appetite and
the perverted taste" (*National Review* 11 [1860]: 401, 405).

45. [G. H. Lewes], "Balzac and George Sand," *Foreign Quarterly Review* 33
(July 1844): 289; Lionel Strachey, "The Books of Emile Zola," *The Lamp* 26 (1903):
411.

46. Stephen, "Balzac's Novels," 17, 39.

47. Hannah Lynch, " 'Fécondité' versus the 'Kreutzner [*sic*] Sonata,' or, Zola
versus Tolstoi," *Fortnightly Review* 73 (January 1900): 69, 75.

48. "French Novels and Novelists," *Dublin University Magazine* 36 (September 1850): 353.

49. Greg, "French Fiction: The Lowest Deep," 403.

50. Barry, "Realism and Decadence in French Fiction," 81.

51. [Linton], "Novels of Balzac, II," 385; Parsons, "Honoré de Balzac," 843.
On the association of sapphism with national otherness in Britain in the late eighteenth and early nineteenth centuries, see Lisa Moore, *Dangerous Intimacies: Toward
a Sapphic History of the British Novel* (Durham, N.C.: Duke University Press, 1997),
12, 81.

52. Emily Crawford, "Emile Zola," *Contemporary Review* 55 (January 1889):
95, 97–99.

53. Richard Stang, *The Theory of the Novel in England, 1850–1870* (New
York: Columbia University Press, 1959), notes how often British critics deemed
French fiction unfit for young readers but does not convey how often female readers
were singled out during the decades he considers (215–17). Only in the 1880s did the
child replace the woman reader as the focus of campaigns against obscenity. On the
female reader in nineteenth-century Britain, see Kate Flint, *The Woman Reader,
1837–1914* (Oxford: Clarendon, 1993); and Ruth Bernard Yeazell, "Podsnappery, Sexuality, and the English Novel," *Critical Inquiry* 9 (December 1982): 339–40, 355.

54. To cite one of many examples: "In France . . . no well-educated girl,
whether noble or bourgeoise, is ever allowed to read novels. . . . It is much to be re-
gretted that French girls do not read the few novels which might safely be put into
their hands, for the unfailing operation of the law of supply and demand would in
that case stimulate the production of works of a purer and healthier tone to suit this
new class of customers" (Honoré de Lagardie [Caroline Peyronnet], "French Novels
and French Life," *Macmillan's* 35 [March 1877]: 389; see also Crawford, "Emile
Zola," 103).

55. For the notion that Frenchwomen required passion in novels because
they lacked it in marriage, see Lagardie, "French Novels and French Life," 393. For an
account of the relationship between the different contents of the French and British

novel and the different marital status women had in each country, and the accompanying notion that French literature should be prohibited to British girls, see "French Novels," *Belgravia* 3 (October 1867): 78–81.

56. Lagardie, "French Novels and French Life," 389.

57. Ibid., 389–90.

58. In addition to the work on the female reader cited above, see Cohen, *Sex Scandal*, 26–72; Thomas Laqueur, "The Social Evil, the Solitary Vice, and Pouring Tea," in *Fragments for a History of the Human Body*, pt. 3, ed. Michel Feher with Ramona Nadaff and Nadia Tazi (New York: Zone, 1989), 334–43; and Philip Stewart, *Engraven Desire: Eros, Image, and Text in the French Eighteenth Century* (Durham, N.C.: Duke University Press, 1992), 94–101.

59. On the frequently positive reception of Sand in England, see Patricia Thomson, *George Sand and the Victorians: Her Influence and Reputation in Nineteenth-Century England* (New York: Columbia University Press, 1977); and Paul Blount, *George Sand and the Victorian World* (Athens: University of Georgia Press, 1979).

60. "French Literature—Recent Novelists," 357.

61. Review of *The Modern Literature of France*, by George Reynolds, *Monthly Review* 149 (August 1839): 463, 462; [Lewes], "Balzac and George Sand," 266.

62. [Greg], "Modern French Literature," 115.

63. Nina H. Kennard, "Gustave Flaubert and George Sand," *Nineteenth Century* 20 (November 1886): 704, 708. Kennard was a novelist and biographer who wrote many articles on Sand and on the French actress Rachel.

64. William Barry, "The French Decadence," *Quarterly Review* 174 (April 1892): 482.

65. In *George Sand and the Victorian World*, Blount recognizes that the preference for Sand was a rejection of realism when he writes that "[i]n contrasting Balzac and Sand, Lewes revealed a dominant Victorian preference for romanticism over realism" (71); however, when discussing Sand and novels, critics used the term *romanticism* far less frequently than they did *idealism*.

66. See Naomi Schor, *George Sand and Idealism* (New York: Columbia University Press, 1993); and Margaret Cohen, *The Sentimental Education of the Novel* (Princeton: Princeton University Press, 1999).

67. On sentimentalism and idealism as the prevalence of moral truth over material truth, see Cohen, *Sentimental Education of the Novel*, 50, and Schor, *George Sand and Idealism*, 13; and as the prevalence of the desirable over the probable, see ibid., 41. On the scarcity of detailed descriptions and muting of the physical register in sentimentalism and idealism, see ibid., 4, 19; and Cohen, *Sentimental Education of the Novel*, 54–57.

68. On idealism and utopianism, see Schor, *George Sand and Idealism*, 15, 21. On sentimental fiction's investment in the tragic collision of principles, see Cohen, *Sentimental Education of the Novel*, 89.

69. J. D. Jump uses the phrase to refer to the *Athenaeum*'s two most important criteria for reviewing literary works ("Weekly Reviewing in the Eighteen-Sixties," 247).

70. Edward Bulwer Lytton, *The Critical and Miscellaneous Writings of Sir Edward Lytton Bulwer,* vol. 1 (Philadelphia, 1841), 52–53, quoted in Stang, *Theory of the Novel in England,* 153.

71. Graham, *English Criticism of the Novel,* 77.

72. Stang begins *The Theory of the Novel in England* by contesting the idea that literary criticism of the novel began in France and was transported from there to England by George Moore and Henry James (ix); he adopts a Jamesian definition of realism and shows that British critics anticipated it, point for point. For a study of the extent to which ethics continued to suffuse even James's theory of realism, see Dorothy J. Hale, *Social Formalism: The Novel in Theory from Henry James to the Present* (Stanford: Stanford University Press, 1998), 21–63. The question of national priority in novel theory seems to misrecognize the basic transnationalism of the novel (see elsewhere in this volume).

73. [Oliphant], "Novels," 261. See also Graham, *English Criticism of the Novel,* 78. My reading of Balzac's reception challenges that of Walter Kendrick, who argues that while reviewers objected to the content of Balzac's plots, they could not resist his realism ("Balzac and British Realism," 10).

74. Wilkie Collins, "Letter of Dedication," *Basil* (1862; reprint, New York: Dover, 1980), iii–iv.

75. George Lewes, "Realism in Art," *Westminster Review* 70 (October 1858): 493–96; the citation appears in an excerpt from the article, reprinted in Skilton, *Early and Mid-Victorian Novel,* 102.

76. [Alfred Austin], "Our Novels: I," *Temple Bar* 29 (May 1870): 183–84, emphasis mine.

77. Lilly, "Age of Balzac," 1006. For a similar defense of Balzac as idealist, see "French Novelists," *London Society* 21 (1872): 308–17.

78. The "Ideal" to which the author refers is Jesus Christ as a principle of the world's transcendence of the material into the spirit. The author notes that British novelists "are yet, as a body, faithful to this, the only beautiful realism," and regrets that materialism has "even tainted the genius of George Eliott [*sic*]" ("French Fiction—Its Better Aspects," *British Quarterly Review* 33 [January 1861]: 110).

79. Lee, "Moral Teaching of Zola," 197. See also J. A. Symonds, "*La Bête Humaine*: A Study in Zola's Idealism," *In the Key of Blue and Other Prose Essays* (London: Elkin Matthews & John Lane, 1892), 111, 112; and Graham, *English Criticism of the Novel,* 57, 61.

80. Edouard Rod, "Emile Zola as Moralist," *Living Age* 222 (July 1899): 137, 143. Other examples abound: Joseph Forster wrote that "[o]ne touch of Zola degrades love, debases friendship, and robs the human heart of its one priceless solace—belief in the perfectibility of human nature" ("Eugene Sue and Emile Zola," *Bel-*

*gravia* 71 [February 1890]: 135). Hannah Lynch took issue with "Zola's strictly material conception of virtue," asserting, "We cannot accept that man was only born for physical sensation"; this anti-idealism is precisely what she associates with Zola's morbidness and perversion (" 'Fécondité' versus the 'Kreutzner Sonata,' " 74, 76).

81. Review of *The Modern Literature of France*, 458–59, emphasis mine.

82. The article "Balzac and His Writings," in the *Westminster Review* 60 (1853), refers to Balzac as "the head of this realist school," committed to "the exact imitation of nature" (203). Another critic wrote that Balzac "accepted life as it was, and described it as he found it," and that his work lacked the moralism that would be opposed to "his hard and sometimes tedious realism" ("Honoré de Balzac," *London Society* 21 [1872]: 316). Throughout his article on the British response to naturalism from 1885–1895, Frierson cites critics who used the terms *realism* and *naturalism* interchangeably to describe Zola's work, which he notes was often linked to Balzac's ("English Controversy over Realism in Fiction," 537 n. 10).

83. "Balzac," *Gentleman's Magazine* 21 (December 1878): 617; Symonds, "*La Bête Humaine*: A Study in Zola's Idealism," 131. See also "Honoré de Balzac," *Temple Bar* 54 (1878): 547.

84. Review of *The Modern Literature of France*, 460; the author is quoting, approvingly, from an article by "Mr. Keratry, a French critic of a very high order of talent in the *Livre des Cent et Un*, and entitled 'The Men of Letters of the present Day (1831–2)' " (459).

85. [Shand], "Balzac," 319.

86. Barry, "Realism and Decadence in French Fiction," 58, 63.

87. [Linton], "Novels of Balzac, III," 499, and "Novels of Balzac, II," 391. This aspect of Balzac's work also linked him to orientalism for British critics who criticized Eastern societies for failing to idealize women's souls and instead treating them as pure flesh subjugated to men's physical desires.

88. As late as 1920 Arthur Symons, whose critical career peaked in the 1890s, wrote apropos of Baudelaire's "Femmes damnées" that lesbians "live only with a life of desire, and that obsession has carried them beyond the wholesome bounds of nature into the violence of a perversity which is at times almost insane." Symons blends the older lingo of idealism with the more recent one of sexology (*Charles Baudelaire: A Study* (New York: Dutton, 1920], 33). Less frequently, realism and sapphism were also both associated with money, the medium of material interests (see Barry, "Realism and Decadence in French Fiction," 62).

89. On the belief that homosexuality and idealized sentiments were incompatible, see the courtroom speech cited in Cohen, *Sex Scandal*, 113–14; Faderman, *Surpassing the Love of Men*; Linda Dowling, *Hellenism and Homosexuality in Victorian Oxford* (Ithaca: Cornell University Press, 1994); and Edward Carpenter, *The Intermediate Sex: A Study of Some Transitional Types of Men and Women* (1912; reprint, New York: Mitchell Kennerley, 1921): "to confuse Uranians (as is so often done) with libertines having no law but curiosity in self-indulgence is to do them a great wrong" (25).

90. [Henry Buxton Forman], "Algernon Charles Swinburne—Poet and Critic," *London Quarterly Review* 31 (January 1869): 371, 374, 373. Forman was a post office employee and literary critic who edited Elizabeth Barrett Browning and William Morris and contributed frequently to *Tinsley's* and the *London Quarterly Review.*

91. Algernon Charles Swinburne, *Under the Microscope* (1872), quoted in Clements, *Baudelaire and the English Tradition*, 73.

92. See Castle, *Apparitional Lesbian*; Moore, *Dangerous Intimacies*, 81; and Valerie Rohy, *Impossible Women: Lesbian Figures and American Literature* (Ithaca: Cornell University Press, 2000).

93. [William Leonard Courtney], "Mr. Swinburne's Poetry," *Fortnightly Review*, n.s., 37 (May 1885): 601.

94. "Mr. Swinburne's New Poems," 145.

95. Baynes, "Swinburne's Poems," 77, 82, 89. The reviewer links Swinburne's poetry to the sensation novel: "As the object of the sensational writer is to produce the strongest effect, he naturally tends not only towards the physical, but towards what is extreme, revolting, and even horrible in our physical experience" (94).

96. Ibid., 77.

97. See Marilyn Farwell, *Heterosexual Plots and Lesbian Narratives* (New York: New York University Press, 1996); Castle, *Apparitional Lesbian*; Moore, *Dangerous Intimacies*; Lynda Hart, *Fatal Women: Lesbian Sexuality and the Mark of Aggression* (Princeton: Princeton University Press, 1994); and White, *UnInvited*. This argument has also been made about queer representation in general (see, e.g., D. A. Miller, *Bringing out Roland Barthes* [Berkeley and Los Angeles: University of California Press, 1992], 45).

98. Castle, *Apparitional Lesbian*, 156.

99. Ibid., 34, 35.

100. "Swinburne's *Poems*," *Edinburgh Review* 134 (1871): 73. On the association of lesbianism with cloisters and harems, see [Ashbee], *Index librorum prohibitorum*, xxxiv–xxxv. On Balzac's exclusion of female readers, see Cohen, *Sentimental Education of the Novel*, 112–18. In his defense of the "realistic novelist" George Moore wrote, "Let us renounce the effort to reconcile these two irreconcilable things—literature and young girls" (*Literature at Nurse* [1885], quoted in Frierson, "English Controversy over Realism in Fiction," 535).

101. Ernest Dowson, "Translator's Preface," in Honoré de Balzac, *La Fille aux yeux d'or*, trans. Ernest Dowson (London: Leonard Smithers, 1896), vii.

EMILY APTER

AFTERWORD

# From Literary Channel to Narrative Chunnel

*The Literary Channel* uses *la manche*, a body of water, as a figurative model for Anglo-Continental literary relations in the period coinciding roughly with the historic "rise of the novel" (1750–1850). In establishing important links between gender and genre, the book points to the formative impact of cross-Channel sentimentality on the history of the novel. Sentiment, sexuality, same-sex intimism, hitherto relegated to the ancillary critical terrain of "themes" or "feminist approaches," now assumes centrality as the very fiber of the novel's self-definition in post-Revolutionary modernity. Meanwhile, the space between the Isles and the Continent becomes rife with significance for literary criticism, calling for renewed attention to the role played by international dialogism in the invention of narrative form.

There have always been logical and substantive comparisons of England and France, two nations distinguished by reciprocal competition as global power brokers in the realms of trade, finance, and imperial expansion; two traditions aligned by their common export of law, standards of universal right, linguistic patrimony, bourgeois subjectivity, and the aesthetics of realism. But the present collection's emphasis on the Channel rather than on the discretely bounded territory of the nation-state shifts the focus away from influence studies and toward a paradigm of "Anglo-Euro" cultural topography that questions the very ground of cross-cultural comparison. The fluid space of the Channel becomes a metaphor for a zone of mutual refraction where Britain defines itself through its incongruent reflection of Frenchness, and vice versa, from the "Brussels" of Charlotte Brontë's *Villette* to the "London" of Joris-Karl Huysmans's *A Rebours*.[1] Whether the genre is in the sentimental novel, the novel of ideas, or the historical novel, national consciousness is captured in the making in a two-way mirror, with Britain's islandness defined through its noncontinentalism and France's hexagonality defined through its noninsular regionalism, or multisided *rayonnement*. The geomorphic boundaries that define national self-image thus become coextensive not only with national mythologies of bedrock and soil but also with the watery in-between of a "channel effect" that over time, and in the contemporary era, has evolved into what one might call a "Chunnel effect," a nation-neutral cultural condition that is part Isles, part Continent.

The narrative Chunnel, at least to my way of thinking, picks up where the literary channel leaves off in suggesting a focus on the relationship between Anglophone and Francophone literary history in the New Europe. The Chunnel imaginary assimilates Britain to Europe and connotes Europe to Europe or intra-European narrative forms that, at their most radical, obfuscate national borders in the Isles and on the Continent. The literary Chunnel might be construed as a middle-management subgenre located in the space of the link—in the network paths of transportation, information, and capital, in the viscous netherworld of "global" identity. In contrast to transnational literature, which, I would submit, preserves the nation in emphasizing minority relations in the novel, Chunnel literature points to a state of postnational borderlessness that sublates regionalist and minority claims in the future history of the novel.

Transnational paradigms, in this scheme, thus stand in stark opposition to the paradigm of the Chunnel. One could imagine a transnational sequel to *The Literary Channel* with chapters devoted to the comparative status of British and French minoritarian languages (Irish, Welsh, Breton, Basque), to comparative pastoral (Scottish highlands versus alpine France, North Sea Atlantic maritime culture versus Mediterranean coastal life), to the impact on the novel of "anomalous states" or interiorized colonies (along the lines of David Lloyd's work), or to postcolonial comparisons between British and French literature beyond the metropole, contrasting Anglophone and Francophone Caribbean and West African literatures, say, or taking up the cultural iconoclasm of a French-speaking enclave on the Indian subcontinent, such as Pondicherry.

Here, transnationalism calls for new paradigms and approaches to literary history that take account of how colonialism and postcolonial theory have altered the shape of European studies, not just in terms of theme criticism (war, world economics, imperial oppression) but internally, in terms of the kinds of questions now asked by disciplines that grew out of national traditions. The issue, for example, of what happens to national literatures when nationalism no longer serves to anchor them impinges with increasing urgency upon discussions of the literary field, from Rey Chow's framework of diaspora studies, to Franco Moretti's paradigms of "distant reading" informed by world systems theory, to Perry Anderson's new cartography in *The Origins of Postmodernity* (1998), which organizes the genealogy of postmodernity according to a map of global cities and intellectual capitals: Lima-Madrid-London; Shaanxi-Angkor-Yucatan; New York–Harvard–Chicago; Athens–Cairo–Las Vegas, and so on. Diasporic canons, distant reading, and cartography all may be seen as representative of a new kind of literary history that circumvents nation-based criticism even as it recognizes that no general theory of literature can dispense with the nation as a crucible of historical and aesthetic comparison.

Though we are far from living a postnational condition in the contemporary world, and though emergent nations still clamor for national status, in academic criticism the nation has come increasingly under attack as the harbinger of Eurocentric values or as the official regulator of a public sphere of letters. The European nation-state's raison d'être has also been challenged by the arrival of large immigrant communities within its borders. France's relationship to its former colonies, particularly Algeria, is being negotiated today as an internal problem of the state, while its integrity as a singular culture has been thrown into question by the increasingly palpable prospect of a "United States of Europe," with its own peculiar brand of "Euro-culture." Euro-culture homogenizes nations and subsumes regionalisms, producing an export-ready cultural product that may one day truly rival its American counterpart. And it is here that England's peculiar status within Europe proves to be particularly important because the linguistic common bond with America, together with the shared legacy of individualism and laissez-faire capitalism (so distinct from the statist models prevalent in the rest of Europe), makes England the obvious mediator of U.S. and European cultures.

And this brings me to the pressing issue of what this Americanized Euro-culture will look like—what shape and form it will take—for it is obvious that the Euro, even if it is ultimately abandoned, has far more wide-reaching cultural implications than its simple designation of a common currency would suggest. Implicit in the notion of the Euro is a homogenized Europeanism, increasingly stripped of national particularisms and increasingly governed by the emergence of virtual communities or cybernations. Some have viewed this move toward postnational identity as a positive advance, hailing the transcendence of cultural parochialism as leading to new forms of cultural cosmopolitanism, or better yet, to a "cosmopolitical" republic of international law and soft-border hospitality. But others see this Euro-culture as a dismal aesthetic prospect, a zone of generic fiction confirming a New European identity that really is no identity at all.

In Euroland, technological transport blurs the cartography of regions, with "in flight" or "below sea level" modes of transport serving to efface the colorful trade routes of medieval Christendom. The romantic tradition of *in genius loci*, hallowed by Britain and France alike, yields to online exoticism and downloaded vignettes. The idea of the Chunnel—a fast train speeding under water with no view from the window—affords the image of a smooth, unmarked spatial continuum, a cross between the blurry walls of the birth canal and an antiseptic test tube. The typical Chunnel traveler is a "netizen," attention riveted to a laptop, undistracted by external scenery. Time supplants place as the measure of subjective experience; antihistoricist chronotypes displace the map, implicitly disorienting historical memory.

This is perhaps why much recent best-selling Euro-fiction may strike readers as being situated in a historical as well as a geographical and political vacuum. Like the NGO or corporate multinational, the literary form of the Chunnel may be associated with posthistorical, postnational fictions. Consider Iain Banks's *The Business*, which traces the airborne peregrinations of a top-level female executive named Kathryn Telman as she negotiates her company's effort to become a nation-state by purchasing a country in the Himalayas, thereby securing a bargaining position as a world power in the United Nations.[2] In Telman's jet-lagged consciousness there is no right time by which to set a watch. She inhabits a no-time zone, moving between bivouacs in London, California, Switzerland, and Kuala Lumpur. The novel devotes more space to describing the quality of take-offs and landings, in-flight amenities, and hotel accommodations than it does to the specific charms of a given locale. If Banks's *The Business* is any indication, regional loyalties in the Euro-novel will be kept to a minimum. Though born of Scottish lower-middle class parents, the heroine loses her roots when she is adopted in childhood by a wealthy businesswoman, given a new name, sent to a Swiss boarding school, dispatched to America for a final entrepreneurial makeover, and then assigned to far-flung geographical outposts in the corporation's vast financial empire. When the dowager queen of the remote Himalayan country of Thulahn asks her where she is from, her stumbling response reveals the condition of the Euro-citizen with no abiding allegiances: "I'm British—Scottish—by birth. I have dual British-US nationality." "I see," the queen responds and then adds: "Well, I don't see, really. I don't see how one can be of dual nationality, apart from purely legally. . . . I mean to say, who are you loyal to?" . . . "Are you loyal to the Queen, or to . . . the American flag? Or are you one of these absurd Scottish Nationalists?" "I'm more of an internationalist, ma'am," replies Telman.

The "internationalism" of Banks's heroine leaves her free to act without fealty to a single nation or principality. In this regard, she is the perfect capitalist tool for a transglobal conglomerate that traces its beginnings back to a time prior to the Holy Roman Empire. The Business is a pseudo-sovereign order, not unlike the papacy or a Freemasonic association, traducing national borders in its exercise of power. And as with these shadowy institutions, there are wild speculations about who and where it is. Depending on which fallacious website is consulted, the Business appears to be:

(a) the major force behind the New World Order . . . ;
(b) an even more extreme, hideous and sinister branch of the International Zionist Conspiracy (in other words, the Jews) . . .;
(c) a long-term deep-entryist group of dedicated cadres charged by the Executive Council of the Fourth International to bring down the entire capitalist system from within by gaining control of lots of shares and then selling them all at once to produce a crash . . . ;
(d) a well-funded cabal of the little known Worshippers of Nostradamus cult intent on bringing about the end of the financial world . . . ;
(e) the militant commercial wing of the Roman Catholic Church . . . ;
(f) a similarly extremist Islamic syndicate sworn to out-perform, out-deal and out-haggle the Jews . . . ;
(g) a zombie-like remnant of the Holy Roman Empire, which has risen from the grave, unspeakably putrid but grotesquely powerful, to re-impose European dominance over the New World in general and the USA in particular through sneaky cosmopolitan business practices and the introduction of the Euro. . . . (98)

It is surely no accident that Banks's narrator, in referring to paranoid projections of what the Business "is," refers to the Euro as the paramount symbol of an Anglo-Continental desire to rescind the reach of American hegemony. The Chunnel is a comparable symbol, an image of superior European technological know-how that affirms intra-European alliance over and against the special fraternity that has existed between Great Britain and the United States ever since the two countries rescued Europe in World War II. This Euro identity, incubating within what we are calling Chunnel narrative, must be read, in this context at least, as a clear counterpoint to the "Anglo" (British-U.S.) cultural nexus.

But of course what is specifically "Euro" about this highly Americanized, virtually postnational Euro-culture is far from clear. And that, ultimately, is what may distinguish Chunnel narrative, at least at the present moment, for it is constantly battling the prospect of its own nebulousness against the backdrop of eroding national traditions. Take, as an illustration of this, Michel Houellebecq's 1994 novel *Extension du domaine de la lutte* (mystifyingly translated into English as *Whatever*), which paints a portrait of the modern European citizen as a subject nationally adrift on the infobahns of the EU.[3] Though the notoriously misanthropic, political correctness–baiting Houellebecq has been billed as a classic new French author—"*L'Étranger* for the info generation" reads a quotation attributed to Tibor Fischer on the cover of the English edition—his short novel belongs to a nation-neutral genre of Euro-existentialism. *Whatever*'s protagonist is a middle-management employee in a computer technology firm whose principal client is the Ministry of Agriculture, itself in constant negotiation with the Common Market. In this world of dairy wars, the Breeder takes the place of God, offering a data-processing plan that promises "the development of a more competitive para-agricultural sector at the European level" and bestowing on humanity the offering of a golden calf, the hyper-bred Breton cow. Regionalism survives in this depiction of Euroland as a geographically dislocated marketing label affixed to the name of a farm animal. The corporate culture of Euroland revolves around motivation seminars, the traffic in acronyms and logos, and the flow of cash, information and technology. Even though the "Maple program," designed for farm subsidy payments, is written in the computer-programming language "Pascal," the narrator only dimly recalls that Pascal is the name of the French seventeenth-century author of the *Pensées*. Mathematical memory thus triumphs at the expense of cultural heritage and *patrimoine*, just as the technobabble of social hierarchy according to data manuals—"a system of global information promulgated by the integration of diversified heterogeneous subsystems"—triumphs over the nostalgic rhetoric of national community (27).

Houellebecq offers a thoroughly pasteurized version of late capitalist everyday life: success is measured by the ability to argue the profitability of a "thyratron inverter" capable of stabilizing "the incoming voltage of the current feeding the server network" (60), and the rural socialist makes good with a book called *Cheesemaking and the Challenge of New Technologies* (33). Existence is hyper-automated and functionalized; dinner can be programmed in advance and delivered by Minitel. Human relationships are "effaced" (posing something of a problem for the novel, as the narrator notes with tongue-in-cheek textual reflexivity), but the absence of intimacy has been redefined as the "multiplication of degrees of freedom" by the resident "information technology thinker," Jean-Yves Fréhaut. The sex drive ebbs, but the narrator manages to suppress his fleeting desire for a "fuck on the moquette" by giving in to the superior satisfaction of throwing up in the toilet (44–45). When the news station flaunts too much human dignity in its report of a political demonstration, he switches to the porn channel or contemplates the grotesque indignity of a man who falls dead in a supermarket amidst congested trolleys and trills of Muzak (61). The decadent depletion of experience portrayed here recalls the sepulchral, simulacral environments of Des Esseintes in Huysmans's *A Rebours* or the blander bouts of spiritual anomie that French writers excel in capturing, from Benjamin Constant's *Adolphe*, a chronicle of post-Revolutionary malaise, to Jean-Paul Sartre's *La Nausée*, a testimonial to liberty as sickness, to Albert Camus's posthumously published *Le Premier Homme*, documenting the peculiar flavor of the pied noir's colonial identity crisis during the Algerian war. Each of these narratives represents a literary cornerstone of French existential ennui, and the critics are justified in placing Houellebecq's novel in the same edifice, but whereas Constant, Huysmans, Sartre, and Camus abstract their characters from history only to mark them, through language and location, as indelibly French, Houellebecq's fictive universe is more anonymously "Euro." Perhaps only Michel Butor's *La Modification*, recording the weak pulsations of a businessman's vacant consciousness as he travels by train between Paris and Rome, or Georges Perec's *Les Choses*, with its modern couples yoked to statistical charts and product surveys, really anticipates the late industrial vacuity of Houellebecq's generic Eurocitizen.

In offering complementary intimations of the diffuse and ultimately confused cultural legacy that awaits the next generation of readers and writers in the era of postnational Europe, the work of Michel Houellebecq and Iain Banks presages the next turn in literary history, in which time travel into the future takes precedence over historical reconstructions of the past, in which literary historians attempt to graph a literary field no longer reliant on the coordinates of discrete national archives, and in which the Channel gives way to the Chunnel as a narrative trope for the European novel.

## Notes

1. *Villette* captures the enchantment-effect of the Channel (a mix of sea-sickness, euphoric wish fulfillment, and imperial ambition), with Brontë's description of Lucy Snowe's crossing: "I was not sick till long after we passed Margate, and deep was the pleasure I drank in with the sea-breeze; divine the delight I drew from the heaving channel-waves, from the sea-birds on their ridges, from the white sails on their dark distance, from the quiet, yet beclouded sky, overhanging all. In my reverie, methought I saw the continent of Europe, like a wide dream-land, far away. Sunshine lay on it, making the long coast one line of gold; tiniest tracery of clustered town and snow-gleaming tower, of woods deep-massed, of heights serrated, of smooth pastur-age and veiny stream, embossed the metal-bright prospect. For background, spread a sky, solemn and dark blue, and—grand with imperial promise, soft with tints of en-chantment—strode from north to south a God-bent bow, an arch of hope." Charlotte Brontë, *Villette* (London: Penguin Books, 1979), 117.

2. Iain Banks, *The Business* (New York: Simon & Schuster, 1999).

3. Michel Houellebecq, *Whatever*, trans. Paul Hammond (London: Serpent's Tail, 1999), originally published in French as *Extension du domaine de la lutte* (n.p.: Éditions Maurice Nadeau, 1994).

# Selected Bibliography

Editors' note: This bibliography includes works cited in the collection that are of general interest to scholars of the cross-Channel novel. We do not, however, exhaust the rich sources relevant to specific aspects of this history contained in the notes to the individual chapters.

Alarcón, Norma, Caren Kaplan, and Minoo Moallem, eds. *Between Women and Nation: Nationalisms, Transnational Feminisms, and the State*. Durham, N.C.: Duke University Press, 1999.

Alliston, April. *Virtue's Faults: Correspondences in Eighteenth-Century British and French Women's Fiction*. Stanford: Stanford University Press, 1996.

Anderson, Benedict. *Imagined Communities: Reflections on the Origin and Spread of Nationalism*. London: Verso, 1983.

Armstrong, Nancy. *Desire and Domestic Fiction: A Political History of the Novel*. New York: Oxford University Press, 1987.

Armstrong, Nancy, and Leonard Tennenhouse. *The Imaginary Puritan*. Berkeley and Los Angeles: University of California Press, 1992.

Auerbach, Erich. *Mimesis*. Trans. Willard R. Trask. Princeton: Princeton University Press, 1953.

Auerbach, Nina. *Communities of Women: An Idea in Fiction*. Cambridge: Harvard University Press, 1978.

———. *Woman and the Demon: The Life of a Victorian Myth*. Cambridge: Harvard University Press, 1982.

Bakhtin, Mikhail. *The Dialogic Imagination: Four Essays*. Ed. Michael Holquist, trans. Caryl Emerson and Michael Holquist. Austin: University of Texas Press, 1981.

Bammer, Angelika, ed. *Displacements: Cultural Identities in Question*. Bloomington: Indiana University Press, 1994.

Barber, Giles. *Daphnis and Chloe: The Markets and Metamorphoses of an Unknown Bestseller.* London: British Library, 1989.

Barbéris, Pierre. *Aux sources du réalisme: Aristocrates et bourgeois: du texte à l'histoire.* Paris: Union générale d'éditions, 1978.

Barthes, Roland. *S/Z.* Paris: Editions du Seuil, 1970.

Baym, Nina. *Woman's Fiction: A Guide to Novels By and About Women in America, 1820–1870.* 1978. Urbana: University of Illinois Press, 1993.

Beebee, Thomas. *"Clarissa" on the Continent: Translation and Seduction.* University Park: Pennsylvania State University Press, 1990.

Berlière, Jean-Marc. *La Police des moeurs sous la IIIe république.* Paris: Editions du Seuil, 1992.

Bhabha, Homi, ed. *Nation and Narration.* New York: Routledge, 1990.

Brooks, Peter. *Novel of Worldliness.* Princeton: Princeton University Press, 1969.

Brown, Homer. *Institutions of the English Novel.* Philadelphia: University of Pennsylvania Press, 1996.

Budick, Sanford, and Wolfgang Iser, eds. *The Translatability of Cultures.* Stanford: Stanford University Press, 1996.

Butler, Marilyn. *Romantics, Rebels, and Reactionaries: English Literature and Its Background, 1760–1830.* New York: Oxford University Press, 1982.

Castle, Terry. *Clarissa's Ciphers: Meaning and Disruption in Richardson's "Clarissa."* Ithaca: Cornell University Press, 1982.

———. *The Female Thermometer: Eighteenth-Century Culture and the Invention of the Uncanny.* Oxford: Oxford University Press, 1995.

———. *Masquerade and Civilization: The Carnivalesque in Eighteenth-Century English Culture and Fiction.* Stanford: Stanford University Press, 1986.

Certeau, Michel de, Dominique Julia, and Jacques Revel. *Une Politique de la langue: La révolution française et les patois.* Paris: Gallimard, 1975.

*The Channel in the Eighteenth Century: Bridge, Barrier, and Gateway.* Ed. John Falvey and William Brooks. Studies on Voltaire and the Eighteenth Century, no. 292. Oxford: Voltaire Foundation, 1991.

Clemit, Pamela. *The Godwinian Novel: The Rational Fictions of Godwin, Brockden Brown, Mary Shelley.* Oxford: Oxford University Press, 1993.

Clery, E. J. *The Rise of Supernatural Fiction, 1762–1800.* Cambridge: Cambridge University Press, 1995.

Cohen, Margaret. *The Sentimental Education of the Novel.* Princeton: Princeton University Press, 1999.

Cohen, Margaret, and Christopher Prendergast, eds. *Spectacles of Realism.* Minneapolis: University of Minnesota Press, 1995.

Colley, Linda. *Britons: Forging the Nation, 1707–1837.* New Haven: Yale University Press, 1992.

Curtius, Ernst. *European Literature and the Latin Middle Ages.* Trans. Willard R. Trask. Princeton: Princeton University Press, 1953.

Davis, Lennard. *Factual Fictions: The Origins of the English Novel.* New York: Columbia University Press, 1983.

Day, Robert Adams. *Told in Letters: Epistolary Fiction before Richardson.* Ann Arbor: University of Michigan Press, 1966.

DeJean, Joan. *Fictions of Sappho, 1546–1937.* Chicago: University of Chicago Press, 1989.

————. *Libertine Strategies: Freedom and the Novel in Seventeenth-Century France.* Columbus: Ohio State University Press, 1981.

————. *Tender Geographies: Women and the Origins of the Novel in France.* New York: Columbia University Press, 1991.

DeJean, Joan, and Nancy K. Miller, eds. *Displacements: Women, Traditions, Literatures in French.* Baltimore: Johns Hopkins University Press, 1991.

Dever, Carolyn. *Death and the Mother from Dickens to Freud: Victorian Fiction and the Anxiety of Origins.* Cambridge: Cambridge University Press, 1998.

DiPiero, Thomas. *Dangerous Truths, Criminal Passions.* Stanford: Stanford University Press, 1992.

Doody, Margaret Anne. *The True Story of the Novel.* New Brunswick, N.J.: Rutgers University Press, 1996.

Douthwaite, Julia V. *Exotic Women: Literary Heroines and Cultural Strategies in Ancien Régime France.* Philadelphia: University of Pennsylvania Press, 1992.

Dowling, Linda. *Hellenism and Homosexuality in Victorian Oxford.* Ithaca: Cornell University Press, 1994.

Dziembowski, Edmond. *Un Nouveau Patriotisme français, 1750–1770: La France face à la puissance anglaise à l'époque de la guerre de Sept Ans.* Studies on Voltaire and the Eighteenth Century, 365. Oxford: Voltaire Foundation, 1998.

Ellis, Kate Ferguson. *The Contested Castle: Gothic Novels and the Subversion of Domestic Ideology.* Urbana: University of Illinois Press, 1989.

Engel, Claire Eliane. *Figures et aventures du XVIIIe siècle: Voyages et découvertes de l'abbé Prévost.* Paris: Editions "Je Sers," 1939.

Engels, Friedrich. *The Condition of the Working-Class in England, from Personal Observation and Authentic Sources.* Moscow: Progress Publishers, 1973.

Favret, Mary A., and Nicola J. Watson, eds. *At the Limits of Romanticism.* Bloomington: Indiana University Press, 1994.

Ferguson, Frances. *Solitude and the Sublime: Romanticism and the Aesthetics of Individuation.* New York: Routledge, 1992.

Fisher, Philip. *Hard Facts: Setting and Form in the American Novel.* New York: Oxford University Press, 1985.

Foxon, David. *Libertine Literature in England, 1660–1745.* London: Shenval, 1964.

Furet, François, and Mona Ozouf, eds. *A Critical Dictionary of the French Revolution.* Cambridge: Harvard University Press, 1989.

Gallagher, Catherine. *Nobody's Story: The Vanishing Acts of Women Writers in the Marketplace, 1670–1820.* Berkeley and Los Angeles: University of California Press, 1994.

Garelick, Rhonda K. *Rising Star: Dandyism, Gender, and Performance in the Fin de siè-cle*. Princeton: Princeton University Press, 1998.

Gelbart, Nina. *Feminism and Opposition Journalism in Old Regime France*. Berkeley and Los Angeles: University of California Press, 1987.

Gellner, Ernest. *Nations and Nationalism*. Ithaca: Cornell University Press, 1983.

Gilbert, Sandra M., and Susan Gubar. *The Madwoman in the Attic: The Woman Writer and the Nineteenth-Century Literary Imagination*. New Haven: Yale University Press, 1979.

Goodman, Dena. *The Republic of Letters: A Cultural History of the French Enlighten-ment*. Ithaca: Cornell University Press, 1994.

Grewal, Inderpal, and Caren Kaplan, eds. *Scattered Hegemonies: Postmodernity and Transnational Feminist Practices*. Minneapolis: University of Minnesota Press, 1994.

Grieder, Josephine. *Anglomania in France, 1740–1789: Fact, Fiction, and Political Dis-course*. Geneva: Droz, 1985.

———. *Translations of French Sentimental Prose Fiction in Late Seventeenth-Century England: The History of a Literary Vogue*. Durham, N.C.: Duke University Press, 1975.

Habermas, Jürgen. *The Structural Transformation of the Public Sphere*. Trans. Thomas Burger. Cambridge: MIT Press, 1989.

Hägg, Tomas. *The Novel in Antiquity*. Berkeley and Los Angeles: University of Califor-nia Press, 1983.

Haviland, Thomas Philip. *The Roman de longue haleine on English Soil*. Philadelphia: University of Pennsylvania, 1931.

Hobsbawm, Eric, and Terence Ranger, eds. *The Invention of Tradition*. Cambridge: Cambridge University Press, 1983.

Homans, Margaret. *Bearing the Word: Language and Female Experience in Nineteenth-Century Women's Writing*. Chicago: University of Chicago Press, 1986.

Huet, Marie-Hélène. *Monstrous Imagination*. Cambridge: Harvard University Press, 1993.

Hunter, J. Paul. *Before Novels: The Cultural Contexts of Eighteenth-Century English Fic-tion*. New York: Norton, 1990.

Hutchinson, John, and Anthony D. Smith, eds. *Nationalism*. New York: Oxford Uni-versity Press, 1994.

Isbell, John Claiborne. *The Birth of European Romanticism: Truth and Propaganda in Staël's De l'Allemagne*. Cambridge: Cambridge University Press, 1994.

Iser, Wolfgang. *The Act of Reading*. Baltimore: Johns Hopkins University Press, 1978.

Jameson, Fredric. *The Political Unconscious*. Ithaca: Cornell University Press, 1981.

Jauss, Hans-Robert. *Aesthetic Experience and Literary Hermeneutics*. Trans. Michael Shaw. Minneapolis: University of Minnesota Press, 1982.

Jones Day, Shirley. *The Search for Lyonnesse: Women's Fiction in France, 1670–1703*. Bern: Peter Lang, 1999.

Kadish, Doris Y. *Politicizing Gender: Narrative Strategies in the Aftermath of the French Revolution.* New Brunswick, N.J.: Rutgers University Press, 1991.

Kohn, Hans. *Nationalism, Its Meaning and History.* Princeton: Van Nostrand, 1955.

La Harpe, Jean-François. *Cours de littérature ancienne et moderne.* 3 vols. 1791–1804. Reprint. Paris: Firmin Didot, 1851.

Langbauer, Laurie. *Women and Romance: The Consolation of Gender in the English Novel.* Ithaca: Cornell University Press, 1990.

Lewis, Jayne Elizabeth. *Mary Queen of Scots: Romance and Nation.* London: Routledge, 1998.

Lieberman, Victor, ed. *Beyond Binary Histories: Re-Imagining Eurasia to c. 1830.* Ann Arbor: University of Michigan Press, 1991.

Lionnet, Françoise. *Autobiographical Voices: Race, Gender, Self-Portraiture.* Ithaca: Cornell University Press, 1989.

Lionnet, Françoise, and Ronnie Scharfman, eds. *Post/Colonial Conditions: Exiles, Migrations, and Nomadisms.* New Haven: Yale University Press, 1993.

Lloyd, David. *Anomalous States: Irish Writing and the Post-Colonial Moment.* Dublin: Lilliput, 1993.

Lukács, Georg. *The Historical Novel.* Trans. Hannah Mitchell and Stanley Mitchell. London: Merlin, 1982.

Lynch, Deidre Shauna. *The Economy of Character: Novels, Market Culture, and the Business of Inner Meaning.* Chicago: University of Chicago Press, 1998.

Lynch, Deidre Shauna, and William Warner, eds. *Cultural Institutions of the Novel.* Durham, N.C.: Duke University Press, 1996.

Macherey, Pierre. *The Object of Literature.* Cambridge: Cambridge University Press, 1995.

Maertz, Gregory, ed. *Cultural Interactions in the Romantic Age: Critical Essays in Comparative Literature.* Albany: State University of New York Press, 1998.

Malchow, Howard L. *Gothic Images of Race in Nineteenth-Century Britain.* Stanford: Stanford University Press, 1996.

Marcus, Sharon. *Apartment Stories: City and Home in Nineteenth-Century Paris and London.* Berkeley and Los Angeles: University of California Press, 1999.

Maxwell, Richard. *The Mysteries of Paris and London.* Charlottesville: University Press of Virginia, 1992.

May, Georges. *Le Dilemme du roman au siècle XVIIIe.* Paris: Presses Universitaires de France; New Haven: Yale University Press, 1963.

McClintock, Anne. *Imperial Leather: Race, Gender, and Sexuality in the Colonial Contest.* New York: Routledge, 1995.

McKeon, Michael. *The Origins of the English Novel, 1600–1740.* Baltimore: Johns Hopkins University Press, 1987.

Meyer, Susan. *Imperialism at Home: Race and Victorian Women's Fiction.* Ithaca: Cornell University Press, 1996.

Miller, D. A. *The Novel and the Police.* Berkeley and Los Angeles: University of California Press, 1988.

Miller, Nancy K. *French Dressing: Women, Men, and Ancien Régime Fiction*. New York: Routledge, 1995.

———. *The Heroine's Text: Readings in the French and English Novel, 1722–1782*. New York: Columbia University Press, 1980.

———. *Subject to Change: Reading Feminist Writing*. New York: Columbia University Press, 1988.

Mitchell, W. J. T. *Iconology: Image, Text, Ideology*. Chicago: University of Chicago Press, 1986.

Moretti, Franco. *Atlas of the European Novel, 1800–1900*. London: Verso, 1998.

———. *The Way of the World*. London: Verso, 1987.

Mornet, Daniel. "Les Enseignements des bibliothèques privées (1750–1780)." *Revue d'Histoire Littéraire de la France* 17 (1910): 449–96.

Musselwhite, David E. *Partings Welded Together: Politics and Desire in the Nineteenth-Century English Novel*. London: Methuen, 1987.

Newman, Gerald. *The Rise of English Nationalism: A Cultural History, 1740–1830*. New York: St. Martin's, 1987.

Nora, Pierre, ed. *Les Lieux de mémoire*. 3 vols. Paris: Gallimard, 1986.

Nussbaum, Felicity A. *Torrid Zones: Maternity, Sexuality, and Empire in Eighteenth-Century English Narratives*. Baltimore: Johns Hopkins University Press, 1995.

Palmer, Stanley H. *Police and Protest in England and Ireland, 1780–1850*. Cambridge: Cambridge University Press, 1988.

Palumbo-Liu, David, and Hans Ulrich Gumbrecht, eds. *Streams of Cultural Capital: Transnational Cultural Studies*. Stanford: Stanford University Press, 1997.

Parker, Andrew, Mary Russo, Doris Sommer, and Patricia Yaeger. *Nationalisms and Sexualities*. New York: Routledge, 1992.

Patterson, Annabel M. *Censorship and Interpretation: The Conditions of Writing and Reading in Early Modern Europe*. Madison: University of Wisconsin Press, 1984.

Pittock, Murray. *The Invention of Scotland: The Stuart Myth and the Scottish Identity, 1638 to the Present*. London: Routledge, 1991.

Poovey, Mary. *The Proper Lady and the Woman Writer: Ideology and Style in the Works of Mary Wollstonecraft, Mary Shelley, and Jane Austen*. Chicago: University of Chicago Press, 1984.

———. *Uneven Developments: The Ideological Work of Gender in Mid-Victorian England*. Chicago: University of Chicago Press, 1988.

Porter, Bernard. *The Origins of the Vigilant State: The London Metropolitan Police Special Branch before the First World War*. Woodbridge, N.J.: Boydell, 1987.

———. *Plots and Paranoia: A History of Political Espionage in Britain, 1790–1988*. New York: Routledge, 1989.

Prendergast, Christopher. *The Order of Mimesis: Balzac, Stendhal, Nerval, Flaubert*. Cambridge: Cambridge University Press, 1986.

Richardson, Alan, and Sonia Hofkosh, eds. *Romanticism, Race, and Imperial Culture, 1780–1834.* Bloomington: Indiana University Press, 1996.

Richetti, John. *Popular Fiction before Richardson: Narrative Patterns, 1700–1739.* Oxford: Clarendon, 1969.

Robbins, Bruce. *Feeling Global: Internationalism in Distress.* New York: New York University Press, 1999.

Sahlins, Peter. *Boundaries: The Making of France and Spain in the Pyrenees.* Berkeley and Los Angeles: University of California Press, 1989.

Sedgwick, Eve Kosofsky, ed. *Novel Gazing: Queer Readings in Fiction.* Durham, N.C.: Duke University Press, 1997.

———. *Tendencies.* Durham, N.C.: Duke University Press, 1993.

Simpson, David. *Romanticism, Nationalism, and the Revolt against Theory.* Chicago: University of Chicago Press, 1993.

Smith, Phillip Thurmond. *Policing Victorian London: Political Policing, Public Order, and the London Metropolitan Police.* London: Greenwood, 1985.

Sommer, Doris. *Foundational Fictions: The National Romances of Latin America.* Berkeley and Los Angeles: University of California Press, 1991.

Spacks, Patricia. *Desire and Truth: Functions of Plot in Eighteenth-Century English Novels.* Chicago: University of Chicago Press, 1990.

———. *Imagining a Self: Autobiography and Novel in Eighteenth-Century England.* Cambridge: Harvard University Press, 1976.

Stead, Philip John. *The Police of Paris.* London: Staples, 1957.

Stewart, Susan. *Crimes of Writing: Problems in the Containment of Representation.* New York: Oxford University Press, 1991.

Streeter, Harold Wade. *The Eighteenth-Century English Novel in French Translation: A Bibliographical Study.* 1936. Reprint. New York: Benjamin Blom, 1970.

Tatum, James, ed. *The Search for the Ancient Novel.* Baltimore: Johns Hopkins University Press, 1994.

Terdiman, Richard. *The Dialectics of Isolation: Self and Society in the French Novel from the Realists to Proust.* New Haven: Yale University Press, 1976.

———. *Discourse/Counter-Discourse: The Theory and Practice of Symbolic Resistance in Nineteenth-Century France.* Ithaca: Cornell University Press, 1985.

Texte, Joseph. *Jean-Jacques Rousseau et les origines du cosmopolitisme littéraire: Etude sur les relations de la France et de l'Angleterre au XVIIIe siècle.* Paris: Hachette, 1909.

Thom, Martin. *Republics, Nations, and Tribes.* London: Verso, 1995.

Thompson, E. P. *The Making of the English Working Class.* New York: Vintage, 1966.

Tompkins, J. M. S. *The Popular Novel in England, 1770–1800.* Lincoln: University of Nebraska Press, 1961.

Trumpener, Katie. *Bardic Nationalism: The Romantic Novel and the British Empire.* Princeton: Princeton University Press, 1997.

Turner, James Grantham. "Novel Panic: Picture and Performance in the Reception of Richardson's *Pamela.*" *Representations* 48 (fall 1994): 70–96.

Walkowitz, Judith. *Prostitution and Victorian Society: Women, Class, and the State.* Cambridge: Cambridge University Press, 1980.

Waller, Margaret. *The Male Malady: Fictions of Impotence in the French Romantic Novel.* New Brunswick, N.J.: Rutgers University Press, 1993.

Warner, William. *Licensing Entertainment: The Elevation of Novel Reading in Britain, 1684–1750.* Berkeley and Los Angeles: University of California Press, 1998.

## CONTRIBUTORS

APRIL ALLISTON is an associate professor in the Department of Comparative Literature at Princeton University.

EMILY APTER is chair of the Department of Comparative Literature at the University of California at Los Angeles, where she is a professor of comparative literature and French and Francophone studies.

MARGARET COHEN is a professor in the Department of Comparative Literature at New York University.

JOAN DeJEAN is Trustee Professor of French at the University of Pennsylvania.

CAROLYN DEVER is an associate professor in the Department of English at Vanderbilt University.

LYNN FESTA is an assistant professor in the Department of English at Harvard University.

DEIDRE SHAUNA LYNCH is an associate professor of English at Indiana University.

FRANÇOISE LIONNET is a professor and chair of the Department of French and Francophone Studies at the University of California at Los Angeles.

SHARON MARCUS is an associate professor in the Department of English at the University of California, Berkeley.

RICHARD MAXWELL is a professor in the Department of English at Valparaiso University.

MARY HELEN McMURRAN is a postdoctoral fellow in the Humanities Program at the University of Chicago.

303

Bonnie Prince Charles, 151, 152, 177, 182n.28
Bourdieu, Pierre, 2, 13
bourgeois nation: British novels and empowered 18th-century, 8–9; faith in policemen model by, 231–32; founded on ideology of separate public/private spheres, 147n.26; pulp detective novels contrast with literature of, 232–33; sympathetic communities as alternative to, 144
Brecht, Bertolt, 113
Britain: changing literary production in, 2; colonial/postcolonial history of, 183–84; conceptual borders of novel genre in, 6–7; French-British conflict and national identity of, 11–13; French women novelists', development in, 40–45; growing social mobility of 18th-century, 135–36; Metropolitan Police of, 225–27, 229, 231; novel development and emerging nationalism within, 125n.9; novelistic core of, 1; novel recognition as new genre in, 28n.2; as "Other" nation-state in French novels, 19–20; political union of "North Britain" with, 177; resistance to French novels in, 62–63, 65–66; rural and urban divisions in 18th-century, 135; sensibility associated with Celtic Fringe of, 136–37, 140; shifting patterns of literary exchange in, 3; spy-police hero as protecting virtuous borders of, 227–28, 238, 240, 246. See also cross-Channel exchanges
British identity: born of British-French struggle, 11–13; cross-Channel invention of novel and, 12–13; importance of marriage market in creating, 135, 144; sensibility association with character of, 136–37. See also national identity
British Metropolitan Police: middle class faith in virtue of, 231; social order provided by model of, 225–27, 229
British Novelists (Barbauld), 54, 57
British novels: anti-Frenchness of 18th-century, 62–63; comparing development of French and, 8–9; empowered 18th-century middle class and, 8–9; French detective figures (19th-century) in, 228, 233–35, 237–40; French origins of historical, 166; French response to translated, 63–65; hybridization of national traits in, 137–38, 143–44; influence of Rousseau on female writers of, 146n.19; marital status of

women and contents of, 281n.55; melodramatic sentimentality of, 119; moral vision/idealism objective of, 267–71. See also Victorian literary culture
British periodical critics: examining rejection of French sapphism by, 266–76; French sapphism reviewed in, 252–54; hostility toward French sapphism by, 254–65. See also Victorian literary culture
British police system: "chivalric ethos" of, 248n.8; distinctions between French and, 238–39; spy-police of, 227–28, 238, 240, 246; Times (1854 report) comparing French and, 225, 229, 230, 248n.11. See also French police system; police hero
Brontë, Charlotte, 228, 261, 286
Brontë, Emily, 140
Brooke, Frances, 51, 117, 136
Buntline, Ned, 23
Burnham, Michelle, 82, 89, 95
The Business (Banks), 289–90
Butler, Josephine, 227, 240
Butor, Michel, 292
Byron, Lord, 206

Cambridge Bibliography of English Literature, 166
Candide (Voltaire), 157
Canler, M., 232, 234–36, 238
Caplan, Jay, 112
Castle, Terry, 254–55, 259, 273, 274
Castle of Otranto (Walpole), 56
Castres, Sébastien de, 64
Caumont de La Force, Charlotte, 41
Celtic Fringe of Britain, 136–37, 140
Les Cent Nouvelles, 26
Cervantes, Miguel de, 22, 53
Channel zone: characterization of, 2–3; colonial/postcolonial literature, 183–92; international development of novel and, 4; opposition of new transnational paradigms to, 287–93; overview of literary, 14–27; transnational culture of, 13. See also cross-Channel exchanges
Charles I, 156
Charles II, 159, 160, 161, 162
Charles Edward (Bonnie Prince Charles), 151, 152, 177, 182n.28
Charrière, Isabelle de, 37, 118, 136
Chateaubriand, François-Auguste-René de, 178, 197

The Dance of Death: Or The Hangman's Plot: A Thrilling Romance of Two Cities (Brownlow and Tuevoleur), 232
Daphnis and Chloe (Longus), 55
D'Arlincourt, 13
d'Arnaud, Baculard, 166
d'Aulnoy, comtesse, 15, 42–43, 44, 45, 48n.7
David Simple, 64
Davies, John, 56
Dawson, Robert, 12
deathbed scenes, 111–13, 128n.28, 132n.60
Defoe, Daniel, 8, 45, 155
De Gondrecourt, 13
DeJean, Joan, 15, 16, 37
Delphine (Staël), 196, 201, 203–5, 207, 214, 216, 218n.5
La Dernière Incarnation de Vautrin (Balzac), 258
La Déroute des Paméla (play), 79
Desfontaines, abbé, 63
Des Grieux, 112, 116
detective fiction: agents provocateurs of, 227–28, 233–38, 240, 246–47; ambivalence and displacement expressed by, 24; British Metropolitan Police model used in, 225–27, 229; British spy-police figure in, 227–28, 238, 240, 246; emergence of pulp, 232–33; female detectives of, 240–44; French detective figures of 19th-century, 228, 233–35, 237–40, 244–47; middle-class faith in police virtue in, 231–32. See also police hero
Dever, Carolyn, 23, 225
The Dialogic Imagination (Bakhtin), 5
Dickens, Charles, 24, 246
Diderot, Denis, 51, 64, 81, 82, 83, 88, 91, 94, 113, 121, 122, 179
Le Dilemme du roman au siècle XVIIIe (May), 8
discursive community, 115
"The (Dis)locations of Romantic Nationalism: Shelly, Staël, and the Home-Schooling of Monsters" (Lynch), 19
Don Bellianis, 55
Donoghue, Emma, 259
Don Quixote (Cervantes), 22, 53, 56
Dora case (Freud), 245
Dowson, Ernest, 275
The Drudge: or the Jealous Extravagant, a Piece of Gallantry (1673), 62
Dublin University Magazine, 263
La Duchesse de Langeais (Balzac), 256

La Duchesse de la Vallière (Genlis), 21
Duhamel (French detective figure), 234, 237–39
Dumas, Alexandre, 13, 153, 178
Du Noyer, Anne-Marguerite, 41, 42, 43

Edgeworth, Maria, 19, 21
Edict of Nantes (1685), 14, 40, 41, 46
Edinburgh Review, 253, 262, 266, 275
Les Egarements du coeur et de l'esprit (Crébillon), 16
18th-century: anti-Frenchness of British novels of, 62–63; British fiction and empowered middle-class of, 8–9; British-French literary cross-Channel zone during, 14–15; cross-Channel zone and historical novels of, 20–21; female communities of, 134, 145n.5; impact of Pamela on French novel of, 76–79; journalistic character of French novels of, 45; literary use of sympathy during, 133–45; nation as political/cultural concept during, 52; national or transnational in context of, 52, 61–66; popularity of novel collections during, 54, 59; translatio and idea of novel during, 55–61; translation market during, 53–61; unique nature of French novel of, 30n.15. See also sentimental novels
Ellis, Havelock, 254, 255–56, 261
Éloge de Richardson (Diderot), 81
Emile (Rousseau), 19
Engels, Friedrich, 9, 231
England. See Britain
English Criticism of the Novel, 1867–1900 (Graham), 268
Enlightenment public sphere: use of pathos in, 129n.37; regarding sentimental novels, 108–9; role of sentimental communities values in, 114–15, 116, 128n.36; Shelley and Staël's examination of, 208–9. See also individual rights; political sphere
epistolary fiction, 186–92, 218n.5
Essay on the First Principles of Government (Priestly), 111
"Essay on Romance" (Scott), 60
Ethiopian Romance (Heliodorus), 22
Euro-culture, 288–91
The Experiences of a French Detective-Officer (Waters), 232, 234, 235, 237, 249n.27
Experiences of a Real Detective (Waters), 232

*Extension du domaine de la lutte* (Houellebecq), 291

fairy-tale genre, 43
family system: as bedrock of French modern state, 221n.27; *Frankenstein* monster as being outside, 209–11; *Frankenstein's* recognition of fatherhood in, 211–12; *Frankenstein's* woman-to-woman transmission within, 212–13; textuality as displacement of, 222n.34
family system metaphor: for colonial/postcolonial political sphere, 192; for imagined community, 134; use of in *Mansfield Park* (Austen), 192; use of in *La Montagne des Signaux* (Humbert), 192
Farwell, Marilyn, 273
*Les Faux Saulniers* (Nerval), 179
Favret, Mary A., 195
female communities, 134, 145n.5
female detective figures (19th-century), 240–44
Fénélon, François de, 15, 53, 171
*Ferragus* (Balzac), 256
Festa, Lynn, 17, 18, 73
Fête de la Fédération (1790), 91
Feuillet, Octave, 13
Fielding, Henry, 8, 16, 62, 120
Fielding, Sarah, 16
*La Fille aux yeux d'or* (Balzac), 26, 255, 256, 258, 259, 260, 262, 275
Fisher, Philip, 85, 108
Flaubert, Gustave, 267
*Les Fleurs du mal* (Baudelaire), 255, 260
Forman, Buxton, 272
*Fortnightly Review,* 252, 253, 257, 272
*The Fortunate Foundlings* (Haywood), 65
France: Anglomania transferred by *Pamela* to, 89–91; British spy-police hero defense against, 226–27, 238, 240, 246; British understanding of justice system in, 235–36; changing condition of literary production in, 2; Code Napoleon regarding status of women in, 202–3; conceptual borders of novel genre in, 6–7; emergence as modern nation, 32n.26; family system as bedrock of modern state of, 221n.27; great pretender novels of, 178–79; model of freedom in, 126n.16; most popular novel collections in 18th-century, 54; novelistic core of, 1; protracted conflict between Britain

and, 11–13; response to British novels in, 63–65; shifting patterns of literary exchange in, 3; *Times* (1854 report) on social disorder of, 229–30; Treaty of Paris (1814) and colonial history of, 183, 184; Wilde's retreat to, 25–26. *See also* cross-Channel exchanges; French Revolution
*Frankenstein* (Shelley): autobiographical narrative by monster in, 206–8; epistolarity used in, 218n.5; exile device used in, 209–10, 211; as extension of Gothic plot, 208–9; fatherhood recognition in, 211–12; imitation notion expressed in, 213–14; letters of naturalization device used by, 197; monster as metaphor of transport in, 207–8; review cataloguing faults of, 195–96; Romantic nationalism expressed in, 210–13; Staël's influence evident in, 205–6; transnational pedagogy center of, 196, 206–7
freedom. *See* individual rights
Freising, Otto von, 58
"The French Decadence" (1892 review), 267
French detective figures (19th-century), 228, 233–35, 237–40, 244–47. *See also* French police system
"The French Detectives" (Canler), 235
"French-English Bellarmine" (Fielding), 62
"French Fiction—Its Better Aspects" (1861 article), 269
French language: fairy tales published in, 43; rising prominence of, 42
French novel: British attitudes toward translation of, 61–66; British resistance to, 62–63, 65–66, 264–76; comparing development of British and, 8–9; considering the transnational history of, 37–39; cross-Channel exchange and development of comic, 21; displacement via England used in, 26; England as "Other" nation-state in, 19–20; French detective figures in, 244–47; French style of manners reflected in, 129n.43; "imagined communities" examined through, 46; impact of history on development of, 30n.14; impact of *Pamela* on, 76–79; journalistic character of 18th-century, 45; marital status of women and contents of, 281n.55; origins of modern, 47n.1; *Pamela* as reforming immoral, 87–88; *Première journée* (1619) as first modern, 45–46; Prévost's impatience with historical, 155–56; sapphism of 19th-century, 251–76; tragic sentimentality of, 119; transla-

The History of Emily Montague (Brooke), 117, 129nn.45, 46
History of English Poetry (Warton), 59
The History of Sir Charles Grandison (Richardson), 136
The History of Sir George Ellison (Scott), 134
Holmes, Sherlock (fictional detective), 231–32
Holquist, Michael, 5
"A Home for Art" (Favret), 195
homosexuality: comparing British/French approach to, 251–52, 271–72, 274–76; French sapphic neutral characterization of, 255–57; visible as pattern of elision, 252. See also lesbianism; sapphism
Houellebecq, Michel, 291, 292
Huet, Pierre Daniel, 39, 40, 47n.2, 57, 58, 60, 62
Hugo, Victor, 13, 266
Humbert, Marie-Thérèse, 21, 183, 184, 186, 187, 190
Humphrey Clinker (Smollett), 62
Hutcheon, Linda, 115
Huysmans, Joris-Karl, 26, 286

idealism: description of British, 283n.78; social norms represented by, 270; Victorian literary blending of realism and, 267–70. See also virtue
Idées sur les romans (Sade), 60
Les Illuminés (Nerval), 179
Imagined Communities (Anderson), 210
imagined community: characteristics of "discursive," 115; as defining characteristic of nation, 133; distinctions between sentimental communities and, 107, 116; examined through French novel, 46; family as, 134; forged by sentimental novels, 75–76, 85–86, 88–89, 106–7; novel genre used to construct national, 50, 88, 123n.2; role of sensibility in, 136–37; romantic friendships of female, 134; sympathetic and sensibility bonds creating, 135–37; utopian sympathetic, 138–40. See also nation-state; sentimental communities
I misteri di Napoli (Mastriani), 23
Indiana (Sand), 135, 266
individual rights: as anguish of choice, 131n.53; British privacy rights attached to, 230; 18th-century sentimental novels on revolutionary labor and, 84–86, 89–96,

101nn.30, 31; French model of, 126n.16; Locke's notion of society and, 126n.13, 127nn.22, 23; negative, 109, 118, 119–20, 121; positive, 109, 119–20; Rousseau's ideal of liberal citizenship and, 114, 119–20; sentimental novel examination of universal vs., 85, 89, 103n.61, 109–12, 114–15; spy-police hero as protector of British, 226–27, 238, 240, 246. See also Enlightenment public sphere; political sphere
Iraihl, Simon, 64

Jacquin, abbé, 59
James, Henry, 268
Jane Eyre (Charlotte Brontë), 13
Johnson, Samuel, 65
Joseph Andrews (Fielding), 62
Journal de Barbier, 87
Journal Étranger, 76
Julia de Roubigné (Mackenzie), 117
Julie, ou la nouvelle Héloïse (Rousseau), 73, 76, 83, 107, 109, 117, 119–20, 137, 139
Justine (Sade), 115

Kennard, Nina, 267
Kock, Paul de, 266
Krestovski, V. V., 23

La Chaussée, Nivelle de, 77
Ladenson, Elisabeth, 255
The Lady's Paquet Broke Open (comtesse d'Aulnoy memoirs), 15
Lafayette, Mme de, 12, 15, 19, 39, 43–44, 45, 155, 156
Lagardie, Honoré de, 265
La Harpe, Jean-François, 24–25
Lang, Andrew, 252
language: awareness of limits of, 188; decentralized by novels of sensibility, 143; fairy tales published in French, 43; Frankenstein's examining learning of, 216; Latin's decline as literary, 41; meaning of novel, 6; 19th-century nationalism and, 215–17; polyglossia discourse, 6; rising prominence of French, 42; spread of sentimental rhetoric, 115–16; Staël's use of self-abjection, 204–5; symbolism of translations into new, 56–57; translatio studii through, 16–17. See also translatio (translation)

values of, 75–76. *See also* imagined community

"Sentimental Communities" (Cohen), 17

*The Sentimental Education of the Novel* (Cohen), 108, 114, 122, 267

*A Sentimental Journey* (Sterne), 114, 125n.7, 136

sentimental novels: descriptions of 18th-century, 81–84; as genuine cross-Channel exchange, 107; historical circumstances depicted by, 88; individual/universal struggle depicted in, 85, 89, 103n.61, 109–12, 114–15; *Julie* (Rousseau) as first French, 76; link between national preference and narrative conflict in, 117–19; mass media afterlife of during 20th century, 107; melodramatic deathbed scene of, 111–13, 128n.28, 132n.60; *Pamela* as first of the, 74–76; and revolutionary labor of 18th century, 84–86, 89–96, 101nn.30, 31; revolutionary movement practices and, 115–16; significance for 18th-century national identity, 75–76, 88–89, 107; tragic sentimentality conflict of, 109–10, 118–20; virtue used in, 79–80, 86, 90–91, 96, 101n.34, 102nn.43, 47, 119–22, 123; "war of duties" plot of, 109–10. *See also* melodramatic sentimentality; *Pamela* (Richardson)

*Séraphita* (Balzac), 255, 258

17th-century: British-French cross-Channel zone during, 14–15; Edict of Nantes/Protestant diaspora of, 14, 40, 41, 46, 48n.3; 18th-century translation of works from, 55; pretender novels of, 151–52

"Sexual Inversion of Women" (Ellis), 254, 261

Shand, Alexander Innes, 271

Shelley, Mary, 19, 189, 194, 195, 206, 209, 211, 212, 213

Shelley, Percy, 195, 196, 206, 210

Smith, Charlotte, 16

Smollett, Tobias, 16, 51, 60, 61, 62

"Some of Balzac's Minor Pieces" (Moore), 257–58

Sommer, Doris, 217

*The Sorrows of Young Werther* (Goethe), 74, 109

*La Souffrance à distance* (Boltanski), 113

Soysal, Yasemin, 11

Spacks, Patricia, 108, 110

*Spectator,* 253

spy-figures: British police as hero, 227–28, 238, 240, 246; as threat to national identity, 246–47. *See also* police hero

Staël, Germaine de, 19, 135, 194, 195, 197–205, 209, 213–17

Stang, Richard, 268

Stendhal, 8, 22

Stephen, Leslie, 252, 256, 257, 259, 262

Sterne, Laurence, 8, 16, 73, 114, 179

Storch, R. D., 231

Stowe, Harriet Beecher, 106

Strachey, Lionel, 262

*Structural Transformation of the Public Sphere* (Habermas), 113

*Studies in European Realism* (Lukács), 4

Sue, Eugène, 107

Swift, Jonathan, 63

Swinburne, Algernon Charles, 257, 272, 273, 275

Symonds, John Addington, 261, 270

sympathetic communities: as alternatives to nations, 142–45; explored in *Corinne,* 135, 146n.20; used as framing device, 112–13; groups included in, 134–35; *Wuthering Heights* (Brontë) rewriting of, 140–42

sympathy: evoked by deathbed scenes, 111–13, 128n.28, 132n.60; as form of nationalism, 137; idealized interpersonal bond of, 133; literary use during 18th/19th-century, 133–45; literary use of sensibility, empathy and, 134; plea of Shelley and Staël's heroines for, 209; romantic friendships/heterosexual couples bonded by, 134–35; utopias of, 138–40. *See also* melodramatic sentimentality

*A Tale of Two Cities* (Dickens), 246

Tallemant de Réaux, 155

Tatius, Achilles, 55

*Télémaque* (Fénelon), 53

Telman, Kathryn (*The Business* character), 289–90

*Temple Bar,* 253, 258, 269

Tennenhouse, Leonard, 75

Terror (French Revolution): Committee of Public Safety during, 91, 92–93, 95, 96, 104n.66; sentimental rhetoric used during, 116

*Theaganes and Chariclea* (Heliodorus), 55

Théophile de Viau, 45–46, 49n.14

*Theory of the Novel* (Lukács), 4

theory of *translatio* in the novel, 58
Thiel, Paul, 23
*Things As They Are; or the Adventures of Caleb Williams* (Godwin), 233
Thiroux d'Arconville, Madame, 65
*The Thirteen* (Saintsbury), 256
Thom, Martin, 198
*Times* (London), 225, 229, 230, 248n.11
*Tom-Jones*, 24–25, 53, 64
Tompkins, J.M.S., 166
tragedy and sentimentality conflict, 109–10, 118–20
*Traité de l'origine des romans* (Hutet), 39, 57, 62
*translatio* (translation): biblical passages and historiographical theory of, 58; British review of French sapphic works and, 254–76, 277n.15, 279n.29, 280n.44; of *Cleveland*, 160; as cultural and literary dynamic, 51; of detective fiction (19th-century), 234–35; of early French novelists, 44, 49nn.9, 12; French and British attitudes toward, 61–66; idea of novel and, 55–61; novel defined by notion of, 57; of *Pamela* (Richardson), 65, 77–81, 98n.10, 124n.5, 125n.6; pseudotranslation device used in, 56, 69n.22; transfer of culture through, 16–17, 51; *translatio imperii*, 16–17, 51
translation market (18th-century): overview of, 53–55; *Pamela's* role in, 65, 77–81, 98n.10, 124n.5, 125n.6; symbolic resonance of, 55–61
transnational culture: of Channel zone, 13; creating new paradigms for, 287–93; cultural formations and new, 11; *Frankenstein's* use of, 196, 206–7; nation-space notion and, 10–14; *translatio* model of, 52; *translatio studii* on transfer of, 16–17, 51
"Transnationalism and the Origins of the (French?) Novel" (DeJean), 16–17
"Transnational Sympathies, Imaginary Communities" (Alliston), 17
Treaty of Paris (1814), 183, 184
*Tristram Shandy* (Sterne), 73
*Trois siècles de la littérature française* (Castres), 64
Troyes, Chrétien de, 58
Trumpener, Katie, 137
Tuevoleur, Monsieur, 232
Tuyll van Serooskerken, Isabella van (Isabelle de Charrière), 37, 118, 136

*Uncle Tom's Cabin* (Stowe), 106, 107
*Une Passion dans le désert* (Balzac), 258
utopian sympathetic communities: described, 138–40; *Wuthering Heights* (Brontë) rewriting of, 140–42. *See also* virtue

*Valentine* (Sand), 266
Van der Weyden, Rogier, 38
Verlaine, Paul, 260
*Le Vicomte de Bragelonne* (Dumas), 178
Victorian literary culture: agents provocateurs of, 227–28, 233–38, 245–47; blending of realism and idealism by, 268–70; British spy-police figures of, 227–28, 238, 240, 246; detective novels of, 23–24, 225–47; "domestic drama" of, 247; erotic politics of, 25; female detectives of, 240–44; French detective figures of, 228, 233–35, 237–40, 244–45; French sapphism reviewed by periodical press of, 252–76, 277n.15, 279n.29, 280n.44; legacy of melodramatic sentimentality to, 122–23; opposition to realism of French sapphism by, 270–76; resistance to French agents provocateurs by, 245–46; use of sympathy in, 133–45; view of lesbianism by critics of, 253–54. *See also* British novels; 19th-century
*Vidocq, Chef de la Police de Sûreté (Detective Force) de Paris* brochure, 233
Vidocq, Eugène-François, 228, 233–34, 235, 246
Villedieu, Mme de, 15
*Villette* (Brontë), 228, 261, 286
virtue: British novel's vision of idealism and, 267–71, 283n.78; British police "chivalric ethos" of, 248n.8; as commerce, 121, 123, 131n.56; corruption of police hero, 236–37, 240; cross-Channel context of melodramatic conflict of, 121–22; female detective display of moral, 240–44; melodramatic negotiations of, 119–22; *Pamela's* model of, 79–80, 86, 96, 101n.34, 102nn.43, 47, 120; as sacrifice, 121; as sacrifice of private freedom, 121; sentimental novel, 90–91
Voltaire, 37, 53, 77, 157

Walpole, Horace, 56, 73
Walpole, Thomas, 194
Warbeck, Perkin, 157, 166

Warburton, Bishop William, 15
Warner, William, 10, 86
Warton, Thomas, 59
Waters, Thomas, 227, 234, 235, 238, 239
Watt, Ian, 7, 8, 185
Waugh, Arthur, 259
*Waverley* (Scott), 12, 21, 22, 177, 178
*Way of the World* (Moretti), 5
Webster, Rev. William, 86
*Westminster Review,* 253
Wilde, Oscar, 25
*The Wild Irish Girl* (Morgan), 199
women: British marriage market and, 135, 144; British refusal to define sexuality between, 251; contents of novels and marital status of, 281n.55; depicted as detectives (19th-century), 240–44; as first modern individual, 185; *Frankenstein* on cultural transmission through, 212–13; Gothic's examination of experience of, 204–5, 221n.28; *Pamela's* invitation to, 83–85; *Pamela's* model of virtue for, 79–80, 86, 96, 101n.34, 102nn.43, 47, 120; postromantic culture ideology on duty of, 223n.47; "romantic friendships" of, 134, 145n.5; Staël's description of legal condition of, 202–3; Staël's identification of nation with, 200–205; tracing correspondences by, 196, 218n.9
women novelists: contributions of colonial/postcolonial, 185–86; English experience of early French, 39, 41–43, 45; as force in creating modern middle-class, 185; influence of Rousseau on British, 146n.19; legacy of Shelley and Staël as, 196–217; Protestant diaspora (17th-century) and, 14, 40, 41, 46, 48n.3. *See also* French novelists
Wraxall, Sir F.C.L., 234–35
Wreford, Henry, 230, 231
*Wuthering Heights* (Emily Brontë), 140–42

Young, Edward, 213

*Zayde* (de Lafayette), 44
*Zingis* (La Roche-Guilhen), 42
Zobel, Joseph, 187
Zola, Émile, 255, 256, 259–60, 261, 262, 269–70

**TRANSLATION** | TRANSNATION

SERIES EDITOR **EMILY APTER**